Evolution of Family Business

Evolution of Family Business

Continuity and Change in Latin America and Spain

Edited by

Paloma Fernández Pérez

University of Barcelona, Spain

Andrea Lluch

CONICET, Argentina and Los Andes University, Colombia

Edward Elgar PUBLISHING

Fundación BBVA

Cheltenham, UK • Northampton, MA, USA

A first version of this book was published in Spanish as *Familias empresarias y grandes empresas familiares en América Latina y España. Una visión de largo plazo*. Bilbao, Fundación BBVA, 2015.
http://www.fbbva.es/TLFU/microsites/EmpresasFamiliares/index.html

Published by
Edward Elgar Publishing Limited
The Lypiatts
15 Lansdown Road
Cheltenham
Glos GL50 2JA
UK

Edward Elgar Publishing, Inc.
William Pratt House
9 Dewey Court
Northampton
Massachusetts 01060
USA

A catalogue record for this book
is available from the British Library

Library of Congress Control Number: 2015950514

This book is available electronically in the **Elgar**online
Business subject collection
DOI 10.4337/9781785363153

MIX
Paper from responsible sources
FSC® C013604
FSC www.fsc.org

ISBN 978 1 78536 314 6 (cased)
ISBN 978 1 78536 315 3 (eBook)

Typeset by Servis Filmsetting Ltd, Stockport, Cheshire
Printed and bound by CPI Group (UK) Ltd, Croydon, CR0 4YY

Contents

Figures

Tables

Contributors

María Inés Barbero, Professor of Economic and Business History, Universidad de Buenos Aires, Argentina. She received her PhD from Universidad Complutense de Madrid, Spain. Current research interests include the history of business groups and Latin American-based multinationals. She has written extensively about the business history of Argentina and Latin America.

Lourdes Casanova, Senior Lecturer, Academic Director, Emerging Markets Institute, Johnson Business School, Cornell University, USA. Co-author of *The Political Economy of an Emerging Global Power: In Search of the Brazil Dream* (2014, with Julian Kassum) and *InnovaLatino, Fostering Innovation in Latin America* (2011, with F. Castellani, J.S. Dayton-Johnson, N. Dutta, C. Fonstad and C. Paunov). Author of *Global Latinas: Latin America's Emerging Multinationals* (2009). She was one of Esglobal's 50 most influential Iberoamerican intellectuals in 2014. Fulbright Scholar. Board Member, World Economic Forum's Global Agenda Council.

Mario Cerutti, Autonomous University of Nuevo Leon, Monterrey, Mexico. Member of the National System of Researchers. His books include *Algodón en el norte de México (1920–1970). Impactos regionales de un cultivo estratégico* (2013, with Araceli Almaraz); *Grandes empresas y grupos empresariales en México en el siglo XX* (2012, with Del Carmen Hernández and Carlos Marichal); and *Propietarios, empresarios y empresa en el norte de México*.

Armando Dalla Costa, PhD from the University of Paris III (Sorbonne Nouvelle, 1997) and postdoctorate from the Picardie Jules Verne University, Amiens, France, 2008. Professor in the Economics Department and PhD Programme in Economic Development of the Federal University of Paraná, Brazil. Coordinator of the Economics Course (2008–10), Masters Professional in Economic Development (2011–13). President of the Brazilian Association of Researchers in Economic History (2011–13). Founded and leads the Center for Research in Business Economics.

Carlos Dávila, PhD from Northwestern University, USA. Professor Emeritus in the School of Management, Universidad de los Andes,

Bogotá, Colombia, where he is also Director of the Business History Group. Author and editor of several books and articles on Colombian and Latin American business history.

Pablo Díaz Morlán, PhD in Economics. Associate Professor, Department of Applied Economic Analysis, University of Alicante, Spain. More than 40 publications including books (six), book chapters and articles on topics related to business history. Research interests include history of companies and entrepreneurs, family business, mining, European steel industry, formation of the European Union.

Allan Discua Cruz, PhD, Lecturer in Entrepreneurship, Lancaster University Management School, UK. He has published in entrepreneurship and family business journals as well as book compilations.

Carlos Eduardo Drumond, Professor of International Economics, UESC (State University of Santa Cruz), Brazil and Professor of Economic Theory, Master of Regional Economics and Public Policy (UESC). His doctorate is from UFPR (Federal University of Parana), Brazil. He conducts research in international economics and macroeconomics.

Paloma Fernández Pérez, PhD in History from the University of California at Berkeley, USA. Fulbright Scholar. Professor of International Business History and History of Family Businesses, Department of Economic History, Universitat de Barcelona, Spain. Co-editor with A. Colli of *The Endurance of Family Businesses: A Global Overview* (2013) and with C. Lubinski and J. Fear of *Family Multinationals* (2013). She received the ICREA Academia Award in 2008 and 2013. Visiting Scholar in Lancaster University (UK), Uniandes (Colombia) and Universidad del Pacífico (Peru).

Lourdes Fortín, PhD, Professor, Catholic University of Honduras. Her research focuses on small and medium-sized enterprises (SMEs), family and family enterprises.

Erick Guillén Miranda, Professor, Instituto Tecnológico de Costa Rica. Family entrepreneur. His MBA is from Universidad Latinoamericana de Ciencia y Tecnología. Academic areas of interest are business strategy, family business, leadership and team work.

José María Las Heras, MS in Economic Development, Postgraduate Programme of the Federal University of Paraná (UFPR), Curitiba, Brazil (2013). His Bachelor's degree is in Economic Science from the National University of Córdoba (UNC), Argentina (2009). His investigations are focused on the economic development, social economy and history of companies. Member of the Board of Directors of the septuagenarian newspaper *Comercio y Justicia Editores* (Córdoba, Argentina), specializing in economic, legal, financial, tax and commercial issues.

Juan Carlos Leiva, PhD in Business Administration from the University of Valencia, Spain. Professor in the Business School, Technology Institute of Costa Rica. His research areas are entrepreneurship, knowledge management and innovation.

Andrea Lluch, Researcher at the National Council of Scientific and Technical Research of Argentina (CONICET-UNLPam) and Associate Professor in the School of Management, Universidad de los Andes, Bogotá, Colombia. Harvard-Newcomen Fellow in Business History at Harvard Business School (2006–07) and Research Fellow (2007–09). She received her PhD from the Universidad Nacional del Centro de Buenos Aires. She researches the business history of Latin America, specializing in the history of direct foreign investment, family business and corporate networks during the twentieth century.

Jon Martínez Echezárraga, PhD in Management from IESE, University of Navarre, Spain. He is the Bci Professor of Families in Business, ESE Business School, University of los Andes, Santiago, Chile. He has taught family business management and business strategy at prestigious academic institutions around the world, like Harvard University, INSEAD (Fontainebleau, France) and University of California, Los Angeles (UCLA). He has authored two books on family business issues and several academic articles published in top journals.

Martín Monsalve Zanatti, PhD, Professor, Humanities Department, Universidad del Pacífico, Lima, Peru and Director of Apuntes, revista de ciencias sociales. His research focuses on the history of family and business groups in Peru. He is the editor of the book *Grupos económicos y mediana empresa familiar en América Latina* (2014).

Nuria Puig, PhD, Professor of Economic History and Institutions, Universidad Complutense de Madrid, Spain and Visiting Professor of History at Ohio State University, USA. Author (with Marta Rey) of 'Globalisation and the organisation of family philanthropy: a case of isomorphism?', *Business History* **55** (2), 2013, 1–28.

Concepción Ramos Rodas, PhD, Professor, Universidad Tecnológica de Honduras. His research focuses on the reform processes for the health sector and alternative methods of health provision programmes.

Claudia Raudales, PhD, Professor, Catholic University of Honduras. Her research focuses on family behaviour and psychology at the social, industrial, clinical and family levels.

Javier Vidal Olivares, PhD from Universidad de Valencia, Professor of Economic and Business History, Universidad de Alicante, Spain. He has worked at the Institute of Historical Research, University of London, European University Institute in Florence and was Visiting Professor in several Latin American universities, including Buenos Aires, Uniandes (Bogotá) and Universidad Nacional Autónoma de México. He has published widely about economic and business history in Spain and Latin America, especially in transport history, entrepreneurship and family firms.

Foreword

There are several reasons for which this book is an important book, a book that deserves the utmost attention by scholars and practitioners.

A first reason is that it is a well-planned, well-written research on family capitalism. Despite a now relatively long and consolidated tradition of research on family firms, evidence and theoretical synthesis is still much needed in order to understand more in depth both similarities and differences in this particular management model, across different countries, cultures, political and institutional frameworks.

A second reason is connected to the approach that the editors have chosen. Everyone familiar with family business research knows that the family/kinship dimension and its relationship with the business sphere are crucial for understanding such a particular form of business organization. The decision to have the chapters written jointly by management scholars and social scientists, and in particular historians has been a crucial choice in providing a well-rounded approach to the subject. Family firms are in fact the inextricable result of the interaction of aspects that are better understood through the synthesis proper of management, and other elements that are understandable only through the approach that characterizes social sciences, oriented towards the use of historical analysis in order to understand the basic components, origins and dynamics of complex phenomena. In this respect, the book is a courageous attempt to put into practice what several historians have suggested about the necessity of (re)introducing a long-term approach in economics and business. The main focus of historical analysis is, in fact, not the past per se but the dynamics of change and evolution, in the case of the business history of organizations and more in general of economic actors.

A third reason is that – beyond these more general aspects – this book is, to my knowledge, the first attempt to have an inclusive and truly comparative analysis of the private enterprise sector in Latin America and Spain, inclusive of smaller and larger countries. This is for sure a big step forward towards a better understanding of the peculiarities of the development of the industrial enterprise in Central and Southern American countries – apart from Spain. Scholars familiar with family business studies know well that comparative studies at a continental or supra-national level are rare. Famous comparative analysis such as *Big Business and the Wealth of Nations* (edited by Alfred Chandler, Franco Amatori and Takashi Hikino in 1997), for instance, focus only on big business and have a very limited focus on family firms. Other research such as the Proceedings of the tenth Fuji Conference held in 1985, *Family Business in the Era of Industrial Growth*, are good examples but now dating quite far back in the past. We are still waiting (hopefully for not too long) for some comparative research on Europe and/or the US family business, and maybe, in the future, on family business on a global scale. In the meantime, luckily, we can have access to books like this, which have certainly a path-breaking role.

This is directly connected to the fourth reason behind the relevance of this book. The comprehensive and longitudinal analysis of the family business enterprise in Latin America provides a precious contribution to the interdisciplinary field of research going under the label 'variety of capitalisms'. Through, in fact, the comparative analysis of different contexts in which family firms develop in Latin America and Spain, the book provides generalizations useful for understanding the characteristics of the capitalist enterprise in that area of the world in comparison with other models of capitalist development. The book is also a key contribution for understanding the relations between particular, national institutional environments and the development of specific forms of business enterprises, including the relationships with the respective governments. One non-trivial contribution of the book in this respect is that through the longitudinal and comparative approach, it moves a step beyond the usual stereotypes concerning the role of family business in countries characterized by widespread familism, corruption and the presence of extractive institutions. The book provides, instead, a much less clear-cut, unidirectional image of the role and perspectives of family firms in Latin American and Spanish contexts, showing how family businesses have tended to co-evolve dynamically with the local context, of course influencing it but also adapting creatively to the changes in the environment.

Last but not least, the book is fundamental for a better understanding of a phenomenon that is today of paramount interest in a variety of research domains, from strategy to organization sciences, to international business. Diversified business groups actively involved in intense processes of internationalization are, in fact, one of the relevant aspects of the most recent process of development and growth of Spain and Latin America's economies. And, as available research makes clear, most of these 'Global Latinas' are multigenerational, family-controlled enterprises that have been developing during the last decades into key components of local economic development.

These – and a series of other reasons that I do not have the space to highlight in this brief Foreword – make this book one seminal and important contribution to the field both of business history and management analysis of family business, at the same time contributing to the concrete cooperation among different fields of research interested in the analysis of business actors. As scholars in the field of family business studies, all of us should be grateful to the authors and to the editors for this fundamental piece of research.

Andrea Colli
Bocconi University, Milan, Italy

Acknowledgements

The authors and editors thank Benedict Hill and Chloe Mitchell for their continuous guidance in the elaboration of this book, and Edward Elgar Publishing for believing in the project from the start. Also, our gratitude goes to Cathrin Scupin and FBBVA for giving us permission to publish this book in English, which is a revision of a recent book originally published in Spanish, *Familias empresarias y grandes empresas familiares en América Latina y España* (Fundación BBVA, Bilbao, 2015, http://www.fbbva.es/TLFU/dat/DE_2015_familias_empresarias.pdf).

An Icrea Academia distinction of the Catalan Institute for Advanced Research (ICREA) provided resources to prepare a first draft in English with the assistance of Kirstin Adams, and to edit the book with the technical support of the University of Barcelona PhD student Jaime López Guauque.

The editors Paloma Fernández Pérez and Andrea Lluch give special thanks to the authors for their long-term commitment and collaborative work. They have made possible a difficult and ambitious project that involved 22 scholars from 11 countries and three academic disciplines, living in two continents. Enthusiasm, optimism and above all team work, as well as a cooperative and positive attitude have made it possible to produce this book, one of the first ones in the English language that has attempted to analyse the continuities and changes of large family businesses in Latin America and Spain in the last century.

Introduction

Paloma Fernández Pérez and Andrea Lluch

In recent years, the concept of emerging countries has become more pervasive and widespread, with an emphasis on the increasing flows of foreign direct investment (FDI) coming from these economies and the growing importance of their enterprises and business groups in rankings of the largest global businesses. The last three decades have witnessed numerous congresses, digital publications, books, monographs and reports from financial institutions (Casanova, 2009; Fernández Pérez, 2012; Guillén and García Canal, 2009, 2013; Jones and Khanna, 2006; Khanna and Palepu, 1997) that attempt to account for this relative boom and the success of the main business players from emerging countries. For many experts, this process reached its point of maximum acceleration towards the end of the 1980s, during the most recent wave of financial globalization, and the increases in deregulation, privatization and global capital flows. With the support of banks and governments, 'new' private giants arose in innovative and strategic sectors such as energy, telecommunications, finance and logistics, and in traditional activities in which technological innovation was key, such as food, construction and commercial distribution (Guillén, 2000; Khanna and Yafeh, 2007).

According to this line of study, the increase in the number of large businesses and business groups from emerging economies in the ranking of the largest groups in the world seems to be a relatively recent and uncharted development, one that is perceived as an opportunity for investment funds, and sometimes as a threat by groups and multinationals from Europe, Japan and the United States.

Business historians and economists interested in a long-term perspective are well aware, however, that many of these businesses and groups are actually not so new, and that they are often strategically controlled by families and family networks.

In this context, this book provides a wealth of empirical evidence that confirms the long-standing presence of business groups in Spain and in the diverse and so-called emerging economies of Latin America, where, in some cases, family groups represent the predominant organizational structure (Barbero, 2011; Cerutti and Marichal, 1997; Dávila, 2013; Valdaliso, 2004). The business groups of the present are larger and more powerful than those of the past, and many families still have an influence on strategic shareholders and those who manage both old and new businesses on their behalf (Casanova, 2009; Fernández Pérez, 2012; Goldstein, 2007; Santiso, 2013).

Based on interviews with consultants in various Latin American countries, some publications have taken a qualitative approach to the reality and corporate governance of Latin American family enterprises (Salazar, 2012). Moreover, there are many quantitative and qualitative analyses of family businesses in various countries, notably Spain, that focus on the post-1990 period (Galve and Salas, 2003; Tàpies, 2009). These publications predominate in the area of business management, and the majority contain analyses with an applied objective, namely providing information about current situations and guiding business practice or company policy. However, their focus tends to be ahistorical, as they provide no more than outlines of the changes, ruptures and learning process that companies go through when faced with sudden long-term changes to their environments.

The acceleration of social change and the diversity of global processes have made it necessary to develop more in-depth perspectives on long-term processes. As a result, there has been a renewed interest in historical analyses of experiences of change, rupture and adaptation in order to learn about the diverse ways in which entrepreneurs and companies act in situations and periods of great uncertainty. Such periods have frequently marked the economies of Latin America and Spain at different points in the twentieth and early twenty-first centuries.

This book therefore seeks to be one of the first collective studies to apply a dynamic, evolutionary methodology to the analysis of the characteristics of, and changes experienced by, large family-controlled businesses over the course of more than a century in eight Latin American countries and in Spain. It includes a variety of quantitative and qualitative empirical evidence and contributions from business historians and management scholars.

How should the evidence presented here be compared, and where is it to be placed within the debates on family enterprise that exist in mainstream academic circles in developed countries? One of the first steps taken by the authors in the book is to precisely identify the most notable business families for different benchmark years from the late nineteenth century to the first decade of the twenty-first century, in eight Latin American countries (Mexico, Brazil, Argentina, Colombia, Costa Rica, Honduras, Peru and Chile) and Spain. It has often been pointed out that family businesses represent – and have represented – the predominant organizational structure for businesses in these countries. However, almost no previous research has attempted the difficult task of collectively identifying, characterizing and analysing the largest family-controlled businesses in Spain and Latin America from the late nineteenth century until now (Fernández Pérez and Puig, 2007). Furthermore, this book identifies clear periods of change in the different countries and sectors it covers, together with the external and internal factors that have given rise to continuity or transformations within large family enterprises.

The result of a joint effort by historians interested in business and entrepreneurial families and specialists in business organization and management, this study presents new evidence about the players who, at various historical moments, occupied the top positions among the large businesses and sectors in their respective countries, regardless of whether or not they remain active today. We thus offer a dynamic perspective that reveals the importance, adaptability, flexibility and (fluctuating) dominance of family firms. We also show how business families have focused on different investment and entrepreneurship activities according to their circumstances.

Even more compellingly, in the case of family firms that relinquished the top positions in business in their respective countries over time, the book analyses their transformations, modifications and, in some cases, failures to continue their activities and adapt to changes in their contexts. When we focus on entrepreneurial families that have managed to maintain their position in their countries' business elites until practically the present day, be it with relative stability or by climbing up the ranking of the world's largest globalized firms, we highlight the dynamics of any such changes, including the internal and external factors that facilitated their expansion or continued success.

Based on both quantitative and, in particular, qualitative analyses, the research demonstrates how and when certain families owned and strategically managed a substantial part of the elite constituted by the largest enterprises and business groups in their respective countries. One intriguing discovery that has emerged from this analysis is that the rise and fall in the importance of large family businesses has differed substantially between the different locations considered here, which illustrates the heterogeneity of Latin America and warns of the difficulty of making sweeping generalizations.

The complex links and connections between enterprise and context have not been linear, and nor has the position of the family company within various private and public business structures in the long term, especially considering the long periods of economic and institutional instability the environment has undergone. In some cases, the periods of strong public interventionism and regulation that characterized the economic development of Spain and Latin America between 1940 and 1980 led to a withdrawal of family businesses, while in other instances of state-driven industrialization, there was a surge in new players and a consolidation of existing ones, which, in contrast, decreased during periods of significant FDI. We, the authors of this book, believe that the explanation for these dynamics lies in the different sectorial structures of the economies studied, the relative diversification of companies and the changing alliances with foreign players and, in particular, the state.

The difficulties this book's authors experienced during their research were enormous. Sources were limited, and there is little tradition of debate around definitions, concepts and methodology that are appropriate for analysing the history of family businesses in the countries in question. The issue is further complicated by the sometimes heedless application of concepts and theories originating in areas with very different historical experiences, such as Asia or the English-speaking world. As such, the first step in this collective work – which involves 22 researchers of 11 nationalities who present current and historical analyses relating to nine specific countries – was to shake off any inferiority complexes regarding the dominant theoretical paradigms from the English-speaking world and to openly discuss how we can, and should, study entrepreneurial families and family-controlled businesses in the context of the countries studied here.

'Family enterprise', 'family business group' and 'entrepreneurial family' are concepts that often appear in this book. Definitions of these concepts have proliferated since at least the late 1970s, especially in the area of family business management. The publishing house Edward Elgar has published various handbooks compiling the diverse definitions and methodological approaches that have appeared in recent decades (Melin et al., 2014). These handbooks, and recent collective works (Fernández Pérez and Colli, 2013; Lubinski et al., 2013), reflect the debates about the problems involved in choosing ahistorical, or historical, definitions when discussing a type of enterprise whose ownership structure and typology has varied enormously in order to adapt to changes in the legal, technological and market environments, not to mention the often dramatic changes in the families themselves over time.

Academics who are more distanced from historical analysis often need clearly established standard definitions to measure and compare very different companies. Experts in family business structure generally accept that: (1) 'family enterprise' means a legally independent business in which ownership and management has been strategically controlled by one or more families for at least two generations; (2) 'family group' tends to identify the partial or total participation in the ownership of various legally independent businesses in which management is strategically controlled;

and (3) 'business family' is a concept that defines families with diverse ties – be they blood or spiritual – that, over the course of several generations, have made productive investments in various businesses in which they do not necessarily control either ownership or management, but within which they aim to ensure the survival of certain values and the continuity of the family over time (Melin et al., 2014). As shown by J. Astrachan, P. Sharma and J. Chua (Melin et al., 2014), for researchers studying family businesses from a management perspective, a family 'company' or 'group' use different organizational forms in accordance with the changing needs of the business and the families in question. These needs change over time and adapt to changing contexts that influence their activity sector and their environment (regulations, technology, markets, gender ideology and war, for instance). Diversity also arises from the evolution of the families in question, such as changes in the demographic structures and gender ideologies.

For business historians and social historians, the concept of 'families in business' seems a more realistic one, and is more in keeping with what historical documents reveal. Archives include records of families that create or participate in companies in very dynamic and flexible ways. For historians of family businesses, families are the real protagonists behind regional and national private business, not the individual companies or groups listed on the official business registers.

This book is the result of an interdisciplinary dialogue between family business scholars and business historians, and it provides abundant new evidence that confirms that it is not the 'family firm' that defines family businesses in the history of Latin America and Spain but rather 'families in business'. In Latin America and Spain, notable entrepreneurial families have appeared in the rankings of the top national firms in national business registers since the late nineteenth century, often as independent companies, and also as business groups, in some capital-intensive sectors. The authors of these chapters show how a significant number of large business groups in the nine countries under analysis began as family firms, though many of these later abandoned the business initially registered in the documents and became entrepreneurial families. Building on what many consultants know about today's top family businesses, the historians in this book provide evidence of a long-standing tradition of survival among large families in business through a tactic not of stubbornly holding onto firms founded by a relative but rather by abandoning the firm when the market points to another direction, and investing in third-party businesses. This book thus provides evidence and lessons that may be useful in other contexts, such as Europe or Asia. For instance, is it not surprising that in some transnational institutions like the European Union so much effort is made to support the survival of small and medium family firms, when business historians have demonstrated that most large family businesses in Europe have survived through planned diversification, often abandoning the family firm or withdrawing from old businesses that seem to be no longer profitable (Fernández Pérez and Colli, 2013). This book on Latin American and Spanish families in business over the course of more than a century may also provide food for thought in this much-needed debate about what real families in business have done in history, and what institutions should really protect.

These historical and evolutionary perspectives on family-controlled business make it necessary to adopt a flexible usage of the operational concepts relating to the study of families in business over time. Concepts, empirical evidence or historical analyses are interesting in themselves, but also because of the ways they may affect the routines of real companies and institutions.

The authors of this book discuss aspects relating to: how to define 'family enterprise', 'family business groups', 'families in business' and 'entrepreneurial families'; the choice of appropriate sources for the quantitative identification of the family business elite at various chronological milestones; the organization of common research topics in order to observe similarities and differences; and the internal and external factors influencing such processes in Latin America and Spain during the twentieth century. During the research and writing process, the team exchanged views in meetings and face-to-face conversations at the Facultat d'Economia i Empresa of the Universitat de Barcelona in 2011, at the École des Hautes Études en Sciences Sociales in Paris in 2012, at the Universidad del Pacífico in Lima in 2013 and at the Goethe University in Frankfurt in 2014, as well as through emails and Skype conversations, so as to keep in close contact despite the geographical distance between them.

The first challenge in compiling the empirical evidence was methodological, to establish a rigorous and comparative up-to-date perspective of the largest family-controlled businesses in eight Latin American countries and in Spain at the present time. Only by establishing a solid analysis of the current situation on the largest family businesses in the nine countries under study could we start asking ourselves questions about how, why, when or who could explain today's problems and realities of family businesses. This has been done in all the national chapters included in this book. Using information from all countries, a database was set up and a quantitative analysis made comparing longevity, specialization and general economic performance of the largest family enterprises and groups in the nine countries in 2010 (see http://192.185.57.7/~centro/fbbva2html/empresas.html).

As shown in Table I.1, in 2010, the sectors that stand out as the main specialization of the largest families in business in Latin America and Spain were retail trade, food and base metals.

Topping the ranking of aggregate sales for 2010 is Spain, represented by a single company with sales figures of over US$20 billion (Figure I.1).

A second group by volume of sales, between US$10 billion and US$20 billion, brings together two Brazilian companies, two Chilean, one Spanish and three Mexican. A third group, with sales between US$5 billion and US$10 billion, comprises two Argentinian companies, five Brazilian, two Chilean, one Spanish and five Mexican. In the fourth group, with between US$2.5 billion and US$5 billion, are three Brazilian, three Chilean, three Spanish and six Mexican family businesses. The fifth group, with sales between US$1251 million and US$2.5 billion, represents, just as the sixth group, the greatest diversity of countries: five Argentinian companies, eight Chilean, one Colombian, ten Spanish, three Mexican and six Peruvian. The sixth group has sales between US$501 and US$1250 million and presents the largest number of companies in the sample: no Brazilian or Mexican, eleven Argentinian, five Chilean, six Colombian, one Costa Rican, four Spanish and fourteen Peruvian. The seventh and last group of family businesses by size, with aggregate sales of less than US$500 million, comprises two Argentinian, thirteen Colombian, nineteen Costa Rican; and almost all the Honduran firms are found in this group.

The top position in total share of sales is occupied by Mexico, followed by Brazil, Spain and Chile and in continuation the remaining countries of the sample. It is interesting to note that Spain, having the company with the greatest sales value of the sample, is in third position in terms of total turnover, somewhat distant from the second position and closer to Chile in fourth position. Spain, Mexico and Chile show the most similarity in segmentation of large family business; Costa Rica, Peru and Colombia show great polarity. For example, eight out of ten companies have more than a thousand employees, and only one out of ten firms have less than 250 employees.

In terms of longevity, Figure I.2 shows for the large family business an average age of 57 years, which would indicate that the companies of the sample are on average into the second generation, with some exceptions in Chile and Mexico where the third generation is in control. Here too, five groups can be identified in relation to age. The group with on average the oldest companies by year of founding is Chile and Mexico, with 77 years. At the other extreme, the youngest is Honduras, with 42 years. In between, there are two groups, one with an average age of between 69 and 55 years (firms of Argentina, Spain and Brazil) and another of between 48 and 43 years (from Peru, Colombia and Costa Rica).

Table I.1 The 180 largest family firms and business groups in eight Latin American countries and Spain in 2010: number of businesses by sector of sample

Sector	ARG	BRA	CHILE	COL	CRIC	SPA	HON	MEX	PERU	Total	%
Retail trade	4	2	3	3	4	5		5	1	27	15.0
Food	6	2	2	3	2			4	2	21	11.7
Base metals	3	3	2	1		1	2		1	13	7.2
Wholesale trade		1	1	3	2	3			1	11	6.1
Financial services	2		3		1			1	4	11	6.1
Construction		2			1	5			1	9	5.0
Beverages			1	2		1		2	2	8	4.4
Air transport		2	1			1				4	2.2
Insurance activities								1	3	4	2.2
Civil engineering				1	2	1				4	2.2
Other minerals				2	1			1	1	5	2.8
Paper manufacturing		2	1	1						4	2.2
Chemical products		2		1						3	1.7
Professional, scientific and technical activities							3			3	1.7
Head office activities	1							2		3	1.7
Programming and transmission		1		1	1					3	1.7
Other manufacturing					1			1		2	1.1
Automotive trade and repair				1	1					2	1.1
Electrical equipment		2								2	1.1
Water transport			2							2	1.1
Machinery and equipment	1					1				2	1.1
Energy and gas			2							2	1.1
Logistics and transport					2					2	1.1

Pharmaceutical products	1			1						2	1.1
Metal ore mining									2	2	1.1
Human health care		1								1	0.6
Electronic equipment	1									1	0.6
Telecommunications								1		1	0.6
Courier					1					1	0.6
Film production								1		1	0.6
Manufacturing of metal products								1		1	0.6
Architecture and engineering activities						1				1	0.6
Travel agents						1				1	0.6
Software engineering, IT consulting			1							1	0.6
Rubber and plastics					1					1	0.6
Manufacturing industries							1			1	0.6
Other mining and quarrying			1							1	0.6
Agriculture, livestock and hunting	1									1	0.6
Other service activities							1			1	0.6
Auxiliary financial activities									1	1	0.6
Activities of associations									1	1	0.6
Without data							13			13	
Grand total	20	20	20	20	20	20	20	20	20	180	

Source: Compiled by Paloma Fernández Pérez and Jaime A. López Guauque from databases set up by Barbero and Lluch (Argentina), Cerutti (Mexico), Dalla Costa and Drumond (Brazil), Discua (Honduras), Leiva and Guillén (Costa Rica), Dávila (Colombia), Martínez (Chile), Monsalve (Peru) and Galve and Hernández (Spain).

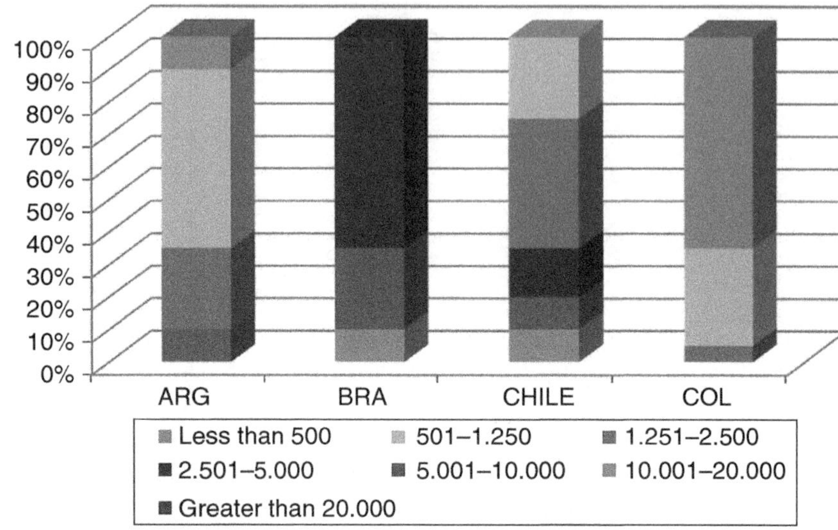

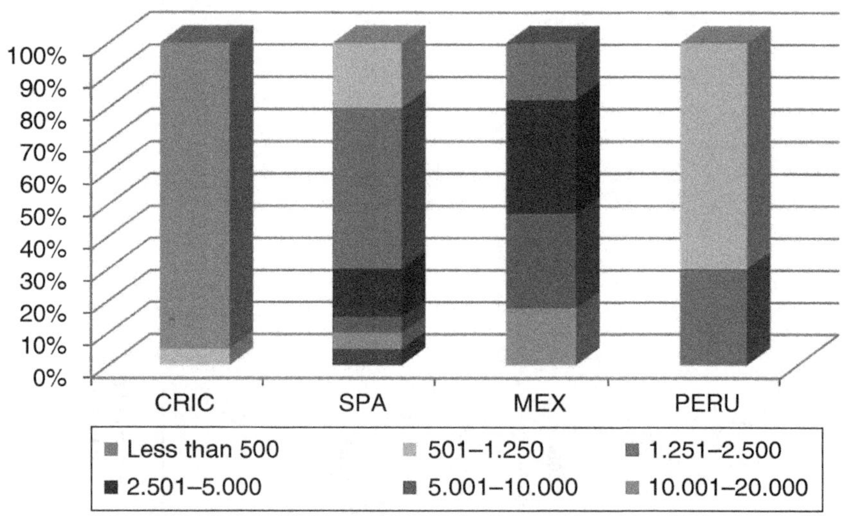

Source: See Table I.1.

Figure I.1 Number of top family businesses by rank of sales in 2010 (US$ million)

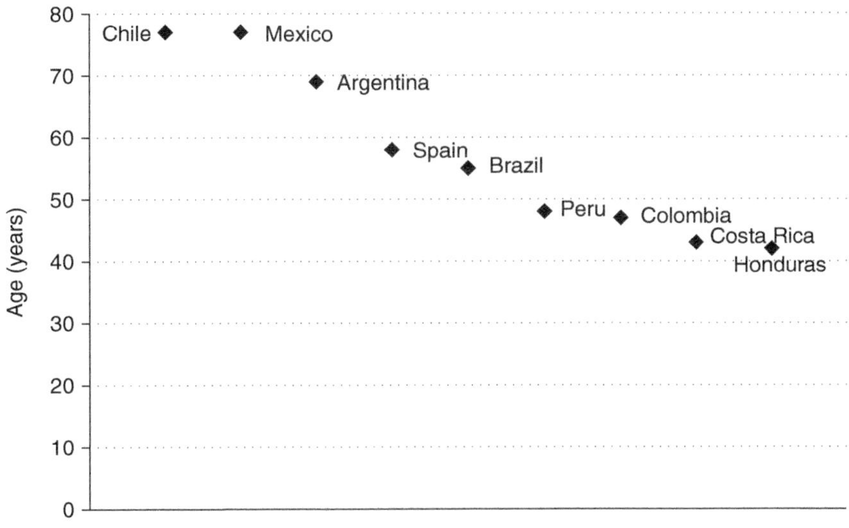

Source: See Table I.1.

Figure I.2 Average longevity of the largest Latin American and Spanish family businesses in 2010 (by year of founding)

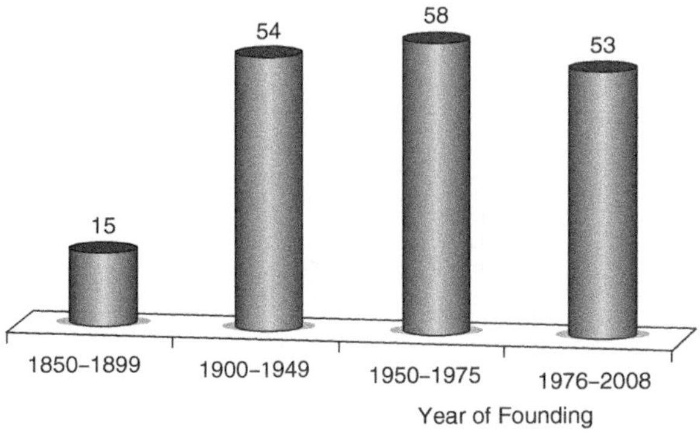

Period	Number
1850–1899	15
1900–1949	54
1950–1975	58
1976–2008	53

Source: See Table I.1.

Figure I.3 Historical periods of creation of the largest Latin American and Spanish family businesses by year of foundation, 2010

Table I.2 Age and sales of largest family firms and groups of top Latin American and Spanish family businesses in 2010

Longevity	ARG	BRA	CHILE	COL	CRIC	SPA	HON	MEX	PERU	Total	%
Less than 30 years	3	4	2	8	5	4	8	1	8	43	2.9
Between 30 and 60 years	7	8	5	5	12	8	11	6	6	68	37.8
Between 60 and 90 years	4	5	7	6	3	5	–	8	2	40	22.2
Between 90 and 120 years	6	3	3	1	–	3	–	5	3	24	13.3
More than 120 years	–	–	3	–	–	–	1	–	1	5	2.8
Average age (years)	66	55	77	47	43	58	42	77	48	57	

Sales	ARG	BRA	CHILE	COL	CRIC	SPA	HON	MEX	PERU	Total	%
Greater than 20 000	–	–	–	–	–	1	–	–	–	1	0.6
20 000–10 001	–	2	2	–	–	1	–	3	–	8	5.0
10 000–5001	2	5	2	–	–	1	–	5	–	15	9.4
5000–2501	–	13	3	–	–	3	–	6	–	25	15.6
2500–1251	5	–	8	1	–	10	–	3	6	33	20.6
1250–501	11	–	5	6	1	4	–	–	14	41	25.6
Less than 500	2	–	–	13	19	–	–	–	–	34	21.3
Total (US$ million)	35 288	105 255	71 902	11 246	2598.5	72 858	–	106 264	20 756	426 167	

Source: See Table I.1.

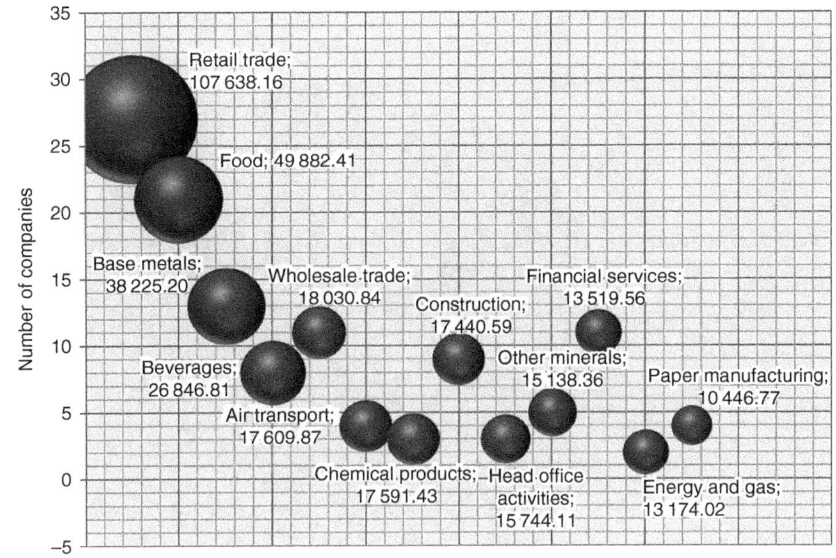

Source: See Table I.1.

Figure I.4 Largest family businesses in Latin America and Spain: sectorial specialization in 2010 (sales over US$10 billion)

With regard to the first year of start of activities of the largest businesses and groups in the sample, 69 began the business between 1850 and 1949, and 111 after 1950. In 2010, three quarters of the businesses of the sample were already in the hands of the second generation, and one quarter under the control of the first generation.

In the figures relating to the specialization of large family business of the sample, in 2010, there is a clear predominance of retail trade, food and base metals (Figures I.4 and I.5). It is here that, according to the sales indicator, a great many of the large family-controlled giants of these countries stand out: 25 per cent of aggregate sales comes from the retail trade sector (ISIC 47), and it is also in this dominant sector where the largest concentration of employees is found (34.9 per cent); second highest in terms of sales, with 11.7 per cent, is the food sector, but reaching only 9.95 per cent in terms of employees. The third sector by aggregate sales is base metals with 8.97 per cent of the total. In fourth position is the beverage sector with 6.3 per cent of the total. Wholesale trade represents 4.23 per cent. Air transport represents 4.13 per cent, identical to the chemical products sector. In eighth position is the construction sector with 4.09 per cent.

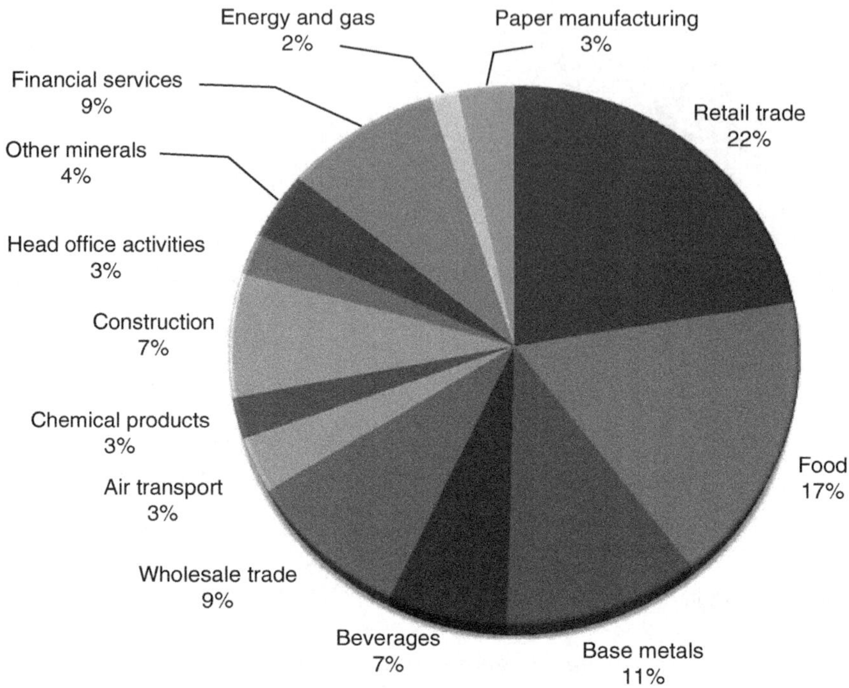

Source: See Table I.1.

Figure I.5 Specialization of the largest family businesses and groups of Latin America and Spain, 2010 (percentage total sales of the sample)

The retail trade sector, which tops the league in terms of sales, is led by Spain (Mercadona, El Corte Inglés); the food sector is led by Mexico (Bimbo); the base metal sector is led by Brazil (CSN) and Argentina (Tenaris); beverages is dominated by Mexico (Femsa, Modelo); wholesale trade is dominated by Spain (Inditex); air transport by Brazil (TAM); chemical products by Brazil (Braskem); construction is dominated by Spain (FCC); head office activities is dominated by Mexico (Alfa); the other minerals sector is dominated by Mexico (Cemex); financial services is shared by Peru (Credicorp), Chile (Banco de Chile) and Argentina (Banco de Galicia y Buenos Aires). The energy and gas sector is dominated by Chile (Copec) and telecommunications is dominated by Mexico (Telmex).

Using a sector performance indicator or proxy, measured with a variant of the RONA[1] indicator (return on net assets) to give a full picture of the efficiency of each sector in our sample, in 2010, information was obtained

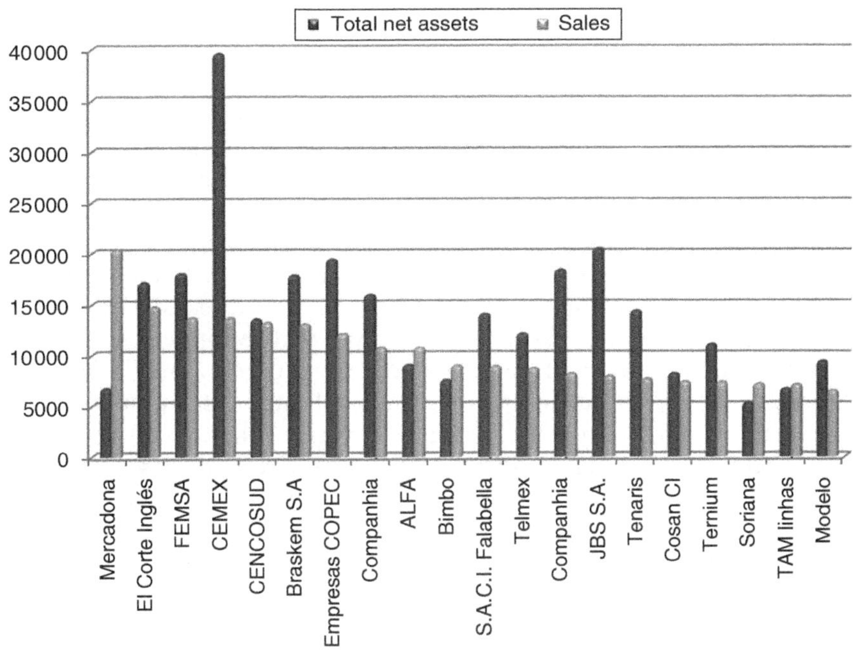

Source: See Table I.1.

Figure I.6 Sales versus assets in the largest businesses and groups of Latin America and Spain, 2010 (US$ billion)

on the performance of the sector in its investment in assets in each of the countries of the sample (Figure I.6). In the retail trade sector, most remarkable is the asset efficiency of Peru (Supermercados Peruanos) and Spain (Mercadona). In the food sector, the performance of assets is led by Alicorp (Peru) and Mastellone Hnos (Argentina). The leadership in base metals is by CI Fundición Escobar of Colombia. In beverages, we find a Peruvian company (Corporación José R. Lindley) and in the construction sector, the Brazilian firm Constructora Norberto Odebrecht.

According to the net assets indicator, in 2010, the family businesses and groups at the top of the ranking for Latin America and Spain in our sample were those specializing in construction, chemicals, metals and telecommunications. This criteria would make particularly visible industries where fixed assets dominate: capital-intensive businesses that dominated in family businesses during the period after the 1980s, when the financial, regulatory and market conditions favoured the expansion of large private family groups in these capital-intensive sectors. Before the 1980s, the state dominated the most technological and capital-intensive industries in all the countries of our sample, not private companies. This means that before the 1980s the largest family businesses could probably be observed in activities less intensive in fixed assets. For this reason, we decided that adopting the criterion of sales could allow a greater visibility for all the other less capital-intensive sectors where families in business usually are, in which state intervention was not so dominant in the history of the countries we studied, and therefore more room for private competition was allowed. Using the sales indicator, the activities of retail trade, food and beverages, transport, accommodation and tourist services were revealed as being the key market niche of the less capital-intensive family businesses in the nine countries under analysis. To measure and compare top family businesses by sales also helped to connect with many publications that point towards the historical importance of informal networks, contact with local and regional markets, the significance of family ties in reducing financial costs and high risk situations. Today, small and medium-sized companies and networks occupy the top 20 in small Central American countries such as Costa Rica and Honduras.

After obtaining a panorama for 2010, the next target involved producing the key contribution of this book: 12 chapters of long-term dynamic analysis that identify the major periods of change and transformation over a century; the most important families in business in each period; and the key determinants of success and failure for the top families in business in each country, during each major historical period. The authors have made a pioneering effort to reconstruct the identity of the elite family firms and business families at various points from the late nineteenth century to the present day and to pinpoint certain benchmarks during this time. They have done so on a large scale, given the book's focus on nine different countries. Their principal aims were to detect periods of transformation and analyse both endogenous factors (family history, organization, structure and strategy) and exogenous ones (market, political and technological shocks) that may shed light on the very diverse evolution of the largest family businesses in each of the countries under analysis. The project adopts flexible historical criteria, focusing on the availability of reliable sources of information, the evolution of the business history of each country and the academic background in management or business history of the researchers responsible for each country in question.

As a consequence, and after our first brainstorming meeting to discuss concepts and methodologies in Barcelona in 2011, the authors of the book's 12 chapters rejected outright the mainstream financial criteria for defining family enterprise as they traced the history of the largest family businesses in Latin America and Spain. Such mainstream quantitative criteria use standardized measures and available estimations and statistics, using only contemporary concepts. A historical study such as the one we have undertaken here implies that contemporary concepts and measures cannot be universally applied to all territories and historical periods. Adopting this approach is proof of the authors' loyalty to the dynamics and diversity of the past, and their recognition of the diversity of the types of family firms. Given the variations in the institutional rules of the game in each period, country or region, and in the size and sectorial specialization of the companies studied, this book demonstrates that one cannot and should not apply a sweeping rigid definition from one period to another, even within the same country. In contrast, what can indeed be compared – as Lourdes Casanova, Javier Vidal Olivares and Nuria Puig do in Part I of this book – are the strategies of family enterprises and business families created in similar environments, of similar sizes and in similar sectors, including the influence of public policies in each of these contexts and at each stage. These three chapters share an analysis of core issues in the current literature on family business, including firms' relationships with the state, the importance of context, internationalization and philanthropy. The next three parts of the book present national long-term studies about the evolution of the largest family businesses in nine countries. Part II focuses on the countries with the largest markets (Mexico, Brazil and Argentina), while Part III looks at the smallest ones, relatively speaking (Colombia, Costa Rica and Honduras). Part IV is a study of three countries (Spain, Peru and Chile) where business families had to adapt their strategies and organizational structures, some more successfully than others, as their contexts went from being deeply interventionist and regulatory institutional and market frameworks to extremely open institutional environments that prompted an accelerated integration into global markets. Following on from these country-specific analyses, the Conclusions chapter attempts to summarize comparative aspects between the cases considered.

A final comment, but not less important, is to acknowledge the generosity, interest and above all the effort and patience of the 22 researchers, and the research fellow Jaime López Guauque, who were involved in this project. Without any doubt, they are key to the successful culmination of an arduous but very stimulating research project that we are proud to present.

NOTE

1. Sales/Assets. Elaboration by Jaime López Guauque.

REFERENCES

Barbero, M.I. (2011). 'Los grupos económicos en la Argentina en una perspectiva de largo plazo. Siglos XIX y XX'. In G. Jones and A. Lluch (eds), *El impacto histórico de la globalización en Argentina y Chile: empresas y empresarios*. Buenos Aires: Temas, pp. 1–37.

Casanova, L. (2009). *Global Latinas: Latin America's Emerging Multinationals*. London: Palgrave Macmillan.

Cerutti, M. and C. Marichal (eds) (1997). *Historia de las grandes empresas en México 1850–1930*. México: Fondo de Cultura Económica.

Dávila, C. (2013). 'The current state of business history in Latin America'. *Australian Economic History Review* **53** (2) (July), 109–20.

Fernández Pérez, P. (2012). *La última globalización y el renacer de los grandes negocios familiares en el mundo*. Bogotá: Universidad de los Andes, Facultad de Administración, Cátedra Corona, p. 21.

Fernández Pérez, P. and A. Colli (eds) (2013). *The Endurance of Family Businesses: A Global Overview*. New York: Cambridge University Press.

Fernández Pérez, P. and N. Puig (2007). 'Bonsais in a wild forest? A historical interpretation of the longevity of large Spanish family firms'. *Revista de Historia Económica. Journal of Iberian and Latin American Economic History* **25** (3), 459–97.

Galve, C. and V. Salas (2003). *La empresa familiar en España. Fundamentos económicos y resultados*. Madrid: Fundación BBVA.

Goldstein, A. (2007). *Multinational Companies from Emerging Economies: Composition, Conceptualization and Direction in the Global Economy*. Basingstoke: Palgrave Macmillan.

Guillén, M. and E. García-Canal (2009). 'The American model of the multinational firm and the "new" multinationals from emerging economies'. *Academy of Management Perspectives* **2** (23), 23–35.

Guillén, M. and E. García-Canal (2013). *Emerging Markets Rule: Growth Strategies of the New Global Giants*. New York: McGraw Hill.

Jones, G. and T. Khanna (2006). 'Bringing history (back) into international business'. *Journal of International Business Studies* **37**, 453–68.

Khanna, T. and K. Palepu (1997). 'Why focused strategies may be wrong for emerging markets'. *Harvard Business Review* **75** (4) (July–August), 3–10.

Khanna, T. and Y. Yafeh (2007). 'Business groups in emerging markets: paragons or parasites?'. *Journal of Economic Literature* **XLV** (June), 331–72.

Lubinski, C., J. Fear and P. Fernández Pérez (eds) (2013). *Family Multinationals: Entrepreneurship, Governance and Pathways to Internationalization*. New York: Routledge.

Melin, L., M. Nordqvist and P. Sharma (eds) (2014). *The SAGE Handbook of Family Business*. London: SAGE Publications Ltd. doi: http://dx.doi.org/10.4135/9781446247556.

Salazar, G. (2012). 'Mambo, Tango o Salsa. . .¿Cuál es el ritmo de la empresa familiar en América Latina?'. http://c.ymcdn.com/sites/www.ffi.org/resource/resmgr/practitioner/practitioner_salazar_spanish.pdf (accessed 19 September 2015).
Santiso, J. (2013). *The Decade of the Multilatinas*. Cambridge: Cambridge University Press.
Tàpies, J. (2009). *Empresa familiar: ni tan pequeña, ni tan joven*. Barcelona: Fundación Jesús Serra.
Valdaliso, J.M. (2004). 'Grupos empresariales y relaciones banca-industria en España durante el franquismo'. *ICE* **812**, 163–78.

PART I

Comparative analysis

1. Latin American multinationals facing the 'new reality'

Lourdes Casanova*

Since 2002, Latin American companies have expanded all over the world becoming *Global Latinas*. Although the biggest ones are natural resources based, we also find them in information technology, steel production, electricity, wine and cosmetics. In times of crisis, their dynamism is a valuable example for European and American multinationals to follow.

1.1 FROM EMERGING COUNTRIES TO ECONOMIC POWERS

The 1990s were marked by the transformation of Latin American economies through market liberalization, privatization of the public sector and tax reforms. Foreign direct investment grew from US$18 billion at the beginning of the 1990s to US$108 billion in 1999. In 2011, the region attracted US$153 billion, which represents 10 per cent of total global direct foreign investment (ECLAC, 2012). In 1998, Europe became for the first time the biggest investor in Latin America and maintains its leadership today. Nevertheless, if we consider each country individually, the United States continues to hold top position with 18 per cent of the total investments in the region.

Increasingly, China's economic power is being felt in the region. China has become the most important trading partner of Brazil,[1] Chile[2] and Peru[3] and trade between the Middle Kingdom and Latin America and the Caribbean reached US$180 billion in 2010 (ECLAC, 2011). Asia receives 16 per cent of Latin American exports.

The Inter-American Development Bank (IADB, 2010) estimates that approximately 90 per cent of Latin American exports to Asia originate in the southern region of the continent: 41 per cent come from Brazil, 23.1 per cent from Chile, 15.9 per cent from Argentina and 9.3 per cent from Peru. China wants access to the raw materials and natural resources of the region, which are abundant but unevenly distributed. While Brazil dominates in iron ore, Chile does so in copper. According to the IADB (2010), the three main products that the region exports to China are raw materials (soya, copper and iron ore) and represent almost 50 per cent of total exports. In contrast, Chinese exports to the region are more diverse and include intermediate and capital goods. China has become the third largest investor in the region and represents 8 per cent of total investments, primarily in natural resources. For this reason, the Asian mergers and acquisitions are in the petroleum and gas sector, such as the purchase of 40 per cent of the Brazilian subsidiary of the Argentinian YPF by Sinopec for US$7.1 billion and the acquisition of 50 per cent of Bridas Corp. in Argentina by the Chinese CNOOC for almost US$4.8 billion.

The presence of multinationals from emerging countries in the ranking of the *Fortune* 'Global 500' (Figure 1.1) has increased fivefold since 1995. In 2013 there were 143, one out of every four, thirteen of them from Latin America (see list in Table 1.1), eight from Brazil (Petrobras, Banco

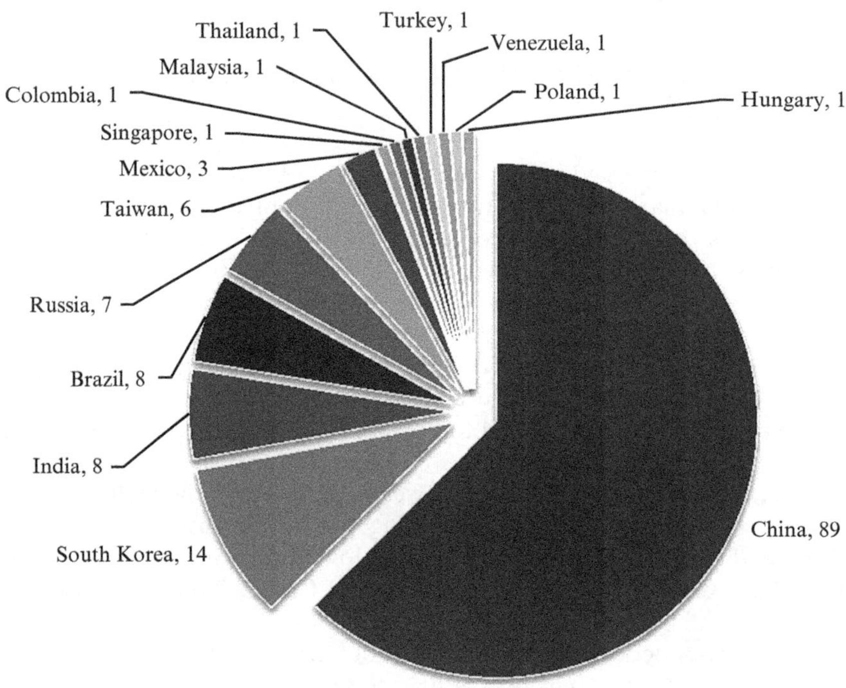

Source: Author's elaboration based on data from *Fortune* Global 500 (July 2013).

Figure 1.1 Emerging multinationals by country of origin in Fortune *Global 500 (2013)*

Table 1.1 Latin American companies in Fortune *Global 500 (2013)*

Ranking 2013	Business	Sales 2012 (US$ million)	Country	2012 profits (US$ million)
23	Petrobras	145.915	Brazil	20121
34	Pemex	125.344	Mexico	−7358
36	PDVSA	124.754	Venezuela	2.640
88	Banco do Brasil	81.887	Brazil	7577
136	Banco Bradesco	65.137	Brazil	6547
159	Vale	58.990	Brazil	22885
176	América Móvil	53.510	Mexico	6664
286	JBS/Friboi	36.921	Brazil	Not available
303	Ecopetrol	35.520	Colombia	8348
311	Itaúsa-Investimentos	34.710	Brazil	2890
380	Ultrapar Holdings	29.083	Brazil	507
399	CBD	27.839	Brazil	Not available
483	CFE	20.143	Mexico	−1381

Source: Author's elaboration based on data from *Fortune* Global 500 (2013).

do Brasil, Banco Bradesco, Vale, JBS/Friboi, Itaúsa, Ultrapar, CBD), three from Mexico (Pemex, América Móvil and CFE), one Venezuelan (PDVSA) and one Colombian (Ecopetrol). And among the ten largest companies in the world by revenues, three are Chinese, two American, four European and one from Saudi Arabia.

It should be noted that although the growth in number and revenues of emerging companies from China continues, the number from Latin America is not growing at the same pace. By number of companies, China occupies second place in *Fortune*'s ranking, South Korea with 14 is the eighth, Brazil with 8 is thirteenth and Mexico with 3 is twenty-first (Figure 1.2).

Figure 1.3 shows the Chinese dominance in these rankings with respect to other emerging economies such as Brazil, India, South Korea and Mexico.

If we consider the stock markets, Shanghai, Hong Kong and São Paulo are among the ten largest stock markets in the world. And innovation is no longer exclusive to the West. The Indian companies Reliance and Tata, the Brazilian Petrobras and the Chinese Huawei, Haier and China Mobile are among the most innovative of the world according to the ranking by Boston Consulting Group published in the American journal *Business Week*.

In light of this revolution, we can see that each industrial sector has

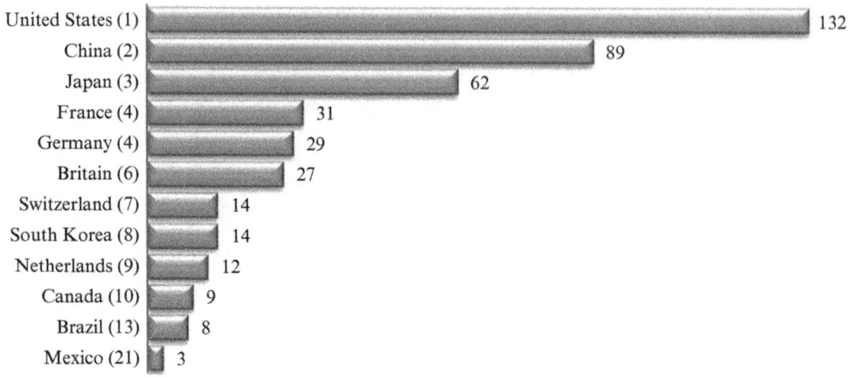

Note: Country (position occupied in the ranking according to the total number of companies) and in the bar number of companies in the ranking from that country.

Source: Author's elaboration based on data from *Fortune* Global 500 (2013), http://money.cnn.com/magazines/fortune/global500/ (accessed 1 November 2013).

Figure 1.2 Fortune *Global 500 (2013) ranking of countries with greatest number of companies compared with Brazil and Mexico*

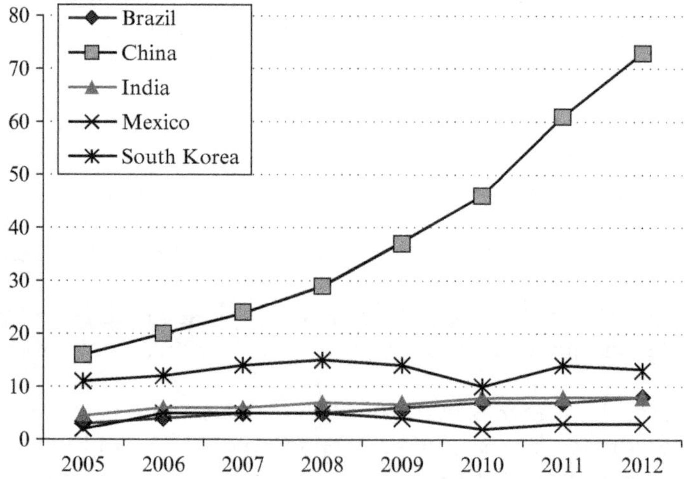

Source: Author's elaboration based on data from *Fortune* Global 500 (2013), http://money.cnn.com/magazines/fortune/global500/ (accessed 1 November 2013).

Figure 1.3 *2005–12 yearly evolution of number of companies in* Fortune *Global 500: China, South Korea, India, Brazil and Mexico*

competing businesses coming from countries with different competitive advantages and diverse economic, political and social contexts. In telecommunications infrastructure projects, Alcatel-Lucent competes with the Chinese Huawei, Spanish Telefónica battles with the Mexican América Móvil and the Brazilian construction company Odebrecht vies with the French Bechtel, to name just a few examples.

1.2 THE LARGEST LATIN AMERICAN BUSINESSES

According to the magazine *América Economía*, in the ranking of 500 largest Latin American businesses,[4] Brazil leads with Petrobras (US$167.8 billion[5]) and also by total number of companies, with 211. It is followed by Mexico with 120, then Chile with 71, Peru with 32, Colombia with 30 and Argentina with 23.

Among the top ten companies in Latin America, Brazil has five: the mining company Vale, the oil companies Petrobras and Petrobras Distribuidora and two family businesses, the construction company Odebrecht and the meat company JBS/Friboi. Mexico has three: Pemex, América Móvil and the American Wal-Mart of Mexico. The last two making the top ten are state-owned companies: the Venezuelan PDVSA and the Colombian Ecopetrol. Oil and gas dominate the results of the ranking by sector.

The ten largest companies in Latin America have greater economic power than the global average. As can be seen in Figure 1.4, and taking

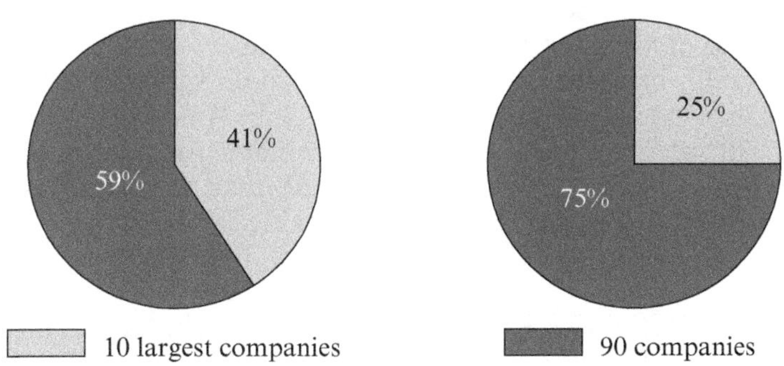

Source: Author's elaboration based on data from *América Economía* and *Fortune* Global 500 (2013 edition).

Figure 1.4 Percentage of concentration of sales of the ten largest companies with respect to the 100 largest in Latin America and the world

into account the data from *América Economía* (2013), the ten largest Latin American businesses account for 41 per cent of total sales of the 100 largest companies, while according to data from *Fortune* Global 500 (2013), the ten largest globally only make up 25 per cent of sales. That is to say, the influence of the ten largest businesses is much greater in Latin America than in the rest of the world.

The importance of family businesses in the region, which we shall look at in the next section, is reflected in the fact that the founder of América Móvil (now with his sons Carlos and Patrick Slim Domit as co-presidents) is the second richest man in the world, with a fortune of US$65 billion.[6] Latin America has seven billionaires in Forbes' ranking of 100 billionaires in the world: two in Brazil, two in Mexico, two in Colombia and one in Chile.

1.3 THE INFLUENCE OF FAMILY BUSINESSES IN LATIN AMERICA

According to the consulting company Exaudi,[7] 85 per cent of private Latin American businesses are family businesses, they were founded in the last decades, with an average of between 11 and 50 employees and annual revenues of about US$3 million. Only 12 per cent of them generate more than US$23 million in annual sales. Of these businesses 47 per cent are managed by the founders, 29 per cent by the second generation and 14 per cent by both generations and only 10 per cent of these businesses are managed by the third or fourth generation.

If we look at the list of the ten largest companies in *América Economía*, four are family businesses, three are local, the Mexican América Móvil and the Brazilian Odebrecht and JBS/Friboi, and one American, Wal-Mart of Mexico. In volatile economies like those in Latin America, family ownership with a long-term focus survive better than a 'traditional' public company that is at the mercy of investors asking for short-term results.

1.4 THE RISE OF EMERGING MULTINATIONALS AND *GLOBAL LATINAS*[8]

The rise of emerging multinationals in the last years has been very noticeable. In 2010 (Ramamurti, 2012), they represented 25 per cent of the global flow of direct investment and their disruptive effect alerted academics. Research in business schools has focused mainly on the differences between traditional multinationals (European, American or Japanese) and these new multinationals (Guillén and García-Canal, 2010), the motivations, the factors that determine their international expansion (Yeoh, 2011) and the factors determining where and how they invest. Some researchers believe that these emerging companies have flourished within protected economic environments and have benefited from subsidized loans and are not part of the technological vanguard (Cuervo-Cazurra, 2012; Guillén and García-Canal, 2010).

In a recent article (Casanova and Losada, 2012), and based on previous empirical work on *Global Latinas* (Casanova, 2009), we argue that these emerging businesses have survived in a competitive environment with leading multinationals thanks to their competitive advantages and their own resources. For example, the Argentinian company Tenaris and the Brazilian firm Petrobras developed technological know-how internally and have used it to provide products and services to clients all over the world. América Móvil managed to defend and increase its market share in the region using its own marketing resources.

Some of the Latin American businesses were created at the beginning of the twentieth century and have managed to survive for more than 100 years despite numerous economic crises. We can distinguish three phases in the internationalization process. The first phase (1970–90) is the beginning of the *multilatinas*, when they expanded in their natural market, the neighbouring countries. Following my own definition in an article in *Foreign Affairs Latinoamérica* (Casanova, 2002), natural markets are those that share the same language or history or are geographically close. The term *multilatinas* was coined at that time and defines the Latin American companies that began their expansion in the region. This phase of international expansion stopped in the 1980s, the so-called 'lost decade', when the governments of the region defaulted on their government debts.

The second phase (1990–2002) corresponds to the Washington Concensus years. It is the big wave of privatizations of telecommunications, energy, water, the financial sector and natural resources. The Latin American press was talking about 'La Reconquista', alluding to the arrival en masse of Spanish companies that knowing the region, saw an opportunity where others saw risk. Twenty years later, the Spanish banks BBVA and Santander are the main players in the financial sector in the region. Spanish Telefónica is one of the leaders in the telecommunications sector. This influx of foreign companies was a catalyst for the *latinas*, who began their own process of internationalization. Some followed the path of the free trade agreements. Argentina, Brazil, Paraguay and Uruguay signed an agreement for a Common Market of the South, and Mexico signed its own accord with the United States and Canada in 1994. Mexican businesses expanded towards the United States: Cemex bought

Southdown there in 2000. Brazilian companies expanded southwards. Petrobras increased its presence in Argentina with investments in the production of gas in UTE Aguaragüe (Salta), the perforation of the exploratory well San Julián (Santa Cruz) and exploratory drilling in Cuenca Neuquina. América Móvil took advantage of the technology sector crisis of 2000 to buy shares in Bell Canada and Bell South, MCI WorldCom, at bargain prices, and overnight became leader of the regional sector.

The third phase (2002–08) is that of the emerging markets in which global Latin American businesses were created. The rise in price of raw materials (oil, copper, silver, gold or iron ore) and agricultural products linked to the increased demand from China and Asia was beneficial to Latin America. According to the Economic Commission for Latin America and the Caribbean (ECLAC), the region achieved, for the first time in 30 years, an average GDP growth of 5 per cent, except in 2009 when, as a consequence of the global crisis, the economy shrank by 1.9 per cent. In 2006, the Brazilian mining company Vale, the largest global exporter of iron ore, bought the Canadian company Inco, specialist in nickel for US$18.9 billion. *Global Latinas* successfully entered Europe, Canada and the United States.

In 2010, the fourth and present phase began, in which the emerging markets reassert themselves while the West struggles to get out of the crisis. Brazil and Mexico are the main players in six of the world's ten largest fusions and acquisitions. According to data from September 2010 published in the British paper, the *Financial Times*, the greatest acquisition was in Mexico, of América Móvil by Carso Global Telecom for a total value of US$24 billion.

1.5 THE COMING OF AGE OF *GLOBAL LATINAS*

In 2006 I began a qualitative study[9] of global Latin American[10] firms in collaboration with the IADB. The sample sought to cover different countries, industrial sectors and sizes in order to find common behaviour among them. The study used case methodology and included interviews with the managers from the companies. We wanted to discover the reasons for internationalization, the strategies they had followed and what their differentiating characteristics were. The results of the research are given in detail below.

1.5.1 Internationalization as a Learning Experience

The macroeconomic context is important in the daily performance of emerging companies. The continent has been characterized by an enormous volatility in the last 30 years: the debt crisis in the 1980s, the Mexican crisis in 1994, the devaluation of the Brazilian real in 1999 and of the Argentinian peso in January 2002 all caused disruption to business in the region. A company's ambition is to enter stable economies that will compensate any domestic instability. The capital cost for Latin American firms has been, and still is, very high, which puts them at a disadvantage when competing with Western businesses, who have cheaper credit facilities. Cemex's acquisitions in Spain in 1992 helped the company to organize its funding at cheaper rates from its Spanish subsidiary. Most countries in the region now have investment grade but it should be remembered that until 2007, the only countries that did have it were Mexico and Chile. When the Spanish firm Repsol bought the Argentinian YPF in December 1999 (which was later nationalized by the Argentine government), some experts pointed out that Repsol was able to do so only because it had access to cheaper credit facilities by being in Europe.

According to the classic work by John Dunning (1993), internationalization of businesses is motivated by three reasons: to seek efficiency, to secure natural resources at reasonable prices or to enter new markets. Latin American businesses are looking, mainly, to enter new markets in order to increase in size. Emerging businesses do not always begin their expansion with a clear competitive advantage, but rather it is something they acquire during the process of internationalization. Thus, a virtuous circle is formed, in which internationalization is seen as a learning process to acquire knowledge, this knowledge is brought home and is then used to gradually build up a competitive advantage. For example, the Guatemalan fast-food restaurant chain Pollo Campero made its first international excursion in 1986 to Miami. Although it was forced to leave the city the following year, Pollo Campero learned to understand the differences in the catering sector between the United States and Central America. After this first failure, it realized that it had to improve its organizational processes, gain the loyalty of its staff and so build a business model that could be transferred to other countries.

1.5.2 First, the Natural Market

The expansion of Latin American multinationals begins in its natural market. Within the natural markets there is more information and thus the competitive panorama is better known, to both clients and suppliers, and it is easier to attract talent. The networks and links between countries in a natural market are tighter than outside it.

The Ibero-American world is a huge natural market that shares a similar culture and has two predominant (and quite similar) languages,

Spanish and Portuguese. The flow of immigrants in both directions across the Atlantic has created constant exchanges of people, information and culture. Since 1991, Ibero-American summits have been held, in which the 22 presidents of the member countries meet. One initiative promoted by these summits has been the Ibero-American Forum of Higher Education. Similar to the Erasmus programme of European university student exchange, there now exists an exchange programme for Ibero-American students within the network of a thousand universities in 11 Ibero-American countries.[11] Between 2005 and 2015, Banco Santander is funding, with 600 million euros, a programme that promotes the movement of 15000 students and researchers within the university network.

Just as the United Kingdom has been the European door for US companies, Spain has opened up Europe for Spanish-speaking firms. Astrid y Gastón, the Peruvian restaurant chain, inaugurated its first European premises in Madrid. Portugal is the bridge for Brazilian companies. Banco Itaú opened its European headquarters in Lisbon in 1994 and Embraer entered Europe via Portugal when it led the consortium that acquired OGMA in 2004.

1.5.3 Are Latin American Multinationals Different?

In Casanova (2009), we found some common characteristics such as strong leadership with a long-term vision. Leaders such as Daniel Servitje from Grupo Bimbo manage the day-to-day affairs of their businesses while at the same time keeping their eye on the long term. These are not firms that copy a strict business plan devised on home ground; rather, they are flexible and capable of adapting with agility to different realities.

State ownership still holds sway in Latin American firms and in the emerging world in general. Five out of the ten largest Latin American companies are partially or totally state-owned and are found in the oil or gas sector: Petrobras and Petrobras distribuidora, PDVSA, Pemex and Ecopetrol.

Family businesses are common and often are organized as a conglomerate. Grupo Carso, for example, comprises hotels, mines, railways and shopping malls. The different sectors of a conglomerate are useful in times of crisis, as losses in one sector can be compensated by the profits in other sectors. The strength of family businesses in the region is described in other chapters of this book.

Other characteristics particular to Latin American businesses are that they know, and adapt their products and services to, the clients at the so-called base of the pyramid. The upper-class market is small in Latin America and if you want to succeed you must attract the general population and adjust to their limited spending power. The Hawaiana flip flops, part of the Brazilian conglomerate Camargo Correa, is a global product that was initially aimed as cheap footwear for the Latin American poor. Through a series of innovations in marketing and in the design of the flip flops, the product became global with a brand image that alludes to the relaxed and outdoor lifestyle in Brazil.

1.5.4 Reverse Innovation

Traditionally, it was the developed world that exported new products, and innovation in general, to the developing world. Now reverse innovation goes from the emerging countries towards the West. Microcredit, the pre-paid card for cell phones, and sugar cane-based ethanol are some of the innovations that have revolutionized the financial sector, telecommunications or biofuels in emerging countries and from there have been imported to Europe and the United States. The Brazilian aeronautics company Embraer, for example, has a business model that some specialists call reverse outsourcing. At the plant in São José dos Campos, aircrafts are designed and assembled, the parts having been manufactured in Europe or the United States. Brazilian aeronautical engineers coming from the Instituto Tecnológico de Aeronáutica (ITA), one of the best aeronautical schools in the world and closely linked to Embraer, are excellent professionals and comparatively cheaper. Thus, Embraer can get quality at a low price.

At a time when alternative energy is in high demand, Brazil offers the world its hybrid engines, which it began to produce in 2003. These engines can work with petrol/gas, ethanol or any combination of the two. The German multinational Volkswagen was the first to commercialize vehicles with these engines. Last year the technology extended to motorcycles and Honda was first to launch a bike with these characteristics. Ethanol is available in all the gas stations of the country and all manufacturers produce these types of flexible engines. Ethanol is the result of the Brazilian government's goal, after the oil crisis of 1973, to be self-sufficient in energy, and of agricultural research done in Embrapa, the governmental research institute that was founded that same year. Embrapa is also responsible for Brazil's status as an agricultural power, achieving a 150 per cent increase in productivity in the sector in the last 30 years. According to Pedro Antonio Pereira, Director of Embrapa, there was only a 30 per cent increase in agricultural land use in that period of time.

The so-called creative industries range from fashion to industrial design, cinematography, audiovisual products and cultural tourism. It is worth pointing out the success of Latin American music: the Colombian

Shakira is one of Latin America's most renowned artists and famous worldwide; the Argentinian tango was declared part of the world's cultural heritage by the United Nations. Apart from music, the region exports television soaps produced by the Brazilian television company Globo or the Mexican Televisa. In Argentina, television programmes are produced and adapted in small and medium-sized companies such as Pol Ka. Argentina exports more than US$500 million in this sector. This is the result of a combination of factors: a highly qualified workforce, a very creative culture of design, plus the commitment of the Government of Buenos Aires, which established the Metropolitan Institute of Design and Innovation (IMDI).

1.5.5 The 'New Reality'

Under these new circumstances, risk is everywhere, not only in emerging countries, and the most volatile currencies have in recent years been those that in the past provided a safe haven in a crisis.

As commented above, Latin American multinationals went to Europe and the United States to learn. At a time when growth and innovation is no longer exclusive to the developed world, are they going to know how to shift their gaze in order to take advantage of opportunities for growth and learning in other emerging countries such as China?

Will the models of business, management and leadership that have for the last 50 years been taught in business schools still be valid for the new emerging multinationals?

The internationalization of Latin American businesses has only just begun. What skills will the Brazilian and Latin American executives need in order to make their business succeed?

The definition of economic success has changed; social and environmental elements have been incorporated. Latin America has the lowest carbon dioxide emissions in the world. The last five years have also seen noticeable social improvements. Will the region and its businesses take advantage of this leadership at a global level?

NOTES

* I am grateful to Paloma Fernández Pérez and Andrea Lluch for their encouragement and support.

1. Please refer to Chapter 5 for more information about Brazilian family businesses by Armando Dalla Costa, Carlos Eduardo Drumond and José María Las Heras.
2. Please refer to Chapter 12 for more information about Chilean family businesses by Jon Martínez Echezárraga.

3. Please refer to Chapter 11 for more information about Peruvian family businesses by Martín Monsalve Zanatti.
4. http://rankings.americaeconomia.com/2012/las-500-empresas-mas-grandes-de-america-latina/ (accessed October 2012).
5. The turnover data of largest businesses in the rankings of *América Economía* and *Fortune* 500 show notable differences. For example, Petrobras in *Fortune* 500 has a turnover of US$145 915 million and in *América Economía* US$167 888.3. It is possible that the results were collected at different times and also that the fluctuations in value of the Brazilian real with respect to the US dollar have a role to play.
6. http://www.forbes.com, December 2013 (accessed 15 December 2013). In 2012, Carlos Slim was the wealthiest man in the world for that year; Bill Gates has returned to first position (at the time of writing).
7. http://www.exaudionline.com (accessed 3 December 2013).
8. *Global Latinas* as defined by Casanova (2009) refers to the Latin American multinationals that have expanded into developed markets such as Europe, the United States and Japan.
9. Casanova, L. and M. Fraser (2009). Casanova, L. (2009).
10. The companies studied were: from Mexico América Móvil, Bimbo, Cemex, Grupo Carso, Grupo Modelo, Televisa, TV Azteca; from Brazil Vale, Embraer, Petrobras, Banco Itaú, CSN, Pão de Açúcar, Sadia; Grupo Luksic from Chile and Techint/tenaris from Argentina; and medium and small firms Concha y Toro (Chile), Natura & Politec (Brazil), Pollo Campero (Guatemala) and Astrid y Gastón (Peru).
11. The 11 countries comprising this network are Argentina, Brazil, Chile, Colombia, Spain, Mexico, Peru, Portugal, Puerto Rico, Uruguay and Venezuela.

REFERENCES

Casanova, L. (2002). 'Lazos de familia: Las inversiones españolas en Iberoamérica'. *Foreign Affairs en español* **2** (2) (May), 67–85. http://www.foreignaffairs-esp.org/20020501faenespessay8472/lourdes-casanova/ (accessed September 2015).

Casanova, L. (2009). *Global Latinas: Emerging Multinationals from Latin America*. New York: Palgrave Macmillan. http://www.globallatinas.org (accessed September 2015).

Casanova, L. and M. Fraser (2009). 'From multilatinas to global latinas. The Latin American multinationals (compilation case studies)' (January). Inter-American Development Bank Working Paper. Washington, DC.

Casanova, L. and M. Losada (2012). 'Resources and internationalization strategies: the case of Latin American multinationals'. INSEAD Working papers.

Cuervo-Cazurra, A. (2012). 'Extending theory by analyzing developing country multinational companies: solving the Goldilocks debate'. *Global Strategy Journal* **2**, 153–67.

Dunning, J.H. (1993). *Multinational Enterprises and the Global Economy*. Reading, MA: Addison-Wesley.

ECLAC (Economic Commission for Latin America and the Caribbean) (2011, 2012). *Foreign Direct Investment in Latin America and the Caribbean*. Santiago: United Nations.

Guillén, M. and E. García-Canal (2010). *The New Multinationals: Spanish Firms in a Global Context*. Cambridge: Cambridge University Press.

IADB (Inter-American Development Bank) (2010). *Ten Years After the Take-off Taking Stock of China-Latin America and the Caribbean Economic Relations*

(October). Washington, DC: Integration and Trade Sector, Inter-American Development Bank.
Ramamurti, R. (2012). 'What is really different about emerging market multinationals?'. *Global Strategy Journal* **2**, 41–7.
Yeoh, P. (2011). 'Location choice and the internationalization sequence; insights from Indian pharmaceutical companies'. *International Marketing Review* **28**, 291–312.

2. State, institutions and impact of economic policies on the historical evolution of family businesses in Spain and Latin America

Javier Vidal Olivares

The historical structure of an economic system based on capitalism has had various formal rhythms and characteristics in different parts of the world. The institutional framework constitutes one of the main determinants of the differences that have molded modern economic growth. Literature has shown repeatedly how the characteristics of institutions and their stability have set the pace (Acemoglu and Robinson, 2012). Along with this, it is worth noting that growth comes from companies, the principal players in economic progress. It is the activity of the firms, therefore, that gives added value to production.

For a good part of the twentieth century, the large corporations stood out as a virtuous system: thousands of workers together, hundreds of managers and thousands of shareholders who gave their capital to an executive board that sought to make the company grow, to raise profits and distribute dividends, permanently improving profitability. The large firm, originating in the United States, expanded internationally as multinationals. After World War II, large internationalized corporate firms were seen as the architects of growth; while establishing themselves on the stock markets and in corporate finance as the ideal mechanism for providing capital to companies, they presented the modern limited company as being the best option for guaranteeing a permanent capacity for growth (Chandler, 1977).

By dint of widespread teaching – to trainee managers and directors in business schools – of the virtues of the large firm, alternative forms of business management were largely ignored. Small and medium-sized enterprises (SMEs) and small family firms came to be considered marginal, their proliferation seen as a symptom of an economy unable to create productive companies. This deeply entrenched paradigm was challenged from the very heart by industrial nations such as Germany and Japan (Odaka and Sawai, 1999). In these countries, and others of later economic development, the small and medium-sized businesses and family firms (as defined by Chua et al., 1999) began to be valued as efficient organizations. Family ownership and its management by groups with family ties were shown to be rational and efficient mechanisms, guaranteeing permanent improvements in the organization and ensuring the durability of its production units (Fernández Pérez, 2003, 2013; Fernández Pérez and Colli, 2013). The problem is not if family firms are obstacles for economic growth; the question is if they are capable of being competitive in research and technological change, in exporting and investing in international markets. There is no doubt that the economic policy put in motion by governments and the relationship with other enterprises in the market, especially with big companies and multinationals, is the scenario where family firms can aim to be competitive (Guillén, 2001; Guillén and García Canal, 2010).

In Latin America and Southern Europe the central role taken by the model of SMEs and family firms constitutes an essential mechanism for understanding and explaining the evolution of economies (Fernández Pérez and Puig, 2007; Haber, 2000).

In order to understand the interactions between economic growth and the role of the SMEs and family businesses – including the minority large ones – we shall firstly address the external factors that condition their evolution. The most important of these is the role of the State and economic policies. Secondly, the focus is on transversal questions: the common elements that span countries and regions. The general aim is to establish which features influence the performance of family businesses in Latin America and Spain. Between these factors the most important has been the State and its capacity to design policies that could interfere in the behavior of enterprises.

2.1 FAMILY BUSINESSES: KEYS TO THE LATIN AMERICAN AND SPANISH BUSINESS NETWORK

In Spain and Latin America, the cycles of the industrialization process show different chronologies but their basis for modern economic growth have common characteristics, especially in the twentieth century when the State played a crucial role in the organization and regulation of the economy and the creation of a State-owned business sector. This characteristic is decisive since it qualifies the dominant theses in the interpretation of the role of the modern company; above all the theses that emphasize the importance of the large corporation (Chandler et al., 1999). This has been the case in advanced economies; but in those with a later development – such as Spain – the tendencies have been different. Even if the large business became prominent, the SMEs maintained their majority, especially dominated by family ownership structures (Salas and Galve, 2003).

The State, as a key element in institutional organization, has been decisive in the historical formation of business structures: as regulator, as source of economic intervention and as Entrepreneurial-State, fundamental in developing strategic interests (Toninelli, 2000). The establishment of economic policies has been a tool used by the State for guiding the macroeconomic aspects, through monetary, commercial, fiscal and financial policies.

In Spain and a great part of Latin America, the structure of the State and its political structure has been the central point when determining the role of SMEs and family businesses. These countries have had very unstable political systems, in which there has been a predominance of cycles of authoritarian regimes. In economic terms, this meant the adoption of policies of commercial isolation and pronounced interventionism – as shown in Part IV of this book. In the business context, these cycles were accompanied by the creation of State-owned enterprises, especially in sectors considered strategic by dominant groups. State intervention led to a reduction in the opening of economies, whereby there was a conscious policy of withdrawal from the international market as a source of growth as export capacity decreased. Nevertheless, State action did not always hinder the arrival of foreign direct investment. The entry of capital and the introduction of multinational companies were supported by the State in some Latin American countries in the 1950s and 1960s, with the idea that this would stimulate industrialization. There were, therefore, cycles of closure to the outside, and others of selective welcoming of capital and companies according to the internal needs of the policies designed by the State. Foreign debt grew due to problems of structural fiscal deficit, restricting the capacity for internal investment and hampering the performance of private companies. Under these conditions, technological progress or innovation was halted, making foreign investment and the introduction of foreign companies even more necessary.

Another element common to Spain and Latin America was the prominent role played by the agricultural sector in their economic structures. But the agricultural sector was not always an ultra-conservative activity or reticent to the introduction of changes. In large areas of the northern states of Mexico and in some agricultural regions of Colombia, the agricultural sector was responsible for significant moves toward the development of commercial agriculture, market-oriented and with an ownership structure based on family businesses with capacity for innovation (Cerutti, 2011; Dávila, 2011). In other cases, the crisis of low crop diversification and low productivity was taken advantage of in order to proceed with a total restructuring toward industrial production, a process in which the agricultural reforms of Mexico in the 1930s and 1940s had a positive impact.

In many parts of Latin America, mining and oil exploitation absorbed a highly significant amount of resources (Bucheli, 2011; Guajardo, 2012). In the producer countries, the State monopoly on the production of raw materials led, in times of concentration of political power, to diseconomies. This was important after the boom period for export, from the 1920s onwards, and particularly in the 1930s. After World War II, the exploitation of these resources by foreign companies – often multinationals – became more common, with different alternatives for mining and oil. The concentration of production activities on raw materials or non-renewable resources for prolonged periods of time hindered the diversification of Latin American economies, generating dependencies and making these countries more vulnerable to the cycles of changes of relative price.

The importance of the State, as well as the dominance, for a good part of the nineteenth and twentieth centuries, of agriculture and activities linked to natural resources and raw materials and relatively little influence from industry gave rise to an overwhelming presence of family firms. Large businesses, already present in Argentina, Mexico and Brazil at the end of the nineteenth century, were, however, a minority in the history of the region. For the most part, large businesses were under State ownership or indirectly controlled by the State, just as multinationals were, especially after the 1930s when in response to the Great Depression, policies were implemented that accelerated the industrialization process through substitution of imports. The SMEs and family businesses were also indirectly stimulated in their development and growth by State intervention, in that many were fueled by large public companies, either as subsidiaries or through subcontracting. Sometimes they were also linked to foreign multinationals when the markets were opened to them, generally in the context of an increase in foreign direct investment.

2.2 CONDITIONING FACTORS IN THE HISTORICAL EVOLUTION OF FAMILY BUSINESS IN SPAIN

The principal characteristic of Spanish economic history was the difficulty in developing industrialization (Tortella and Núñez, 2011). The increase in industrial activities in the first third of the twentieth century noticeably reduced the importance of the agricultural sector in total production, even though the produce of the primary sector still had a very much higher participation in relative terms than in other Western European economies. The Civil War (1936–39) and the Franco dictatorship (1939–75) interrupted the process of diversification and expansion of industrial activities. For a long period, 1940–60, the Spanish economy was in a state of pronounced stagnation.

State intervention increased in the 1920s, but it was with Franco's regime that it became the norm. In this period, a public enterprise sector was formed to set up public companies in sectors such as oil and its derivatives, telecommunications and all industry related to armaments. What had been a common occurrence in the 1920s and 1930s on the Continent, became in Spain an exaggerated creation of businesses controlled by the public sector. State intervention and the overwhelming presence of public companies in the economy reduced entrepreneurial initiative, leading to market inefficiency and the creation of oligopolies and monopolies.

Intervention was relaxed in the 1960s, making room for a recuperation of private initiative. In the first third of the twentieth century, there was, as Chapter 10 shows, an increase in family business groups in sectors that were not excessively regulated. The periods that provided the most important opportunities for these firms were in the years 1900–36 and 1960–2010. One of the advantages that favored their growth was that less capital was needed for funding. The opportunities to facilitate the diversification of many activities improved the expectations of business groups, but family firms could only develop in sectors where no significant increase in size was necessary for growth. This was the case with firms in the textile, food and agriculture, paper, pharmaceuticals and furniture sectors.

Family businesses found it difficult to develop, given the historical structure of the Spanish financial system. This system, in the first third of the twentieth century, was oriented toward an industrial bank with close ties to State financing, thus hampering the organization of a universal banking system focused solely on trade, with credit facilities for family businesses. The self-financing, which the majority of SMEs were forced to take on, made the fiscal system and its treatment of companies another important element in the shaping of survival strategies for family businesses (Durán et al., 1982). The complications of creating a modern fiscal system in which family firms are not discriminated against by non-differentiation of individual and corporate taxation was an obstacle to the development of family businesses. The changes made to the fiscal system after the return to democracy at the end of the 1970s, the preparation for joining the European Community and the formation of a lobby group by family firm all opened up opportunities for better treatment of these firms by the taxation system in the 1990s.

Behind the organization of the interests of family businesses lie the regional traditions of Spain (García Ruiz and Manera, 2006). In comparative terms, family SMEs have tended toward greater development in economies on the Mediterranean seaboard (Vidal, 2006). In these areas, economic activities were centered on manufacturing, where family business ownership predominated. Since the late eighteenth century, the textile industry had expanded at a great pace in Catalonia, in the wool and cotton sectors. Similarly, it is worth noting the production of agriculture and food, paper, furniture, and wood, chemicals and its derivatives, including pharmaceutical products or light metals (Fernández Pérez, 2003; Fernández Pérez and Puig, 2007). Businesses established themselves early on in these regions, at the same time as local production systems became organized. This does not mean that in other regions there was not the same development of activities or that a different type of business organization was in use.[1] On the contrary, in the 1960s the production activities organized under the family SME system predominated (Caruana et al., 2011). At the end of the 1970s, access to the European Economic Community accelerated the creation of large businesses, aimed at being able to compete with other large companies in Europe, but the SMEs maintained their ground right through the decade of the 1980s. The relevance of this type of firm emerged institutionally with the creation in 1992 of the Instituto de la Empresa Familiar (Association of Family Business), the principal defensive group of the interests of this type of firms.

2.3 THE STATE AND PUBLIC POLICIES: CONDITIONING FACTORS IN THE HISTORICAL EVOLUTION OF THE FAMILY FIRM IN LATIN AMERICA

It is a complex task to establish the standards that fixed the characteristics of family firms in Latin America. The huge size of the region and its historical differences makes it hard to find common denominators for all nations and economies. The elements discussed here refer to some large countries that can be used as examples for what occurred in the region: Mexico and Argentina. We also consider Colombia where family firms and business groups have had a decisive influence in the political system.

It is the cyclic conditions and structural variables that have influenced each country's configuration of business structure. In Argentina, the phase as agricultural exporter in the late nineteenth and early twentieth centuries, and in Mexico, the period of the *Porfiriato* had different effects on the structure of businesses (see Chapters 4 and 6). In the Argentinian economy, the export from the pampas (meat, leather) was in the hands of creole family businesses, with a significant contribution from foreign entrepreneurs. European immigration supported economic expansion from the Argentinian border inwards, based on a model of small family producers and groups of landowners. There were, however, relevant and diversified economic groups – explained in Chapter 6 – that had arisen in the 1860s and had continued into the first third of the twentieth century, constituting the elite of Argentinian large business.

During the *Porfiriato*, Mexico channeled the entry of foreign capital toward the setting up of large-scale service and industrial firms that brought inflows of investment to stimulate internal growth. Only the direct or indirect intervention of the State led to better development of business groups, large companies and State-owned businesses. In some cases it was the State itself that took the initiative to create companies that dealt with the production of strategic goods and services; in other cases, the establishment of firms by private entrepreneurs and investors was encouraged through direct stimulation by the State itself.

In the inter-war period, family business groups consolidated and became diversified in countries like Argentina; in parallel, the arrival of multinationals to the local market generated a wide range of subsidiary companies and created supply links with family SMEs in the host countries, transferring knowledge and technology (Barbero and Lluch, 2013). Also in the case of Argentina, the opportunities that arose with the arrival of foreign investment boosted local family businesses, which, through the acquisition of foreign licenses and patents, could adopt new distribution, marketing and publicity techniques (Lluch, 2010). This was significant in the manufacturing industry, in the automotive industry, and in pharmaceuticals and chemicals, branches in which Argentinian SMEs were beginning to excel. There is evidence that in the first third of the twentieth century, local industry expanded, with a parallel process of concentration and formation of large businesses; this in turn stimulated the creation of family SMEs whose growth was fueled by the development of big businesses. At the same time, also in the service sector, the expansion was keenly felt, especially when mass consumerism opened the way for trade circuits, department stores and other retail distribution chains in the cities; in Buenos Aires as well as in metropolitan areas in the interior of the country (Rocchi, 2006).

In Mexico, the Revolution changed the institutional conditions for enterprises, orienting general economic policies toward a more protectionist economic nationalism that stimulated new industrial branches and strengthened existing ones. The revolutionary process had a negative impact on businesses due to its destructive effects, confiscations and the lack of support given by the revolutionaries to business sectors. Family businesses with links to the oligarchy that supported the political system of *Porfiriato*, some of them from the north of the country in new sectors such as cement, metals and cotton, suffered greatly in the Revolution. In contrast, small family firms in Mexico City grew and expanded with the Revolution, in particular Spanish firms that were decisive in textile and food, as well as in the retail trade and distribution, and also in the financial sector.

One relevant question concerns the role the financing system played in Mexico, given that family firms and the SMEs in general depended on the supply of capital. A regional banking system started to take shape at the end of the nineteenth century, after a long time without any institutionalized formal banking. With banking legislation deeply entrenched in the issue conditions of 1897, the strong push of regional banking began to make itself felt. Researchers who have studied the formation and evolution of these banks emphasize this was an expression of entrepreneurs' needs for funds in order to operate at a greater capacity than that being generated by their own business activities. The need to count on greater possibilities of capital to support the agricultural, commercial and industrial development of companies and those of the whole regional systems was solved through the creation of formal credit institutions (Cerutti and Marichal, 2003). Cases such as the entrepreneurs of Sinaloa and La Laguna region show how, even before the existence of banking legislation, entrepreneurs turned to these mechanisms in order to guarantee permanent funding channels that gave continuity to the prevailing forms of credit in economies that were still under development. Family firms linked to very active regional entrepreneurs in Mexico could thus count on a mechanism to help their operations.

In Mexico, the 1920s brought a process of recuperation before the crisis provoked by the international recession in the following decade. In Monterrey, new family firms emerged. The Zambrano family in 1920 founded Cementos Monterrey, a firm that in 1931 would merge with that of the Hernández y Muguerza family to create Cementos de México (CEMEX), destined to become, by the end of the twentieth century, one of the most important Mexican multinationals. Out of the line-up of families from Monterrey with a history in business, other prominent companies emerged. Metal and steel, food and breweries were the favorite industries of family businesses in the state of Nuevo León. The Garza Sada and Sada families, owners of the Cuauhtémoc Brewery and Monterrey Glass Company, were an example of the climate of business creation that reigned in the capital of Nuevo León; but there were other families too that developed the productive, successful and diversified economic base of the richest state in the north of Mexico. In addition to the fertile conditions for business in Monterrey since the end of the colonial period, State and federal legislation favored industrial development and funding for productive activities, anticipating the policies of substitution of imports that Mexico put into operation in the 1930s.

Family firms emerged in Colombia in the first part of the twentieth century, bringing about business groups. This process had a regional base where family firms were firmly rooted. Six business groups created during this period were founded as family firms (Rodríguez, 2014). At the end of the twentieth century, three of the four more important business groups were controlled by family firms and their capacity to press and impose decisions at the political level were decisive. Those business groups avoiding employers' organizations activity (Schneider, 2004) had the capacity to develop their interests by imposing the economic policy followed by the State, as explained in Chapter 7. The political influence developed by business groups controlled by family firms over the State is the most relevant feature of the evolution of family businesses in Colombia.

The international economic depression forced Latin American economies to adopt new economic policies. These were centered on monetary devaluations, associated with the abandoning of the gold standard and the raising of tariffs. Not only was the response circumstantial through the adoption of these instruments of economic policy but it was also broadened through the introduction of more integral elements that took shape in what has become known as the process of import substitution industrialization (ISI) (Cardoso and Helwege, 1993).

The impact of the crisis led to the adoption of these measures of monetary and fiscal policies, in Argentina as well as in Mexico (Díaz Fuentes, 1994), while the adoption of the ISI was accelerated due to the consequences of World War II on the region. These policies were spurred on by price instability of raw materials, deterioration in conditions for trade and the need to support a nascent industry through protectionism. Policies of State intervention had their starting point in distinct prior circumstances in Argentina and Mexico, where the degree of industrial development differed. The ISI was applied using a wide range of instruments: authorization of import permits, tariffs, overvalued exchange rates and deployment of direct State investment in selected industries. The effects of the ISI exaggerated the growth of industry, especially if that industry was boosted by the State apparatus. That said, the effects of the ISI should not be overemphasized, nor can it be claimed that its approach was completely new. In reality, the ISI went beyond the substitution of imports, for the State had an increasingly significant role in economic and social promotion, while protectionism had been in discussion years before and exports were still playing a relevant role (Bértola and Ocampo, 2013).

The impact of policies based on the ISI on SMEs and those under family control are still not known. It should be pointed out that State interventionism and its direct action of creating a business sector of public ownership diminished the entrepreneurship, damaging the possibilities for development of private companies. It is likely that this was the case for sectors such as the automotive industry, steel and others that needed significant investment of capital and technology. In contrast, the intermediate manufacturing industries took advantage of the opportunities of a restricted competitive environment to boost SMEs and family businesses. Another question is how companies that had just come through the depression and were in a new cycle of protectionism responded to the new policies. Here, we refer to business groups of family ownership or family business networks that were facing different rules of internal market behavior. In Monterrey and Nuevo León, these businesses responded to the crisis through the process of productive integration, adapting to the application of the ISI. Family businesses of the area played a central role in a second process of industrialization, with special significance in the more capital-intensive branches such as base metals, cement and glass, and automotive, and less importance in branches of light industry, like textile, leather and footwear. In addition, the family business groups supported each other by creating, in parallel, societies of financial intermediation, which they used to cover their capital needs in the new industrial branches. This growth process continued with the broadening and diversification of new sectors that the ISI permitted until the 1970s. From then on, and stimulated by the State itself, a completely new phase began in the impact of the ISI on private businesses. The Mexican State, through authorization of subsidies for the integration of firms, supported family business groups who owned various companies that went on to diversify in unrelated sectors (Cerutti, 2000). These groups were the response to the internal evolution of the ISI's application to the previous characteristics of the business and industrial fabric of Monterrey that had been formed during the nineteenth century and that in the twentieth century had developed and adapted to external cycles and their repercussions, in the national market as well as the international. When the ISI ran out in Mexico and the opening up of markets generated a new situation of international competition, these same groups transformed themselves rapidly, integrating themselves in the process of internationalization, whether in the direction of the United States and Canada with the North American Free Trade Agreement (NAFTA) or toward the creation of multinationals (Cerutti et al., 2006). This move has demonstrated the robustness of these entrepreneurs and their family-owned and controlled businesses in their ability to adapt to cyclic – and also institutional – changes.

In the case of Argentina, the adoption of protectionist policies associated with the application of the ISI came simultaneously with an increasingly more business-oriented State, reinforced by the characteristics of Perón's regime. The repercussions of these policies on private companies and in particular on SMEs and family firms varied according to the different phases of import substitution and the fluctuations in internal and institutional policies in Argentina (Barbero and Lluch, 2013). The historiography of Argentina has concentrated on the reconstruction of industrial policies in order to understand how the phase of ISI affected the progress of the sector as a whole. The divergences are significant in relation to the role of the public sector, the affected sectors and the accrual of its effects, and the literature has produced new evidence from further-reaching research. The 1944 legislation of the industrial promotion system was the start of the policy of State support to boost the process of industrialization. Although one cannot define this as a long-term model of industrial policy, the State put into operation various instruments of economic policy, almost always related to monetary and fiscal policy, with the originality of including among the most important ones those of a financial character (Rougier, 2001).

It is hard to know what the impact of the State measures on private companies were in the long run between 1950 and 1980, except for what is reported in a few case studies. These suggest that business initiative in Argentina was strongly driven and did not generate an atrophied industry, technologically backward and dependent on protectionism in order to grow. Family businesses in sectors such as electronic component manufacture, agricultural machinery and machine tools production were able to innovate, export and show organizational capacity for production oriented toward competitive markets. If many of them failed – although others remained – it was due to macroeconomic turbulence or institutional conditions between 1950 and 1980. Another contributing factor was the retreat and later return of foreign companies and especially the invasion of multinationals (Barbero and Lluch, 2013; Rougier, 2007). What seems clear, on the other hand, is that during the ISI, large Argentinian firms and traditional business groups were disintegrating and transforming because of the impact of the arrival of multinationals; this fragmentation led to the coordination of a network of interests between the companies and entrepreneurs, which was consolidated in the 1970s by the institutional changes and instabilities suffered by the country. It should be underlined that the business groups remained a viable organization for family businesses due to their adaptation to the new circumstances and to the interests tied to the industrial policy of the State. New groups were also formed, different to the traditional ones, whereby the industrial businesses predominated over the older, more commercial companies. In the individual family businesses, changes in the environment as well as the transition to second or third generations produced structural renovations from 1950/60 (Barbero and Lluch, 2013).

After the dismantling of the ISI in 1980, one of the big changes felt in the business structure of many Latin American countries was the increased importance of family firms with influence on economic structure. In the Argentinian case, family firms strengthened their position in the face of companies bolstered by foreign capital, and family business groups even managed to grow and become internationalized despite financial difficulties but the privatizations in the 1990s changed the situation. Market liberalization and globalization of the economy increased the opportunities for family businesses, especially those organized through the system of business groups. In Mexico in 2001, out of the 100 largest businesses, 34 were family-owned (Hoshino, 2006). Family firms have retained their influence in emerging economies and have been the most novel element in the emergence of family-owned Latin American multinationals, a process that was envisaged at the end of the 1980s and that in the following years became a defining feature of how companies coming from new groups created in countries like Mexico, Argentina and Brazil are establishing themselves in the international economy (Barbero, 2014). Other cases dealt with family-owned firms that had internationalized very quickly, practically from the moment they were founded: they constitute the so-called 'born global firms' (Gabrielsson and Manek Kirpalami, 2012). Small and large companies respond to the same logic of growth, with the logical differences of capacity allowing the latter more opportunities of success. It is possible that the greater capacity and experience of second or third generations to increase the size of their business was related to the seizure of institutions in many Latin American countries. The size would be correlated with the capacity of the family businesses to act through political influence in order to favor their own strategic interests in certain periods. Large family businesses have had greater capacity to exert pressure on the design of economic policy, especially in countries where it is easier to influence decision-making due to the absence of robust democratic institutions representative of majority coalitions. In any case, the tensions between small and large family businesses were measured more in the context of influence on economic policy, rather than in growth mechanisms and autonomy in design of survival strategies.

2.4 TRANSVERSAL THEMES: FAMILY BUSINESSES IN SPAIN AND LATIN AMERICA

Family firm has played a central role in the economic and business history of the Hispanic world. In the case of Spain and Latin America, the initiative has been in the hands of entrepreneurs who adopted an ownership and management structure based on the networks that are inherent in family organizations. Risks are minimized through trust; family relationships guarantee that the uncertainties of business are kept within the family, and so the cycle of economic activity is managed with more efficiency.

This way of working meant that the continuity of entrepreneurial initiative has depended – more than in other societies and economies with more stable institutional frameworks – on periods of recession or on cycles of great intensity of State intervention as a consequence of brusque political changes. It is the State that has played the central role in the regulation of markets, with particular influence on the legal codification of the limited company and its links to the conditions of family law. The responsibility at the heart of the State, in the face of conditions of business functioning, was the unique conditioning factor, not experienced in the same way by the Anglo-Saxon or Scandinavian societies, where external regulations determined the operating of companies, and where rules were fully assimilated by the entrepreneurial families themselves.

Family usually meant 'extended family,' and the strong links within this circle and the strength of blood ties were transferred to law and from there to the companies. Ownership of shares and its responsible handling in front of the founding entrepreneur or chief executive officer has common ground in Hispanic societies; customs reinforced by common religious beliefs, based on Catholicism, are an important common denominator that pivots on the exaltation of family values. In this way, family and company have come to form a single entity, central to the functioning of the economy, by playing a fundamental role in Hispanic societies, deeply etching the path of their economic evolution as an institution.

These last features establish the relationship between the taxation system and the family firm (Fernández Pérez and Hernández, 2009). In Latin American and Spanish economies, fiscal policy has been different for large businesses than for small and family-owned firms. Tax problems are decisive because of the difficulties they cause companies when the tax base in a company is confused with family assets. Little diversification between different types of assets explains the high concentration of equity in small and medium-sized family businesses, which increases risk and accelerates the mortality rate of these types of companies. In addition, a large part of the shares in family businesses are not very liquid and of low profitability in comparison to shares with the same characteristics in similar investments made in non-family businesses.

The distinctive features of family firms were not contemplated from this perspective by governments in the course of the business cycles, which made family-owned companies – the exception being some of the larger firms – more vulnerable. Fiscal policy has also been more benign with large businesses than with SMEs and family companies, because of their reduced capacity for institutional organization and pressure on the State, as opposed to the power of the elite executive boards of large firms.

Family firms have virtues that are inherent to their constitution and functioning, making them ideal for operating as a network and cooperating within business networks that work as a bonding mechanism in industrial districts or local production systems. This makes them particularly important in their relationship to the impact of the arrival of foreign direct investment (FDI) or the establishment of multinationals during the periods of market opening in many Latin American countries. In the 1960s, the effect of these aspects was not so important for many industrial sectors, even having a non-conciliatory effect on the local business network of SMEs and family businesses in countries such as Argentina; but in other periods, FDI had decisive implications in stimulating these businesses.

Corporate governance of family firms is another of the elements in the transversal analysis of the role played by them in Latin America and Spain. Given that a large number of companies do not distinguish between ownership and management in their historical evolution, the confusion or overlapping of roles between the organization of the family and the business can lead to conflict and the possible demise of the company, due to dynastic problems or because the difficulties encountered in the economic cycle become embedded in the heart of the company. The majority of family businesses have functioned with a single governing body for family and firm, without being equipped with instruments of corporate governance to ensure the survival of the business or to avoid family conflicts. It is fundamental, from this perspective, to know the historical organization that family businesses in different countries have followed, keeping in mind that in Mexico the biggest companies are controlled, or majority owned, by a not too extensive group of families, and their influence is also significant in other Latin American countries (Hoshino, 2006; La Porta et al., 1999; Mazzarol and Reboud, 2011; Morck and Steier, 2007). The spread of corporate governance good practice with the establishment of codes of conduct gives family firms transparency for investors, clients, suppliers and cooperating and/or associated companies, and contributes intangible value, preparing the companies for raising capital in the markets. Its adoption is an almost unavoidable prerequisite to ensuring growth and expansion, especially since the opening up of international markets after the liberalization of the 1980s and 1990s, not only in Latin America with the disappearance of the ISI but also in Spain after access to the European Community.

One basic aspect of family firms' performance is its capacity to innovate through the introduction of new management and commercialization practices (Mazzarol and Reboud, 2011). Increased specialization in the context of globalization has accelerated the process of innovation, not necessarily in what is referred to as the introduction of technical change but in the adoption of new logistic systems or agreements with companies in product distribution (Audretsch, 2003). Organizational improvements historically arrived with the adoption of organizational structures of large companies such as the holding system. Business groups introduced these ways into Mexico, Argentina and Colombia, but they also spread, albeit more slowly, to smaller family firms. The diffusion of these structures was associated with the professionalization of management that companies tried to incorporate through external evaluation by consultancy firms in the 1950s and 1960s (Kipping and Puig, 2003).

The professionalization of management is also linked to the creation of a corporate culture that family businesses have been able to develop and that helps to overcome the inertia of traditional forms of governance and management, along with overcoming the inefficiencies associated with the dependency on anachronic methods of working. Only very recently have business associations been formed for the defense of family firms, comprised of groups of companies that try to enter the institutional dynamic to protect their own interests (Fernández Pérez and Puig, 2009). Historically, this has been a disadvantage for family firms, since official or unofficial employers' associations, formal or informal, have tended to represent mainly the interests of large corporations in most of the Latin American countries and Spain, with some exceptions (Schneider, 2004). Where family firms have lobbied for, or insisted on, the recognition of their interests, they have been able to support their longevity (Fernández Pérez and Casanova, 2012).

2.5 RECAPITULATION WITH SOME SUGGESTED CONCLUSIONS

There is some common ground in the historical study of family business in Latin America and Spain. The first element is the impact of the cycles of economic policy and the role of the State as two determining aspects of the formation, evolution and characteristic features of family-owned enterprises. Secondly, and just as important, are the different opportunities each economic sector generate within the production system for the development of the companies; the sector conditions not only the size of the business but also its organization as based on business and ownership management mechanisms. The agricultural sector, predominant in economies of late industrialization – as is the case with Latin America and Spain – has historically linked its development to small family-managed ownership. The manufacturing industry is another sector in which family business has had great significance, constituting as it does the bulk of the first phases of industrial growth. The role of the retail and wholesale trader as leader in the creation of small and medium-sized family businesses should also not be understated. In contrast, the intervention of the State before, and above all with, the application of the ISI, introduced a different dynamic, with industrial sectors more oriented toward greater capital needs, such as the production goods industry: steelworks and metal-mechanical.

The introduction of tariff protection policies and the ISI led to the formation of processes of concentration in family firms that in turn went on to form business groups, as in Mexico, Argentina, Colombia and Brazil. In the main, these groups came from the initial phases of development in open economies, such as the period of incorporation of agricultural and livestock products into the world market by Argentina at the end of the nineteenth century. Or as seen in the region of Monterrey in Mexico, entrepreneurial families entrenched in their ways since the end of the colonial period, moving toward processes of integration, alliances with other families and permanent adaptation to the cycles. In the case of Colombia, business groups controlled by family firms maintained their capacity to control political changes. The survival of business groups shows that the cycles and macroeconomic policies change the conditions, but entrepreneurial families, and the family firms in particular, have become one of the fundamental levers of economic growth in Latin America.

The capacity for adaptation and the flexibility of entrepreneurs and family firms in market fluctuations show that even in unfavorable conditions, this type of company has intrinsic qualities that allow it to detect and take advantage of opportunities offered by the productive system, especially those linked to the existence of previous specializations. The existence of path dependence and business networks, historically formed and with the will to stay, can be explained by the existence of family firms. These firms have the special asset of cooperation, the basic instrument in the forming of collaborative relationships in local productive systems.

The fact that family firms have intrinsic virtues for surviving and maintaining their longevity stands in contrast with the difficulties in assimilating changes that guarantee their viability and improve their capacity to survive. The incorporation of practices of corporate governance that ensure efficient business management and the permanent modification of organizational structures is worth further investigation in order to appreciate the limitations this type of business has had in its development in Latin America and Spain. While many companies have managed to retain their capacity for adaptation thanks to the adoption of modern systems of corporate governance, others – the majority – have disappeared in their first or second generation due to problems of inefficiencies in their management or, more commonly, insurmountable difficulties associated with ownership.

The key to the success of the family firms in Latin America has been their capacity for developing innovation, investing abroad and to access global markets. In every country there were different combinations between public policies, internal conditions and economic cycles. This explains why the same economic policies created different results. It is because there were variations in the process of adaptation and development of the family firms and also from the path dependence of the economic sector in every country.

The conditions of economic policy did not change the strategies of growth of the business groups controlled by family firms. For SMEs' business families the conditions of development, perdurability and longevity depended on their relationships with public enterprises, foreign multinationals and FDI investment and with their links with local policy makers. There was not only a model of development for family firms in Latin America, there were many ways to success and to pressure political powers was an important instrument to assure growth and stability – as the Colombian case showed – for family firms. In other cases it was the capacity of being open to international markets; but often family firms assured their capacity to survive by State protection and government action. The adaptation capacity to different economic and political environments and cultural assets based on local particularities were the guarantee of perdurability of family firms.

NOTE

1. The family SME is hegemonic in Spain. See Chapter 10.

REFERENCES

Acemoglu, D. and J.A. Robinson (2012). *Why Nations Fail: The Origins of Power, Prosperity and Poverty*. New York: Crown Business.

Audretsch, D.B. (ed.) (2003). *SMEs in the Age of Globalization*. Cheltenham, UK and Northampton, MA, USA: Edward Elgar.
Barbero, M.I. and A. Lluch (2013). 'El capitalismo familiar en Argentina: modelos y dinámicas en el largo plazo'. In P. Fernández and A. Lluch (eds), *Un siglo de cambios: Familias empresarias y grandes empresas y grupos familiares en América Latina y España*. Barcelona: FBBVA.
Barbero, M.I. (2014). *Multinacionales latinoamericanas en perspectiva comparada. Teoría e historia*. Bogotá: Cátedra Corona, Universidad de los Andes.
Bértola, L. and J.A. Ocampo (2013). *Desarrollo, vaivenes y desigualdad. Una historia económica de América Latina desde la independencia*. México: Fondo de Cultura Económica.
Bucheli, M. (2011). 'Oil nationalism, property rights, and political regimes: a comparative study of Colombia and Mexico in the twentieth century'. In A. Beltran (ed.), *Oil Producing Countries and Oil Companies: From the Nineteenth to the Twenty-first Century*. Brussels: Peter Lang, pp. 201–22.
Cardoso, E. and A. Helwege (1993). *La economía latinoamericana. Diversidad, tendencias y conflictos*. México DF: Fondo de Cultura Económica.
Caruana, L., C. Larrinaga and J.M. Matés (2011). 'La pequeña y mediana empresa en la edad de oro de la economía española: Estado de la cuestión'. *Investigaciones de Historia Económica* **7**, 322–33.
Cerutti, M. (2000). *Propietarios, empresarios y empresa en el norte de México*. México DF: Siglo XXI Editores.
Cerutti, M. and C. Marichal (eds) (2003). *La Banca regional en México (1870–1930)*. México DF: El Colegio de México-Fondo de Cultura Económica.
Cerutti, M., C. Marichal, I. Ortega and L. Palacios (2006). 'Cemex, IMSA, FEMSA: apertura y respuesta empresarial en Monterrey (1982–2002)'. In M. Ángeles Pozas (ed.), *Estructura y dinámica de la gran empresa en México: cinco estudios sobre su realidad reciente*. México DF: El Colegio de México, pp. 177–213.
Cerutti, M. (2011). 'Agricultura, tejidos productivos y dinámica empresarial en el Norte de México (1925–1965)'. *Revista de Historia de la Economía y de la Empresa* **V**, 25–54.
Chandler, A. (1977). *The Visible Hand: The Managerial Revolution in American Business*. Cambridge, MA: Harvard University Press.
Chandler, A., F. Amatori and T. Hikino (eds) (1999). *Big Business and the Wealth of Nations*. Cambridge: Cambridge University Press.
Chua, J.H., J. Christman and P. Sharma (1999). 'Defining the family business by behaviour'. *Entrepreneurship Theory and Practice* **23** (4), 19–39.
Dávila, C. (2011). 'Empresarios, diversificación de inversiones y nexos con la propiedad territorial en cinco regiones colombianas, 1880–1930'. *Revista de Historia de la Economía y de la Empresa* **V**, 89–116.
Díaz Fuentes, D. (1994). *Crisis y cambios estructurales en América Latina. Argentina, Brasil y México durante el período de entreguerras*. México DF: Fondo de Cultura Económica.
Durán, J.J., V. Salas and I. Santillana (1982). *La actividad económico-financiera de la empresa española en la crisis: especial referencia a las pequeñas y medianas empresas*. Madrid: Instituto de la Pequeña y Mediana Empresa Industrial, Ministerio de Industria y Energía.
Fernández Pérez, P. (2003). 'Family firms in the age of globalization: cooperation and competition in Spanish metal manufacturing, 1870s–1970s'.

Business and Economic History on line **1**. http://www.thebhc.org/publications/BEHonline/2003/Fernandez.pdf (accessed 9 May 2015).
Fernández Pérez, P. and N. Puig (2007). 'Bonsais in a wild forest? A historical interpretation of the longevity of large Spanish family firms'. *Revista de Historia Económica* **XXV** (3), 459–98.
Fernández Pérez, P. and A. Hernández (2009). 'The role of the State in the promotion of family businesses. The case of Spain in a long-run perspective'. *Entrepreneurial History Discussion Papers* **5** (5), 712–20 (wew.ehdp.net).
Fernández Pérez, P. and N. Puig (2009). 'Global lobbies for a global economy: the making of the Spanish Institute of Family Firms in an international perspective'. *Business History* **51** (5), 712–33.
Fernández Pérez, P. and L. Casanova (2012). 'Algunas claves de la longevidad de las grandes empresas familiares brasileñas'. *Apuntes. Revista de Ciencias Sociales* **70**, 273–300.
Fernández Pérez, P. (ed.) (2013). *La profesionalización de la empresa familiar*. Madrid: Lid Empresarial.
Fernández Pérez, P. and A. Colli (2013). 'A global revolution: the endurance of large family businesses around the world'. In P. Fernández Pérez and A. Colli (eds), *The Endurance of Family Businesses: A Global Overview*. Cambridge: Cambridge University Press, pp. 1–10.
Gabrielsson, M. and V.H. Manek Kirpalami (eds) (2012). *Handbook of Research on Born Globals*. Cheltenham, UK and Northampton, MA, USA: Edward Elgar.
García Ruiz, J.L. and C. Manera (eds) (2006). *Historia empresarial de España: un enfoque regional en profundidad*. Madrid: Lid Empresarial.
Guajardo, G. (2012). 'Aprendizajes de innovación y negocios en el petróleo y los ferrocarriles de México, 1952–1992'. In G. Guajardo (ed.), *Innovación y empresa: estudios históricos de España y América Latina*. Buenos Aires: Lenguaje Claro, pp. 301–20.
Guillén, M. (2001). *The Limits of Convergence: Globalization and Organizational Change in Argentina, South Korea and Spain*. Princeton, NJ: Princeton University Press.
Guillén, M. and E. García Canal (2010). *The New Multinationals. Spanish Firms in a Global Context*. Cambridge, MA: Cambridge University Press.
Haber, S. (2000). 'Institutional change, economic growth, and economic history'. In S. Haber (ed.), *Political Institutions and Economic Growth in Latin America. Essays in Policy. History and Political Economy*. Stanford, CA: Hoover Institution Press, pp. 1–20.
Hoshino, T. (2006). 'Estructura de la propiedad y mecanismos de control de las grandes empresas familiares en México'. In M.A. Pozas (ed.), *Estructura y dinámica de la gran empresa en México: cinco estudios sobre su realidad reciente*. México DF: El Colegio de México, pp. 111–46.
Kipping, M. and N. Puig (2003). 'De la teoría a la práctica: las consultoras y la organización de empresas en perspectiva histórica'. In C. Erro (ed.), *Historia empresarial. Pasado, presente y retos del futuro*. Barcelona: Ariel, pp. 101–31.
La Porta, R., F. López De Silanes, A. Scheleifer and R. Visnhy (1999). 'Corporate ownership around the world'. *Journal of Finance* **54** (2), 471–520.
Lluch, A. (2010). 'Redes comerciales en la distribución de maquinarias agrícolas y automóviles en el interior argentino (1900–1930)'. *Anuario del Centro de Estudios Económicos de la Empresa y el Desarrollo* No. 2, Buenos Aires: UBA, pp. 97–134.
Mazzarol, T.W. and S. Reboud (eds) (2011). *Strategic Innovation in Small Firms:*

An International Analysis of Innovation and Strategic Decision Making in Small to Medium Enterprises. Cheltenham, UK and Northampton, MA, USA: Edward Elgar.

Morck, R.K. and L. Steier (2007). 'The global history of corporate governance'. In R.K. Morck (ed.), *A History of Corporate Governance Around the World: Family Business Groups to Professional Managers*. Chicago, IL: Chicago University Press, pp. 1–64.

Odaka, K. and M. Sawai (1999). *Small Firms, Large Concerns: The Development of Small Business in Comparative Perspective*. Oxford: Oxford University Press.

Rocchi, F. (2006). *Chimneys in the Desert: Industrialization in Argentina during the Export Boom Years, 1870–1930*. Stanford, CA: Stanford University Press.

Rodríguez, B. (2014). 'Grupos económicos en Colombia (1974–1998): entre pequeña emmpresa familiar y gran familia de empresas'. In M. Monsalve (ed.), *Grupos económicos y mediana empresa familiar en América Latina*, Lima: Universidad del Pacífico, pp. 41–87.

Rougier, M. (2001). *La política crediticia del Banco Industrial durante el primer peronismo*. Buenos Aires: CEEED-FCE-UBA.

Rougier, M. (ed.) (2007). *Políticas de promoción y estrategias empresariales en la industria argentina, 1950–1980*. Buenos Aires: Ediciones Cooperativas.

Salas, V. and C. Galve (2003). *La empresa familiar en España: fundamentos económicos y resultados*. Madrid: Fundación BBVA.

Schneider, B.R. (2004). *Business Politics and State in Twentieth-century Latin America*. Cambridge: Cambridge University Press.

Toninelli, P. (2000). *The Rise and Fall of State-owned Enterprises in the Western World*. Cambridge: Cambridge University Press.

Tortella, G. and C.E. Núñez (2011). *El desarrollo de la España contemporánea. Historia económica de los siglos XIX y XX*. Madrid: Alianza.

Vidal Olivares, J. (2006). 'Empresas y empresarios en el País Valenciano, 1890–2000'. In J.L. García Ruiz and C. Manera (eds), *Historia empresarial de España: un enfoque regional en profundidad*. Madrid: Lid Empresarial, pp. 57–77.

3. The origins of modern family foundations in Spanish-speaking countries: a preliminary study

Nuria Puig*

This chapter examines the rise of organized family philanthropy in Venezuela, Spain and Mexico during the second half of the twentieth century. It focuses on the crucial role played by local business groups and North American foundations and the enduring networks established by leading entrepreneurial and philanthropic families across and beyond these three countries.

3.1 THE PHILANTHROPIC DIMENSION OF FAMILY BUSINESSES IN SPANISH-SPEAKING COUNTRIES

Since the end of the 1970s, the relevance and visibility of large family firms and entrepreneurial families have increased significantly worldwide. Specialized consultants, professors, institutes and lobbies have contributed very effectively to professionalize and institutionalize family business, create a favourable atmosphere for family capitalism and consolidate family business studies as a new academic field (Fernández Pérez and Puig-Raposo, 2013; Puig, 2015). This movement has extended quickly and efficiently from the United States, where it originated, to the rest of the world, adapting to very different legal, political and economic cultures, and taking on very diverse forms.

One of the most interesting effects of this process is the proliferation and growing social impact of foundations linked to or controlled by family firms and entrepreneurial families all over the world. Family foundations are not easy to research, as they have evolved within very diverse traditions and legal frameworks, rarely disclose relevant quantitative information and often overlap with related phenomena such as the third sector and corporate social responsibility.

The baseline hypothesis of this work is that the rise of family business has helped fuel a global transformation and coordination of institutionalized philanthropy by family businesses and entrepreneurial families worldwide. These two facts invite a closer look at the most influential ideas, people and institutions that have been involved, and to examine them in terms of convergence as well as diversity of philanthropic cultures. Although this chapter is essentially qualitative and based on secondary sources, it forms part of a more ambitious research project that seeks to integrate family philanthropy in the historical analysis of strategies and organization of family capitalism, verifying the usefulness of various theoretical proposals in the Spanish-speaking environment (Gersick, 1990; Gersick et al., 2004; Lungeanu and Ward, 2012; Rey-García and Puig-Raposo, 2013).

In the following we examine the history of organized family philanthropy in Spanish-speaking countries, focusing on four issues: the international activity of large US family foundations during the Cold War; the philanthropic initiatives of the Venezuelan group Mendoza; the Spanish foundation movement; and the new Mexican philanthropy.

3.2 THE FAR-REACHING INFLUENCE OF AMERICAN FOUNDATIONS

Modern philanthropy emerged during the first globalization wave under the influence of a few American entrepreneurial families, such as Carnegie, Rockefeller and Ford. In contrast to the traditional charitable institutions, modern foundations approached social needs with scientific methods and professional management (Hall, 2006). American business dynasties have continued to influence large-scale philanthropy to the present day, promoting global philanthropy and philanthrocapitalism (under the lead of Warren Buffet and Bill Gates) and inspiring European, Latin American and Asian foundations.

Despite its promising start and enduring influence, the American foundation developed among social criticism and public scrutiny (Kiger, 2000). During the First World War, the Walsh commission denounced the control of the American economy by a group of rich men (and their foundations). In the 1930s, the fiscal incentives provided by the New Deal to corporate foundations ignited new debates. The controversy continued until a tax reform passed in 1969 put all the foundations under severe controls, restrictions and obligations (Kiger, 2000). However, family foundations became a visible and powerful force in American society during the middle decades of the twentieth century (Nielsen, 2001). How? First, through the coordinated action of the large foundations, which under Rockefeller's lead encouraged the creation of thousands of new foundations in an improved fiscal framework for philanthropic giving. Second, through the growing competition of the postwar American governments in some of the foundations' traditional areas, such as higher education and research, which forced the foundations to reinvent themselves. Third and most important, through the new opportunities opened up by the Cold War. The largest foundations, most notably Ford and Rockefeller, became strong supporters of US foreign policy and economic diplomacy. In doing so, they successfully explored new areas of activity, such as international economic cooperation and the dissemination of modern management and new paradigms for the social sciences (Gemelli, 1998).

As a result, the large American foundations became major players in the Americanization of the political allies of the United States during the Cold War. In 1947 the Rockefeller Foundation organized in Salzburg and Bellagio a series of transatlantic meetings that not only prepared the ground for the operations of the American private foundations in Europe, but also helped institutionalize European philanthropy (Gemelli and Macleod, 2003). The European Cultural Foundation (1954), established in this context, became the seed of the European Foundation Center (1989) and a network of foundations and national umbrella associations across Europe (Kiger, 2007). The Ford Foundation sponsored similarly relevant initiatives. In 1964 it funded a conference with entrepreneurs, leaders and representatives of foundations and the European civil society in Berlin. This was followed by a series of annual conferences (London, Ditchley, Rome, Bad Godesberg, Bellagio) leading to the establishment of the Club of The Hague (Kiger, 2000). It should be noted that most of the 26 foundations represented in this club in the 1980s were family-based (Puig, 2015). The four Spanish foundations were General Mediterránea, Juan March, Santillana and Universidad Empresa. March and Santillana have both played a significant role in our story, the former introducing the American model in Spain and the latter building bridges with the Latin American foundation movement.

American scholars usually refer to Ford and its contemporaries as the large liberal foundations. How did smaller and less liberal foundations evolve during the golden age of American philanthropy? Historian Oliver Zunz explains that the most conservative foundations launched a new movement, led by the Pew Memorial Trust (1948), critical of the secular outlook and international outreach of the liberal foundations (Zunz, 2012). However, the main threat to both liberal and conservative foundations came from President Johnson's Great Society project, which made private foundations increasingly dependent on the Administration.

In the 1970s and 1980s, the most influential American foundations helped create a broad network of institutions and an emerging academic field around the new concepts of the third and the independent sector, and continued to lobby for a new legal and fiscal framework. But times were changing. The industrial crisis hit the cradle of the big foundations in the northeast of the country hard, while fuelling criticism of the American welfare state and the values associated with liberal philanthropy. Meanwhile, in the Midwest a new generation of family foundations emerged around the Philanthropy Roundtable (1987) and supported by the Board of Trade, Republican think tanks and neoconservative intellectuals. Many of their demands were met by the Welfare Reform Act of 1996: reduced social public spending, a less strict division between Church and state and more room for lobbying.

In Latin America, the modern foundation was introduced by large local family groups working closely with American firms and foundations. Pioneered by the Venezuelan Mendoza group in the early 1940s, modern family philanthropy expanded rapidly across the continent, influencing non-family foundations as well. Colombia followed its own, very interesting path from the 1960s onwards, with local family groups (Santo Domingo, Carvajal, Echevarría) and the Bank of Colombia as main drivers. In Mexico, the catalyst of the foundation movement and corporate social responsibility since the end of the 1980s was the entrepreneur Manuel Arango.

Three academic works on Latin American private philanthropy are relevant for our purposes. The first one is a study commissioned by the Pan American Development Foundation and published by the Russell Sage Foundation (Stromberg, 1968). Author Ann Stromberg relied on local partners to produce the first Latin American foundation directory. She pointed at the extraordinary diversity of the foundation landscape, despite the common institutional and ideological heritage, and the promising awakening of the business community to new approaches to philanthropy. Decades later, José Luis Piñar Mañas coordinated an ambitious study on philanthropic regimes in the Iberian Peninsula and Latin America (Piñar Mañas and García, 1997). This project was closely related to the Ibero-American foundation meetings discussed below. Finally, in 2005 Cynthia Sanborn and Felipe Portocarrero undertook a comparative and critical analysis of the sociopolitical dimension of Latin American philanthropy in association with the David Rockefeller Center on Latin American Studies at Harvard University (Sanborn and Portocarrero, 2005).

3.2.1 Venezuela

The history of Venezuelan philanthropy is inseparable from Eugenio Mendoza (1906–1979). His life and the development of the business group

Mendoza have been chronicled extensively, mostly in a hagiographical vein (Acedo Mendoza, 1973; Aurrecoechea, 1966; Consejo de Coordinación Empresas Mendoza, 1976; Fundación Eugenio Mendoza, 1961, 1986; Jaén, 1987; Polanco Alcántara, 1993; Uslar Pietri, 1983). A dropout student born into a well-off family in Caracas, Mendoza started his successful business career in the construction industry. The Great Depression provided him with the opportunity to enter the import-export business, establish himself in the expanding market for construction materials and build a business group. Mendoza's political trajectory, however brief and controversial, and the economic order that emerged from the Second World War are crucial to understand how this focused, essentially commercial group became Venezuela's largest private group, and a very diversified one, in a short period of time. Appointed Minister of Development and the Economy by General Isaías Medina, Mendoza nationalized the oil refining industry, paving the way for the nationalization of the oil industry and the rise of state capitalism in Venezuela that took place later under the Presidency of Carlos Andrés Pérez (Jaén, 1987). Protinal (1942), Venezolana de Cementos (1943), Financiadora Inmobiliaria Nacional (1945), Maquinarias Mendoza (1948), Sherwin Williams Venezolana (1953), Venezolana de Pulpa y Papel (1954), Financiera Mendoza (1956), Banco Hipotecario de la Vivienda Popular (1961) and Construcciones Viviendas Populares (1966) made Mendoza a major player in Venezuela's emerging industry and real estate market.

A paradigmatic business group, Mendoza was based on economic nationalism, proximity to political power, privileged access to foreign capital and know-how and a team of well-prepared and loyal professionals, among them many exiled Spaniards. However, Mendoza's relationship to power was not always straightforward. In 1953 he came up against General Pérez Jiménez. Not only was Mendoza's project to nationalize the steel industry rejected, but he was accused of funding the exiled opposition. Without access to official credit, the Venezuelan entrepreneur turned to North American capital, established his own financial firm and moved to New York. He returned to Caracas in 1958, right after the fall of Pérez Jiménez.

Having travelled for the first time to the United States in 1928, Mendoza always acknowledged American philanthropy as the main source of inspiration for his own philanthropic activity. Like other Latin American business groups, Mendoza provided its employees with comparatively extensive social benefits, such as soup kitchens, credit and saving instruments, sport facilities and activities, and internal mechanisms of training and promotion. An outbreak of polio in 1942 prompted the transformation of this rather paternalistic approach to capitalism into modern, organized philanthropy: the 'nationalization of Mendoza's social action' (Jaén, 1987). In association with other Venezuelan capitalists and the Rockefeller Foundation, Mendoza created the Foundación para la Prevención de la Parálisis Infantil, which built the Orthopaedic Hospital for Children and inspired him to establish the Eugenio Mendoza Foundation in 1951 (Jaén, 1987). A year later, the death of his only son Eugenio Andres gave new significance to the project.

Among the reduced number of Mendoza's direct collaborators were two exiled Spaniards: Pedro Grases (1909–2004) and Justino Azcárate (1903–1989). The educator and historian Grases began to work for Mendoza in 1939; the lawyer and politician Azcárate joined him in 1946 as advisor to the real estate firm Financiadora Inmobiliaria Nacional (Grases, 1995). From 1951 onwards, both of them focused their activity on the Mendoza Foundation and its main institutional initiatives: Sala de Exposiciones (1956), Fundación Vivienda Popular (1958), Fundación Dividendo para la Comunidad (1964) and Fundación Universidad Metropolitana (1970).

The mobilization of other Venezuelan capitalists to engage in collective philanthropic projects remained a major goal and characteristic of Mendoza's foundation. The most successful example is the Fundación Dividendo para la Comunidad, which emerged in the early 1960s. A prominent businessman from Maracaibo, Iván Lansberg Henríquez (father of one of the founders of family business studies, Ivan Lansberg) explained in 1968 that this initiative came about through the 'new attitude' of the Latin American business elite (Lansberg Henríque, 1968). Individuals like E. Mendoza, M. Carvajal, C. Mariotti, J. Ross, G. di Tella, P. Ayres, F. de Sola and E. Garza Sada, among others, would have realized that the social inequalities of the region were not the responsibility of governments alone, but ought to be addressed by the business community. In 1963, Lansberg organized a meeting in Maracaibo under the slogan 'Corporate Responsibility and Social Progress' that was attended by nearly 100 business leaders and led to the establishment of the Fundación Dividendo para la Comunidad, a 'national movement of private business against the social effects of underdevelopment'. Around 500 corporate members of this foundation invested 2–5 per cent of their profits in social and educational programmes in the late 1960s.

Another prominent Venezuelan philanthropist was Gustavo Cisneros, chairman of the Organización Cisneros. This business group, created by his father in 1929, was based on three pillars: licensing from US manufacturing companies (such as Pepsi-Cola and Studebacker), political connections and the domestic media industry (Venevision). Educated in the United States, Cisneros junior was able to increase the number of joint ventures with North American companies (Sears Roebuck, Pizza Hut,

Apple, AOL), expand its market share of the media business, cultivate the relationship with high calibre politicians (Carlos Andrés Pérez, David Rockefeller, Henry Kissinger, George Bush, Felipe González) and launch an ambitious internationalization strategy in Spain, Portugal and the United States. At the beginning of the 1970s, Gustavo Cisneros and his wife Patricia Phelps (linked to Radio Caracas) created the Cisneros Foundation. In tune with the 'new attitude' described by Lansberg, this institution sought to disseminate free market, entrepreneurship and corporate social responsibility in Venezuela, as well as encourage education and the arts. Like Mendoza, Cisneros would greatly influence the institutionalization of philanthropy in Spain.

3.2.2 Spain

In Spain, foundations constitute a typical legal instrument of organized philanthropy. On the eve of the Great Recession, Spain stood among the five countries of the European Union with the highest number of registered foundations (Asociación Española de Fundaciones, 2007). The sector went through a period of exponential growth after the restoration of democracy in 1978 (Rey-García and Puig-Raposo, 2010). Until then, foundations had been limited by the traditional hegemony of the Catholic Church (built over time through private donations and legacies, but challenged by expropriation during the liberal revolutions); by a restrictive legal framework (Ley General de Beneficencia 1849); and by a chronically weak civil society, the consequence of Spain's economic and social backwardness. This situation, however, did not prevent the emergence of philanthropic initiatives in the late nineteenth and early twentieth centuries, supported by local entrepreneurs, many of whom were emigrants returning home after making their fortunes in the New World (the so-called 'indianos').

Paradoxically, during General Franco's dictatorship (1939–75) a number of foundations were established by leading entrepreneurs: Juan March (1955), Marcelino Botín (1964), Pedro Barrié de la Maza (1966) and Ramón Areces (1976), linked respectively to Banca March, Banco de Santander, Unión Fenosa-Banco Pastor and El Corte Inglés. American scientific philanthropy served as a role model for at least the first of these foundations. Meanwhile, in Catalunya, the cradle of the industrial revolution in Spain, family philanthropy also flourished, with foundations such as Francisca M. Roviralta (1959) and Lluís Carulla (1973), linked to Uralita and to Gallina Blanca (both associated with North American companies). Although smaller, these Catalan foundations were numerous and firmly established in the vigorous Catalan civil society (Coordinadora Catalana de Fundacions, 2008).

Three legal milestones helped bring the development of the foundational sector into the democratic era: the recognition of the right to found in the Spanish Constitution of 1978; the Law of Foundations of 1994; and the Law of Foundations and Philanthropy of 2002. It should be mentioned that the first modern fiscal system in the history of Spain, established in 1978, by eliminating many of the tax privileges related to philanthropy caused a legal, fiscal and political confrontation between the new political and administrative elite and the leaders of the foundation movement, who advocated for a modern legal and fiscal framework for private philanthropy (Centro de Fundaciones de España, 2003). Although the law of 1994 established a series of tax breaks, the battle continued until 2002. This new law acknowledged the specific legal framework for 15 of the 17 regions of Spain, improved the tax regime for foundations and paved the way for corporate foundations. Nevertheless, the 2002 regulatory framework still did not satisfy the foundation sector that continued to demand a more favourable framework while trying to promote professionalization, transparency and accountability among Spanish foundations (Pérez-Díaz, 2008).

The origins of the Spanish foundation movement go back to the 1960s, when the economic modernization of Spain allowed the strengthening of civil society in general and non-profit organizations in particular. Interestingly, many of these organizations were linked to private corporations and their missions went beyond traditional charity. The Centro de Fundaciones, created between 1973 and 1977 under the subtle leadership of Fundesco (a foundation linked to the semi-public corporation Telefónica), can be regarded as the departing point of the institutional history of modern Spanish philanthropy (Centro de Fundaciones de España, 2003). Emerging in the midst of the Spanish democratic transition, the Centro had two main objectives: to produce a directory of Spanish foundations and to adapt the legal framework to the needs of the new foundations and the new Spanish society, using the United States and Western Europe as role models. According to the intellectual architects of the Centro de Fundaciones, the new foundation regime was crucial because it implied a definition of the boundaries between state and society. The Magna Carta of the new Spanish democracy, they argued, should embrace the spirit of civil society. In 1978, Catalan foundations established the Coordinadora Catalana de Fundacions. This new entity not only collaborated closely with the Centro, but had an important role of proselytizing in Catalan civil society, and published in 1995 the first directory of private Catalan foundations (Coordinadora Catalana de Fundacions, 1995).

One of the most influential people in the institutionalization of the foundation movement was Justino Azcárate, a close collaborator of

Eugenio Mendoza between 1946 and 1977 (Boletín de la Institución Libre De Enseñanza, 2009). In the 1960s, Azcárate began travelling to Spain with the financial and social support of Banco Urquijo and the Spanish liberal elite. Urquijo was a private investment bank and Spain's largest private industrial group (Puig and Torres, 2008). Between 1940 and 1970, under the leadership of Juan Lladó, Urquijo supported numerous artistic and intellectual projects through the Sociedad de Estudios y Publicaciones, and in the 1960s became the local partner of the Ford Foundation (Anes and Gómez Mendoza, 2009; Puig et al., 2011). The extensive Urquijo family and many of the non-family managers of the group had a long-standing relationship with North American investors as well as with Spanish expatriate networks in Latin America, particularly in Venezuela and Mexico. All this helps understand the crucial role played by Urquijo in the dissemination of American-style philanthropy in postwar Spain (Puig and Torres, 2015). Additionally, Jaime Carvajal Urquijo, who took control of the bank and the group in the late 1970s, was well integrated within the international business and philanthropic circuit.

In 1977 Azcárate, who had just become a member of the Spanish Senate, proposed to improve the fiscal status of private foundations. Although he had successfully connected the Spanish emerging foundation movement with Mendoza and other prominent Latin American and North American philanthropists, introduced new philanthropic concepts among the Spanish cultural and artistic elite and encouraged corporate philanthropy, his project had to wait until 1994. Moreover, Urquijo did not meet the expectations of Azcárate to become the equal partner of Mendoza and other big Latin American foundations in Spain, because the political context forced Lladó to act with great discretion until 1977, and because internal and external factors made the management of both the bank and its new foundation (Fundación Banco Urquijo, 1980) difficult until the final collapse of the two of them in 1982. Therefore, Spain's first business group did not live up to the expectations it had created, but did promote the circulation of ideas and personal ties among many of the key people in the history of modern philanthropy. As a result, the influence of Urquijo Group and the social group adhering to it moved more in the direction of inspiration and support for the initiatives of others. The legal heir to Urquijo's philanthropic activities is the Fundación Xavier Zubiri, which is controlled by the Lladó family. José Lladó, main shareholder and president of the engineering firm Técnicas Reunidas, serves or has served on the boards of major cultural institutions he helped modernize in association with Azcárate, Arango, Cisneros and others.

At the end of the 1980s, Spain's full integration into the international economy and fast economic growth contributed to enhance the social status of entrepreneurs and private philanthropy. It was the beginning of the golden age for family capitalism, driven and capitalized by the Instituto de la Empresa Familiar, and a new phase in the history of family philanthropy, whose expectations had still not been fulfilled (Fernández Pérez and Puig-Raposo, 2009; Instituto De La Empresa Familiar, 2001; Rey-García and Puig-Raposo, 2010).

3.2.3 Mexico

As in most of Latin America, in Mexico the development of private charity was strongly influenced by the Catholic Church and by local elites (Verduzco Igartúa, 2003). However, a new legal framework for philanthropy emerged from the liberal revolutions, which eroded the Church's power by confiscating many of its assets, and the long tenure of General Porfirio Díaz (1876–1910), under which many philanthropic initiatives, religious and secular, indigenous and foreign, flourished. In 1910, the Revolution opened a new phase, characterized by the pre-eminence of the state on Mexico's economic and social life. Regarded as state subsidiaries, charitable institutions started to be supervised by boards comprised of representatives from philanthropic institutions and from the government. From 1943 onwards, non-profit associations were legally recognized and given significant tax incentives (Villalobos Grzywobicz, 2010).

How did Mexican entrepreneurs respond to the new institutional framework? The existing evidence indicates that, in contrast to Venezuela, in Mexico the revolutionary regime prevented the large North American foundations from operating or having any direct influence in the country at least until the 1980s. The driving force of modern philanthropy came from some entrepreneurial families from Nuevo León, in the north of Mexico. This is the case of the Garza family (Cuauhtémoc Group), which had been socially aware and proactive since the beginning of the past century and would serve as role models to Mexican philanthropic entrepreneurs during the central decades of the century (Centro Mexicano de Instituciones Filantrópicas, 1990). It was also in Nuevo León where in the 1940s a local group of entrepreneurs established the prestigious Instituto Tecnológico de Estudios Superiores de México (ITESM), which aimed to provide their own staffs with state of the art managerial education. Another local family, Zambrano (Cemex Group), also stood out in the field of philanthropy, through the Cemex foundations, which are currently operational in various continents, supporting the group's international investments.

The Nuevo León initiatives inspired entrepreneurs from other areas of the country. In Mexico DF, a group of business people launched the Mexican Institute of Technology in 1946. The Servitje family (Bimbo

Group), also from the DF and a proactive, Christian-inspired philanthropist, helped create the Mexican Institute of Social Christian Doctrine in 1982. Together with other prominent entrepreneurs, such as Jerónimo Arango, Servitje established in 1985 the Mexican Health Foundation, which played a crucial role in the national health system. Interestingly, during the long revolutionary-institutional regime the large Mexican family businesses that stood behind institutional philanthropy became very involved in the organized defence of their business interests through successful institutions such as the Confederación Patronal de la República Mexicana (Coparmex), founded by Luis Sada in 1929, or the Consejo Mexicano de Hombres de Negocios Mexicano, created at the beginning of the 1960s by Raúl Bailleres (BUDA Group).

Since the mid 1980s, the role of Mexican family businesses and entrepreneurial families in organized Mexican philanthropy has increased significantly (Villalobos Grzywobicz, 2010). The earthquake that hit Mexico City in 1985 was a turning point. It mobilized civil society, exposed the incapacity of the government to respond to disasters of this magnitude and gave private initiative the legitimacy it had lacked in the Mexican political and ideological framework (Agüero, 2005). The person that contributed more effectively and visibly to seize this opportunity and reshape Mexican private philanthropy was Manuel Arango Arias. The son of an Asturian emigrant, Arango was born in Tampico in 1936. After graduating in Economics in the United States in 1958, Arango founded with his father and older brothers (Jerónimo, born in 1927, and Plácido, born in 1931) the supermarket chain Aurrerá in Mexico DF. It was a textbook adaptation of the American model to the Mexican market with Mexican capital and management, and a very successful enterprise that allowed the Arangos to create the CIFRA Group and become one of the wealthiest families in Mexico. In 1991, the Arango family formed a strategic alliance with Wal-Mart that led to the full acquisition of the Mexican chain by Wal-Mart in 1997.

Long before this, in 1985, Manuel Arango created the Fundación Universo Veintiuno (renamed Manuel Arango Foundation in 1994), which focused on the defence of the environment and the dissemination of modern philanthropy. This initiative was followed by Centro Mexicano de Filantropía (CEMEFI) in 1988 and Fundación Caracol de Plata in 1999 (Arango, 2002). Whereas CEMEFI seeks to promote private philanthropy and civic engagement in Mexico, Caracol de Plata aims to promote social responsibility and civic participation in the media. Modern philanthropy, according to Arango, differs from traditional charity in that it is broad and inclusive. It promotes the organized and voluntary participation of civil society, weakened by the historical hegemony of the Catholic Church and the state, which have created a paternalistic and dependent culture (Arango, 2002). Philanthropy is 'any private, voluntary and non-profit activity that pursues the common good' (Arango, 2002). To be precise, CEMEFI seeks to strengthen civil society (regulated by private business and the third sector, which includes religious organizations and political parties), improve the legal framework, mobilize resources, professionalize the management of institutions of the third sector, increase its visibility, promote the culture of philanthropy and community service, sponsor studies in philanthropy, support community foundations and disseminate corporate social responsibility. Needless to say, the activity and public image of CEMEFI benefited greatly from Mexico's conservative regime between 2002 and 2012.

CEMEFI also played a part in the publication of Mexico's first directory of foundations (Centro Mexicano de Instituciones Filantrópicas, 1990). Moreover, it took on very ambitious projects in collaboration with US-based institutions working in the international arena, such as Johns Hopkins, CIVICUS and Synergos. A comparative study on grant-making foundations (those that support projects of other organizations) in Ecuador, Brazil and Mexico, directed by Synergos, concludes that Mexico was, at the beginning of this century, one of the few Latin American countries with tax incentives for philanthropy; that foundations saw themselves as the bridge between the government and the private sector; and that private companies and the promotion of corporate social responsibility had a central role in the development of the sector (Sanborn and Portocarrero, 2005).

Significantly more critical is Felipe Agüero's analysis on the evolution of corporate social responsibility in Mexico (Agüero, 2005). In contrast to other philanthropy scholars, Agüero argues that corporate social responsibility cannot be considered philanthropy, as it does not pursue the common good, but rather to improve the reputation and performance of the firm that promotes it while simultaneously contributing to the community. Corporate social responsibility, explains this scholar, emerged in the historical context of globalization, which has enhanced the social visibility and strengthening of the private sector and facilitated the construction of transnational networks. The promotion of corporate social responsibility in Latin America as a whole took place in collaboration with North American institutions such as Business for Social Responsibility (founded in 1992 in San Francisco), Inter-American Foundation, Kellogg Foundation, Synergos Institute, Ford Foundation and Avina, on the one hand, and with pan-American networks such as Forum Empresa, on the other. This constellation of organizations (which includes the active participation of CEMEFI) has its own agenda with obvious macropolitical and economic motivations and implications. CEMEFI can be considered the dean of corporate social responsibility, not only in Mexico, but in the whole of Latin America. It was Manuel Arango who in 2000 organized the first conference on corporate social responsibility in the continent, bringing together a large number of institutions that until then had been dispersed, creating ALIARSE and a credit system of corporate social responsibility for businesses. Essential players in the development of this initiative were the entrepreneurs Lorenzo Servitje (Bimbo), Roberto Hernández (Banamex) and Carlos Slim (Telmex). The companies and the family groups, in short, have also been crucial for the diffusion of corporate social responsibility in Mexico.

Arango's Spanish connection is very revealing of the global outreach of modern family philanthropy. In 1965, Plácido Arango moved to Spain, where he founded Aurrerá and ten years later Vips, a successful chain of convenience stores and fast-food restaurants and the cornerstone of Sigla Group. In the early twenty-first century Vips went into partnership with Goldman Sachs and Starbucks aimed at increasing its financial muscle and facilitating Starbuck's entry into the Spanish market. Vips ended up acquiring 100 per cent of Starbucks Coffee in Spain and Portugal. Since 2005, Sigla Group has been managed by a son of Arango, Plácido Arango García-Urtiaga.

The relevant point here is that Plácido Arango integrated easily into the group of people and the institutions that led the modernization of Spanish philanthropy. A personal and business friend of Justino Azcárate and Jaime Carvajal, among others, and a prominent art collector, Arango was key in launching the Fundación Príncipe de Asturias in 1980. He became chairman of the board of trustees (where he was represented through Sigla Group) between 1987 and 1996. Arango was also appointed member and chairman of the Board of Trustees of the Museo del Prado in 1985 and 2007, respectively, and trustee of the Museo de Arte Reina Sofia and the Academia de Bellas Artes de San Fernando. Discretely but effectively, Arango, like other Spanish emigrants and exiles, would contribute to the spread of American-style philanthropy in Spain, a phenomenon that reinforces and is reinforced by family capitalism.

3.3 A TRANSCONTINENTAL NETWORK: THE IBERO-AMERICAN MEETINGS OF FOUNDATIONS

The experiences of Venezuela, Spain and Mexico reveal that formal and informal cooperation among foundations, driven by family business groups in most cases, was crucial to consolidate private philanthropy. These associations encouraged the preparation and publication of national directories and databases that, albeit incomplete, provide an insight into the extraordinarily opaque world of the foundations.

The association of foundations began in the pioneering countries after the Second World War. The Mendoza Foundation used the journal *Fundaciones* (1964–73) to instigate the creation of national federations and the publication of foundation directories and conference proceedings across the continent. The first directory of Venezuelan private foundations appeared in 1973. One year later, Mendoza hosted the first meeting of American foundations and entrepreneurs, which was attended by representatives from Latin America, the United States and Europe (Fundación Eugenio Mendoza, 1973). From this meeting emerged in 1977 the Venezuelan Federation of Private Foundations, supported by 24 philanthropic institutions under Mendoza's lead. The second meeting, held in Caracas in 1981, was also sponsored by the Mendoza Foundation under the slogan 'Strengthening private initiatives for social welfare'. However, the third meeting was organized by the Council of Latin American Development Foundations and the Council of Foundations. 'The participation of the private sector in social promotion and economic progress in Latin America and the Caribbean' was the slogan chosen for this openly pro-American and market-friendly gathering. Despite the political and institutional changes that have taken place in Venezuela ever since, Mendoza's leadership has remained solid to this day.

In Spain, the foundation movement crystallized into two associations: the Centro de Fundaciones de España (1977), predecessor of the leading Asociación Española de Fundaciones, and the Coordinadora Catalana de Fundacions (1978). The relationship between the foundation movements on either side of the Atlantic intensified in the 1980s thanks to bilateral contacts between the Centro de Fundaciones and various Latin American entities. Justino Azcárate from the Eugenio Mendoza Foundation and two Mexican non-profits, the Domecq Cultural Institute and the Miguel Alemán Foundation, were key to institutionalize these contacts.

In the long run, the most relevant outcome was the Encuentros de Fundaciones Iberoamericanas (Ibero-American Foundation Meetings, subsequently renamed Encuentros Iberoamericanos del Tercer Sector and Encuentros Iberoamericanos de la Sociedad Civil). The celebration of the 500th anniversary of the discovery of America provided a unique opportunity to intensify the bonds between Spain and the Americas on many levels, an opportunity shaped and seized by many private corporations (such as the media group Prisa-Santillana, a founding member of the Club of The Hague with growing business interests in Latin America) and official Spanish organizations (such as the Instituto de Cooperación Iberoamericana, linked to the Spanish Ministry of Foreign Affairs). A preliminary meeting, held in 1983 in Santillana del Mar, was attended by representatives of 20 foundations from Argentina, Brazil, Colombia, Spain, Mexico, Peru and Venezuela (Centro de Fundaciones de España, 2003). The first institutional meeting took place in Cáceres (Spain) in 1992 around the topic 'Challenging Ibero-American civil society'. Other meetings followed in Guadalajara (Mexico) in 1994, Rio de Janeiro (Brazil) in 1996, Buenos Aires (Argentina) in 1998, Cartagena de Indias (Colombia) in 2000, Barcelona (Spain) in 2002, Sao Paulo (Brazil) in 2004, Mexico City (Mexico) in 2006, Guayaquil (Ecuador) in 2008, Rosario (Argentina) in 2010, Madrid (Spain) in 2012, Rio de Janeiro (Brazil) in 2013 and Puebla (Mexico) in 2014. Worth mentioning is the growing role of the CEMEFI that led Manuel Arango to chair the Board of Directors of the Ibero-American Meetings in 2000. Both the Domecq Cultural Institute and the Miguel Alemán Foundation have continued to support this unique social, economic and political platform. The following entities were particularly supportive during the early history of the Ibero-American meetings: GIFE and Roberto Marinho Foundation, Brazil; Federación de Fundaciones Agentinas, FEDEFA, and Foro del Tercer Sector, Argentina; and Fundación Mario Santo Domingo, Colombia. Borghi (Argentina), Martini (Argentina), Cambó (Spain), Nobis (Ecuador), Voigt (Brazil) and Falcao (Brazil) have also actively served on the Advisory Board of the Encuentros Ibero-Americanos de la Sociedad Civil. Interestingly, most of them are foundations linked to or controlled by family firms and business groups with stable relationships with the American market and American business and philanthropic institutions.

3.4 CONCLUSIONS AND FUTURE RESEARCH

The early history of institutionalized family philanthropy in Venezuela, Spain and Mexico shows that foundations are part of the strategy and organization of the firms and families that support them. Our research provides new evidence on three issues that are at the heart of this collective volume: (1) the key role of entrepreneurial families, more than firms, in family capitalism; (2) the diversity and organizational flexibility of family entrepreneurship in Spanish-speaking countries; and (3) the ability of business dynasties (most notably of founders) to influence their institutional framework. This chapter also sheds light on the instrumentality of organized philanthropy to ensure continuity and provide legitimacy to the firm and the family. However, in its present form it offers more questions than answers. If philanthropy is such an appropriate instrument to achieve the purposes of the family business, why are there so few family foundations? What are the determinants of philanthropic activity, innovation and leadership? Are foundations fiscal and public relations tools available to business families? When and how do foundations serve corporate strategies? Mendoza, the Spanish foundation movement, Arango and the global networks they contributed in building are just the tip of the iceberg of a fascinating research topic.

The early history of Spanish family philanthropy is inseparable from the transatlantic institutional infrastructure built during the Cold War by American foundations and a small number of local business groups. This indicates, first, that many of the foundations examined here perform as agents of globalization, and second, that the development of family capitalism in Latin American and Spain is underpinned by personal ties, shared interests and communication flows that make it more compact and homogeneous than usually assumed. We suggest two broad research directions to improve our knowledge of family philanthropy in Latin America and Spain. On the one hand, new empirical evidence should be gathered by identifying the most relevant companies and philanthropic families, estimating the philanthropic propensity of each country, analysing the interplay between foundations and their associated firms and assessing the effects of generational change on philanthropic activity. On the other, the philanthropic dimension of family firms should be examined with the long-term vision and tools of the historian in light of the theoretical contributions of other social sciences.

NOTE

* The author acknowledges financial support by the Spanish Ministry of Science and Innovation under grant number ECO2009-10977 and the research framework provided by the Center for European Studies at Harvard University (2012).

REFERENCES

Acedo Mendoza, M. (1973). *Por qué Eugenio Mendoza*. Caracas: Talleres de Gráficas Armitano.

Agüero, F. (2005). 'The promotion of corporate social responsibility in Latin America'. In C. Sanborn and F. Portocarrero (eds), *Philanthropy and Social Change in Latin America*. Cambridge, MA: David Rockefeller Center on Latin American Studies (DRCLAS), pp. 103–33.

Anes, G. and A. Gómez Mendoza (2009). *Cultura sin libertad. La Sociedad de Estudios y Publicaciones (1947–1980)*. Madrid: Pre-Textos.

Arango, M. (2002). 'Philanthropy in Mexico'. *ReVista. Harvard Review of Latin America*. Revista.drclas.harvard.edu/book/philanthropy-mexico (accessed 18 September 2015).

Asociación Española de Fundaciones (2007). *Directorio de Fundaciones Españolas*. Madrid: Asociación Española de Fundaciones.

Aurrecoechea, J.L. (1966). *Nace una organización*. Caracas: Talleres Gráficos Ituarte.

Boletín de la Institución Libre de Enseñanza (2009). *Número especial sobre Justino de Azcárate Flórez* No. 76 (December).

Centro de Fundaciones de España (2003). *El Centro de Fundaciones: Memoria de 25 años (1977–2002)*. Madrid: Centro de Fundaciones de España.

Centro Mexicano de Instituciones Filantrópicas (1990). *Directorio de Instituciones Filantrópicas*. Mexico: Centro Mexicano de Instituciones Filantrópicas.

Consejo de Coordinación Empresas Mendoza (1976). *50 años dedicados a Venezuela*. Caracas: Talleres de Gráficas Armitano.

Coordinadora Catalana de Fundacions (1995). *Directori de fundacions privades catalanes*. Barcelona: Coordinadora Catalana de Fundacions.

Coordinadora Catalana de Fundacions (2008). *Identitat, Valors, Futur. 30 Anys*. Barcelona: Coordinadora Catalana de Fundacions.

Fernández Pérez, P. and N. Puig-Raposo (2009). 'Global lobbies for a global economy: the creation of the Spanish Institute of Family Firms in international perspective'. *Business History* **51** (5), 712–33.

Fernández Pérez, P. and N. Puig-Raposo (2013). 'The emergence of family business studies: a historical approach to key centres, ideas, and scholars'. In A. Colli and P. Fernández Pérez (eds), *The Endurance of Family Businesses: A Global Overview*. Cambridge: Cambridge University Press, pp. 13–33.

Fundación Eugenio Mendoza (1961). *Diez años de la Fundación Eugenio Mendoza 1951–1961*. Caracas: Cromotip.

Fundación Eugenio Mendoza (1973). *Fundaciones privadas de Venezuela*. Caracas: Fundación Eugenio Mendoza.

Fundación Eugenio Mendoza (1986). *Ideario y acción de un venezolano. Eugenio Mendoza 1906–1979*. Caracas: Fundación Eugenio Mendoza.

Gemelli, G. (ed.) (1998). *The Ford Foundation and Europe (1950s–1970s). Cross-fertilization in Social Sciences and Management*. Brussels: European Interuniversity Press.

Gemelli, G. and R. Macleod (eds) (2003). *American Foundations in Europe: Grant-giving Policies, Cultural Diplomacy and Trans-Atlantic Relations, 1920–1980*. Brussels: Peter Lang.

Gersick, K.E (1990). 'Editors' notes'. *Family Business Review* **III** (4), 327–30.

Gersick, K.E., D. Stone, M. Desjardins and K. Grady (2004). *Generations of Giving: Leadership and Continuity in Family Foundations*. Lanham, MD: Lexington Books.

Grases, P. (1995). *Venezolanos del Exilio Español*. Madrid: Instituto de Cooperación Internacional.

Hall, P.D. (2006). 'A historical overview of philanthropy, voluntary associations, and nonprofit organisations in the United States, 1600–2000'. In W.W. Powell and R. Steinberg (eds), *The Nonprofit Sector. A Research Handbook*. New Haven, CT: Yale University Press, pp. 32–65.

Instituto de la Empresa Familiar (2001). *Fundaciones familiares*. Barcelona: Instituto de la Empresa Familiar.
Jaén, G. (1987). *Eugenio Mendoza. Apuntes para una interpretación*. Caracas: Ediciones Centauro.
Kiger, J.C. (2000). *Philanthropic Foundations in the Twentieth Century*. Westport, CT and London: Greenwood Press.
Kiger, J.C. (2007). *Philanthropists and Foundation Globalization*. New Brunswick, NJ: Transaction Publishers.
Lansberg Henríquez, I. (1968). 'Corporate responsibility in social progress'. In A. Stromberg (ed.), *Philanthropic Foundations in Latin America*. New York: Russell Sage Foundation, pp. 183–7.
Lungeanu, R. and J. Ward (2012). 'A governance-based typology of family foundations: the effect of generation stage and governance structure on family philanthropic activities'. *Family Business Review* **25** (4), 409–24.
Nielsen, W.A. (2001). *Golden Donors: A New Anatomy of the Great Foundations*. New York: E.P. Dutton.
Pérez-Díaz, V. (2008). *La filantropía: tendencias y perspectivas*. Madrid: Fundación de Estudios Financieros – Fundación Profesor Uría.
Piñar Mañas, J.L. and J.A. García (1997). *Las fundaciones en Iberoamérica: régimen jurídico*. Madrid: McGraw-Hill.
Polanco Alcántara, T. (1993). *Eugenio Mendoza. Un destino venezolano*. Caracas: Grijalbo.
Puig, N. (2015). 'Brokering trust: the construction of transnational family business networks, 1980–2010'. *Jahrbuch für Wirtschaftsgeschichte* **56** (1), 111–35.
Puig, N. and E. Torres (2008). *Banco Urquijo. Un banco con historia*. Madrid: Turner.
Puig, N. and E. Torres (2015). 'Grupos empresariales en la España contemporánea: El Grupo Urquijo, 1851–1982'. *América Latina en la Historia Económica* **22** (2) (May–August), 160–97.
Puig, N., F. Santisteban and E. Torres (2011). 'Juan Lladó, el Banco Urquijo y la España de su tiempo'. Unpublished manuscript.
Rey-García, M. and N. Puig-Raposo (2010). 'Understanding the organised philanthropic activities of entrepreneurial families'. *Business and Economic History On-Line* **8**.
Rey-García, M. and N. Puig-Raposo (2013). 'Globalization and the organization of family philanthropy: a case of isomorphism?'. *Business History* **55** (2), 1–28.
Sanborn, C. and F. Portocarrero (eds) (2005). *Philanthropy and Social Change in Latin America*., Vol. 16. Cambridge, MA: David Rockefeller Center on Latin American Studies (RCLAS).
Stromberg, A. (ed.) (1968). *Philanthropic Foundations in Latin America*. New York: Russell Sage Foundation.
Uslar Pietri, A. (1983). *Biografía de Eugenio Mendoza*. Caracas: Cromotip.
Verduzco Igartúa, G. (2003). *Organizaciones no lucrativas: visión de su trayectoria en México*. México: El Colegio de México-Centro Mexicano para la Filantropía.
Villalobos Grzywobicz, J. (ed.) (2010). *Filantropía y acción solidaria en la historia de México*. Mexico: Centro Mexicano para la Filantropía.
Zunz, O. (2012). *Philanthropy in America: A History*. Princeton, NJ: Princeton University Press.

PART II

Large national markets and large family groups (Mexico, Brazil, Argentina)

4. Large businesses and entrepreneurial families in Mexico

Mario Cerutti

4.1 USEFUL CONCEPTS

This chapter presents a brief explanation of the prominent entrepreneurial families of Mexico in the twentieth century, families that were also the driving force behind important companies still in operation today. It will not deal with the individual family business nor will it discuss what is usually understood by family business (Chrisman et al., 2005, 2010; Chua et al., 1999; Fernández Pérez, 2003, 2012; Sharma, 2004, among others). What follows is an analysis of the developmental path of some of the most powerful and long-standing expressions of Mexican kinship, which are based on the following concepts:[1]

1. The positioning of large business in the arena of peripheral societies,[2] whose dynamics were not – and are still not today – the same as those of developed societies. There is no reason for the size of a company, in its indigenous form, to be similar in the 1950s to that of General Motors or Siemens.
2. Large businesses in societies such as Mexico were interlinked with two complementary realities: the entrepreneurial family and the business group. Their characteristics, behaviour and dimensions (assets, number of employees, level of turnover) must be seen in the context of the family-group pairing. The empirical evidence shows that groups and their mother companies were born and survived through links with entrepreneurial families. In other words, kinship cores connected their surnames to other relevant families, thus, generation after generation could succeed each other in business.
3. We assign the concept of entrepreneurial family to a broad kinship group that, in its itinerary, starts up multiple companies[3] among which there can be: (a) a mother company that builds up a business group (examples for Mexico: Cemex and Vidriera Monterrey); (b) companies connected in a variety of ways to the mother company

(suppliers, financial intermediation, distributors, agro-industry) that can be owned by those who participate in the mother company or also brothers, cousins, sons-in-law or grandchildren; (c) and very importantly, undertakings that have little to do with the mother company but rather constitute private businesses of members of the family (urban construction, public works, real estate agencies, supplies, services such as education, hospitals, transport).

4. Entrepreneurial families form a core component of the business fabric that prevails in a region, city or economic area, and that can attain national importance. This texture as a whole is what guaranteed a certain degree of permanence, of intergenerational survival; it sustained progress even when a large business fell by the wayside. The company could fail, but the families and the business fabric remained in place.[4]
5. A strong business fabric would be formed: (a) through the historical multiplying of investments in the area studied; (b) due to significant portions of these investments being made by local families; (c) because of the gradual interlinkage through marriage; (d) by the simultaneous interlinking of interests that the limited company facilitated in Mexico from the end of the nineteenth century onwards; and (e) with the arrival of executive boards, through the incorporation of players from other families.
6. The mother company and/or family are basic components of the central business; complementary businesses would be those connected to the dynamics of this large company or group under development; and private businesses would be those that start up independently. Another phase of interlacement is through marriage or corporate unions.
7. Entrepreneurial families and business fabric are useful concepts for explaining the durability of a productive fabric. A frequent base for subsequent launches, both national and international, the productive fabric emerges as another concept-guideline that includes: (a) the interrelations that owners, producers and companies located in the same region maintain over the long term; (b) the multipliers that branch out throughout the productive system, thereby involving a diversity of players, from producers of raw materials and supplies to services, credit, processing and distribution; (c) the externalities that derive from proximity, mutual recognition and cooperation between players; (d) the economic and organizational links and the bonds of trust that are built up between agents, with their ramifications and diversification.[5]

This conceptual framework will orient the analysis of a reduced sample of families that were clearly important in the entrepreneurial evolution of Mexico. Empirical research shows that the everyday activities of these families seem to fit easily into the above-mentioned theoretical arena.

4.2 THE SAMPLE

It is convenient to begin with some information on the twenty-first century so that the following questions can be posed: (a) does historical research have anything to say about entrepreneurial projects, trajectories, characteristics and durability?; (b) when did the most relevant families at the start of the twenty-first century – the largest companies, the most renowned groups – emerge? And above all, from which corners of the Mexican geography did they come?

In order to answer these questions, a source was used that would be useful for the chosen procedure.[6] The collected data was organized into two areas: (a) *Entrepreneurs/owner families*; (b) *Large businesses/owner families*. For the first, records were reviewed for two years previous to the 2006–08 crisis (2003 and 2004), for another two from the middle of the crisis (2007 and 2008) and from one that can be considered post-crisis (2011). For the second case (*Large businesses/owner families*) a similar course was taken, using 2001 and 2002 for the pre-crisis years, 2006 and 2008 for the most recessive years and 2011 for the possible exit out of the depression. Then a selection was made of: (a) the most prominent private Mexican entrepreneurial businesses and/or groups[7] (not including State-owned or foreign); and (b) the 12 most prominent entrepreneurs. The aim was to show which surnames/families were most often mentioned when referring to the principal companies and groups of the early twenty-first century. Slim, Zambrano, Garza Sada, Garza Sada-Sada, Bailleres González and Servitje were named or included in every year; two surnames (Fernandez González and Martin Bringas) on four occasions. The Slim family, although seeming to be in the top position in the first decade of the century, does not offer the trajectory of families operating from the northern city of Monterrey (Figure 4.1) where the intercrossed surnames Garza/Sada are as visible today as they were in 1900.

A similar operation was done on the pairing *Entrepreneurs/owner families*. In this case, the search was for which and how many families were cited when referring to the most prominent entrepreneurs and the largest Mexican companies in the early twenty-first century. Six surnames also appeared every year (Slim, Zambrano, Garza Sada,[8] Garza Sada-Sada, Larrea Mota and Salinas Pliego); and five were positioned in second place (González Barrera, Bailleres González, Fernández González, Servitje and Martín Bringas).

Source: Author's elaboration.

Figure 4.1 Map of north of Mexico

Table 4.1 Selected family groups, Mexico

	Slim-Heliú-Domit	Zambrano	Garza Sada	Garza Sada-Sada
Origin	Mexico DF	Monterrey	Monterrey	Monterrey
Generations	2	4	4	4
Tendency	diversification	specialization	specialization	diversification
International	yes	yes	yes	yes
Internal market	yes	yes	yes	yes
Base sector	communications	cement	beverages	automobile parts-food-petrochemical
Group(s)	Carso-Inbursa	Cemex	FEMSA	ALFA

Source: *Expansión*, 2001–12.

If the two samples are put together, the following can be observed:

1. The Slim, Zambrano, Garza Sada and Garza Sada-Sada families were mentioned in all the selected years, in the context of large companies as well as prominent entrepreneurial players.
2. As mentioned above, the Slim family is leader in significant areas of entrepreneurial activity in the first decade of the twenty-first century, but it was the families of Monterrey, in northern Mexico, that had a longer track record at the head of large companies and economic groups. This can be seen in Table 4.1, which quantifies the generations. Thus, priority in this chapter is given to the development of these kinship cores originating from northern Mexico, a multi-regional area closely linked to the economy of the United States.

4.3 MEXICO (1890–2010)

It is necessary to present an overview of the economic, socio-political and institutional evolution of Mexico between the *Porfiriato* and the start of the twenty-first century.

The initial date (1890) is linked with a significant institutional change: the Commerce Code defined the scope of the limited liability company, which in turn would stimulate the growth of large companies. But, in addition, 1890 marked the maturity of the *Porfiriato*, which could be defined as a regime of oligarchic profiles that: (a) stabilized Mexico and defined multiple ground rules in economic matters; (b) encouraged local and foreign investment with identical enthusiasm and levels of protection; (c) installed more than 20 000 km of railway track and integrated the central-northern area with the US economy. These innovations had two striking consequences: (a) they helped to structure the internal market; (b) they converted Mexico into a complementary economy of the United States, especially the extensive northern region. The regional dynamics and subsequent appearance of long-standing entrepreneurial families were nourished by both markets.

The revolution (1911–17) and reconstruction during the 1920s changed this panorama. The emerging manufacturing sector was not affected; not only that, it would, in time, become the activity that was most protected, particularly after 1940. What changed profoundly was agriculture. The most impressive process was that of agriculturizing the northern deserts through vast irrigation works, a task that continued until the 1970s. With additional effects provided by agrarian reform, the agricultural sector became a spur for the internal market, a spectacular generator of currency, a veritable entrepreneurial hothouse and a vibrant component of the productive fabric of the country.

Between 1940 and 1975 Mexico experienced import substitution. It coincided with the golden era of the one-party state, many of whose participants moved from politics to business, or from prosperous rural environments to the urban world. For authors such as Leff (1974), it was during these decades that entrepreneurial groups became consolidated, moved by the over-protectionism of the market, the inflow of currency from agricultural competitiveness and by the wisdom acquired through various generations. In some cases, such as the pioneering example of Monterrey, which was the most defined, these groups were organized as holding companies, very similar to the Japanese *zaibatsu*. Powerful families from the *Porfiriato* era remained prominent, although adapted to the post-revolutionary institutional framework and with links to the newcomers that the new order nurtured.

The crisis of 1982, the nationalization of banking and the bankruptcy of the State led to an aggressive liberalization, set up by the party that had governed since 1930. Mexico entered the General Agreement on Tariffs and Trade (GATT) (1986), negotiated a trade treaty that linked it with the United States, multiplied its agreements in Latin America, Europe and Asia and announced its entry into globalization. There were success stories, but also failures. Little by little, some large companies and/or families abandoned activities of low profitability or competitiveness – steel production,[9] for example – and redirected capital towards areas with a better perspective: agro-industry,[10] food products,[11] communications,[12] the automotive sector,[13] trade,[14] services.[15] Others, such as Cemex, became global players.[16] Who were these selected families and companies, and how did they operate in such diverse phases?

4.4 CHARACTERISTICS

Which elements characterize the origin and development of the selected families? What do the sources suggest? In other words, where did the chosen surnames come from and what did they do in the twentieth century? In terms of their trajectories, is it correct to define them as entrepreneurial families? Let us see.

- Durability: core data for recognizing the capacity of a company, group or family to adapt. The Zambrano family, for example, had been operational in northeastern Mexico and in nascent Texas (Cerutti, 1983, 1992) since the times of war with the United States (1846–47). Without counting the activity of its founder (Gregorio Zambrano, 1802–1873), we find four generations involved in the founding, financing, direction and management of companies.[17] We can even classify each generation by the era: the porfirians (1875–1915); the post revolutionaries (1915–40); the substitutes or protected (1940–80); and the globalizers (1985 onwards).
- Kinship texture: these families demonstrate, among other things, two efficient mechanisms of formation: marriage and the limited liability company. The former had to do with the abundance of inheritors that older generations tended to engender, and with the opportunity for being linked with distinguished families. This led to intercrossed surnames that branched generation after generation until arriving at the present day.[18] In this sense, women must be included in the historical foundation of entrepreneurship: (a) as a mechanism of socio-economic formation that accompanied the centralization of capital as well as the structuring of the bourgeoisie itself, its values and ideology; (b) as a tool destined to endure as a strategic component for the consistency of entrepreneurship itself.
- Limited company, networks: the nineteenth century was crowned by a significant occurrence: the Commercial Code of 1889 defined the regime of limited companies, which would have strategic importance. As the operational capacity of capital increased and the risks were mitigated through sectorial or geographical diversification, the limited company stimulated a cross-linked activity. Sectorial diversification implied investments in various areas: agriculture, livestock, services, finance, manufacturing industry, mining. Geographical diversification implied that owners with different regional roots collaborated to establish large companies. By favouring the unification of dispersed capital, local businessmen began to associate with others from north and central Mexico and from abroad. It should be

of no surprise, then, that around 1910, the principal families were connected with dozens of limited companies.

- Additional characteristics: briefly, another four: (a) these families had built up a manufacturing base since the early twentieth century, which favoured their development under protectionism; (b) they maintained close links to the United States, which allowed them to operate in two markets, transfer technology, form human resources and find alternative financing; (c) they knew how to play at a certain remove from central power, meaning they had moments of rapprochement and others of confrontation; (d) they had the capacity to adapt to the ups and downs of the Mexican economy, to moments of extreme political crisis (the revolution), to the impact of both international crises (the Great Depression) and national crises and to diverse economic policies.

4.5 ENTREPRENEURIAL FAMILIES AND LARGE COMPANIES

4.5.1 The Sada Family

Birth of an entrepreneurial family

The Sada family, and their closest relatives, the Garza Sada, can be seen as a representative case for three reasons: (a) they were a kinship grouping with many branches from the first generations onwards; (b) although they were always in close association with their cousins, they had their own individual profile; and (c) through both routes, they formed links with other families from the late nineteenth century onwards.

Without going further back in time, the developmental path of this group can be traced to the lawyer Francisco Sada y Gómez who, in times of war with the French and in the US Civil War, was already active with local business people.[19] Other observations on Francisco Sada: (a) he married Carmen Muguerza; (b) he had 11 children; (c) among the sons were Francisco G. (one of the founders of Cervecería Cuauhtémoc) and Alberto Sada Muguerza, who would both become business figures during and after the *Porfiriato*; (d) he had various daughters: the best remembered being Consuelo, Rosario and Concepción Sada, who would all marry well-known entrepreneurs. As had occured with the Zambrano, Garza, Madero and González Treviño, the Sada family connected with other families, and they exemplify the method followed by the great entrepreneurs to construct a veritable spider's web of cousins, nephews, brothers-in-law, brothers, children and grandchildren.[20]

Entrepreneurial activity, first generation

The historical launch of Sada as an entrepreneurial family, the first generation creator of companies, occurred with Francisco G. and Alberto Sada Muguerza, who integrated the most conspicuous cadre of parental groups that nurtured the outbreak of manufacturing in Monterrey between 1890 and 1910. At that time it was possible to observe: (a) the participation of the Sada family – as either founders or associates – in the big projects of the time, Cervecería Cuauhtémoc, Fundidora de Fierro y Acero, Fábrica de Vidrios y Cristales (which would give rise to the Vidriera Monterrey in 1909), Banco Mercantil; (b) its significant participation in mining; (c) and the extensive network of connections established through shared ownership.

It should be pointed out that these were the years when Consuelo, Rosario and Concepción Sada all married. Their husbands were from other distinguished families, and henceforth the surname Sada became linked to important characters in the region. The most frequently mentioned marriage was that of Consuelo Sada with Isaac Garza, which brought with it three consequences: (a) the composite surname Garza Sada that would have a wide influence on the history of industrialization in Monterrey; (b) the birth of Eugenio Garza Sada, the future founder of the Institute of Technology and Superior Studies of Monterrey (1943), and who would later become iconic for his career path as well as for his murder in 1973; and (c) the importance of the surname Muguerza, being linked for decades with Garza Sada and Sada.[21]

The post-revolution (1930–45)

Francisco G. Sada Muguerza and his brothers did not only launch companies. As with the Garza Sada cousins and the very closely linked Muguerza family, the Sadas produced many children, nephews, daughters-in-law and sons-in-law. From these came numerous composite surnames. One of the most productive branches grew from the marriage between Francisco G. Sada Muguerza and Mercedes García Fuentes.[22]

Roberto G. Sada García headed the second generation, forming companies of the family, either as founders or shareholders. To add to the diversity of their activities, the following can also be mentioned: (a) among the limited companies, prominent were those linked to the second technological revolution – chemical, petrochemical, electricity; (b) the mother company and the group of companies connected to glass production generated a holding company; this was established in 1936 with Fomento de Industria y Comercio SA (FICSA); [23] (c) close links with the core family promotor Cervecería Cuauhtémoc (Garza Sada, Muguerza, Calderón); (d) links with other important families were maintained; (e) the appearance of new surnames – Elizondo, Barragán, Benavides, Chapa, Santos; (f) entry into parallel projects, generally by a member of the family (among the auspicious businesses were real estate and construction); (g) increasing participation in the service sector, most notably financial activities.

4.5.2 The Zambrano Family (1870–1950)

From trade to mining-manufacturing

The founder of this family was Gregorio Zambrano. Head of a trading house that had been operating on the northeastern frontier since the mid nineteenth century, he was among those who had prospered after the war with the United States and the definition of the border on the Rio Grande. Together with the surnames Madero, Garza, Belden, Milmo, Sada, González Treviño and Ferrara, the Zambrano family excelled among those who promoted manufacturing in the city during the *Porfiriato*. Gregorio, deceased in 1873, had ten children: the most active were Ildefonso, Eduardo, Onofre and, in particular, Adolfo. As in the case of the Sada family, his offspring married relevant persons of the region.

One measure of this family's importance at the end of the nineteenth century is that between 1890 and 1910, decades in which Monterrey gave birth to an industrial outbreak based on heavy metal industry and in its connection to mining, the Zambrano family founded or participated in 65 limited liability companies, 39 of which corresponded to the mining sector. It kept capital in trade, invested in finance, developed strong relations with the rural community and, of course, played a big role in the takeoff of manufacturing. Among major companies that participated, the Zambrano family was at the forefront of those devoted to heavy metallurgy, transport, banking and glass.

In the family context, the Zambrano were becoming interlinked with the regional elite. The twentieth century saw the emergence of, among many others, the following composite surnames: Zambrano Madero, Zambrano Treviño, Sada Zambrano, Garza Zambrano, Sada Gómez de Zambrano, Garza Sada Zambrano, Lagüera Zambrano de Garza Sada, Lagüera Zambrano, Zambrano Gutiérrez.

The post-revolutionaries (1930–45)

As with the Sadas and other business families of Monterrey, the Zambranos shared the following characteristics: diversification of investments, association with members of other families, the use of technologies of the second industrial revolution, participation in the services sector, direct links with the banking sector, gradual occupation of the internal market, taking advantage of the existing relations with the United States and the use of increasingly protectionist policies of the State.

4.6 FROM THE PROTECTED MARKET TO GLOBALIZATION

This section concentrates on ventures undertaken by two families: the Sadas and their mother company, Vidriera Monterrey, and the Zambranos and their largest enterprise, Cemex. These two examples were chosen because (a) they are century-old projects, and still running; (b) they were witness to the protected industrialization and the subsequent opening in 1985; (c) they reveal mechanisms of adaptation to the global arena; (d) they were present in times of booms and crisis; (e) they allow observation of the behaviour of members of the family pairing.

4.6.1 Vidriera Monterrey-Vitro: 1909–2010

The Sada family and glass

The entry of the Sada family into the world of glass had a marginal beginning: the first company of the branch in Monterrey was Fábrica de Vidrios y Cristales, promoted by Cervecería Cuauhtémoc. At the founding of this company (1899), the executive board of Cuauhtémoc included the manager Francisco G. Sada Muguerza. The seed of the idea originated with Isaac Garza, creator of the Garza Sada family. When Vidriera Monterrey was established, the situation changed. Vidriera was the result of a pact between entrepreneurs from La Laguna, Chihuahua and Monterrey (see Figure 4.1). The local negotiator was Garza, while Juan Brittingham represented the outsiders. When Vidriera was founded, Francisco G. Sada was prominent as director, but relevant here is the fact that one of his sons, the engineer Roberto G. Sada, educated in the United States, was named manager. Even though the company-group never stopped being part of the Garza Sada-Sada network, glass production went on to become the responsibility of the Sada family (Barragán and Cerutti, 1993).

Vidriera gradually started to convert its departments into limited companies and during the 1930s and 1940s various firms were founded: Vidrio Plano, Cristalerías, Vidrios y Cristales, Productos Alcali and Fabricación de Máquinas. This itinerary also included the acquisition or creation of plants in other regions: Vidriera México, Distribuidora Nacional, Vidriera Los Reyes, Vidriera Guadalajara, Cristales Mexicanos.

The increasing complexity of the operations, the need for geographical expansion, the uncertainty generated by post-revolutionary policies, plus skillful legal consulting, all led to the founding of the holding company Fomento de Industria y Comercio SA in 1936. In the records of the Cervecería Cuauhtémoc, it is stated that a consultant and 'some of the main shareholders' had considered this alternative since 'the growth of business' amounted to 'a volume of assets, capital and activities' that needed to be separated and organized 'rationally'.[24] As pointed out by Recio (2008, pp. 235–7), the Sada-Garza Sada family wanted to retain 'absolute control of (its) diverse businesses' and pushed for a model that would 'hide the level of expansion that was being reached'. Holding companies were set up. As far as is known today, FICSA and VISA were the first in Mexico.

The internal leap

The holding company FICSA became the predecessor of Vitro SA (1978). As the main shareholder of Vidriera Monterrey, Vidrio Plano, Vidriera México and Cristalería, among others, the controlling company comprised the most prominent axis of the Sada branch of the extensive Sada-Garza Sada-Muguerza family; in two senses: (a) within the strict segment of glass; (b) as a base for ventures involving banking, services, multiple manufacturing investments, construction and any profitable business.

Diverse authors and sources (Flores, 2000; Torres Martínez, 1998) affirm that between the 1930s and 1975, FICSA promoted or acquired Vitro Fibras, Materias Primas Monterrey, Industrias del Alcali, Silicatos de Sodio, Vidrio Plano de México, Enboplast, Vidriera Los Reyes, Vidriera Guadalajara, Cristales Mexicanos, Nacional Distribuidora, Industria del Plástico, Cristales Mexicanos and Cristales Inastillables.

However, two further areas promoted by Vidriera or by the prolific extended family should be mentioned. One consisted of big infrastructure projects with other limited companies. For example, Grupo Industrial, which in 1943 initiated the Planta Generadora de Energía, y Gas Industrial de Monterrey, in 1944, a project aimed at supplying gas from Texas.[25] Secondly, they were decades ahead in their association with foreigners, especially from the United States. In order to produce sheet glass, co-investments were made with the British company Pilkington. In 1957, relations with Owens were established. In 1964, it linked up with Philadelphia Quartz to launch Silicatos de Sodio.

The second half of the 1970s and the years of the oil boom saw expansion reach its peak, both of FICSA/Vitro as well as its sister companies VISA, ALFA and CYDSA.[26] In this environment, 'the development of the group was greatly accelerated when Vitro acquired around 17 national companies'. Among others, it merged Arcillas Trituradas, Ampolletas, Imex, Tubo Plast and Vitrocrisa Cubiertos. It took over the control of companies linked to Pilkington and Owens, installing subsidiaries in Brazil, Costa Rica and Guatemala; and it founded Vitrocrisa Toluca, Vitro Flotado, Regioplast, Crisa Parras, Farmoenvases, Vidriera Querétaro, Vitroflex and the research centre known as VitroTec (Torres Martínez, 1998).

The problems of internationalization

The terminal crisis of 1982 was proof that the internal market was insufficient for continuing the process of protected industrialization. If there were any players in Mexico who understood this problem, they were to be found in Monterrey. Vitro was among those who made the biggest effort to respond to the opening up of the economy in 1985. And like Cemex, its international expansion had both success stories and problems.

Vitro was hit in 1982 by its high dollar debt. For this reason, among the mechanisms used to survive the crisis, it entered the financial sector through a brokerage house that gave short-term help. This strategy also involved exports to the United States and investments in that country. Its external sales grew from 8.3 per cent in 1982 to almost 17 per cent of the total in 1986 (Torres Martínez, 1998). The group was forced to undergo a severe restructuring that constituted changes in costs, management, markets, technology and relocalization, and it managed to firmly establish its process of internationalization. In 1982 it installed distributors in Miami and Texas. In 1986/87 it entered New York and California. In Dallas it established Vitro Packaging, its largest distributor in the United States. In Guatemala it founded Enboplast. And in 1989 it formalized its most risky acquisition in the United States: Anchor Glass.

In the 1980s it reconverted the plant in Toluca, set up a unit in Nuevo León directed at the automotive sector, opened a mine in Coahuila and processing plants in Hermosillo and El Bajío, reduced staff, entered the white goods trade, and during the 1990s concentrated on the production of glass and its derivatives. Simultaneously, with its acquisition of Vidriera Oriental, it installed a packaging manufacturer in Mexicali and established Autotemplex in Nuevo León. In the 1990s, it facilitated strategic alliances with Toyo Glass and Ishizuka (Japan), Azko (Netherlands), Kimble, Corning, American Silver, Owens and Anheuser-Busch (United States) and Pechinery (France). Thanks to the merger of Anchor Glass and Latchford Glass, it managed to occupy almost 30 per cent of the market of glass containers in the United States. In addition, it invested in Peru, Bolivia, Colombia and Ecuador.

For reasons that will not be discussed here, operations with Anchor

Glass generated serious problems for Vitro that, as a group, entered the twenty-first century in a very weakened position. This forced a new and more profound restructuring between 1995 and 2010. According to its report to the stock market, it comprised only two business units: Envases de Vidrio and Vidrio Plano (54 and 46 per cent of sales, respectively). Its plants were spread over ten countries, it exported to more than 15 and managed distribution centres 'throughout the American continent and Europe'. Its turnover in 2010 increased to US$1892 millions. The chairman of the executive board was Adrián Sada González (7.65 per cent of shares). Federico Sada Melo, commercial director of Vitro América, had another 7.56 per cent. Also present were Adrián Sada Cueva, Tomás González Sada, Álvaro Fernández Garza and Jaime Rico Garza.[27] Other members of the family divided the share package, always within control of the founding core.

4.6.2 Cemex (1931–2005)

The Zambrano family in cement

This step in the developmental path of the Zambrano family began in 1920, when it founded Cementos Monterrey. As with its predecessor Cementos Hidalgo (managed in 2006 by Juan Brittingham), it had to compete with firms from central Mexico. To this was added the penetration of cement from the United States, the uncertainties of the 1920s and the crisis of 1929. At this point, in 1931, Hidalgo and Cementos Monterrey decided to merge, and Cemex was born. The growth of the internal market favoured the evolution of the sector. Production was increased and Cemex began to take hold in the northeast, Cementos Guadalajara in the Bajío, Tolteca in central Mexico, Anáhuac in the central area and the Gulf of Mexico, San Luis Mining in the Pacific and Cruz Azul in the central-southern area. Like its competitors, Cemex took advantage of the cycle of substitution. Between 1948 and 1970, its capacity grew to 1.14 million tons, 15 per cent of the market. But it was not until the 1970s that its participation increased: with 3.3 million tons it reached 26 per cent of the national total. Therefore, for the almost 30 years after 1940, the company had gone from being local to multi-regional.

Restructuring and the oil boom

Between 1970 and 1976, Mexico witnessed a process of sector concentration that strengthened Cemex and Tolteca. It was with this background that a business model was designed for Cemex in which various plants would manage themselves independently and would count on a support structure formed by the CEO and staff. An unprecedented phase began:

Cemex reconverted its productive apparatus and integrated itself vertically. The acquisition of Cementos Guadalajara was a significant step, establishing it as number two in Mexico. The increase in oil prices had repercussions on the sector. The Alianza para la Producción (Alliance for Production), called for by the government, led in 1980 to the Programa de Fomento a la Industria Cementera (Program for the Development of the Cement Industry). The entrepreneurs commited themselves to supplying the internal market and exporting the surplus; Cemex, for its part, announced that it would triplicate its production capacity. But such optimistic actions did not foresee the phenomenal collapse that the 1982 crisis would cause. Although the industry was rocked to its foundations, Cemex continued its investments and in 1985 inaugurated the most modern plant in the country, located in Hidalgo, with which it reached 10.7 million tons: 35.5 per cent of the national total. As it maintained its strategy with a minimum of debt, it did not face financial problems. In parallel, thanks to its administrative structure and technological restructuring, it managed to reduce its costs of 55 dollars per ton to 42 dollars between 1982 and 1987, making it competitive in the international market.

Lorenzo Zambrano

Although there were stops and starts, the internal market favoured the evolution of the sector. However, during the 1980s there began to appear signs of alarm. The Europeans began to expose an aggressive attitude on the continent and entered the United States, Canada and Latin America. The Mexican opening hinted at what could happen to Cemex on home ground if it did not counteract the offensive. Given that the future of the industry was to be dominated by a few global companies, if it wanted to survive, it had to play in the same league. Adaptation required in-depth changes. It was at this moment, in 1985, that Lorenzo Zambrano Treviño (fourth generation) was nominated CEO. From then on, Cemex underwent a revolution.

The first step in the Lorenzo Zambrano era was the acquisition in 1987 of Anáhuac: it controlled 13 per cent of the national market, had an excellent export platform, owned the first shipping terminal of Mexico, managed another in Florida, and since 1981, exported to the United States. Cemex strengthened its position: its capacity rose to 15.2 million tons, 48 per cent of the national total. Two years later, in 1989, Zambrano made the surprise acquisition of Tolteca (with a capacity of 6.7 million tons).[28] For Cemex this acquisition signified taking control of 67 per cent of national production. As exporter it added installations in California and Arizona, plus a terminal in Guaymas. At this point it became the first international group with terminals on both oceans and the sixth producer in the world.

Inevitable internationalization

The next phase was linked to the export dimension. The appearance of Mexico derived, on the one hand, from the drastic fall in internal consumption, a consequence of the 1982 crisis, and, on the other, from the demand in the United States. From 1983 onwards, exports to the neighbouring country increased. In 1987 they rose to 4.6 million tons, 20 per cent of local production. Mexico became the principal seller in a market that imported more than 12 million tons annually. With the arrival of a new board of directors, Cemex established an aggressive policy for its conquest, but an anti-dumping lawsuit mitigated the euphoria and, around 1991, sales to the United States plunged.

Zambrano understood that concentrating exports on only one country was very risky, bringing him to two conclusions: (a) in order not to depend on the United States, it was necessary to install plants within its territory; (b) greater diversification of markets was needed. That is: the simple concept of exporter should be abandoned in order to begin the process of internationalization. The cement industry was well on its way to becoming concentrated. Cemex had solid bases in a peripheral country, dominated the practical side of the new technological revolution and could sustain an efficient organization. The experience in the United States helped to evaluate capacities. And since the opening of the Mexican market tended to favour those who were internationalizing, it was decided to move towards globalization.

The first opportunity arose in Spain. Embedded in the demanding European Union, the Spanish put Valenciana and Sansón up for sale. They totalled a capacity of over 11 million tons, controlled 28 per cent of the market and had presence in 70 per cent of the territory. Their acquisition by Cemex awakened interest on both sides of the Atlantic: it was the biggest acquisition made by Latin Americans in Europe (US$1840 million). With its entry into Spain, Cemex became part of the global elite: its 35 million ton annual capacity placed it in fourth position.[29] From a strategic point of view, this step meant competing with global rivals and, at the same time, having access to mechanisms of finance that were unusual in Latin America.

Subsequent steps included the acquisition of Venezolana de Cementos, which covered 45 per cent of the country's consumption, and Bayamo, in Panamá. In 1995, with the latest financial crisis in Mexico, it was decided that the penetration into the global market should be intensified.[30] But the greatest innovation in the mid 1990s was the exploration of the provocative Asian market. The acquisition of 30 per cent of Rizal, in the Philippines, opened this cycle. In 1998 Cemex took over 14 per cent of PT Semen Gresik in Indonesia, it began the building of a container terminal in Egypt and sales transactions in China. In 1999, it expanded its presence in the Philippines and Indonesia. In the year 2000 Cemex bought the giant US company Southdown.[31]

Cemex began the twenty-first century with a capacity close to 80 million tons, dozens of maritime terminals and commercial operations in 60 countries spread across four continents. It registered more than 50 of its own factories, participation in an additional 17, nearly 500 concrete plants, 164 distribution centres and 55 maritime terminals. Simultaneously the company laid out its business model: (a) strengthen its core business; (b) be present in the most dynamic markets in the five continents; (c) a high rate of expansion. In other words, specialization, search for active markets and high geographical diversification. In this way, Cemex became one of the first global companies to come out of Mexico. For this evaluation to be correct, it had to distinguish itself from others (Vitro, FEMSA, Modelo, Gruma, Televisa, Bimbo), which at that moment could be said to be internationalized or with foreign implantation.

Global company

The development of Cemex into a global company was connected to the emergence of new economic powers. Having managed to rise through the ranks within a backward economy, its experience taught it to focus on similar societies that had high potential: the emerging markets. Among the large companies, Cemex was alone in having developed inside a peripheral society, which enabled it to quickly detect both opportunities and limitations: markets such as Latin America were subject to cycles of high instability, so they demanded constant anticipatory actions. Added to this was an incisive administrative restructuring, its ambition to be situated at the technological vanguard and the ever-dependable support of the internal market.

Its evolution in the years prior to the 2007 crisis[32] included the following stages: (a) strength in the internal market (1975–87), giving it a solid base for foreign ventures; (b) recognition in foreign markets through exports (1982–89); (c) establishment of a transnational structure through the acquisition of plants abroad but within the known cultural environment: the United States, Spain and Latin America (1989–94); (d) recognition outside its cultural environment through trading (1992–2000); (e) arrival in Asia, Africa and Oceania (1997–2007); (g) implementation of a competitive model enabling it to compete with the big firms, Holderbank and Lafarge.

4.7 FINAL COMMENTS

Which and how many of the concepts presented at the beginning of the chapter can be applied? To what extent does the empirical material allow an evaluation of the reality uncovered by these conceptual tools? Let us see.

The initial concepts seem not to present a problem. We discussed large companies in the context of a peripheral economy. And it is a well-known fact that in Mexico, these large-scale organizations were involved with two complementary realities: the entrepreneurial family and the business group. The evolutionary path of the Sada-Garza Sada family and the development of the Zambrano family clearly illustrate this.

In the comparison between the detailed empirical register and the concepts, one can see that the permanence of these mother companies, and of the groups that were being formed, was very linked to what were called entrepreneurial families. Were the Sada and the Zambrano entrepreneurial families? The list of companies that they founded or participated in, their remarkable variety and diversification, would seem to confirm this. The fact that they reached the fourth generation also endorses it, and it has even more support when we look at the business fabric: this very dense interlinkage of prominent intercrossed surnames, kinship bonds and corporate formation via share packages or through the executive boards.

What about the relationship of the business texture with its material structure, the productive fabric? Here is the key question: How has the original productive fabric been affected by Vitro's problems, by those faced by Cemex, by the traumatic bankruptcy of Fundidora de Fierro y Acero (1986) or by the recent sale of the Cervecería Cuauhtémoc? Have these events dismantled the fabric from its economic activities? If Vitro still survives, if CYDSA is beginning to be operational again, if FEMSA (the prosperous heir of Cuauhtémoc) and ALFA (almost bankrupt in 1982) find themselves in 2013 at a remarkable juncture, is it not due to – among other factors – having been sustained by the now age-old business fabric?

The impression given is that not only has this structure not disappeared, but many of the old families responsible for it are still active. It would also seem that the two phenomena provide a foundation that could offer mutual guarantees of durability, of intergenerational permanence, especially in times of crisis. As suggested above, in an entrepreneurial-regional development of these characteristics, a large company may go bankrupt, but the business fabric (the group, the spider's web, the frame) has many possibilities of survival.[33]

NOTES

1. In obtaining concepts that are efficient for systematizing the enormous amount of data usually collected, the historian faces a dilemma: should concepts from other social sciences be borrowed? Or, faced with the lack of tools that help to analyse efficiently the subject under investigation, should one generate instruments derived from the research itself? In our case, we used a combination, although in principle what prevailed was derived from the experience of the agents being researched.
2. Societies that did not undergo an industrial revolution in the nineteenth century.
3. In terms of generations, those that form companies will be considered. The founder of the core family, the initial accumulator of fortune multiplied by his heirs in diverse companies, will not necessarily be considered.
4. And the productive fabric will continue to exist, although damaged by the bankruptcy of the large business.
5. A concept derived from debates on local productive systems (LPS) and industrial districts (ID) in Southern Europe. Some differences: (a) the productive fabric (and its business texture) expands in agricultural areas and is not restricted to the industrial-urban areas; (b) includes small as well as medium and large companies; (c) does not require the levels of specialization that the concepts of LPS and ID seem to demand; (d) strictly includes personal relations, especially based on kinship and trust.
6. *Expansión*, 2000–12, on the 500 'most important' companies. Details on procedure used in Cerutti (2015).
7. Companies and groups were mixed.
8. José Antonio Fernández, current CEO of FEMSA, was son-in-law of Eugenio Garza Lagüera, who had no male offspring. Garza Lagüera (now deceased) was part of the third generation Garza Sada.
9. Alfa, IMSA, Proeza.
10. Gruma, Bimbo, Bachoco.
11. Bimbo, Gruma, Modelo, Alfa, Bachoco.
12. Televisa, Grupo Salinas, Carso.
13. Alfa, Proeza.
14. Soriana, FEMSA, Grupo Salinas.
15. Proeza, Televisa, GNP, Grupo Salinas.
16. Among the new players, beneficiaries of the post-1982 privatizations, emerged a champion: Carlos Slim.
17. See note 3.
18. For this reason it is appropriate to use combinations such as Garza-Sada-Muguerza. This way the itinerary of surnames, such as Calderón, Madero, Ferrara, Milmo, Rivero, Elizondo and many more besides can be followed.
19. General Archive of the State of Nuevo León (GANL), notaries, Pacheco, 3 August 1864.
20. During the twentieth century the Sada family helped build, among others, the following cross surnames of the business universe: Sada Madero, Sada González, Sada Zambrano, Garza Sada, Sada Garza, Sada Santos, Sada Gómez de Zambrano, Rivero de Sada Gomez, Garza Sada Sada, Salinas de Sada, Sada Muguerza and Sada Salinas.
21. Concepción and Rosario Sada, for their part, would each marry sons from the very extensive González Treviño family, producing the surname González Sada. See GANL, notaries and Cerutti (1983, 1992).
22. Two sons excelled: Roberto G. Sada and Luis G. Sada. But the star wedding was with Margarita Sada García and her cousin Roberto Garza Sada, one of the most active entrepreneurs. Margarita and Roberto would perpetuate the composite surname Garza Sada.
23. Together with Valores Industriales SA, acting as guide for Cervecería Cuauhtémoc.
24. Cervecería Cuauhtémoc, Report, 24 May 1935.

25. Group of 16 companies, 13 of them from the Sada-Garza Sada-Muguerza core.
26. Founded after the murder of Eugenio Garza Sada, in 1973.
27. Stock market, annual report. The report added that six of the board members were related 'by blood or through marriage'. Adrián Sada González was 'father of Adrián Sada Cueva, cousin of Tomás González Sada and uncle of Federico Sada Melo. Álvaro Fernández Garza is nephew-in-law of Adrián Sada González and cousin-in-law of Federico Sada Melo and of Adrián Sada Cueva. Jaime Rico Garza is nephew-in-law of Adrián Sada González.'
28. Tolteca had lost strength in 1970 due to the weakening of its main shareholder, the British company Blue Circle.
29. It became the principal producer and exporter of white cement.
30. Expansion began again in 1996 with Samper y Diamante, in Colombia.
31. After this merger, business operations began in Thailand, Puerto Rico and California.
32. At the beginning of 2007, it constituted one of the three largest groups, was the principal producer of white cement and appeared among the first international traders. Its most recent acquisitions were the British company RMC (2005) and the Australian firm Rinker, whose acquisition was completed in 2007. This operation implied such a high level of debt that, on the eve of the financial crisis, Cemex was on the brink of bankruptcy.
33. And a substantial part of the productive fabric would also survive, despite damage by the hypothetical bankruptcy of the large business.

REFERENCES

Barragán, J. and M. Cerutti (1993). *Juan F. Brittingham y la industria en México, 1859–1940*. Monterrey: Urbis Internacional.

Cerutti, M. (1983). *Burguesía y capitalismo en Monterrey (1850–1910)*. México DF: Claves Latinoamericanas.

Cerutti, M. (1992). *Burguesía, capitales e industria en el norte de México (1850–1910)*. México DF: Alianza Editorial.

Cerutti, M. (2015). 'Familias empresariales y grandes empresas en México (1890–2010)'. In P. Fernández Pérez and A. Lluch (eds), *Familias empresarias y grandes empresas familiares en América Latina y España. Una visión de largo plazo*. Bilbao: Fundación BBVA, pp. 153–88.

Chrisman, J., J. Chua and P. Sharma (2005). 'Trends and directions in the development of a strategic management theory of the family firm'. *Entrepreneurship Theory and Practice* **31**, 555–75.

Chrisman, J., J. Chua, A. Pearson and T. Barnett (2010). 'Family involvement, family influence, and family-centered non-economic goals in small firms'. *Entrepreneurship Theory and Practice* **36**, 267–93.

Chua, J., J. Chrisman and P. Sharma (1999). 'Defining the family business by behavior'. *Entrepreneurship Theory and Practice* **23**, 19–39.

Fernández Pérez, P. (2003). 'Reinstalando la empresa familiar en la Economía y en la Historia. Una aproximación a debates recientes'. *Cuadernos de Economía y Dirección de la Empresa* **17**, 45–63.

Fernández Pérez, P. (2012). *La última globalización y el renacer de los grandes negocios familiares en el mundo*. Bogotá: Universidad de los Andes.

Flores, O. (2000). *Monterrey Industrial (1890–2000)*. Monterrey: Universidad de Monterrey.

Leff, N. (1974). 'El espíritu de empresa y la organización industrial en los países menos desarrollados: los grupos'. *El Trimestre Económico* **3** (XLI), 521–41.

Recio, G. (2008). 'El abogado y la empresa: una mirada al despacho de Manuel Gómez Morín, 1920–1940'. Doctoral thesis, El Colegio de México.
Sharma, P. (2004). 'An overview of the field of family business studies: current status and directions for the future'. *Family Business Review* **17**, 1–36.
Torres Martínez, J. (1998). 'Estrategias empresariales en México. El caso del grupo Vitro, 1982–1994'. Masters thesis, Universidad Nacional Autónoma de México.

5. Brazilian companies and business groups from a historical perspective

Armando Dalla Costa, Carlos Eduardo Drumond and José María Las Heras*

5.1 INTRODUCTION

According to Dalla Costa (2009), family businesses represent around 90 per cent of economic entities in Brazil. The *Melhores e Maiores* report from the journal *Exame* (2010) indicates that of the large corporations that are active in this country, more than 50 per cent are family businesses.

Nevertheless, this business structure has a reduced survival rate in the long term. According to the consultants Hoft, only 33 per cent of the economic entities reached the second generation and only 4 per cent the fourth (Amorim, 2012, p. 85).

That said, it is important to study the evolution of the principal Brazilian family businesses in the twentieth century, in an attempt to identify and understand the actions and strategies that allowed them to survive over time. In this sense, we will try to present a broad vision of these institutions through an analysis of the most representative firms in the periods in question.

In the available literature there is no concensus on the most precise concept of family business; as underlined by Dalla Costa (2009) and Chua et al. (1999), there are multiple and various definitions for this type of productive unit.

The concept developed by Chua et al. (1999) is the one best suited to the aims of the authors: it describes the objects of study as organizations founded on a coalition of one or more families with the intention of ensuring that the company be managed according to a shared vision. Thus, a family company is one in which the management structure allows the values of the family groups to be perpetuated over time and across generations.

It can be seen that this evaluation comes close to that suggested by Dalla Costa (2009, p. 26), who says: 'the family business is created by the entrepreneurial spirit of one (or various) founders, its majority capital and control is in the hands of a single (or a few) family/families and there is a reciprocal influence from entrepreneurial and family systems, regardless whether management is in the first generation or the subsequent'.

These clarifications made, the aim of this work consists in presenting an analysis of Brazilian family businesses in the historical context of the country's economy in the twentieth and twenty-first centuries. It is clear that with such a broad and diverse time span, there will be particular aspects of each firm and of the economy in each period that cannot be covered in detail. Nevertheless, it is hoped that the text will be a useful point of departure for future research.

The classification of the family businesses came from the ranking of *Maiores e Melhores* from the journal *Exame*, based on the criterion of turnover, with the exception of the interval 1890–1930 when the list was configured using the criterion founding of business, supported in the best-known literature of research for that time, such as Marcovith (2005, 2006, 2007), Dean (1976), Suzigan (1986) and Silva (1976).

The analysis focuses on four important periods. The first begins on the symbolic date of the Proclamation of the Republic, 1889, and ends with the Revolution of 1930. The second features industrialization through substitution of imports, between 1930 and 1960. The third seeks to understand the role of the multinationals, state-owned and national private companies (in this case the majority were family-owned) in the period denominated *milagre brasilero* (Brazilian miracle) and during the big crisis of the 1980s. Lastly, the fourth incorporates the Brazilian economy and its family businesses since the start of the new millennium.

In conclusion, there will be some reflections, challenges and suggestions for new studies to be undertaken, as well as details of references used.

5.2 THE GROWTH OF FAMILY BUSINESS IN THE CONTEXT OF THE EVOLUTION OF THE BRAZILIAN ECONOMY

During the twentieth century, various family businesses made important contributions to the development and industrialization of the Brazilian economy. Interestingly, as confirmation of the data presented at the beginning of the chapter, many did not last the course, so that when looking at the largest family conglomerates in the early twenty-first century (see Table 5.6), an important part of the history of family business in Brazil is absent.

Thus, we seek to briefly relate the developmental path of some of these companies, which, despite their historical importance, no longer exist. Two paradigmatic examples are the Empresas Reunidas Matarazzo and the business group in the area of communication Diários Associados, belonging to Assis Chateaubriand.[1]

The two cases share the characteristics of having been examples of innovation and strategic behaviour, and not having survived over time or, in the case of Diários Associados, having lost relative importance with respect to its past position.

It is understood that in order to offer a dynamic explanation it is not enough to look at isolated extracts from the history of family business in Brazil, therefore these institutions will be studied in the context of Brazilian economic history. To this end, four periods are identified, from the declaration of the Republic onwards, which will make it possible to follow the evolution of the family groups within – and across – each period.

5.2.1 The Milk Coffee Republic or the Old Republic: 1889–1930

The beginning of this phase is recognized as being the declaration of the Republic, in 1889, and it lasts until 1930; it is characterized by the existence of an agro-export economy sustained principally by coffee production. In 1929, the population of the country was 33 million inhabitants and the GDP per capita around US$1000 (American dollar of 1990); between 1870 and 1929, the GDP grew at a rate of 2.8 per cent (Bértola and Ocampo, 2010, p. 108).

The abolition of slavery in 1888 attracted a great number of immigrants who joined the coffee plantations, contributing to the substitution of slave labour by wage earners. This transition occured gradually; in 1876 there were 1 600 000 black slaves, reduced to 720 000 in 1887.

Between 1870 and 1930, a total of 2 589 962 immigrants[2] entered the country (the Brazilian population was 17 434 400 inhabitants in 1900, according to data from the Brazilian Institute of Geography and Statistics, IBGE) and formed part of the workforce on the coffee plantations. Out of this total, 48.3 per cent were originally from Italy, and the majority settled in the state of São Paulo; some of them, as we shall see later, becoming industrialists.

To satisfy the demand of the incipient internal market, and financed by coffee exports, the first national industries began to appear. Some of the establishments that emerged at this time are still active today.

Warren Dean (1976, p. 16), in a well-known study on Brazilian industrialization, mentions for the year 1895 the existence of 121 companies in the city of São Paulo, of which 52 were industrial. The author identifies that 11 of these establishments employed more than 100 workers (three

Table 5.1 Companies, capital, production, employees and value of production, Brazil, 1907 and 1920

Year	Number of companies	Capital (in contos réis)	Production (in contos réis)	Production value	Number of employees
1907	3258	653 555	731 292	109 284	149 018
1920	13 336	1 815 156	2 959 176	310 424	275 512

Source: Dean (1976).

spinning mills, one brewery, three hat factories, one match factory, one foundry and two railway depots).

In another report for the year 1901, for the same city, 170 factories are identified, 50 of which generated employment for more than 100 workers (17 spinning mills and 7 foundries; there were also potteries, cement factories, production of sugar, wheat flour, glass objects, shoes, clothing and paper).

The first decades of the twentieth century were significant for industrialization; between 1907 and 1920 not only did the number of companies increase, but also the production and amount of workers employed. Table 5.1 presents the details of this evolution.

Table 5.2 shows the entrepreneurial families and their founders.[3] From its analysis one can see the strong presence of immigrants and their descendants in the founding as well as the continuation of businesses.

To get an impression of the evolution of Brazilian family conglomerates, we will discuss the experience of four large groups, each from a different area of the country and within diverse areas of activity. Specifically, the cases of the following groups will be looked at: Gerdau, metalworking plant from the south of the country; Casas Pernambucanas, belonging to the textile trade branch, and from the northeast; Klabin Papel e Celuluse, from the south; and the Votorantim group, a business conglomerate immersed in diverse economic sectors, from the southeast.

The Gerdau group began its activities in 1901 with the establishment of the nail factory Pontas de Paris, in the city of Porto Alegre. The company was founded by João Gerdau[4] and his son Hugo Gerdau, who put up the capital of 114 contos and 700 000 réis, respectively (Marcovitch, 2005, p. 273).

German immigrants, they arrived in Brazil at the end of the nineteenth century and became involved in trade in the interior of the state of Río Grande do Sur, an activity that led to an accumulation of capital sufficient for them to enter industrialization.

Diversifying his business, in 1914 Hugo Gerdau opened the doors of the

Table 5.2 Brazil, 20 largest family businesses in 1890

Company	Year of founding	Founder	Generation	Activity sector
Prado family	1817	Antonio Prado	3	Tax collector, livestock, sugar producer, coffee producer, railway, banks, export
Casas Pernambucanas	1861	Herman Lundgren	1	Gunpowder, textile
Santa Maria	1865	Marchiso, Loureiro, Silveira & Cia.	1	Cotton weaving plant
Cia. Têxtil Bernardo Mascarenhas	1872	Bernardo Mascarenhas	1	Textile
Fábrica Santa Francisca	1874	Luiz de Queiroz	1	Textile
Fábrica de Massas Cristofani	1878	Ludovico dal Portoz e Francisco Casini	1	Pasta manufacturer
Fábrica de Toldos, Colchões e Almofadas	1879	Scorzato & Cia.	1	Manufacturer of awnings, cushions and mattresses
Fábrica de pianos	1881	Isidoro Nardelli	1	Piano manufacturer
Indústrias Reunidas Matarazzo	1882	Francesco Matarazzo	1	Trade, metallurgic, textile, bank, edible oil manufacturer
Luiz Trevisan & Irmão	1886	Luiz Trevisan & Irmão	1	Liquors, confectionary
Fracalanza	1886	Angelo Fracalanza	1	Manufacturer of brooms and baskets
Gaffrée, Guinle & Cia.	1888	Cândido Gaffrée e Eduardo Guinle	1	Manufacturer of matches, railways, hydroelectric plants, Docas de Santos company, trams, Boa Vista bank
Antonio de Masso	1888	Antonio De Masso	1	Furniture manufacturer
Klabin Irmãos & Cia.	1890	Maurício Klabin	1	Typography, paper and wood pulp
L'Artística	1890	Innocencio M. Pagani	1	Lithography
Fábrica a Vapor de Tecido e fiação de Corda e Barbante	1890	Enrico Maggi	1	Spinning mills, manufacturer of rope and cord
Estabelecimento dos Irmãos Falchi	1890	Emígdio, Pamphilo, Bernardino Falchi	1	Ceramic, fabrics and bitumen

Table 5.2 (continued)

Company	Year of founding	Founder	Generation	Activity sector
Cia. Empório Industrial do Norte	1891	Luiz Tarquinio	1	Textile
Indústria Votorantim	1891	Lacerda Franco	1	Textile
Sociedade Anônima Derby Club	1899	Valdomiro Gouveia	1	Textile, trade and hydroelectric

Source: Author's elaboration based on Marcovitch (2005, 2006, 2007), Dean (1976), Suzigan (1986) and Silva (1976).

Companhia Geral de Indústrias, an enterprise that unified the production of three match factories: Jung Secco & Cia., Manoel Valente da Costa Leite and João Aydos & Cia. The first, and largest, employed 185 workers and produced 1200 boxes of matches a day.

The origin of Casas Pernambucanas dates back to 1861 when Herman Lundgren[5] founded the gunpowder manufacturer Pernambuco Power Factory; it was active until 2001 when, after the attack on the World Trade Center, the United States stopped importing this product.

According to Marcovitch (2007, p. 36), in order to facilitate distribution, Lundgren established gunpowder depots in Bahia, Espírito Santo, Rio de Janeiro, São Paulo, Paraná, Santa Catarina, Río Grande do Sur, Ceará, Maranhão, Pará and Amazonas.

In 1904, looking to expand his activities, he created a textile factory. After his death in 1907, his heirs Frederico and Arthur Lundgren took over the business and the following year they opened the first retail store of Casas Pernambucanas. A short time later, they inaugurated the Praça da Sé subsidiary, a reference point in the city of São Paulo.

Around 1920, the network of establishments extended towards Porto Alegre, Florianópolis and Teresina, with approximately 200 subsidiaries that sold a wide range of products, but predominantly fabrics from its own manufacturing plants.

The Klabin (Cony and Lamarão, 2001) and Lafer families, both originally from Lithuania, are responsible for the formation of one of the largest Brazilian business groups, Industrias Klabin. Its beginnings go back to 1890, when Maurício Freeman Klabin found employment in the development of typography in a print shop in São Paulo. Ten years later, together with his brothers (Salomão and Hessel) and his cousin, Miguel Lafer, he founded the company Klabin Irmãos e Cia.

In 1902, they leased the Fábrica de Papel Paulista, in the city of Salto de Itu, an initiative that with the involvement of 44 employees allowed them to produce 700 tons of paper a year.

According to Marcovitch (2005), in 1909 the two families created in São Paulo the Companhia Fabricadora de Papel, with an initial investment of 1500 contos de réis. After the death of the founder, in 1923 the management of the company was taken over by the second generation, led by Wolff Klabin and Horacio Lafer.

The ventures undertaken by Antonio Pereira Inácio, born in 1874 in Portugal, constitute the main antecedent of the business conglomerate Votorantim.

His trade skills[6] allowed him to accumulate a capital of 3000 réis that he later invested in a retail shop in São Manoel, São Paulo, at the tender age of 18.

Later he would attempt diverse enterprises in various cities in the interior of São Paulo. Thus, in 1905 he inaugurated the Fábrica de Óleos Santa Helena, in Sorocaba, with equipment acquired in the United States. In 1924 he reorganized his establishments: the Limited Company Industrias Votorantim incorporated the fabric manufacturers of São Paulo, the vegetable oil plant in Sorocaba and the cotton processing units. At that time, the company generated around 3400 jobs.

In 1925, José Ermírio de Moraes, son-in-law of A. Pereira Inácio, took over as CEO of the group, joined by his brothers-in-law João Pereira Inácio and Paulo Pereira Inácio as commercial and financial directors, respectively. This second generation's management led to an increase in accumulated capital from 5000 réis to 20 000 contos de réis in 1926.

5.2.2 Industrialization Through the Substitution of Imports: 1930–64

'The Great Depression of the 1930s and the disruptions to world trade generated by the Second World War were fatal blows to export-led growth' (Bértola and Ocampo, 2010, p. 151). It is in this context that a large part of Brazilian family businesses emerged.

Between 1930 and 1964, the Brazilian economy closed its doors, stimulating its growth almost entirely through the dynamics of internal demand, a situation that allowed the beginnings of an industrialization process.

In 1950, the population rose to more than 50 million inhabitants and the economy was in rapid expansion, signifying a relative loss of importance for the agro-export model compared with the new model driven by industry and services.

The process of industrialization in Brazil (as with the other Latin American countries) was closely related to three well-defined phenomena:

the First World War, the Great Crisis of 1929 and the Second World War. These events brought about a sharp drop in exports from Latin American economies, a situation that led to an approximately 50 per cent decrease in the capacity to import goods.

The solution came through the process of substitution of imports, defined by Tavares (1977, p. 35) as 'a partial and closed process of development that, responding to restrictions on external trade, attempted to repeat, at an accelerated pace and under different historical conditions, the experience of industrialization in developed countries'.

In Brazil, the experience of the industrialization of intermediate goods was preceded by strong investments by the state in base industry, through the creation of the Companhia Vale do Rio Doce in 1943, the Companhia Siderúrgica Nacional in 1941 and Petrobras in 1953 (Dalla Costa, 2011).

The government, in turn, developed the necessary instruments for financing the process, through the already existing Banco do Brasil and the Banco Nacional de Desenvolvimento Econômico (BNDES), founded in 1952. These initiatives were of fundamental importance for President Juscelino Kubitschek to carry out his economic plan, known as *Plano de Metas* and later for the military government to implement its development strategies (first and second National Development Plans), seeking to put an end to the process of substitution of imports.

The great leap forward of the 1950s was the above-mentioned *Plano de Metas*, '50 years in 5'. According to Villela (2005, p. 55), the model 'contemplated investments in the areas of energy, transport, base industries, food and education, with a total budget of almost 5 per cent of GDP in the period 1957–61'.

It is in this new political and economic context that the companies and family ventures will be analysed.

Among the principal companies of the time, the development of Indústrias Reunidas Matarazzo is remarkable. According to Marcovitch (2006, p. 111), in the 1960s the group 'employed more than 30 000 people, working in more than 100 companies'. The successors of Conde Matarazzo were not able to continue the expansion of the businesses and with the passing of time they lost strength, finally going bankrupt some years later.

It was a similar story in the case of Diários Associados, founded in 1924 and owned by Assis Chateaubriand. This lawyer from the northeast of the country, later based in Rio de Janeiro, began his professional career in journalism before becoming involved in the area of radio. His skill and entrepreneurial spirit led him to become a pioneer in the introduction of television in Brazil, and allowed him to build a media empire of radio stations and television channels (Morais, 1994), as well as a strong presence in the printed press.

As with the case of Indústrias Reunidas Matarazzo, the group over time began to lose ground when faced with new competitors, especially the television network Red Globo, owned by Roberto Marinho (seventh largest Brazilian company in 2010, see Table 5.6). Even though it occupies a modest position, Diários Associados is currently still active – in stark contrast to the companies of Conde Matarazzo.

In this period there was also a notable emergence of companies such as Perdigão[7] (1934) and Sadia[8] (1944), which towards the end of the first decade of the new millennium merged into Brasil Foods (BRF), thus creating one of the largest international food conglomerates. Grandchildren of Attilio Fontana, founder of Sadia, are today in charge of the group and control almost 12 per cent of shares.

It is also worth mentioning the 1953 creation of JBS-Friboi, a company that today represents, like BRF, one of the largest food producing groups in the world, out-performing traditional multinationals like the US giant Thysson Foods. Table 5.3 shows the importance of the movement initiated in the 1930s, when industry became a priority concern for the representatives of the national elite.

According to Caldeira (2007, pp. 59–60), this process began in 1928 with the Manifesto Votorantim, Matarazzo e Klabin, which led to the founding of the Centro de Indústrias do Estado de São Paulo. It included in its steering committee such well-known figures as Francisco Matarazzo, Roberto Simonsen, José Ermírio de Moraes and Paulo Pereira Inácio, to mention just a few of the main players.

Looking a bit further into the history of the prominent companies, it can be seen that Gerdau went through periods of profound change and complex developments. In 1939, after the death of Hugo Gerdau, the second generation gave up control of the enterprises. His daughter married Curt Paul Johannpeter, a specialist in finance who was working in Argentina, a determinant for the couple to reside in that country.

Returning to Brazil in 1946, Johannpeter took control of the company. Shortly after, the Siderúrgica Riograndense was acquired and in 1955 the Usina II was constructed in the city of Sapucaia do Sul (Rio Grande do Sul), with a production capacity of 18 000 tons a year.

The success of Casas Pernambucanas is the result of clearly defined circumstances. According to Marcovitch (2007, p. 29), in addition to the undeniable administrative capacity of Herman Lundgren and his sons, other reasons should be mentioned.

The northeast of the country was the supplier of abundant and high quality raw materials, as well as having relatively cheap labour costs

Table 5.3 Brazil, 20 largest family companies in 1930

Company	Year of founding	Founder	Generation	Activity sector
Família Prado	1817	Antônio Prado	4	Tax collector, livestock trade, sugar, coffee producer, railways, banks, exports
Casas Pernambucanas	1861	Herman Lundgren	2	Textile, retail trade
Cia. Têxtil Bernardo Mascarenhas	1872	Bernardo Mascarenhas	2	Textile
Klabin Irmãos & Cia.	1890	Maurício Klabin	2	Tiles, paper, wood pulp
Indústria Votorantim	1891	Antônio Pereira Ignácio	2	Textile, cement, vegetable oil
Cia. Empório Industrial do Norte	1891	Luis Tarquínio	2	Textile
Nami, Jafet & Irmãos	1896	Nami Jafet	1	Trade
Grupo Gerdau	1901	João Gerdau	2	Nail manufacturer, iron and steel
Indústrias Nardini	1908	Família Nardini	2	Lathe manufacturer
Cia. Frigorífica e Pastoril de Barretos	1910	Antônio Prado	2	Frozen meat production
Indústrias Reunidas Francisco Matarazzo	1911	Francesco Matarazzo	1	Metalworking, trade
Metalúrgica Dedini	1920	Família Dedini	1	Manufacture and repair of sugar mill machinery
Cia. Eletrometalúrgica Brasileira	1921	Flávio de Mendonça Uchôa	1	Steel production
Usina Queiroz Junior	1922	Queiroz Junior	1	Iron and steel production
Lorenzetti & Cia.	1923	Alessandro Lorenzetti	1	Manufacture of showers, sanitary materials and domestic appliances
Diários Associados	1924	Assis Chateaubriand	1	Communication
Organizações Globo	1924	Irineu Marinho	1	Communication
Cia Bras. de Mineração e Metalurgia	1924	Alexandre Siciliano	1	Iron beams, sheet iron, wire
Genésio Queiroz & Cia.	1927	Família Queiroz	1	Trade, gas distribution
Indústria Romi SA	1928	Família Romi	1	Parts for agricultural machinery, lathes

Source: Author's elaboration based on Marcovitch (2005, 2006, 2007), Dean (1976), Suzigan (1986) and Silva (1976).

compared to the south. The essential question, however, resided in the distribution system designed by the founders, which allowed them to cut out the intermediaries and deal directly with clients through their establishments. Here, fabrics were traded from external producers, but their strength lay in their own production.

In the 1930s, with the aim of overcoming the difficulties imposed by poor communication, he began to use a procedural manual devised in the company, a guide for managers in, above all, the practical aspects of running the business.

In addition, the network was innovative in launching a publicity campaign in circuses and cinemas, at a time when the marketing industry was taking its first steps. 'Farmgates, walls, stones, lampposts and circus awnings, all became transformed, thus the first outdoor advertizing in the country was introduced.'[9]

In the case of Indústrias Klabin, the expansion of its businesses came when Wolff Klabin acquired the Manufactura Nacional de Porcelanas in 1931. According to Marcovitch (2005, p. 208), after importing new machinery and redesigning the production process, 'it became ten years later the largest tile producer in the world'.

Seeking to diversify their activities, W. Klabin and Horacio Lafer acquired in Paraná the hacienda Monte Alegre, with 144 000 hectares of araucarias, or monkey puzzle trees. Here, in 1941, Indústrias Klabin do Paraná de Celulose SA was established.

A short time later, the industrial plant was inaugurated, an event of such size and importance that it included the participation of then president of the Republic, Getúlio Vargas. This factory went on to supply 80 per cent of the national paper market.

Wolff Klabin died on 15 March 1957 and his elder son, Israel Klabin, together with Horacio Lafer and other members of the family, continued the leadership of the business. Horacio Lafer died in 1965 and his heirs took over his role in the group.

The expansion of the Votorantim groups's activities was strongly stimulated in the 1940s and 1950s, based on its incursion into diverse sectors and regions out of São Paulo. In 1938, it entered into steel production and in the following year opened the Barra Mansa power plant in Rio de Janeiro.

Two years later, the company began the construction of a cement plant in the city of Itajaí, Santa Catarina, and in 1944 it inaugurated a new cement production plant in Pernambuco.

This sectorial and territorial diversification led to the acquisition of the paper manufacturer Pedras Brancas in the state of Rio Grande do Sul, of Cimento Portland Rio Branco in Paraná and with the entry into the sugar sector through the acquisition of the power plant São José en Igarassu in Pernambuco.

After the death of Antonio Pereira Ignácio in 1951, Antonio Ermírio de Moraes took control of the group.[10]

5.2.3 The Industrialization of Brazil with the Help of Multinational and State-owned Companies and Private Firms with National Capital: 1964–90

In the 1960s, the state was clearly incentivized by the arrival of foreign capital, by public investment and private enterprise.

Among the government policies that were introduced, notable were the National Development Plans I and II (NDP-I and -II). The former took place during the presidency of Emílio Garrastazu Médici (1972–74) and its aim was the development of large projects of integration (transport, export corridors, telecommunications, the Rio de Janeiro-Niterói bridge, the transamazonic highway, the hydroelectric plants of Três Marías e Itaipu), the structuring of special plans of regional development; and the expansion of state investments, to mention the most important.

The latter was to complement the policies of the previous Plan, focusing on the process of substitution of imports. It was introduced by Ernesto Geisel (1974–79) to promote the development of base industries, capital goods, energy and to achieve autonomy in certain basic supplies. It also included scientific and technological development through specific policies such as the Primer Plan Nacional de Post Grado.[11]

According to the data presented by Bértola and Ocampo (2010), in 1980 the population of Brazil exceeded 120 000 inhabitants, and had become more urban than agricultural. According to Castro (2005, p. 143), 'in the period 1950–1980, the GDP of Brazil grew at an average rate of 7.4 per cent per year'.

This growth, obtained to a large extent through the implementation of the economic plans, allowed the family-controlled, state-owned and multinational companies to progress; they were the principal players that contributed to the development of the economy and its change of profile, both in the period called the *milagre brasileiro*[12] and later, in the 1980s.

As a result, there was a reduction of basic goods for export, from 65 per cent in 1973 to 32 per cent in 1984 (Castro, 2005). This variation was compensated for by the increase in relative importance of manufactured goods, going from 23 per cent to 56 per cent. Table 5.4 is a reflection of the family initiatives in this period.

The Brazilian economy, like the others in Latin America, went through some difficulties between 1980 and the mid 1990s. Above all, it had to deal

Table 5.4 Brazil, 20 largest family companies in 1974

Company	Year of founding	Turnover (in Cr$ 1000)	Generation	Activity sector
Varig-SA Viação Aérea Rio-Grandense	1927	1 617 324	n.a.	Air transport
SA Inds. Reunidas F. Matarazzo	1911	1 450 673	3	Wholesale trade
Eletroradiobraz SA	1949	1 383 530	n.a.	Supermarket
Supermercados Pão de Açúcar SA	1959	1 206 069	1	Supermarket
Copersucar	1959	1 200 000	n.a.	Wholesale trade (alcohol, sugar, ethanol)
Construções e Comércio Camargo Correa SA	1939	1 022 510	2	Construction, iron and steel
Mesbla SA	1912	930 098	n.a.	Retail trade
Casas Sendas Com. Ind. SA	1960	925 168	2	Retail trade
Cia. Cervejaria Brahma	1888	845 847	n.a.	Beverages
Arthur Lundgren Tecidos SA (Casas Pernambucanas)	1908	827 000	4	Retail trade
Hermes Macedo SA	1932	720 000	1	Retail trade
Cia. Siderúrgica Mannesmann	1952	684 892	n.a.	Metalwork
Construtora Norberto Odebrecht SA	1944	648 802	3	Construction and petrochemical
Construtora Andrade Gutierrez SA	1948	611 017	1	Construction
SA Indústrias Votorantim	1891	610 689	3	Cement, others
Abril SA Cultural e Industrial	1950	604 710	2	Media groups
Cia. Ultragás SA	1937	521 360	3	Oil derivatives
Paes Mendonça SA	1959	520 000	n.a.	Supermarket
Cia. Industrial de Conservas Alimentícias – CICA	1941	496 504	n.a.	Agricultural producer
C.R. Almeida SA Engenharia e Construções	1958	459 349	2	Construction

Source: Author's elaboration based on the journal *Exame, Mayores y Mejores* (1974).

with a high level of foreign debt, hyperinflation and low growth rate of GDP.

In the early 1990s, a strong presence of family enterprises became noticeable in the areas of food and construction. In relation to the former, prominent were the supermarkets Pão de Açúcar, Casas Sendas, Paes Mendonça, Bompreço, Casas da Banha, and the food producing groups Ceval, Sadia and Perdigão (Table 5.5). Construction companies also strengthened their position in this period, among them Norberto Odebrecht, Camargo Corrêa, C.R. Almeida and Andrade Gutierrez.

The growth of these groups occurred both in the internal market and abroad. The companies that had had problems positioning their products in the local arena began a cautious process of internationalization, as in the case of Sadia, which made its first exports in 1963, or the construction firms that intensified their participation in foreign markets in the 1980s.

In the analysis of the evolution of the selected companies, it is clear that in the years 1960–90, the Gerdau group was oriented towards the national arena, expanding its activity in various sectors and regions. Thus, it established a wire manufacturing plant in São Paulo, a metalworking plant in Pernambuco and others in Rio de Janeiro and Paraná.

During the phase of privatization of the national economy, the group strengthened its presence through the acquisition of the Barão de Cocais power plant in Minas Gerais and of Usiba, in Bahia. A determining aspect for the growth of the group was the beginning of the process of internationalization in 1980, through the incorporation of the metalworking plant Laisa, in Uruguay. After almost a decade of apprenticeship, in 1989 it acquired another unit, the Courtice Steel in Canada.[13]

In the case of Casas Pernambucanas, it should be mentioned that it reached a total of approximately 800 subsidiaries and 40 000 employees.[14] In 1970 it was among the first retail companies to offer credit and its own financing. Nevertheless, as in the case of other family firms, it succumbed to family disputes among the heirs in the next decades.

Once separated, the operations developed in the states of Pernambuco and Ceará disappeared. The businesses in Rio de Janeiro went bankrupt. Only Arthur Lundgren Tecidos, with operations in São Paulo, prospered and continued to compete with the big players in retail trade.

In the early 1960s, the Klabin Irmaõs & Companhi group intensified its process of sectorial diversification and occupation of national territory,[15] based on the founding in 1961 of the Unidad Vila Anastácio (São Paulo), considered the largest paper manufacturer in Latin America.

In 1969 began the activities of the Papel e Celulose Catarinense factory in Lages (Santa Catarina), a pioneering industry in Brazil in the area of wood pulp bleaching by chlorine dioxide. In 1973 began the production

Table 5.5 Brazil, 20 largest family companies in 1989

Company	Year of founding	Turnover (in Cr$ 1000)	Generation	Activity sector
Supermercados Pão de Açúcar SA	1959	2425172	2	Supermarket
Construtora Norberto Odebrecht SA	1944	1976632	3	Construction and petrochemicals
Varig-SA Viação Aérea Rio-Grandense	1927	1880637	n.a.	Air transport
Construções e Comércio Camargo Correa SA	1939	1257037	2	Construction, metalworking
C.R. Almeida SA Engenharia e Construções	1958	1144836	2	Construction
Ceval Alimentos SA	1972	1135190	n.a.	Food
Mesbla SA	1912	1071176	n.a	Retail trade
Casas Sendas Com. Ind. SA	1960	992260	2	Retail trade
Construtora Andrade Gutierrez SA	1948	982887	1	Construction
Paes Mendonça SA	1959	934577	n.a.	Supermarket
Cia. Cervejaria Brahma	1988	779044	n.a.	Beverages
Mendes Júnior SA	1953	722453	2	Construction
Bompreço	1966	714434	n.a.	Supermarket
Sadia Concórdia SA	1944	688845	3	Food
Casas da Banha	1955	663058	n.a.	Supermarket
Arthur Lundgren Tecidos SA (Casas Pernambucanas)	1908	630212	4	Retail trade
CCE	1964	618391	1	Electronics
Cofap	1950	615696	n.a.	Automobile parts
Klabin Fabricadora	1899	603234	1	Paper and wood pulp
Perdigão Agroindustrial	1934	595910	2	Food

Source: Author's elaboration based on the journal *Exame, Mayores y Mejores* (1989).

of the company Papelão Ondulado do Nordeste, Goiana (Pernambuco), precursor in the manufacture of wood pulp from sugar cane bagasse.

With the enactment of the new Law of Limited Companies in 1973, the Supervisory Board was established, comprising the shareholders of the company. This led to a process of professionalization of the group, with directors chosen by the Board.

In the 1960s and 1970s, the Votorantim corporation continued its path of growth and diversification. It established cement plants across the country, from the south to the northeast, and expanded its activities into sectors such as orange juice production and the construction of hydroelectric plants and manufacturing plants of paper and wood pulp.

A crucial moment in the history of the group was the transition from the first to the second generation. In 1973, after the death of José Ermírio de Moraes, his sons took control of the companies. José Ermírio de Moraes junior was responsible for the sector of cement; Antonio focused on the area of metals; Ermírio Pereira de Moraes on nitro-chemicals; and his son-in-law, Clovis Scripilliti, took over the business in the northeast of the country.[16]

5.2.4 From Privatization to Internationalization of Brazilian Family Business: 1990–2010

In the period 1980–94, one of the main problems faced by the Brazilian economy was the control of inflation. In these 15 years, five plans were introduced, namely: (1) Cruzado (1986); (2) 1909 (1987); (3) Verão (1989); (4) Collor I (1990); and (5) Collor II (1991). In the short term, they all met their objectives, but none were effective as a long-term solution. They were useful, however, as preparation for the *Plano Real* (1994) that incorporated the lessons of the previous plans and inaugurated a new era of control of inflation for the country.

In the early 1990s, the economic climate was characterized by high inflation, trade openings and the implementation of a national plan of privatization. This latter process did not advance much during the presidencies of Fernando Collor and Itamar Franco (1990–94), during which only 33 state-owned companies were sold. The main sectors, according to Giambiagi et al. (2005), were iron and steel, petrochemical and fertilizers, and total revenue reached US$8.6 billion, with transfer for the private sector of US$3.3 in debt.

Later, during the two presidencies of Fernando Henrique Cardoso (1994–2002), privatization led to revenue of approximately US$100 billion (Giambiagi et al., 2005, p. 187). This model profoundly changed the tripod that had sustained previous economic development, based on multinationals, state-owned and private national companies.

With this panorama, a new phase in the internationalization process of Brazilian companies was begun. Among them, some state-owned companies such as Petrobras and Banco do Brasil, internationalized since the 1970s, saw an opportunity in this environment to strengthen their presence abroad.

Nevertheless, the most representative experiences occurred with the large family groups. According to Canuto et al. (1997), there were four institutional changes in economic policy in the vectors of productive restructuring: (1) trade and financial liberalization; (2) the programme of integration of the countries of Mercosur; (3) the implementation of the Plano Real; and (4) the programme of privatizations.

It is worth mentioning other factors that allowed family conglomerates to enter the external market: (a) the policies of revenue distribution promoted by the governments of Lula da Silva (2003–10); (b) the strengthening of the internal market; (c) the reduction of poverty, allowing the incorporation of more than 30 million new consumers into the national economy; (d) the increase of operations in the stock market (Bovespa), making possible an increase in funding for companies; and (e) the new role of the National Bank of Economic and Social Development (BNDES), which contributed to the formation of conglomerates with the potential of becoming international players.

In Table 5.6 it is possible to see the strengthening of the traditional groups that were already active abroad. One can also observe the presence of recently formed companies with a solid internationalization behind them.

Among the traditional groups, prominent are both Gerdau and the construction firms Norberto Odebrecht and Camargo Corrêa. From those that followed, it is worth mentioning JBS-Friboi that began its process of internationalization in 2005 and currently holds the top position globally in beef cattle management.

According to Dalla Costa (2011, p. 153), the group had 'installations capable of dealing with the slaughter of 65.2 thousand heads per day. It had 22 industrial plants in Brazil, 6 in Argentina, 16 in the United States, 10 in Australia and 10 in Italy, giving employment to 125 thousand workers globally.'[17]

The role of BNDES was of fundamental importance in the financing of companies in general. The institution closed in 2011 with total borrowings of nearly 139.7 billion reales,[18] and the resources directed towards small and medium-sized companies reached a record 36 per cent of total borrowings, in this way bringing democracy to the financing process.

In the last decade, the bank offered resources to large national conglomerates that were in a position to become international.[19] In this context it

Table 5.6 Brazil, 20 largest family companies in 2010

Company	Year of founding	Turnover (in US$ million)	Generation	President	Activity sector
Braskem SA*	2002	13070.00	3	Carlos Jose Fadigas de Souza Filho	Petrochemical
Pão Açúcar	1952	10786.00	2	Abílio dos Santos Diniz	Supermarket
Cia. Siderúrgica Nacional	1946–93	8223.40	2	Benjamin Steinbruc	Metalworking
JBS-Friboi	1953	7975.50	2	Wesley Mendonça Batista	Food
Cosan	1936	7421.80	4	Rubens Ometto Silveira Mello	Energy, food, logistics, infrastructure
TAM	1976	7142.90	2	Líbano Miranda Barroco	Aviation
Gerdau Aços Longos	1901	6014.50	5	André Bier Gerdau Johannpeter	Metalworking
Globo	1965	4814.30	2	Roberto Irineu Marinho	Telecommunications
Gol Varig	2001	4508.70	1	Constantino de Oliveira Jr	Aviation
Alesat Combustíveis	1996	4394.70	1	Marcelo Henrique Ribeiro Alecrim	Fuel retail
Natura	1969	4004.30	1	Alessandro Giuseppe Carlucci	Perfumes, cosmetics
Norberto Odebrecht	1944	3773.00	3	Marcelo Bahia Odebrecht	Construction and petrochemical
Camargo Corrêa	1939	3246.10	2	Vitor Hallack	Construction, metalworking
Gerdau Açominas	1986	3178.70	5	André Bier Gerdau Johannpeter	Metalworking
Magazine Luiza	1957	3084.50	2	Luiza Helena Trajano Inácio Rodrigues	Retail trade
Suzano Papel	1924	2990.20	3	Antônio Maciel Neto	Paper, wood pulp
Klabin	1889	2792.60	3	Fabio Schvartsman	Paper, wood pulp
Casas Pernambucanas	1908	2632.40	3	Anita Louise Harley	Retail trade
Amil	1978	2602.40	1	Edson de Godoy Bueno	Medical insurance
Weg Equipamentos	1961	2599.20	2	Harry Schmelzer Júnior	Motors, equipment

Note: *The company is in the third generation and began in 2002 because the majority shareholders belong to the Odebrecht family.

Source: Author's elaboration based on the journal *Exame, Mayores y Mejores* (2010).

is worth pointing out the contribution BNDES made to the formation of Brasil Foods and to the strengthening of some groups like Friboi, Marfrig and Gerdau, to mention the most significant.

The current situation of the four companies analysed in the text is presented next.

The Gerdau group reached its centenary under the management of the fifth generation of family directors, led by André Bier Gerdau Johannpeter. Thanks to its growth in the internal and foreign markets, it reached 2011 with a structure of more than 337 industrial units, and a presence in around 100 countries. The company's turnover reached 35.4 billion reales, with profits of 2.1 billion.

With respect to the origin of its revenue, 35.9 per cent corresponds to Brazil, 30.5 per cent to North America, 12.4 per cent to Latin America and the remaining 21.2 per cent to operations developed in other countries (Gerdau, 2011, pp. 5–28).

With the slogan, 'everything for your home', Casas Pernambucanas began the second decade of the twenty-first century under the leadership of Anita Louise Harley, part of the third generation of the family. The group's turnover in 2011 was close to 3.8 billion reales, with profits of 100 million, obtained through a network of 283 subsidiaries staffed by 15000 employees.[20] Out of the four companies studied in the text, it is the only one that did not venture into the international market.

Fábio Schvartsman, belonging to the third generation, is at the head of the Klabin group, managing operations that develop 16 factory units installed in eight Brazilian states and one Argentinian. The company has commercial offices in nine states of its country of origin, one subsidiary in the United States and a logistics distributor in Europe, as well as representatives in the rest of the world. It closed the year 2011 with a staff of 13831 employees, of which 8556 are directly employed, 5140 outsourced and 135 interns or young apprentices.

It sold 1739000 tons of paper and packaging, with a turnover of close to 3889 million reales and profits of more than 183 million (Klabin, 2011, p. 13).

Votorantim began the second decade of the twenty-first century with a structure of 100 per cent national capital, operating in more that 15 countries and immersed in the following areas of activity: (1) cement, concrete and complementary products; (2) mining, metalworking, steel, aluminum, zinc and nickel; (3) wood pulp; (4) self-generation of energy; and (5) production of concentrated orange juice.

These activities are developed through 55 factories, 44 mines, 111 concrete plants and 52 distribution centres, as well as 35 hydroelectric generators. The operations give the group a turnover of 23.7 billion reales with profits of 1.3 million. The revenue of the group can be divided as follows: cement, 41 per cent; metals, 33 per cent; iron and steel, 12 per cent; wood pulp, 11 per cent; others, 3 per cent (Votorantim, 2011, pp. 20, 21, 65).

Currently the group has a staff of 38 700 000 employees and another 36 700 000 outsourced, distributed over its factories in Argentina, Bolivia, Canada, Chile, China, Colombia, the United States, Paraguay, Peru, Portugal and its commercial and logistic units in Australia, Austria, Belgium, Hungary and Switzerland.

5.3 FINAL CONSIDERATIONS

Over the course of the twentieth century, the Brazilian economy went through a series of transformations that allowed it to leave behind its initial profile of being purely an agro-exporter and to make way for an industrial and service-led economy.

The productive initiatives undertaken by certain family groups emerged out of the transition from slave labour to wage earners in the late nineteenth century, and with the arrival of immigrants. Nevertheless, a large part of these companies were formed in or after the 1930s, when industry began to be a priority for governments and the national economic elite.

Analysing the previous paragraphs of this chapter, it can be seen that traditional family groups like Gerdau, Casas Pernambucanas, Klabin and Votorantim, which are more than a century old, coexist with important young companies that have been stimulated by a recent scenario in the Brazilian economy. Among these latter a few stand out: Marfrig, which began its activities in the twenty-first century; Natura and O Boticário in the perfume and cosmetics branch; Gol and Tam in the aviation sector; Organizações Globo in telecommunications, to mention just a few of the most prominent.

Table 5.6 distinguishes the presence of two female CEOs: Magazine Luiza and Casas Pernambucanas. Despite the fact that there has been, since the Second World War, an ever-increasing insertion of women into the working environment and within all types of activities, it is still not often that they occupy positions of leadership in companies, especially if these are family-controlled.

Having made these general observations, there now follows a description of the limits and challenges that were presented in the writing of this text.

The first question refers to the production and industrialization of coffee. For centuries Brazil has held the top position in coffee production and export; however, there is in the country not a single company with national capital – whether family-controlled or not – that dominates in this area.

There is a void in the historiography when attempting to understand why none of the family groups studied were interested in the benefits provided by the cultivation of coffee, an activity in which the country has always held clear comparative advantages.

Another area in which no local participation is seen is the automotive sector. Systematically, since the 1940s, the emerging national companies did not manage to break the entrance barrier to this industry, dominated by multinationals.

Currently, Brazil is one of the largest markets for automobiles in the world; it would therefore be a promising proposal to identify the reason why family firms are absent in this sector. This research should, among other things, include a comparative analysis considering countries where family groups have a strong presence in the production of this type of vehicle.

Expanding the discussion on the evolution in this area, there is the curious matter of two family corporations that are currently internationalized: Marcopolo and Randon. Both firms are active in areas of the sector that have not attracted the interest of multinationals, the former producing body shells for omnibuses and the latter components for trucks.

That said, the research proposal suggested above could include the question of why none of these firms, considering the relative success in their performance, entered into the traditional sector of cars, trucks and omnibuses.

Without wanting to undermine the importance of the research issues presented, the authors agree on the necessity of emphasizing the challenge of understanding correctly the role of the 'Shumpeterian entrepreneur' in large family businesses of Brazil.

There is no lack of examples of this model of entrepreneurship; one has to go no further than Francisco Matarazzo and Assis Chateubriand who were active in the twentieth century and represent perfectly the role of innovative entrepreneur. Even though the text does not focus further on this subject, it is a promising aspect that has been little investigated in the literature.

A valuable contribution to enrich the research would be the inclusion of an analysis of the internationalization strategies of Brazilian family business groups. In this context, there are diverse examples, such as JBS-Friboi, Gerdau, Natura, Odebrecht, Votorantim and so on that stand out and should therefore be considered for future research.

Also worth incorporating into the research agenda are aspects such as the existence of some strategic common pattern adopted by the surviving groups. Large Brazilian family conglomerates, such as Indústrias Reunidas Matarazzo, went bankrupt. What was the component that differentiated the groups that disappeared from the ones that were successful, like those mentioned in the text?

Another point to be kept in mind comes from the relation between family companies and the state. In the majority of countries in the world, the link manifests itself either through the direct involvement of entrepreneurs in politics or in the form of agreements and funding.

In the Brazilian case, firms such as Odebrecht and Camargo Corrêa played a crucial role in important projects for the country's economic development; on the other hand, groups like JBS-Friboi and Gerdau have in the last years received significant support from the state in their internationalization strategies.

Finally, it is necessary to point out that the greatest contribution this chapter offers is simultaneously one of its weaknesses. The time span under consideration allows a panoramic vision of the history of family business in the country; nevertheless, each of the determined periods is a source of research in its own right and deserves a more in-depth investigation in the future.

NOTES

* The authors are grateful for the collaboration of Mariana Tozo Wichinewsky and Dalila Analy Goes Labor Hennel, students of Economy at the Universidade Federal do Paraná and fellows in the scientific initiation programme for the elaboration of the tables on the 20 largest businesses in 1974, 1989 and 2010.

1. For an initial approach to the vast amount of literature on these groups, see Morais (1994) and Costa Couto (2004a, 2004b).
2. Data available at http://www.diasmarques.adv.br/artigo_ImigracaoEstadao2.pdf (accessed 30 July 2012).
3. From the methodological point of view, it is very difficult to find data on the companies existing at the end of the nineteenth and early twentieth centuries. Therefore, in the tables on 1890 and 1930, the available information is used. Various information is missing that is found in the following paragraphs. It was decided to present the tables regardless, because they represent the beginnings and the founders of the main family companies of each period.
4. For more details on the entrepreneurs of this family, see, among others, Carmo (1991), Teixeira (2001) and Werlang (2002).
5. For information on the Lundgren family, see Alvin (1977), Góes (1963) and Stein (1979).
6. For more details on the Votorantim group, see Caldeira (2007), Pastore (2013) and the Memorial Center Votorantim (http://www.memoriavotorantim.com.br, accessed 30 July 2012).
7. Tassara and Scapin (1996).
8. Fontana (1980) and Teixeira (1994).
9. http://chimbica91.wordpress.com/2011/07/21/casas-pernambucanas/ (accessed 12 August 2012).

10. http://www.memoriavotorantim.com.br/NossaHistoria/linha_do_tempo/Paginas/Linhadotempo.aspx (accessed 4 September 2012).
11. Data from NDP-I and -II, available at http://www.pralmeida.org/05DocsPRA/1369PlanejBr1946-2005.pdf (accessed 16 August 2012).
12. Between 1968 and 1973, the Brazilian GDP grew at an average annual rate of more than 10 per cent, hence its designation as the 'Brazilian miracle'.
13. Data available at http://www.gerdau.com/sobre-gerdau/memoria-gerdau-linha-do-tempo.aspx (accessed 4 September 2012).
14. Information on the Casas Pernambucanas from http://chimbica91.wordpress.com/2011/07/21/casas-pernambucanas/ (accessed 4 September 2012).
15. http://www.klabin.com.br/es-es/paginas/historia (accessed 4 September 2012).
16. http://www.memoriavotorantim.com.br/NossaHistoria/linha_do_tempo/Paginas/Linhadotempo.aspx (accessed 4 September 2012).
17. The text by Dalla Costa (2011) gives other examples of internationalization of Brazilian family companies, such as Gerdau, Marcopolo, Randon, JBS-Friboi, BRF-Brasil Foods and Marfrig.
18. http://www1.folha.uol.com.br/fsp/opiniao/21512-ajustes-no-bndes.shtml (accessed 4 September 2012).
19. For more information on the role of BNDES in the internationalization process of Brazilian companies, see, among others, Alem and Cavalcanti (2005), Carvalho et al. (2002), Dalla Costa and Souza Santos (2010) and Instituto Alvorada (2011).
20. Data available at http://chimbica91.wordpress.com/2011/07/21/casas-pernambucanas/ (accessed 5 September 2012).

REFERENCES

Alem, A.C. and C.E. Cavalcanti (2005). 'O bndes e o apoio à internacionalização das empresas brasileiras: algumas reflexões'. *Revista do BNDES* **24** (12) (December), 42–76.

Alvim, R. (1977). *A sedução da cidade. Os operários camponeses e a fábrica dos Lundgren*. Rio de Janeiro: Graphica.

Amorim, L. (2012). *Recomeço aos 100 anos*. Fundada em 1910, a vinícola gaúcha Salton reformulou a gestão para sobreviver ao período mais crítico de sua história, a morte de seu presidente em 2009. *Revista Exame* (April). São Paulo. edição 1.010, **46** (3), (22 February), 84–6.

Bértola, L. and J.A. Ocampo (2010). *Desarrollo, Vaivenes y Desigualdad: una Historia Económica de América Latina desde la Independencia*. Madrid: SEGIB.

Caldeira, J. (2007). *Votorantim. Uma história de trabalho e superação*. São Paulo: Mameluco.

Canuto, O., F.M. Rabelo and J M. Silveira (1997). 'Abertura e grupos econômicos na indústria brasileira'. *Revista Paranaense de Desenvolvimento Econômico* (September–December), 33–52.

Carmo, V. (1991). 'Curt Heinrich Paul Johannpeter'. In *Pense Grande*, Vol. 2. São Paulo: Prêmio Editorial.

Carvalho, C.E., R. Studart and A.J. Alves Jr (2002). 'Desnacionalização do setor bancário e financiamento das empresas: a experiência brasileira recente'. IPEA, Textos Para Discussão 882.

Castro, LB. (2005). 'Privatização, abertura e desindexação: a primeira metade dos anos 90'. In F. Giambiagi et al. (eds), *Economia Brasileira Contemporânea (1945–2004)*. Rio de Janeiro: Elsevier, pp. 141–65.

Chua, J., J. Chrisman and P. Sharma (1999). 'Defining the family firm by behavior'. *Entrepreneurship Theory and Practice* **23** (4), 19–39.
Cony, C.H. and S.T. Lamarão (2001). *Wolff Klabin: a trajetória de um pioneiro*. Rio de Janeiro: FGV.
Costa Couto, R. (2004a). *Matarazzo: A travessia*. São Paulo: Planeta do Brasil.
Costa Couto, R. (2004b). *Matarazzo: Colosso brasileiro*. São Paulo: Planeta do Brasil.
Dalla Costa, A. (2009). *Sucessão e sucesso nas empresas familiares* Vol. 4. Reimp. Curitiba: Juruá.
Dalla Costa, A. (2011). *Internacionalização de empresas brasileiras. Teoria e experiências*. Curitiba: Juruá.
Dalla Costa, A. and E.R. de Souza Santos (2010). 'Internacionalização de empresas brasileiras: restrições de financiamento e papel do BNDES'. *Revista Economia & Tecnologia* **6** (23) (October–December), 167–74.
Dean, W. (1976). *A industrialização de São Paulo (1880–1945)*, 2nd edn. São Paulo: Difel.
Exame (2010). *Melhores & Maiores*. April.
Fontana, A. (1980). *História da minha vida*. Petrópolis: Vozes.
Gerdau (2011). *Relatório Anual, 2011*. http://www.gerdau.com.br/relatoriogerdau/2011/ra-br/download/RA2011-GERDAU-Completo.pdf (accessed 5 September 2012).
Giambiagi, F. et al. (2005). *Economia Brasileira Contemporânea 1945–2004*. Rio de Janeiro: Elsevier.
Góes, P. de (1963). *Um sueco emigra para o Nordeste*. Rio de Janeiro: José Olympio.
Instituto Alvorada (2011). *O papel do Estado na formação de grandes conglomerados nacionais, 2011*. http://institutoalvorada.org/wp-content/uploads/2010/04/conglomerados_alvorada.pdf (accessed 29 August 2012).
Klabin (2011). *Relatório Anual, 2011*. http://www.klabin.com.br/arquivo/document/RS2011-PT.pdf (accessed 5 September 2012).
Marcovitch, J. (2005, 2006, 2007). *Pioneiros e empreendedores. A saga do desenvolvimento no Brasil*. Vols I, II, III. São Paulo: Saraiva/Edusp.
Morais, F. Chatô (1994). *O rei do Brasil, a vida de Assis Chateaubriand*. São Paulo: Companhia das Letras.
Pastore, J. (2013). *Antonio Ermírio de Moraes. Memórias de um diário confidencial*. São Paulo: Planeta.
Silva, S. (1976). *Expansão cafeeira e origens da indústria no Brasil*. São Paulo: Alfa-Omega.
Suzigan, W. (1986). *A indústria brasileira: origem e desenvolvimento*. São Paulo: Braziliense.
Stein, S. (1979). *Origens e evolução da indústria têxtil no Brasil, 1850–1950*. Rio de Janeiro: Campus.
Tassara, H. and A. Scapin (1996). *Perdigão. Uma trajetória para o futuro*. Videria: Empresa das artes.
Tavares, M. da C. (1977). *Da substituição de importações ao capitalismo financeiro*, 6th edn. Rio de Janeiro: Zahar.
Teixeira, F. (1994). *Sadia. 50 anos construindo uma história*. São Paulo: Prêmio Editorial.
Teixeira, F. (2001). *Chama empreendedora. A história e a cultura do Grupo Gerdau 1901–2001*. São Paulo: Prêmio Editorial.
Villela, A. (2005). 'Dos anos dourados de JK à crise não resolvida (1956–1963)'. In

F. Giambiagi et al. (eds), *Economia Brasileira Contemporânea (1945–2004)*. Rio de Janeiro: Elsevier, pp. 45–68.

Votorantim (2011). *Relatório Anual, 2011*. http://votorantim.mzweb.com.br/votorantim/web/arquivos/Votorantim_Industrial_2011_Relatorio_Anual_v2.pdf (accessed 5 September 2012).

Werlang, W. (2002). *A família de Johannes Heinrich Kaspar Gerdau: Um estudo de caso sobre a industrialização no Rio Grande do Sul*. Agudo: Editora Werlang.

6. Family capitalism in Argentina: changes and continuity over the course of a century

María Inés Barbero and Andrea Lluch

6.1 INTRODUCTION

The aim of this chapter is to analyse the distinctive features and long-term evolution of Argentinian family capitalism in order to compare this case to other historical experiences and contribute to the international debate on family businesses in emerging countries. We investigate the relevance and organizational forms of the largest Argentinian family firms and provide evidence on how to explain their longevity, survival and failures from a long-term perspective.

This chapter presents, for the first time, a quantitative evaluation of the significance and characteristics of the largest Argentinian family firms between 1923 and 2010, based on the nominal analysis of a series of rankings available for the 100 largest businesses for ten benchmark years (1923, 1937, 1944, 1954/56, 1970, 1980, 1990, 2004 and 2010), and the subsequent individualization of family-owned firms.[1]

This data allows us to evaluate the relevance and role of family firms between the 1920s and the 2000s. In order to analyse these processes, we have combined quantitative and qualitative analysis, using information from case histories, institutional histories, biographical dictionaries and other research relating to large Argentinian business families and Argentinian family firms.[2]

The following criteria were considered in identifying family businesses: strategic ownership by at least two members of one family, or by one member of each of the participating families in the case of plurifamily businesses; the presence of at least two family members on the board of directors; and the participation of various generations of the family in the ownership and/or management of the business, showing a desire for continuity over time (for more information on these criteria, see the Introduction to this volume). We have also included businesses managed by the founder that have remained under the control of the original family.

We argue that in the period under study, large-scale Argentinian capitalism has been family-based, and has retained some enduring features over the years, in particular the notable presence of diversified business groups (DBGs). We also note that sales, mergers and failures have had a strong impact on the dynamic reconfiguration of Argentinian family capitalism in the long term. This innovative longitudinal approach therefore allows us to identify transformations and discontinuities in the environment and the players and sectors that have made up the family business elite at various moments in the period under study.

6.2 FAMILY BUSINESS DURING THE FIRST PHASE OF THE IMPORT SUBSTITUTION INDUSTRIALIZATION PERIOD (1918–54)

6.2.1 The Context

The first phase of the import substitution industrialization (ISI) period spans various decades in which the Argentinian economy went through fundamental changes in terms of its productive structure and its regulatory framework, as a result of transformations in the international context and a reorientation of internal public policies.

During the first global economy (*c.* 1870–1914), Argentina's economy grew at an exponential rate, largely due to its entry into international markets as an exporter of raw materials and food products. With the outbreak of World War I (WWI), and above all after the crisis of 1929, it was forced to adapt to a new phase in which growth depended fundamentally on the expansion of the internal market.

The manufacturing sector became the most dynamic in the economy between the early 1920s and mid 1950s. The process of import substitution that had begun at the end of the nineteenth century accelerated after WWI and was consolidated in the 1930s during the Great Depression and World War II (WWII) (Barbero and Rocchi, 2003).

Following worldwide tendencies, the state began to take on an increasingly active role in the economy. In the 1930s, industrial growth was boosted pragmatically by measures adopted by the authorities in order to deal with the global crisis (devaluations, tariffs, exchange controls, higher levels of regulation, public investment). Interventionism intensified in the early 1940s. The authorities introduced industrial policies that deliberately enhanced protectionism and the provision of public credit for the manufacturing sector and encouraged the creation of public-owned businesses in strategic sectors. These measures were reinforced during Juan Domingo Perón's administrations between 1946 and 1955, in which state intervention was increased and many transportation and public service companies owned by foreign capital were nationalized.

The industrialization process was riddled with tension and conflicts that affected the strategy and performance of individual businesses. From the end of the 1940s, there were frequent crises in the external sector, which generated austerity policies and devaluations, which in turn resulted in mediocre economic performance up to the beginning of the 1960s. These so-called stop-go cycles were accompanied by high levels of inflation that reached an average of 26 per cent annually between 1949 and 1962 (Di Tella and Dornbusch, 1989).

The political scene became increasingly unstable from 1930 onwards. The coup d'état of September 1930 signified the defeat of constitutional legality and an alternating cycle of civilian- and military-led governments began. Perón's electoral victory in 1946 led to more social transformation. After Perón was overthrown in 1955, a phase of great socio-political conflict began, which has since become one of the characteristic features of Argentinian political life.

6.2.2 Family Businesses

The rankings of the 100 largest firms (by share capital) in 1923, 1937, 1944 and 1954 reveal that the market share of domestic-owned firms declined up to 1944, while that of foreign companies grew. This tendency was reverted at the end of WWII due to the nationalizations that took place during the Perón administration, which reduced the proportion of foreign companies in the top 100 and raised that of domestic private firms to 60 per cent by 1954. Throughout the entire period, there were more family businesses than non-family businesses among the domestic-owned companies.

By focusing on the 30 largest (by share capital) family businesses over this period, one characteristic of Argentinian capitalism emerged: the dominant presence of businesses founded by foreigners. A second notable trait, as mentioned above, is the importance of DBGs that have successfully adapted their investment profile to the new business conditions. In the four different benchmark years analysed, at least a third of the family firms in the country's 30 largest firms belonged to DBGs, including the notably long-standing Bunge & Born Group, owned by the Bunge, Born, Hirsch and Oster families (Green and Laurent, 1988; Schvarzer, 1989); the Tornquist Group, owned by the Tornquist family (Gilbert, 2003) and the Bemberg Group, owned by the Bemberg family (López, 2001; Russo,

2006). In 1954, the presence of DBGs intensified, accounting for almost 50 per cent of the 30 largest firms, an indication of how these had been strengthened during Perón's term in office (1946–55), despite the fact that some companies were expropriated (specifically those of the Bemberg Group, which recovered its companies after 1955).

The three aforementioned DBGs were created between the 1860s and 1880s by foreigners or second-generation foreigners with close links to European investors, giving them privileged access to capital, information and managerial talent and human resources. They all began by carrying out commercial activities and later diversifying their investments as the economy grew (Barbero, 2015). In addition to the long-standing presence of the DBGs mentioned above, the rankings for 1923–54 also show a rotation of groups entering and leaving the 30 largest firms (Table 6.1).

A third general point to emphasize is the sustained presence of sugar refineries, mostly created by landowners in the northwest of Argentina. These firms benefited from a high level of tariff protection from the 1880s onwards, even though from the 1920s they faced recurring crises of overproduction, which only a few of the largest refineries were able to recover from (Moyano, 2015). A fourth topic is the presence of agriculture and livestock businesses among the 30 largest firms. This is most notable up to the mid 1940s, after which their share begins to decline, in parallel with the stagnation of the primary sector from the 1930s onwards.

A third of the 30 largest family businesses between 1923 and 1954 was made up of standalone industrial firms. This proportion is similar to that of businesses belonging to DBGs, with the exception of 1954. From 1937 onwards, more complex manufacturing activities appeared, such as metalworking (SIAM Di Tella, owned by the Di Tella family, founded in 1910), cement (Loma Negra, owned by the Fortabat family, founded in 1926) and steel (Siderca, part of the Techint Group, owned by the Rocca family, founded in 1954), all of which would give rise in the future to new business groups through diversification (Castro, 2012; Cochran and Reina, 1962).

Throughout this phase, we observed remarkable continuity in terms of players from pre-WWII onwards. It is noteworthy that until 1944, almost all standalone firms had been founded before 1914 by foreigners of various origins, as was the case with DBGs and agricultural and livestock businesses. Many of these firms went through generational processes and managed to successfully adapt to the economic changes of the interwar period and Perón's first two terms in office (1946–55).

With regard to the sectorial structure of the largest Argentinian family businesses between 1923 and 1954, the most represented activity was industry. The food sector continued to predominate but its share was decreasing participation by 1954, while there is a growing diversification

Table 6.1 The 30 largest family firms and family business groups, Argentina, 1923 to 1954, by share capital

Top 30	1923	1937	1944–45	1954
1	BUNGE & BORN LTD (Bunge, Born, Hirsch and Oster Families; Bunge & Born Group) Cereals' exports	ARGENTINA DE NAVEGACIÓN MIHANOVICH LTDA (Dodero Family) Transportation	BUNGE & BORN LTD (Bunge & Born Group)	ALBA (Bunge & Born Group) Chemical products
2	PICCARDO Y CIA. LTDA (Piccardo Family) Tobacco manufacturing	PICCARDO Y CIA. LTDA (Piccardo Family)	INGENIO Y REFINERÍA SAN MARTÍN DEL TABACAL SA (Patrón Costas Family) Food industry – sugar	ASTRA (Grüneisen, Sánchez Caballero and Aguirre Families)
3	ERNESTO TORNQUIST Y CO. (Tornquist Family and Group) Finance-holding	FÁBRICA ARGENTINA DE ALPARGATAS (Fraser Family – Roberts Group)	ARGENTINA DE NAVEGACIÓN DODERO (Dodero Family)	ATANOR (Bunge & Born Group) Chemical products
4	CERVECERÍA ARGENTINA QUILMES (Bemberg Family and Group) Food industry – beer	SANSINENA (Tornquist Group)	PICCARDO Y CIA. LTDA. (Piccardo Family)	AZUCARERA CONCEPCIÓN (Guzman Family)
5	LEDESMA SUGAR STATES AND REFINING COMPANY (Wollmann Family) Food industry – sugar	TORNQUIST Y CIA LTDA. (Tornquist Family and Group)	LEDESMA SUGAR STATES AND REFINING COMPANY (Wollmann-Arrieta Families)	BAGLEY (Mosoteguy Family) Food industry

Table 6.1 (continued)

Top 30	1923	1937	1944–45	1954
6	SANSINENA DE CARNES CONGELADAS (Tornquist Family and Group) Food industry – meat packing	TERRITORIAL RIO DE LA PLATA (Tornquist Group)	MENENÉNDEZ BEHETY SA GANADERA ARGENTINA (Menéndez Behety Family)	BENEGAS HNOS. (Benegas Family) Food industry
7	INDUSTRIAL Y COMERCIAL NICOLÁS MIHANOVICH (Mihanovich Family) Holding (diversified)	PEREDA LTDA. (Pereda Family) Livestock – lands	CAMPOMAR SA (Campomar Family) Textiles	BUNGE Y BORN LTD (Bunge & Born Group)
8	IMPORTADORA Y EXPORTADORA DE LA PATAGONIA (Braun Menendez Family) Trade and lands – Patagonia	BUNGE & BORN LTD (Bunge & Born Group)	MOLINOS RÍO DE LA PLATA (Bunge & Born Group)	CAMPOMAR SA (Campomar Family)
9	BARTOLOMÉ GINOCCHIO E HIJOS (Ginocchio Family) Livestock – agriculture	LEDESMA SUGAR STATES AND REFINING COMPANY (Wollmann-Arrieta Family)	FÁBRICA ARGENTINA DE ALPARGATAS (Fraser Family – Roberts Group)	CASA JACOBO PEUSER (Peuser Family) Publisher
10	MINETTI Y CIA. (Minetti Family) Food industry – Flour	MOLINOS RÍO DE LA PLATA (Bunge & Born Group) Food industry	SOCIEDAD FINANCIERA E INDUSTRIAL SUDAMERICANA (Bunge & Born Group)	CENTENERA (Bunge & Born Group) Cans

11	GANADERA ARGENTINA MENENDEZ BEHETY (Menendez Behety Family) Livestock – agriculture – lands	AZUCARERA TUCUMANA (Tornquist Group) Food industry – sugar	LOMA NEGRA SA COMPAÑÍA INDUSTRIAL ARGENTINA (Fortabat Family)	COMPAÑÍA QUÍMICA (Bunge & Born Group) Chemical products
12	LEACH'S ARGENTINE ESTATES LTD (Leach Family) Food industry – sugar	BARTOLOMÉGINOCCHIO E HIJOS (Ginocchio Family)	BARTOLOMÉ GINOCCHIO E HIJOS (Ginocchio Family)	COMEGA CIA. MERCANTIL Y GANADERA (Bunge & Born Group) Livestock – agriculture – lands
13	SAINT HERMANOS (Saint Family) Food industry	MINETTI Y CIA. (Minetti Family)	MINETTI Y CIA. (Minetti Family)	CRISTALERIAS RIGOLLEAU (Rigolleau Family, Roberts Group)
14	SIMON MATTALDI LIMITADA (Mattaldi Family) Lands – beverages	GANADERA ARGENTINA MENENDEZ BEHETY (Menéndez Behety Family)	IMPORTADORA Y EXPORTADORA DE LA PATAGONIA (Braun Menendez Family)	SIDERCA DALMINE (Rocca Family Rocca) Metals and metal products
15	CAMPOMAR Y SOULAS (Campomar and Soulas Families) Textiles	CAMPOMAR Y SOULAS (Campomar and Soulas Families)	TALLERES METALÚRGICOS SAN MARTÍN TAMET SA (Tornquist Group) Metals	EZRA TEUBAL HERMANOS (Teubal Family) Textiles
16	AZUCARERA BELLA VISTA (Manuel García Fernández Family) Food industry – sugar	CARLOS CASADO LTDA. (Casado Family) Lands – livestock	S.I.A.M. (Di Tella Family) Metals and machinery	FÁBRICA ARGENTINA DE ALPARGATAS (Fraser Family – Roberts Group)

Table 6.1 (continued)

Top 30	1923	1937	1944–45	1954
17	AZUCARERA CONCEPCIÓN (Guzmán Family) Food industry – sugar	AZUCARERA CONCEPCIÓN (Guzmán Family)	AZUCARERA CONCEPCIÓN (Guzmán Family)	FERRUM (Tornquist Group) Ceramics – bathroom fittings
18	FINANCIERA E INDUSTRIAL SUD-AMERICANA (Bunge & Born Group) Finance	INDUSTRIAL Y COMERCIAL NICOLÁS MIHANOVICH (Mihanovich Family) Holding (diversified)	PRIMERA MALTERÍA ARGENTINA SA (Bemberg Group) Food industry	FINANCIERA E INDUSTRIAL SUDAMERICANA (Bunge & Born Group)
19	DROGUERÍA DE LA ESTRELLA (Demarchi Family) Chemical – pharmaceutical products	LEACH'S ARGENTINE ESTATES LTD (Leach Family)	COMEGA. CÍA MERCANTIAL Y GANADERA SA (Bunge & Born Group)	SANSINENA (Tornquist Group)
20	ASTRA (Grüneisen, Sánchez Caballero and Aguirre Families) Oil	IMPORTADORA Y EXPORTADORA DE LA PATAGONIA (Braun Menendez Family)	ESTANCIAS UNIDAS DEL SUD SA (Fortabat Family) Lands – livestock	GAROVAGLIO Y ZORRAQUIN Garovaglio and Zorraquín Families) Finance-holding
21	FÁBRICA ARGENTINA DE ALPARGATAS (Fraser Family – Roberts Group) Textiles	ASTRA (Gruneisen, Sánchez Caballero and Aguirre Families)	PEREDA LTDA. GANADERÍA, COMERCIO, INDUSTRIA SA (Pereda Family)	GRAFA (Bunge & Born Group) Textiles
22	ESTANCIA Y COLONIAS TRENEL (Devoto Family and Group) Lands – livestock	COMERCIO E INDUSTRIA (Tornquist Group)	LEACH'S ARGENTINE ESTATES LTD (Leach Family)	GUILLERMO KRAFT (Kraft Family) Publisher

23	TIENDA SAN JUAN (Cibrián Family) Retail – textiles	INTRODUCTORA DE BUENOS AIRES (Tornquist Group)	BRASSERIE ARGENTINE QUILMES SA (Bemberg Group)	GUILLERMO PADILLA (Padilla Family) Food industry
24	SANTA ROSA ESTANCIAS LIMITADA (Bemberg Family and Group) Lands – livestock	CRISTALERIAS RIGOLLEAU (Rigolleau Family, Roberts Group) Glass products	ASTRA (Grüneisen, Sánchez Caballero and Aguirre Families)	IMPORTADORA Y EXPORTADORA DE LA PATAGONIA (Braun Menendez Family)
25	LUIS MAGNASCO Y CIA. (Magnasco Family) Food industry	EMPRESA MATE LARANGEIRA MENDES (Mendez Family)	ECHESORTU Y CASAS SA (Casas Family) Livestock – agriculture – lands	INGENIO Y REFINERÍA SAN MARTÍN DEL TABACAL SA (Patrón Costas Family)
26	INTRODUCTORA DE BUENOS AIRES (Tornquist Group) Import – export	LA MARTONA (Casares Family) Food industry	EMPRESA MATE LARANGEIRA MENDES SA (Mendez Family)	INTRODUCTORA DE BUENOS AIRES (Tornquist Group)
27	EMPRESA MATE LARANGEIRA MENDES SA (Mendez Family) Food industry	JUAN GALLI E HIJOS LTDA. (Galli Family) Agriculture – livestock	MANUFACTURA DE TABACOS PARTICULAR SA (Greco Family) Tobacco manufacturing	LEDESMA SUGAR STATES AND REFINING COMPANY (Wollmann-Arrieta Family)

Table 6.1 (continued)

Top 30	1923	1937	1944–45	1954
28	TALLERES METALÚRGICOS (Tornquist Group) Metal industry	SIMÓN MATTALDI LTDA. (Mattaldi Family)	MASLLORENS HERMANOS SA (Masllorens Family) Textiles	LUIS MAGNASCO Y CIA. (Magnasco Family)
29	NOUGUÉS HERMANOS (Nougués Family) Food industry – sugar – lands	LOMA NEGRA (Fortabat Family) Cement	JUAN GALLI E HIJOS LTDA. SA AGRÍCOLA, GANADERA Y COMERCIAL (Galli Family)	MOLINOS RÍO DE LA PLATA (Bunge & Born Group)
30	SAN PABLO DE FABRICACIÓN DE AZÚCAR (Nougués Family) Food industry – sugar – lands	SOCIEDAD FINANCIERA E INDUSTRIAL SUDAMERICANA (Bunge & Born Group) Finance and manufacturing	SAINT HERMANOS SA (Saint Family) Food industry	PICCARDO Y CIA. LTDA. SA (Piccardo Family)

Source: Authors' elaboration based on the database built by the project 'The evolution of the corporate networks in Argentina and Chile, 1901–2010', coordinated by Dr Erica Salvaj and Dr Andrea Lluch. The rankings included the largest non-financial corporations, according to their share capital. Sources listed in the main sources references section.

within manufacturing activities, with a large number of textile and tobacco firms and the introduction of non-metallic minerals (cement, glass) and metalworking.

6.3 FAMILY BUSINESSES DURING THE SECOND STAGE OF ISI (1956–74)

The second phase of the import substitution process took place between 1956 and 1974. State policies in this period promoted the development of new industries – particularly capital-intensive and intermediate goods – and aimed to integrate production and reduce imbalances in the external sector. This was also the objective of energy policies during this time, which sought oil self-sufficiency, and policies promoting industrial exports. Up to the end of the 1950s, national capital firms had been one of the main beneficiaries of ISI policies, but from that point on, and until the end of the 1960s, the focus was on attracting foreign capital. This was the so-called second stage of the state-led industrialization process, which took place in a context marked by the application of development programmes all over Latin America in what was a new era of global expansion for multinationals. The results of this transformation began to be felt around the mid 1960s. The stop-go cycles that had begun in Argentina in 1949 continued until 1963. Then came a period of expansion that lasted until 1974, sustained as much by the growth of industry as by the recuperation of agricultural and livestock exports. In parallel, Argentina continued to have high inflation levels: between 1963 and 1973 the average annual rate was 29 per cent (Di Tella and Dornbusch, 1989).

As mentioned above, the entire period was characterized by high levels of institutional instability in which civilian-led governments alternated with de facto military governments and there were frequent about-turns in economic policies. It was an environment of acute political and social conflict that became more marked towards the end of the 1960s with the emergence of the first guerrilla groups and then of paramilitary squads, leading to increasing levels of violence.

6.3.1 Family Businesses

The changes mentioned above had direct effects on businesses, which varied due to the specificities of public policies and to the changing relationships established between entrepreneurs and the state during the various governments. In terms of players, the most notorious change was the significant advance of foreign companies (or multinational corporations,

MNCs), particularly in sectors that required high levels of investment and know-how (the automobile, chemical, pharmaceutical and oil sectors). In a comparison of the 100 largest industrial businesses between 1956 and 1970, foreign firms doubled their share of the total, going from 25 per cent to 51 per cent, while the share of state-owned companies also increased. These figures correlated with the decline of family firms (from 45 per cent to 25 per cent), and non-family domestic-owned firms (from 25 per cent to 11 per cent).

During this phase, Argentinian capitalism went from having a strong national and family-owned component in the 1950s to a new state of affairs in which MNCs, mainly of US origin, predominated. Among family businesses, DBGs became more significant as an organizational form: firms belonging to DBGs made up almost 50 per cent of the 20 largest industrial firms in 1956 and 1970, with the notable presence (as in 1923–54) of Bunge & Born and, to a much lesser degree, of the Tornquist and Bemberg Groups. This fact confirmed the capacity of some of the largest, most traditional DBGs to adapt to a new stage in the Argentinian economy and their ability to benefit from state-led industrialization policies.

However, together with the 'traditional' groups, there was a growth of 'new' groups emerging from individual firms that had been started before and after 1930 and that had begun to diversify and acquire new organizational structure from the 1940s onwards, within the context of a closed, regulated economy. In contrast to traditional DBGs, which had been created from commercial firms, these new groups originated in industrial businesses and underwent diversifications that both were related (SIAM, Techint) and unrelated (Fortabat) (Barbero, 2015).

The year 1970 saw the appearance of the Soldati Group, one of the groups that would excel in the 1980s, and the return of the Bemberg Group, which recovered its businesses, which had been expropriated during Perón's term in office. Also worth mentioning is the Fábrica Argentina de Alpargatas, which increased the diversification of its investments in the 1950s and could therefore be included in the DBGs category (Gutiérrez and Korol, 1988).

Some standalone family businesses that had managed to survive among the elite of the largest companies until the mid 1950s were no longer present by the early 1970s. Their departure was due to a number of factors: takeover by foreign capital in the 1960s, sectorial crises, the transition from one generation to the next or the fact that they were simply replaced by other firms on the list of the largest 100. In the 1960s there was a process of transfer of local business control to foreign interests, favoured by the devaluation of local currency, the drop in the level of internal demand and difficulties in gaining access to long-term credit.

All the evidence presented shows that by virtue of the changes in the context and/or the transition to the third generation, a renewal occurred between the end of the 1950s and the early 1960s. In contrast, other companies founded by immigrants before 1914 joined the ranking at this time; for instance, the food companies Bagley and Terrabusi, which had gone through generational transitions without many conflicts and retained a strong position up to their acquisition by foreign companies at the beginning of the 1990s.

At the same time, the rankings of 1956 and 1970 reveal the incorporation of more recently founded businesses, including Acindar (owned by the Acevedo family), a steel company that was created in 1949 and is, together with Siderca and Gurmendi, representative of the new branches that emerged during the second period of ISI. Also worth mentioning is Fate, a manufacturer of rubber products and tyres that was created in 1940 and eventually gave rise to the Madanes-Quintanilla Group, which expanded rapidly with the development of an automobile industry at the beginning of the 1960s.

Concerning sugar refineries, the firm showing most continuity is Ledesma. Between 1945 and 1970, the business – which was already producing sugar and alcohol – started to manufacture paper and paper pulp, basing its expansion on an increase in scale as well as on diversification, gradually transforming itself into an agro-industrial complex.

The importance of the food sector continued to decrease among the 30 largest family businesses, while there was an increase in metals, metalworking and chemicals (Table 6.2). At this point, the family business elite begins to reflect the increased diversification of Argentina's industrial sector.

6.4 LIBERALIZATION THROUGH RESTRUCTURING AND GLOBALIZATION (1974–2004)

In the mid 1970s, a new period of institutional transformations began in Argentina, which involved a first attempt at the liberalization and deregulation of the economy, bringing the period when industrialization and full employment had been a sustained state policy to a gradual end.

This was not a linear process, but rather one that involved many advances and setbacks, in that there was an initial phase of liberalization between 1976 and 1981, a decline in the 1980s and a new phase of accelerated liberalization in the 1990s. These changes marched in time to transformations in the global economy and changes in Argentina's economic policies from the early 1970s onwards, with the crisis in the Keynesian consensus and the

Table 6.2 The 20 largest family firms and family business groups, Argentina, 1956 to 2010, by annual sales

Top 20	1956–57	1970	1980	1990	2004*	2010
1	MOLINOS RÍO DE LA PLATA (Bunge & Born Group) Food industry	MOLINOS RÍO DE LA PLATA (Bunge & Born Group)	MOLINOS RÍO DE LA PLATA (Bunge & Born Group)	DALMINE SIDERCA (Rocca Family – Techint Group)	TECHINT GROUP + TENARIS (Rocca Family)	TENARIS (Techint Group – Rocca Family)
2	ALPARGATAS (Fraser and Roberts Families) Textiles	ACINDAR (Acevedo Family)	ACINDAR (Acevedo Family)	ACINDAR (Acevedo Family)	ACEITERA GENERAL DEHEZA SA (Urquía Family)	TERNIUM (Techint Group – Rocca Family)
3	FRIGORÍFICO SANSINENA (Tornquist Group) Food industry	ALPARGATAS (Fraser and Roberts Families)	PROPULSORA SIDERÚR-GICA (Rocca Family – Techint Group)	MOLINOS RIO DE LA PLATA (Bunge & Born Group)	MOLINOS RIO DE LA PLATA/PCA SA (Pérez Companc Family and Group)	MOLINOS RIO DE LA PLATA/ PCA SA (Pérez Companc Family and Group)
4	SIAM di Tella (Di Tella Family) Metals and machinery	LOMA NEGRA (Fortabat Family) Cement	EDITORIAL CLARÍN (Noble Family)	MASTELLONE (Mastellone Family) iFood Industry	ARCOR GROUP/ ARCOR (Pagani Family)	ARCOR GROUP/ ARCOR (Pagani Family)
5	ACINDAR (Acevedo Family) Metals and metal products	SIAM DI TELLA (Di Tella Family)	ALUAR (Madanes Family) Metals	BRIDAS (Bulgheroni Family)	COTO CICSA (Coto Family) Retail – supermarkets	ACEITERA GENERAL DEHEZA (Urquía Family)
6	MANUFACTURA DE TABACOS PARTICULAR (Grego Family) Tobacco industry	ACEROS GURMENDI (Gurmendi Family) Metals and metal products	SADE (Pérez Companc Family) Construction and engineering	ALUAR (Madanes Quintanilla Family and Group)	CLARÍN GROUP/ AGEA GROUP/ MULTICANAL (Noble Family)	VICENTÍN SAIC (Vicentín and Nardelli Families)

7	PICCARDO Y CÍA. (Piccardo Family) Tobacco industry	FATE (Madanes Family) Rubber industry	TERRABUSI (Reyes, Terrabusi and Montagna Families)	PÉREZ COMPANC (Pérez Companc Family)	MADANES QUINTANILLA GROUP (Aluar, Fate, Futaleufu) (Madanes Quintanilla Family)	BANCO DE GALICIA Y BUENOS AIRES (Ayerza, Braun and Escasany Families) Finance – bank
8	TALLERES METALÚR-GICOS SAN MARTÍN (Tornquist Group) Metals and metal products	DALMINE SIDERCA (Rocca Family – Techint Group)	DALMINE SIDERCA (Rocca Family – Techint Group)	ASTRA (Gruneisen Family)	VICENTÍN SAIC (Vicentín and Nardelli Families) Food industry	COTO CICSA (Coto Family)
9	GRAFA (Bunge & Born Group) Textiles	LEDESMA (Blaquier – Arrieta Family) Food industry	LOMA NEGRA (Fortabat Family) Cement	TIENDAS TÍA (Deuscht and Steuer Families) Retail – supermarkets	TEMIS GROUP (Drogueria del Sud and Laboratorio Temis Lostaló) (Macchiavello Family) Pharmaceutical	GARBARINO (Garbarino Family) Retail – electrical appliances
10	LOMA NEGRA (Fortabat Family) Cement	GRAFA (Bunge & Born Group)	LEDESMA (Blaquier – Arrieta Family) Food industry	ARCOR (Pagani Family)	MASTELLONE HNOS. SA (Mastellone Family)	LA ANÓNIMA IMPORT-ADORA Y EXPORT-ADORA DE LA PATAGONIA (Braun Family)

Table 6.2 (continued)

Top 20	1956–57	1970	1980	1990	2004*	2010
11	COMPAÑÍA QUÍMICA (Bunge & Born Group) Chemical products	COMPAÑÍA QUÍMICA (Bunge & Born Group) Chemical products	PÉREZ COMPANC (Pérez Companc Family) Oil	SADE (Pérez Companc Family)	SAIEP LA ANÓNIMA IMPORT-ADORA Y EXPORT-ADORA DE LA PATAGONIA (Braun Family) Retail – supermarkets	BANCO MACRO (Brito Family) Bank
12	INGENIO Y REFINERÍA SAN MARTÍN DEL TABACAL SA (Patrón Costas Family) Food industry – sugar	TALLERES METALÚRGICOS SAN MARTÍN (Tornquist Group)	BRIDAS (Bulgheroni Family) Oil	PROPULSORA SIDERÚR-GICA (Rocca Family – Techint Group)	GRUPO FORTABAT (Loma Negra-Ferrosur-Estancias Unidas del Sud) (Fortabat Family)	GRUPO LOS GROBO (Grobocopatel Family) Agriculture – exports
13	LEDESMA (Blaquier – Arrieta Family) Food industry	ALBA (Bunge & Born Group)	ACEROS GURMENDI (Gurmendi Family) Metals and metal products	TECHINT (Rocca Family, Techint Group)	MOLINO CAÑUELAS (Navilli Family) Food industry	MASTELLONE HNOS. SA (Mastellone Family)

14	JABÓN FEDERAL (Delbene Family) Chemical products	QUILMES (Bemberg Group) Food industry – beer	BAGLEY (Mosoteguy and Shoobridge Families)	IMPSA (Pescarmona Family) Machinery – engineering	LEDESMA SA (Blaquier – Arrieta Family)	IMPSA (Pescarmona Family)
15	ALBA (Bunge & Born Group) Chemical products	ISAURA (Elicabe Family) Oil	TECHINT (Rocca Family, Techint Group) Engineering and construction	LEDESMA (Blaquier – Arrieta Family) Food industry	SIDECO AMERICANA SA /ESTANCIAS DEL SUR (Macri Family) Construction – public services infrastructure	ALUAR (Madanes Quintanilla Group)
16	DALMINE SIDERCA (Rocca Family – Techint Group) Metals and metal products	MINETTI MOLINOS (Minetti Family) Food industry	ALBA (Bunge & Born Group)	GATIC SA (Bakchellian Family) Textiles	GRUPO SPM (Tim, Galeno Life, Amsa) (Julio Fraomeni) Medical services	FRÁVEGA (Frávega Family)
17	CRISTALERÍAS RIGOLLEAU (Rigolleau Family) Glass	EDITORIAL CLARÍN (Noble Family) Publishers – information and communication	ASTRA (Gruneisen Family) Oil	TERRABUSI (Reyes, Terrabusi and Montagna Families)	FRÁVEGA (Frávega Family) Retail – electrical appliances	DROGUERÍA DEL SUD (Temis Group, Macchiavello Family)

Table 6.2 (continued)

Top 20	1956–57	1970	1980	1990	2004*	2010
18	SAINT HNOS. (Saint Family) Food industry	TERRABUSI (Reyes, Terrabusi and Montagna Families) Food industry	ISAURA (Elicabe Family)	ACEITERA CHABÁS-ACEITERA GENERAL DEHEZA (Urquia Family) Food industry	DIARCO (Roberto Goldfard) Wholesale	CLISA (Clisa Group – Roggio Family) Holding, financing and others
19	LUIS MAGNASCO Y CIA (Magnasco Family) Food industry	BAGLEY (Mosoteguy Family) Food industry	LA NACIÓN (Saguier and Mitre Family) Information and communication	LOMA NEGRA (Fortabat Family) Cement	SADESA SA (Galperín Family) Leather industry	BGH (Hojman and Teubal Families) Electronics and computer industry
20	BAGLEY (Mosoteguy Family) Food industry	COMPAÑÍA GENERAL DE COMBUSTIBLES (Soldati Family and Group) Oil	ARCOR (Pagani Family) Food industry	ATANOR (Bunge & Born Group) Chemical products	GRUPO JOSÉ CARTELLONE/ JOSÉ CARTELLONE CONSTRUC-CIONES (Cartellone Family) Construction	LEDESMA (Blaquier – Arrieta Family)

Note: * That year the ranking Mercado consolidated sales of companies that belonged to BGs.

Source: Authors' elaboration from 100 largest companies' sales rankings. Sources listed in the main sources references section.

advance of neoliberalism. In order to deal with the specifics of these cycles of advances and setbacks, we have subdivided this period into two phases (1976–90 and 1990–2004).

6.4.1 Initial Reforms, Advances and Setbacks: 1976–90

Between 1976 and 1981, a new military dictatorship tried to deregulate the market by means of a programme of financial and trade liberalization, though part of the pre-existing industrial incentives were maintained or extended. These planned reforms were hindered by tax deficits and inflation (which remained above 100 per cent annually), culminating in an acute financial crisis at the beginning of 1981.

The macroeconomic conditions became even more unfavourable from 1981 onwards, with Latin America's external debt crisis, beginning in 1982. The democratic government that came into power in 1983 inherited a significant external and fiscal imbalance. Various efforts were made to stabilize the macro economy, but all failed due to the persistent nature of the imbalances and the influence of the external debt, which in 1989 was equivalent to 85.6 per cent of gross national product. The measures adopted during the 1980s concentrated on the short-term administration of a highly volatile and conflict-ridden economy, until culminating in two episodes of hyperinflation, in 1989 and 1990, with a growth rate of the consumer price index at 3079 per cent and 2311 per cent, respectively. All said, the performance of the economy in the period 1975–90 was the worst in Argentinian history since the mid nineteenth century.

6.4.2 Family Businesses

In this context of disruption, family businesses strengthened their position in the ranking of the largest 100 firms in comparison to foreign and non-family-owned firms in both 1980 and 1990. A parallel phenomenon was the increase in the representation of state-owned companies, which reached its peak in 1980 and 1990, when they comprised 17 per cent of the 100 largest firms. In contrast, the share of MNCs shrank from 51 per cent in 1970 to 38 per cent in 1990. Most foreign firms considered their chances of continued expansion in the Argentinian market to be slight, given the new macro and regulatory scenario (López, 2015). The military government of 1976–83 and the democratic administration of 1983–89 both maintained a series of industrial incentives for national businesses, albeit with differences, in a context of debate and tension concerning the policies to be introduced (Azpiazu, 1989). This context was particularly beneficial for some businesses linked to more recently founded family DBGs. However, a reduced internal demand and rising inflation caused many companies to experience delicate financial circumstances. As a consequence, a large number of bankruptcies and mergers took place, in association with the tariff reduction applied during the military administration of 1976–83.[3]

The list of the 20 largest family businesses by annual sales in 1980 presents an ambiguous picture. On the one hand, there are no great changes in comparison with 1970 (12 companies are still there), indicating that the family business elite (as a whole) was less severely affected by the economic changes discussed above than other firms during this troubled time.

On the other hand, if we focus on the fraction of companies entering and leaving the ranking, a structural change did indeed take place, one associated with the definitive crisis of long-standing industrial firms, some of which were owned by traditional DBGs. Paradigmatic situations of this time were the disappearance of the SIAM Di Tella Group, which was nationalized in 1974; the decline of the Tornquist Group, also in the midst of liquidation at this point; the transfer of a company that was emblematic of the first phase of Argentinian industry to foreign capital, as was the case with Alpargatas; and the relative decline of the powerful Bunge & Born Group within Argentina (although its food company Molinos remained among the three largest firms between 1970 and 1990).

The most novel feature of the 1980 ranking was the consolidation of family businesses linked to the new DBGs. Some of these had already been represented in previous rankings, such as Techint or Fortabat. Others joined the ranks of the 20 largest firms in 1980 and were still there in 1990, such as the aforementioned Madanes-Quintanilla Group (represented by Aluar), Pérez Companc (founded in 1946 by two brothers from the Pérez Companc family), Bridas (controlled by the Bulgheroni family) and Arcor (owned by the Pagani family).

The process was also related to significant changes in the industrial sector where, as a whole, activity dropped 25 per cent from 1975 to 1990, and the food sector lost its relative importance. The most interesting aspect at this level is that Arcor became one of the 20 largest family businesses in 1980. Founded as a candy manufacturer in 1951, it has been one of the most dynamic groups of the last 30 years, during which it has undergone a significant process of vertical integration and diversification (Kosacoff et al., 2002).

Another representative feature of this phase was the strengthening of businesses from family groups in the sectors of metal-based products, construction-engineering and oil, where notable features include both the presence of new firms and the return of ASTRA (already included in the rankings from 1923 to 1954). In 1990 there was evidence of a high level of continuity, in that 65 per cent of the companies among the largest 20 in 1980 were still present (13 cases). Also noteworthy is the expansion of groups like Pérez Companc and Techint, which in the 1980s had secured direct outside investment.

This study therefore illustrates that the 1980s was a time of consolidation for some of the largest DBGs, while they also continued to enjoy the benefits of incentive schemes for investment and export, market reserves and public contracts. This process, however, was not homogeneous since the composition of the family business elite in 1990 also reflected the relative decline of traditional players such as Bunge & Born, who had already redirected their activities towards Brazil and, later, to the United States.

Balancing out this process, new players appeared among the 20 largest firms in the 1990 ranking, such as IMPSA, a metalworking business from the IMPSA Group, owned by the Pescarmona family, which originated in a workshop founded by an Italian immigrant in 1907; and two firms that have remained amongst the largest family firms in the food sector from this point on: La Serenísima, a dairy company founded in 1942 by the Mastellone brothers, two Italian immigrants; and Aceitera General Deheza, a vegetable oil company created in the 1960s and controlled by the Urquía family (Table 6.2). The presence of these new players is explained in part by the different repercussions of the crisis of the 1980s. Those most affected by this were industrial firms, such as those from the metalworking and textiles sectors, which suffered as a consequence of the new policies and the shrinking of the internal market, even though the impact was very heterogeneous at the sectorial level as well as in terms of its effect on individual companies (Beccaria et al., 1993). In contrast, certain branches that had a competitive advantage or could direct their production to the international market became stronger – the vegetable oil industry is a perfect example of this process (Gutman and Bisang, 1989).

6.4.3 The 1990s and the Situation After the Crisis of 2001

In the 1990s, in parallel with the situation in other Latin American countries, the Menem administration (1989–99) made a series of reforms that focused on macroeconomic stabilizing, market liberalization and the privatization of state-owned companies (Galiani et al., 2002). With the aim of halting inflation, the Convertibility Plan was introduced in 1991, which legally pegged the Argentinian peso to the US dollar at a parity of one to one. The economy progressively opened up, tariffs were reduced and there was a liberalization of capital exchange (Berlinski, 2003). Another relevant change was the creation in 1991 of a regional market, the MERCOSUR, comprising Argentina, Brazil, Paraguay and Uruguay.

One feature that had a huge impact on the ownership structure of

Argentinian businesses was the massive privatization process, which took place with remarkable speed, in that 80 per cent of it was completed between 1990 and 1993 (Azpiazu and Schorr, 2002). The programme covered the majority of state-owned firms, as well as other public assets. In 2004, not a single state-owned company was among the 100 largest firms by annual sales. The macroeconomic situation worsened in the second half of the 1990s, when the economy lost dynamism and became highly sensitive to external shocks. In 2001, the experiment of convertibility reached its end under the effects of an acute economic, social and political crisis.

6.4.4 Family Businesses

The process of neoliberal reform and the subsequent crisis had an enormous impact on the structure of businesses, with an inverse dynamic to that observed in the previous years. The most obvious and significant result was the notable increase in foreign takeover. This is explained to a large extent by the opening up of markets through privatization, the return of foreign companies to Argentina or their arrival there, the dissolution of some important joint ventures and, in 1993, the sanctioning of a law that was favourable to foreign investment.

What consequences did this context bring for large family businesses? In the ranking of the largest businesses by annual sales in 2004, which reflects the 2001–02 crisis, the most notable feature is the impact of the privatization process and the massive arrival of foreign direct investment (FDI). The second notable characteristic is the sale of various family businesses. In 2004, MNCs represented 70 per cent of the largest 100 businesses (a long-term historical record), and family businesses lost importance within the business elite, their share reduced to 22 per cent, the lowest on record in the period under study (although it is very close to the figure for 1944–45, 23 per cent).

The scenario became a lot more competitive with the massive influx of foreign companies. However, the experience of the large family businesses in the 1990s was ambiguous and heterogeneous. The key feature to highlight is that this context of reform and crisis led to a much higher rate of company turnover than in previous periods, and also to the disappearance of many traditional firms. Some structural features remained, such as the predominance of family businesses within domestic-owned firms and the decisive role of DBGs, despite their reduced relative share in the 100 largest firms after the 2001 crisis.

As explained above, DBGs came under serious threaten in the 1990s, as their capacity to accumulate earnings and profit exclusively in the local market was weakened (Kosacoff, 1999). Nevertheless, in this same environment, some firms became stronger by opting for processes of internal restructuring and actively seeking business opportunities, which was facilitated in the 1990s by price stability, the loosening of financial restrictions and the availability of supplies and capital goods. Groups like Techint, Arcor, Pérez Companc, Urquía, IMPSA and Madanes Quintanilla (Aluar) strengthened their positions in the local market, often withdrawing to their respective core business, and increased their presence in external markets through exports and FDI operations, professionalization of management and the renewal of organizational structures (Bisang, 1996).

However, for another cluster of family businesses, this was a time of challenges and crisis: only ten family businesses from the 20 largest firms in the 1990 ranking were still present on the 2004 list. Several factors account for this change. These include the discontinuation of certain industrial incentive schemes, the opening up of trade (the average tariff fell from 26 per cent in 1989 to 10 per cent in 1991) and the new exchange rate. All these factors signified a change in the rules of the game for companies that had been protected from outside competition through various types of tariff barriers for decades. Indeed, one factor shared by almost all the large family businesses was the need to restructure their investment profiles and/or organizational structures.[4]

Some firms went through financial difficulties. For example, for the dairy firm Mastellone, the presence of MNCs signified a need to introduce new business strategies. The firm was able to maintain its sector leadership only through the sale of some of its brands and product lines to Danone, by associating itself with a group of foreign investors (relinquishing its hold on 15 per cent of its capital) and by taking on high levels of debt. This case was not an exception: many businesses saw themselves forced to take on foreign partners.

A correlative phenomenon was the gradual disappearance of historical firms that were bought up by foreign businesses. These operations took place in the 1990s and after the crisis of 2001. The first significant such operations were the transfer of Terrabusi (1994) and Bagley (1994) to the multinationals Nabisco and Danone, respectively. This process intensified in the second half of the 1990s, with the continued arrival of international players, the acceleration of the aforementioned restructuring processes within DBGs and the worsening financial situation of some firms. As such, other companies that were among the 20 largest in 1990 but were taken over by foreign firms in these years were ASTRA, bought by Spanish-owned Repsol (1996), and Bridas (1997), which merged with the multinational Amoco.

The acute crisis of 2001–02 generated new challenges and problems for local businesses. The devaluation of the Argentinian peso in 2002 worsened financial conditions for many (Kosacoff, 2007). As a consequence, a third wave of sales of large family businesses began. Among these were Compañía General de Combustibles (Soldati Group) and Acindar, the latter of which was sold to Belgo Mineira (today part of Arcelor Mittal) in 2006. Another paradigmatic sale was that of the historical brewery and malthouse Quilmes (formerly part of the QUINSA Group, which succeeded the Bemberg Group), which ended up in foreign hands in 2006 after the Belgian-Brazilian Group InBev acquired it.

This complex process of readjustments, transfers and sales also paved the way for ten new players in the 20 largest family businesses in 2010, indicating the dawn of a new era in local capitalism. The analysis of the profiles of these firms reveals explosive bursts of growth (some of these companies were created a century ago, but only recently achieved prominence), and, in particular, a lower proportion of firms associated with DBGs. Meanwhile, the sectoral profile of the largest family firms signals the advance of services and the retreat of industry. A new phenomenon is the significant increase in retail trade (Coto, Diarco, La Anónima, and major home appliances chains such as Frávega), in services in areas like construction (Grupo José Cartellone/José Cartellone Construcciones), medical insurance (Grupo SPM), and in exports of primary products as demonstrated by the presence of Molino Cañuelas, Sadesa SA and Vicentín. Another player joining the group of the 20 largest firms in this 2010 ranking is the Temis Group, a manufacturer of pharmaceutical products, another area of noticeable expansion that underwent a strong process of internationalization during the 1990s.

6.5 THE POST-CONVERTIBILITY PERIOD (2005–10)

In the context of a significant international price increase for primary commodities, the Argentinian economy registered an average cumulative annual growth rate of 8.2 per cent between 2002 and 2007 (Kosacoff, 2007). However, in 2008 and particularly 2009, during the global financial crisis, there was a marked slowing down, followed by a slight recuperation in 2010, even if at that point some macroeconomic imbalances began to be discernable, especially the reappearance of inflation.

6.5.1 Family Businesses

Studies that analyse the changes in the Argentinian corporate elite suggest that it has been affected by the huge transformations in the country in the years after the 2001–02 crisis. Santarcángelo (2012) maintains that the process of foreign takeover of large businesses was consolidated in the post-convertibility phase, and that in 2009 foreign capital dominated around 65 per cent of the country's 500 largest firms.

Foreign takeover was also prevalent, although to a lesser degree, among the largest 100 firms by annual sales in 2010. Between 2004 and 2010, the share of MNCs was reduced to almost 60 per cent, that of national non-family businesses rose to 11 per cent and that of state-owned firms increased to 6 per cent, the result of the renationalization of some of the businesses that were privatized in the 1990s. Meanwhile, the relative importance of family businesses and DBGs remained unchanged at 22 per cent, and 12 firms continued to be among the ten largest from 2004 onwards. The continuity of large family business in this short period is supported by the fact that changes in companies' positions in the ranking is relative, and did not necessarily mean that they had disappeared, had gone bankrupt or had been taken over, with the exception of Loma Negra, which was sold in 2005 to the Brazilian firm Camargo Correa, thus constituting another example of the issue of takeovers discussed in the previous section.

The departure of century-old family firms made room for new protagonists, who positioned themselves as models of the new Argentinian family capitalism, which is no longer dominated by DBGs (36 per cent), but rather by a majority of standalone firms. The only new DBG to be found among the 20 largest firms in the 2010 ranking is Los Grobo, which is yet another case (as are vegetable oil companies) of the consolidation of businesses exporting primary commodities. Furthermore, it is a clear example of the important changes taking place in the primary sector at that time, due to the increase in demand from international markets as well as the aforementioned increase in the price of agriculture and livestock commodities. As such, the activities of the largest family businesses in 2010 are examples of the general tendency towards sectorial restructuring in favour of services and activities that are linked to natural advantages. This phenomenon is a characteristic of Argentina and of Latin American countries in general. Other sectors that continued to play a relatively more central role were wholesale and retail activities.

6.6 CONCLUSIONS

This chapter has offered, for the first time, a quantitative long-term evaluation of the characteristics and dynamics of the Argentinian family business elite and has revealed a series of key features of local family capitalism. With respect to the first question formulated in the introduction – how relevant family businesses have been over the last century – the evidence presented here has confirmed that Argentinian capitalism is and has been based on family-owned businesses. Throughout the period under study, family firms numbered higher than non-family firms within the largest Argentinian businesses.

With respect to the second question – which forms of organization have been dominant among the largest family businesses – the importance of DBGs is notable, at least until 2004. The proportion of companies belonging to DBGs among the 30 largest family firms between 1923 and 1954 ranged between 30 per cent and 50 per cent, while between 1956 and 2010 it varied between 29 per cent and 48 per cent of the 20 largest family firms.

It is therefore evident that as an organizational form, DBGs were already playing a significant role by the early 1920s and that several such groups were able to adapt successfully to the context of ISI. This reinforces the arguments presented previously in qualitative works on the creation of business groups during the primary export-led growth phase, when the economy was open and deregulated. But another point that has been stressed is the appearance of new DBGs that originated in industrial firms founded before and after 1930, which diversified and gradually took on this organizational form. Some of these (such as Alpargatas, SIAM and Loma Negra) were already present among the 30 largest family firms in the rankings of various years before 1954. Traditional and new DBGs benefited from the industrial policies of the mid 1940s to the end of the 1980s, as well as from privatizations in the early 1990s. However, a decline was observed between 1990 and 2010, a subject we shall return to.

The Argentinian scenario in the twentieth century contains almost all the reasons identified in the literature as an explanation for the presence of DBGs (Khanna and Palepu, 1997; Leff, 1978; Morck and Steier, 2007, among others). Some specific cases mentioned in this study confirm the advantages of this organizational pattern. Nevertheless, the unrelated diversification that some groups underwent in the 1990s, within the framework of privatization, negatively affected several of them, increasing the internal transaction costs and their need for capital.

Another point that emerges from our analysis is the high proportion of large family businesses founded by immigrants or foreigners. The relationship between immigration and entrepreneurship has been emphasized by specialized literature. In the case of Argentina, it is notable that in 1914, a third of the country's total population had been born abroad, and this proportion was even higher in the big cities or among the male workforce. Many immigrants brought technical know-how from their countries of origin, and/or had valuable social capital that they were able to use to set up new ventures in a phase of accelerated expansion of the internal market. In

Argentina, in any event, immigration led to the presence of a wide range of entrepreneurs. The foreign and immigrant communities maintained close ties with their countries of origin, which contributed to the creation of the first DBGs. Some of the corporate networks created at the end of the nineteenth century lasted until well into the twentieth century: the founding of Techint by Agostino Rocca in Buenos Aires was due to a large extent to the strength of the Italian-Argentinian business community.

The third question was how to explain the longevity of family businesses. In general terms, family businesses both gained and lost their positions in the historical rankings as a result of the cyclical expansion and contraction of FDI, which affected all domestically controlled businesses. They became stronger during the phases when there was a relative decrease in FDI as a result of nationalizations or the withdrawal of MNCs. Family businesses also became weaker during the cycles of peak FDI due to policies that aimed to attract foreign capital (in the 1960s and 1990s) or during critical moments that alienated many national companies (such as in the 1960s and 1994–2005). In contrast, there were phases (1940s–53, 1970–89) in which incentive schemes, state demand and government contracts contributed to the strengthening of domestic companies (including family businesses), especially DBGs (between 1970 and 1990). The presence or absence of state-owned companies among Argentina's 100 largest firms was also a determining factor for the representation of family businesses in the corporate elite.

The survival of domestic firms, including family-owned firms, was also affected by the volatility of the macroeconomic conditions, which were subject to the significant variations in economic policies, to recurrent crises, austerity programmes and devaluations, all of which had a direct impact on business performance, even though this was heterogeneous at the level of sectors and firms. These imbalances were accentuated in the mid twentieth century and reached their peak with the 2001–02 crisis, leading to the subsequent sale of some of the most characteristic and long-standing firms representing local capitalism. It is still too early to identify all the changes generated by pro-market reforms of the 1990s and the crisis of 2001, but some features (such as foreign takeovers among the 100 largest firms, the decline of DBGs in comparison with standalone companies and the decline of family businesses with respect to non-family businesses) could mean a rupture with previous decades. Over these years, a significant number of firms that had been present throughout most of the twentieth century disappeared, some of which had been emblematic of Argentinian family capitalism. Nevertheless, during the same period, new players emerged.

Despite the often volatile environment, a significant proportion of family businesses managed to expand, even in difficult conditions, and many survived successfully for various generations. Diversification turned out to be a suitable strategy for remaining and growing in the turbulent Argentinian market, as long as it did not reach unmanageable levels. Internationalization was a second form of securing continued growth and to be independent from local macroeconomic conditions. Prudent financial strategies and manageable levels of debt also contributed to the firms successfully surviving the most critical moments. And, of course, other necessary conditions for successful performance included the capacity to handle the transition from one generation to the next without conflicts and the gradual professionalization of management (be it within the family or outside it).

The long-term perspective and analysis of the relationship between businesses and their context clearly reveal the extent to which the characteristics and evolution of family business have responded to firms' own intrinsic features as well as to the peculiarities of a complex and volatile environment, wherein endogenous and exogenous factors both play a part in the development of Argentinian family capitalism. Likewise, over the period under study, changes have taken place not only in the role of family firms in the business elite, but also within the sectors in which such firms are active. In conclusion, we believe that this analysis has allowed us to identify some of the keys to the success of certain Argentinian family-owned businesses through the generations, just as it has shown the main causes of failures in a process that has been, as we have described, far from linear.

NOTES

1. The rankings for 1923, 1937, 1944 and 1954 were drawn up as a result of considerable effort in terms of the organization of information, a process that was facilitated by the research project 'Description and evolution of corporate networks in Argentina (1901–2010)', coordinated by Dr Erica Salvaj and Dr Andrea Lluch. The rankings included the largest non-financial corporations, according to their share capital. For 1956 onwards, the rankings used were from evaluations by business journals based on companies' annual sales. We are aware that these listings could contain errors and omissions and we have, as far as possible, tried to minimize these. Unfortunately, there is no uniform data available on annual turnover that might allow the use of uniform criteria to identify the 100 largest Argentinian businesses throughout the whole period under study.
2. Due to space restrictions, bibliographical references and historical commentaries on family businesses have been reduced to a minimum in this version. For a more complete version, see Barbero and Lluch (2015).
3. Regarding this, the high inflation rate during this period generates enormous distortions and means that any analysis of companies' financial and accounting situations is a complex task that must be undertaken with much caution (in both 1980 and 1990).
4. The 'Creating emerging markets' oral history project at the Harvard Business School

provides new evidence for family firms such as Acindar, Bunge & Born, Arcor, Loma Negra and Sociedad Anónima Importadora y Exportadora de la Patagonia, among others. These interviews are publically available at http://www.hbs.edu/businesshistory/emerging-markets/Pages/default.aspx (accessed 15 September 2015).

MAIN SOURCES

Cámara de Sociedades Anónimas (1972). *Guía de Sociedades Anónimas*. Buenos Aires: Cámara de Sociedades Anónimas.
Dorr Mansilla, A. (1924). *Guía de Sociedades Anónimas. Anuario 1923–24*. Buenos Aires: A. Dorr Mansilla.
Dorr Mansilla, A. (1938). *Guía de Sociedades Anónimas, responsabilidad limitada y cooperativas, 1937–1938*. Buenos Aires: A. Dorr Mansilla.
Dorr Mansilla, A. (1946). *Guía de Sociedades Anónimas 1944/45, responsabilidad limitada y cooperativas*, Buenos Aires: A. Dorr Mansilla.
El Accionista (1954). *Guía de Sociedades Anónimas*. Buenos Aires: El Accionista.
Revista Mercado, Las empresas que más venden (1971). No. 106, Buenos Aires.
Revista Mercado, El ranking de las empresas que más venden (1981). No. 620, 27 August, Buenos Aires.
Revista Mercado, Las empresas que más venden en la Argentina (1990). August, Buenos Aires.
Revista Mercado, Las 1000 empresas que más venden (2005). June, Buenos Aires.
Revista Mercado, Las 1000 que más venden (2011). June, Buenos Aires.
Revista Panorama de la Economía Argentina, Los ingresos de las grandes empresas (1958). No. 4.

REFERENCES

Azpiazu, D. (1989). 'La promoción de la inversión industrial en la Argentina. Efectos sobre la estructura industrial. 1974–87'. In B. Kosacoff and D. Azpiazu (eds), *La industria argentina: desarrollo y cambios estructurales*. Buenos Aires: CEAL/CEPAL, pp. 35–98.
Azpiazu, D. and M. Schorr (2002). *Privatizaciones, rentas de privilegio, subordinación estatal y acumulación del capital en la Argentina contemporánea*. Buenos Aires: FLACSO.
Barbero, M.I. (2015). 'A long-term view on business groups in 19th and twentieth century Argentina'. In G. Jones and A. Lluch (eds), *The Historical Impact of Globalization in Argentina and Chile*. Cheltenham, UK and Northampton, MA, USA: Edward Elgar, pp. 6–44.
Barbero, M.I. and A. Lluch (2015). 'El capitalismo familiar en Argentina: modelos y dinámicas en el largo plazo'. In P. Fernández Pérez and A. Lluch (eds), *Familias empresarias y grandes empresas familiares en América Latina y España: Una visión de largo plazo*. Bilbao: Fundación BBVA, pp. 219–60.
Barbero, M.I. and F. Rocchi (2003). 'Industry and industrialization in Argentina in the long run: from its origins to the 1970s'. In G. Della Paolera and A. Taylor

(eds), *The New Economic History of Argentina*. Cambridge: Cambridge University Press, pp. 261–94.

Beccaria, L., G. Bezchinsky, R. Bisang et al. (1993). 'La industria argentina. Un proceso de reestructuración desarticulada'. In B. Kosacoff (ed.), *El desafío de la competitividad*. Buenos Aires: CEPAL/Alianza, pp. 11–67. http://www.cepal.org/cgi-bin/getProd.asp?xml=/publicaciones/xml/2/25572/P25572.xml&xsl=/argentina/tpl/p9f.xsl&base=/argentina/tpl/top-bottom.xsl (accessed 21 September 2015).

Berlinski, J. (2003). 'International trade and commercial policy'. In G. Della Paolera and A. Taylor (eds), *The New Economic History of Argentina*. Cambridge: Cambridge University Press, pp. 197–232.

Bisang, R. (1996). 'Perfil tecno-productivo de los grupos económicos en la industria argentina'. In J. Katz (ed.), *Estabilización macroeconómica, reforma estructural y comportamiento industrial*. Buenos Aires: CEPAL/Alianza, pp. 375–478.

Castro, C. (2012). 'Una multinacional dirigida desde Buenos Aires. La internacionalización temprana de Techint, 1946–1976'. In G. Guajardo (ed.), *Innovación y empresa. Estudios históricos de México, España y América Latina*. Buenos Aires: Lenguaje Claro, pp. 221–48.

Cochran, T. and R. Reina (1962). *Entrepreneurship in Argentine Culture: Torcuato Di Tella and S.I.A.M.* Philadelphia, PA: University of Pennsylvania Press.

Di Tella, G. and R. Dornbusch (eds) (1989). *The Political Economy of Argentina (1946–1983)*. Houndmills: Macmillan.

Galiani, S., D. Heymann and M. Tommasi (2002). 'The political economy of economic reforms in Argentina'. *Journal of Policy Reform* **5** (2), 75–88.

Gilbert, J. (2003). 'Entre la expansión y la crisis de la economía argentina. Ernesto Tornquist y Cía'. *Ciclos* **25–26**, 65–92.

Green, R. and C. Laurent (1988). *El poder de Bunge y Born*. Buenos Aires: Legasa.

Gutiérrez, L. and J.C. Korol (1988). 'Historia de empresas y crecimiento industrial en la Argentina. El caso de la Fábrica Argentina de Alpargatas'. *Desarrollo Económico* **28** (111), 401–24.

Gutman, G. and R. Bisang (1989). 'El proceso de industrialización y dinámica exportadora. Las experiencias de las industria aceitera y siderúrgica en la Argentina'. Documentos de Trabajo No. 32, CEPAL, Santiago de Chile.

Khanna, T. and K. Palepu (1997). 'Why focused strategies may be wrong for emerging markets'. *Harvard Business Review* July–August, 41–51.

Kosacoff, B. (1999). 'El caso argentino'. In D. Chudnovsky, B. Kosacoff and A. López (eds), *Las multinacionales latinoamericanas. Sus estrategias en un mundo globalizado*. Buenos Aires: Fondo de Cultura Económica, pp. 65–164.

Kosacoff, B. (ed.) (2007). *Crisis, recuperación y nuevos dilemas: la economía argentina 2002–2007*. Buenos Aires: CEPAL.

Kosacoff, B., J. Forteza, M.I. Barbero, A. Stengel and F. Porta (2002). *Going Global from Latin America: The Arcor Case*. Buenos Aires: McGraw Hill.

Leff, N. (1978). 'Industrial organization and entrepreneurship in the developing countries: the economic groups'. *Economic Development and Cultural Change* **26** (4), 66–175.

López, A. (2015). 'Multinational enterprises in Argentina: from primary commodity exporter to the new liberal era'. In G. Jones and A. Lluch (eds), *The Historical Impact of Globalization in Argentina and Chile*. Cheltenham, UK and Northampton, MA, USA: Edward Elgar, pp. 108–34.

López, S. (2001). 'Integración y especialización como estrategias empresariales.

El caso de la Cervecería Quilmes (1890–1990)', Master thesis in History, Universidad de San Andrés, Buenos Aires.
Morck, R. and L. Steier (2007). 'The global history of corporate governance: an introduction'. In R. Morck (ed.), *A History of Corporate Governance Around the World: Family Business Groups to Professional Managers*. Chicago, IL: University of Chicago Press, pp. 1–64.
Moyano, D. (2015). *Desde la empresa. Firmas familiares y estructura empresarial en la industria azucarera tucumana (1895–1930)*. Buenos Aires: Prometeo Ediciones.
Russo, C. (2006). 'Entreprises et territoire: construction de l'identité industrielle au sud de la région métropolitaine de Buenos Aires. Brasserie Quilmes et Cristallerie Rigolleau'. PhD thesis in History, Université Paris III – Sorbonne Nouvelle.
Santarcángelo, J.E. (2012). 'Concentración, rentabilidad y extranjerización en Argentina. Una mirada desde la cúpula empresaria'. *Ensayos de Economía* **40**, 39–59.
Schvarzer, J. (1989). *Bunge & Born. Crecimiento y diversificación de un grupo económico*. Buenos Aires: CISEA.

PART III

Business families and politics in small and medium-sized markets (Colombia, Costa Rica, Honduras)

7. Politics and endurance of entrepreneurial families: the case of 'presidential families' in a Latin American economy (Colombia, 1850–2010)

Carlos Dávila*

7.1 INTRODUCTION

Family business's relationship with politics and the state has received little attention in the literature on family businesses, which has mostly focused on endogenous over exogenous factors. However, it constitutes a key skill in family business's performance and survival. Holding public office is one of the forms this relationship can take, and the chief of state is the highest position possible. This chapter explores this relationship in an emerging Latin American economy, Colombia. In the period studied, 1850–2010, ten of the 45 presidents of the republic have been members of six entrepreneurial families. These families have all played leading roles in Colombian life for at least 100 years. The chapter comprises five sections. The first refers to the growing interest in various disciplines and, in particular business history, on entrepreneurial families and family business as key forms of business organization in capitalist development. Departing from the current ('Manichean') critique of family business, the second section approaches the diverse forms of interaction of entrepreneurial actors with politics and the state. The third section presents the case of one of the presidential families; the fourth compares the six families using a series of variables (longevity/dynastic character, education, intergenerational social mobility and business diversification). The final section provides a series of considerations on content, method and theory for further research.

7.2 FAMILY CAPITALISM, BUSINESS HISTORY AND FAMILY STUDIES: A NEED FOR MULTIDISCIPLINARY RESEARCH

Family business is not an anomaly of capitalist development, nor is it an obsolete player on the way to extinction. It is a form of business organization that for the purpose of research requires a multidisciplinary approach. Recent international publications agree on its contemporary relevance and the need to study its historical path. In Spain and Latin America, on which most of the chapters of this volume are focused, there are emblematic family groups of entrepreneurial families whose origin can be traced back to the second half of the nineteenth century. They represent a form of business organization different from that of the large multidivisional firm characteristic of US managerial capitalism (Chandler, 1977).

This form of organization has gradually aroused scholarly interest, not only in the field of management and entrepreneurship (Chrisman et al., 2005; Fernández Pérez, 2012), but also from researchers in other disciplines, particularly business history and economists interested in corporate governance. In the case of the former, this is reflected in recent international publications (Colli, 2011, 2013; Colli and Rose, 2007; Fernández Pérez, 2012; Fernández Pérez and Colli, 2013); likewise, it has been recognized (if also stereotyped) by some studies on corporate governance (Morck and Steir, 2005). What is certain, in this new historical phase of globalization, is that the reality of the diverse forms of ownership, governance structures and organization that family businesses have taken on defy those who predicted their progressive demise. The example of the family multinationals and their strategy and structures in various parts of the world is evidence of this (Colli et al., 2013; Lubinsky et al., 2013). The Latin American multinationals (*multilatinas*) are already recognized in the literature, and the most prominent are those owned and controlled by entrepreneurial families (Casanova, 2008; Santiso, 2013). Even in markets such as Colombia, smaller and less developed than Argentina, Brazil, Mexico or Chile, various family economic groups advanced in their process of internationalization and were poised to enter the group of *multilatinas* from the beginning of the new century.[1] A handful of family business groups made their name between 1880 and 1930 and established themselves in the main cities of this 'country of regions'. In 1975, among the 24 largest conglomerates, nine were family-owned (Superintendencia de Sociedades, 1978). In those years, an economic group from a traditional family of the country's capital city elite, Grupo Grancolombiano of the Michelsen Uribe family, with barely five years of existence, suddenly became the most powerful group in the country. But this was short-lived:

in the financial crisis of 1982, the government intervened and the main bank was nationalized. The Group was later liquidated amid a notorious scandal involving private loans and inappropriate handling of investment funds (Donadio, 1983, 1984; Echavarría, 1983; Semana, 1989).

In the following decades, business groups multiplied and gained importance in the country's economic activity to become a central player in Colombian business (Dávila, 2013; Rodríguez-Satizábal, 2010). Three of the four largest business groups are family-owned (Sarmiento Angulo, Santo Domingo and Ardila Lulle) and have been in this position for a quarter of a century (Dinero, 2013; Portafolio, 2013; Rodríguez-Satizábal, 2010). With their influence and connection to recent key episodes in Colombia's political and economic situation, they have displaced the employer associations (Rettberg, 2003; Semana, 2013) by deftly cultivating politics/state relations in their various forms. It should be emphasized that the presidential families we are looking at in this chapter are not owners of any of the mentioned groups. In fact, having lasted for more than a century, they have witnessed – since the mid 1970s – the rise and consolidation of new, proactive groups with greater economic power and wide diversification in their investments, facing the new phase of globalization.

7.3 THE RELATIONSHIP OF BUSINESS FAMILIES WITH POLITICS AND THE STATE: BEYOND MANICHEAN CRITICISM

A starting point for this study is the recognition of the different developmental paths of capitalism and, more precisely, the variation in forms of business organization in different societies, for example, in emerging economies. In other words, our aim is to study the evolution of entrepreneurial families and family businesses, rather than following the 'teleological hierarchy' marked by the development of the United States as archetype for business historians (Herrigel and Zeitlin, 2010, p. 667). Another starting point states that institutional structures, that is, the systemic relationships between firms and public authorities and the way the market is organized, condition business strategy; public institutions, in turn, could be seen as a resource for the firms, to the extent that they have influence on the formation of the institutional framework (Iversen, 2010, pp. 464–6). This approach is complemented by the perspective of the theory of resource dependency, which studies the relationship between organizations and their environment (Pfeffer and Salancik, 1978). Particularly, the focus is on the strategies and tactics of power and management control in inter-organizational relations; in this case, between entrepreneurial families and the state, as well as between the families themselves when faced with other players in the market. Over the years, these families and their businesses and groups evolved strategies to operate and consolidate themselves, oriented by the idea that power (not only profit or efficiency) is a key objective (Davis and Cobb, 2010).

Thus, this chapter does not focus on endogenous factors that determine the permanence, performance and entrepreneurship of family businesses in the long term. Although it shares with other chapters in this book a historical perspective and an interest in gaining insight into common features – as well as national differences – in the track record of family business in Spain and Latin America, it revolves around a different analysis: the entrepreneurial family per se and its long-term relationship with politics and the state. Its purpose is to show the need for opening the field in this direction and underline the potential for future research, especially of a comparative historical nature.

The hypothesis is that in the emerging Latin American economies, large economic groups hierarchically controlled by entrepreneurial families are key players in economic development. Under such circumstances, the skillful handling of the relationship with power and the state, a central but not unique element of the context, leads to the accumulation of resources of political power and builds up a capacity over the long term. It is akin to the organizational capabilities of firms studied by Chandler (1992). This capability is crucial in turbulent and uncertain economic, political and social environments, typical of Latin America. It has evolved over many generations of these entrepreneurial families, giving them a distinctive competence, similar to the core competencies of firms, in their business activities, and of significance because of their enduring nature.

To study this political capability, the approach on productive, unproductive and destructive functions that entrepreneurs deploy in response to the payoff structure (incentives) and the constraints that institutional frameworks (institutions in general and rules of the game in particular) offer in each historical period are worth considering (Baumol, 1968, 2010; Torres, 2003).[2] This perspective, although still under elaboration, is thought-provoking and provides an insightful perspective on the relationship between business and politics, rather than blindly accepting the easy and trite option that stigmatizes this relationship.[3] In addition to being dynamic, the institutional framework is not neutral in the face of different social actors, nor does it embody the 'common good'. Likewise, it is not perceived by everyone in the same way. Its formation (including organization of the state), implementation and modification are influenced by the intervention of the business actors, acting in their own interests. In addition, the behaviour shown by social and economic actors, entrepreneurs, entrepreneurial families and business lobby groups is marked by restricted rationality, incomplete information and opportunistic conduct.

For this reason, the conditions of the market in which they operate should be studied, but it is also fundamental to consider the institutional environment in which they are immersed. Thus, entrepreneurs seek efficiency through adequate management and, at the same time, they exert influence (through one or many forms of political entrepreneurial action) on the state. Entrepreneurs have to act simultaneously on both fronts. And in the cases where institutional development is precarious, as in Colombia, characterized by the instability of the rules of the game, their political action has a special significance. Under these conditions, the entrepreneur or the entrepreneurial family may either deploy productive functions, aim for rent-seeking and related unproductive functions or engage in the destruction of resources (not only ecological). Whether a specific time and space is prone to any of these functions, or a combination of them, is a matter for empirical research. It cannot be taken for granted. It should be made clear that these functions are not present in a pure form in empirical reality. They are unveiled through research, and illustrate, for example, that in a lifetime, an entrepreneur and his or her family, plus the social and political networks they weave can display one or other entrepreneurial functions, in one moment or another, in a given business or another.

The empirical evidence analysed here relates to a very special type of entrepreneurial family, dynasties that, being part of the economic and political elite, have more than once held the position of head of state in Colombia between 1850 and 2010. It should be clarified that being elected to public office is only one of a whole spectrum of ways that an entrepreneur can engage in politics. To study them, a typology has been developed that covers a dozen ways the entrepreneur can participate in politics and relate to the state (Dávila, 2012, pp. 67–70). They include:

1. voting in elections
2. funding of political campaigns
3. leadership responsibilities in political parties or groups
4. discharge of public office by appointment, especially high level public administration, at a national, departmental or local level
5. holding of public office by popular election (presidency of the nation, senator, house representative, council person)
6. government contracts and concessions (public works of infrastructure, service delivery; handling concessions, rents and so on)
7. purchaser of services and products from state enterprises
8. ownership and management of mass media and public opinion channels (newspapers, television channels, radio networks and so on)

9. organization of business associations, lobbying
10. promotion of and participation in social, voluntary, civic and non-governmental organization (NGO) movements; promotion and management of private foundations.

It should be mentioned that the presidential families have had members of various generations active in many of these ways of political participation. Those members who have reached the pinnacle of power (becoming head of state) had previously pursued a substantial political career, either by elected office (council persons, members of regional chambers, congressmen/women) or through appointment to positions at a high level of state administration (ministers, management of national and regional public organizations, diplomatic positions and so on). Some, such as ex-presidents, have continued to be politically active, and not only as ambassadors for their country or representatives in international organizations. At the same time, they have rejoined their businesses. It would be interesting to examine if this wide-ranging portfolio of relationships with politics has been exclusive to emerging economies, in this case Latin America, or if it is also present in economies of other continents, where entrepreneurial families continue to have hierarchical control over business groups. It is a subject that would make comparative research very attractive. In particular, it could provide evidence that departs from the 'Manichean critique' (Fernández Pérez, 2003, p. 3) raised by scholars of corporate governance in large businesses with regard to ownership and family capitalism in the more advanced countries. These scholars contrast it with other forms of capitalism, such as shareholder capitalism or Anglo-American capitalism and bank capitalism: 'The studies in this volume provide ample evidence of powerful family economic groups that behave like establishments or like oligarchies, or first the one and then the other' (Morck and Steir, 2005, p. 33). Basing themselves on Thurow (1989), Morck and Steir (2005, p. 33) point out that both are able to lead their countries but, while the establishment seeks assurance that its country is functioning in order to reap benefits for itself, the oligarchy has only its own interests in mind, without giving any thought to the future of the country. One of the evils attributed to it, is the 'risk of systematic mismanagement' of its businesses leading to macroeconomic instability (Morck, 2009). According to these authors, instead of 'healthy institutions' (those of advanced economies), poor countries with a short industrial history have 'oligarchical institutions' that do not protect the minority investor and, in contrast, bring about economic backwardness.

From a wider perspective than that of corporate governance, two renowned economists have recently asked themselves: 'Why are some nations rich and others poor? Why do nations fail?' Like their colleagues from corporate governance, they reach a similar verdict: nations fail because of the presence of 'extractive institutions' (economical as well as political) based on elites who design them in a such a way as to make themselves rich and perpetuate their power at the cost of the majority of the population. 'Vicious circles' are created that must be converted to 'virtuous circles' (convert 'extractive institutions' into 'inclusive institutions' and so end the 'iron rule of the oligarchy' (Acemoglu and Robinson, 2012, pp. 399, 430–1, 388).[4]

The generalizations of these authors are reminiscent of other generalizations made about underdevelopment in the 1960s and 1970s. They were fodder for academic debates and international development policies. They originated in ideologically opposite shores. On the one hand, the theories of modernization, rooted in the United States and embedded in the structural functionalism of Talcott Parsons, gave priority to non-economic factors of development (cultural, ethnical and psychological) (Dávila, 2010). On the other hand, the theory of dependence and imperialism elaborated in Latin America underlined the inequality (asymmetry) in the economical and political relations between centre (empire) and periphery (Miller, 2010b). Both arrived at a deadlock because of something they both, ironically, had in common: a fragile empirical base and lack of rigorous empirical research. In both currents, ideological and political considerations prevailed over considerations of academic research.

In contrast to these simplistic views that nevertheless still enjoy a recurrent glamour in the international academic world, the growing economic and business historiography of Spain and Latin America point towards a renewed, nuanced understanding of the relationship between entrepreneurial families and politics. However, this as well as other exogenous factors that are primarily institutional in nature have not received due attention in the family business literature (Colli, 2013).

The historical perspective offers a promising path to remedy this neglect. More precisely, it allows for the possibility of dialogue between family business scholars and business historians, in tune with recent debates on the future of this latter discipline on a global scale (de Jong et al., 2015; Friedman and Jones, 2011; Kobrak and Schneider, 2011). In any case, it should be kept in mind that business historians from emerging nations must be alert to avoiding the 'traps' that may ensnare the discipline (Scranton and Fridenson, 2013). One of these is ignoring the role of the state as an actor in capitalist development; another is to assume that the experiences of the United States and Europe are 'the one best way', as 'normal and normative' ('something done so often that you hardly even notice it') (Scranton and Fridenson, 2013, pp. 16–22, 47–50, 45).

In this context, the chapter is not concerned with the evolution of the main family businesses in the different periods of Colombian economic development, nor does it in particular allude to the 20 largest family businesses in 2010, the data collected for the quantitative comparative analysis among the nine countries covered by the comparative international project in which the present book is based. However, it does contribute to exploring a subject (the relationship of entrepreneurial families with politics and the state) that is a fundamental part of the capability for adaptation of entrepreneurial families to the perennial Latin America environmental turbulence.

7.4 ENTREPRENEURIAL AND PRESIDENTIAL FAMILIES IN COLOMBIA, 1850–2010

In talking about presidential families, we refer to those entrepreneurial families that, in addition to being characterized as having an important, diverse and continued economic activity, have also had, in the last 150 years, one or more members as head of state in the Republic of Colombia. The category 'presidential families' as such is not explained in the specialized literature, although they could be considered family dynasties (Fernández Pérez and Puig, 2010; Landes, 2006). The study presents a clear example of what nascent business historiography regards as one of the characteristics of Latin American and Colombian entrepreneurship (Barbero, 2008; Dávila, 2013); that is, a close relationship between business and politics and the state resulting in a high concentration of economic and political power. Exemplified in the case of Colombia by a tightly closed elite with great influence in this country's development. Out of the total of 45 presidents of the Republic of Colombia between 1850 and 2010, ten of them, almost a quarter, belong to six entrepreneurial families, all of whom have been a feature of Colombian life for over 100 years. Specifically, 'the' Ospinas (three presidents): Mariano Ospina Rodríguez, 1857–61; Pedro Nel Ospina Vásquez, 1922–26; Mariano Ospina Pérez, 1946–50; 'the' López (two presidents): Alfonso López Pumarejo, 1934–38 and 1942–46; Alfonso López Michelsen, 1974–78; 'the' Santos (two presidents): Eduardo Santos Montejo, 1938–42; Juan Manuel Santos Calderón, 2010 to the present; 'the' Reyes (one president: Rafael Reyes Prieto (1904–09); 'the' Restrepos (one president): Carlos E. Restrepo Restrepo (1910–14); 'the' Sampers (one president): Ernesto Samper Pizano, 1994–98.

A series of economic, political and social features of Colombian society that have conditioned the evolution of family businesses and entrepreneurial families in the last 150 years can be synthesized as follows.[5] The slow economic development of the Colombian economy in the nineteenth century was marked by a weak link to the international market in comparison with other Latin American countries like Mexico and Brazil and regions such as the southern part of Latin America. The country went through a succession of ephemeral agro-export bonanzas between 1850 and 1880 (tobacco, quinine, indigo); gold was the only stable export product until the rise of coffee in the 1880s (lasting a century – in 1989 the International Pact of coffee ended) made the Colombian economy a mono-exporter of this product (Ocampo, 1984). The evolution of the Colombian economy occurred in a bipartite political context (Liberal and Conservative parties) with numerous (regional) civil wars during the nineteenth century that ended in the Thousand Days' War (1899–1901), and affected the business activity of the families who, due to their political affiliations, were not isolated from these conflicts. Many business families were proud of having war generals among their number. Perhaps with the exception of the conservative region of Antioquia, whose entrepreneurs displayed certain pragmatism ('make business' instead of becoming involved in political conflicts), it was not the same situation in other regions of the country: not in Cauca Valley and the region of Cauca in the southwest of the country, nor in Santander, in the northeast. The 'conservative hegemony' (1900–30) stimulated the beginnings of industrialization in the first two decades of the twentieth century, saw the dispossession of Panama by the United States in 1904, was the boom period of coffee as principal export and a decade (the 1920s) characterized as the 'dance of the millions' (because of private loans obtained in the United States and the income from coffee). Then came the sudden rise to power of the Liberal party (1930–45), the bloody confrontation between liberals and conservatives (known as the Violence, 1945–58), the bipartite peace pact (the Frente Nacional, 1958–74), armed conflict involving many sides (the state, guerrilla, drug traffickers, paramilitarists, from 1965 to the present day), the illegal economy of drug trafficking since the second half of the 1970s, the change in economic model and the neoliberal economic opening (in 1990) and the greatest economic crisis of the twentieth century, between 1998 and 2002 (Safford and Palacios, 2002). It was against this backdrop that ten members of six prominent entrepreneurial families became heads of the Colombian state.

The pertinence of the phenomenon of presidential families was seen in presidential elections in 2014. An heir of one of them (the López family) stood against the current president, another member of a presidential family (the Santos family) who was re-elected. A third candidate belongs to the third generation of an entrepreneurial family (the Zuluaga) from the coffee-growing region, whose business group became a steel *multilatina*, although his family's political path cannot be compared to that of the López nor the Santos families (Semana, 2013, p. 17). In addition, he was elected by his right-wing coalition party in a bitter contest with another member of the Santos family, Francisco Santos, cousin of the current president (Juan Manuel Santos) as well as his opponent. Francisco Santos was vice president of the country in 2002–10, during which time the current president was a member of the Cabinet.

7.5 COMPARATIVE ANALYSIS OF THE SIX PRESIDENTIAL FAMILIES

In this section, a brief comparative analysis of the families studied is presented, according to the following variables: dynastic longevity (number of generations) and nature, regional origin, social intergenerational mobility, education abroad, geographical mobility, family size and sectors of business activity.[6]

One variable related to the longevity of these families is its dynastic character. This characteristic is uniform within the sample studied. The Ospina, Restrepo, López and Samper families are all now entering the fifth generation; the Santos, the fourth. Only one family, the Reyes, disappeared as such after the first generation in which one of its members, an export trader of quinine and rubber, became president (Rafael Reyes, 1904–09). Regarding their political affiliations, three families have been champions of the Liberal party (López, Samper and Santos), and three of the Conservative (Ospina, Reyes and Restrepo). They come from two regions: the central-east (four families) and Antioquia (Ospina and Restrepo); none of the families have immigrant origins. Only the Samper family has some foreign link, given that the second generation on the maternal side (Samper Brush) in the early twentieth century was English. One demographic data should be added: the size of the families in the first two generations was very large, especially among those from Antioquia. A family with ten children was commonplace.

Three of these families in the first and second generations (Ospina, López and Samper) sent their children to study abroad (the United States, Great Britain, France); the other two (Santos and Restrepo) did so in the third and fourth generations. In particular, they studied engineering and business administration in the case of the two families from Antioquia; law, journalism and administration in the case of the families who had long ago settled in the capital (Bogotá) (López, Santos, Samper). Of the ten presidents, members of the six presidential families, half completed secondary or university studies abroad. Nine lived for some time in another country, usually as part of the diplomatic service. For the different generations, but most especially for the first, these international contacts and experiences meant privileged circulation of business information, knowledge of the international market, technology, familiarity with international management practices and so on.

As far as social mobility in the first generation is concerned, it is only observed in the López family, whose trunk (Pedro A. López) was son of an artisan (tailor). None of the other families have working class or peasant roots and already in the first generation there was a tendency towards relatively important business activity in an economy that had only just entered industrialization in the first decade of the twentieth century. The exception is the Santos family, whose original head (Eduardo Santos, son of a provincial politician) was not a businessman. Francisco Santos Calderón, vice president of the Republic (2002–10), and cousin of the current president Juan Manuel Santos Calderón, indicated that his father (second generation) 'had never made a deal in his life' (Santos, 2013, pp. 30–1). However, he, his brothers and cousins from the third generation in the early 1990s combined the political role of the family newspaper, founded in 1911 and with great influence on Colombian life throughout the twentieth century, with the formation of a powerful economic group (Casa Editorial El Tiempo, CEET) in the communications sector (print media, publishing houses, television channels) with managerial support from family business consultants (Santos, 2013, p. 111). In 2007 the group was bought by a Spanish family media group (Grupo Planeta) that subsequently sold it to one of the largest Colombian family business groups (Grupo Aval/Sarmiento Angulo).

Regarding the economic sectors in which these six families had their business activities, with the exception of the Santos family, the first generations were linked to foreign trade (import of European and US merchandise, and export of agricultural and livestock products, especially coffee, the main export product from the 1870s to 1989[7]). The Ospina family also made money in gold mining in the second half of the nineteenth century, and in 1927, still held executive positions in the mining association; it invested heavily in livestock and came to have one of the main cattle ranches of the country in the early twentieth century. The Restrepo family roots were initially from land colonizers, traders, representatives of foreign trading houses and partners of nascent textile industries in Medellín (the industrial capital of Colombia). In banking and finance, in the middle of the 'free bank' period (1872–1922), two of the families from the capital intervened directly, one with their own bank (López in the 1910s), the other as founding partners of a bank (Banco de Bogotá in 1870); and the other two (Ospina and Restrepo) developed financial activities as part of their trading house.

In general, these families were very diversified in their businesses, especially in the first generations. The Samper family was involved in the nascent manufacturing activity of the capital (electric power, cement, glass) until 1950, when they lost majority control of the Bogotá cement works and stepped out of its management. The Ospina and Restrepo families intervened in the manufacturing activity of Medellín (textile), as promotors and partners. Well into the next generations (and until today), the Restrepo family has continued to play a decisive role in the industrial, commercial and financial development of Medellín, for example, by holding key executive positions in the only business group out of the four that, since the 1980s, is not family-owned (Grupo Empresarial Antioqueño), but distinctively regional. Its origins are rooted in the 1920s through the association of rich families from this area of the country to form 'companies of companies'. Since the beginning, this family has held other positions of entrepreneurial leadership (national association of industrialists, organization for the promotion of Antioquia, interventions in peace processes and so on) going beyond the sphere of business, being involved in civic, cultural and educational initiatives and holding public office, especially at local and regional levels. Even though, since the second generation (1910–14), there was not another president of the Republic with their name, they have never stopped being intensely involved, very noticeably at a regional level but also with economic power at a national level.

In the case of the Ospina family, which, like the Restrepos, is a conservative presidential family from Antioquia, it has held the presidency of the Republic three times (more than any other family studied here) and at very different moments of the country's development (1857–61, 1922–26, 1946–50). Although it had been active in the manufacturing industry since the third generation it has concentrated its main activity on services (construction industry and urbanization) in Bogotá, where it founded a large company (Ospina & Cía.) that celebrated 80 years of existence in 2010. Before becoming president of Colombia in the mid twentieth century, Ospina was at the head of this company and also led a key organization in Colombia's development (the National Federation of Coffee Growers, created in 1927) at a critical moment in time (1930–34).

Four of the families (Santos, López, Restrepo and Ospina) have been involved in mass media for various generations. They have also, from the beginning, been part of cultural and educational activities (principally the Samper family in second and third generations, the Restrepo family since the second generation and the Ospina family in the second and third generations) without suffering from the 'Buddenbrook syndrome' (Allende, 2009; Fernández Pérez, 2003). That is, they did not follow the route of progressive decline of the family business that often leads to members of the third or fourth generation showing less inclination for business and more for spending their time involved in cultural, artistic and journalistic activities, and 'la dolce vita'.

7.6 BY WAY OF CONCLUSION

Below we present a few considerations on content, method and theory related to the relationship between family businesses and politics in an emerging Latin American economy. Regarding the first, although it is complex and requiring further empirical research, it seems more relevant to encourage this type of study rather than dogmatically condemn (or praise) the entrepreneurial families, their ways of operation, their relationship with the state and their role in the development of capitalism in societies in different stages of economic development.

Certainly, the existence of presidential families studied in this chapter is not to be taken as an example of an institutional trajectory to praise or as an open, inclusive democratic society model to follow. Nor is it explained by encompassing generalizations on the existence of 'extractive institutions' designed for their own benefit by elites that supposedly embody the 'iron law of oligarchy'. To carry on this caricature leads nowhere; neither does it open any avenue for further research that illuminates the nuances of their rule throughout the period under study. What the empirical evidence demonstrates, perhaps taking the case of the presidential families as an extreme example, is that in emerging economies relationships with politics and the state constitutes a key capability ensuring the endurance of entrepreneurial families.

The impact of this concentration of presidential power in the hands of six families over 150 years is a subject for research, and towards this end examining their productive, unproductive and destructive functions seems to provide fertile ground (Baumol, 1968; Torres, 2003). Thus, for example, nearly half of these six families played an important role in the export-based model, particularly in the case of the coffee economy in the 1880–1930 period. They deployed productive entrepreneurial functions, perhaps in contrast to combining them with unproductive, rent-seeking functions in the following six decades (1930–90) marked by state protectionism that favoured the coffee sector. The deployment of destructive functions does not seem evident in the presidential families during either of these two periods. On the other hand, the outline presented here of a great variety (nine or ten) of modalities of involvement in politics allows for examination of the vast array of combinations of political action open to entrepreneurial families (Dávila, 2012). Undoubtedly, this poses a more demanding intellectual challenge and yet is a more promising approach than stereotyping the political relationships of entrepreneurial families in terms of a simplistic dichotomy of good and evil.

We are not ignoring the entrepreneurial families that, although not having reached the political apex, managed to forge across generations a capability for handling the relationship with politics and the state as a strategic resource for their entrepreneurial activity, by recourse to the various methods shown here. Exemplifying this are the 'merchant houses' of the powerful families in the gold-mining region of Antioquia, which since the mid nineteenth century, even before the emergence of the coffee economy (from the 1880s onwards) had excelled thanks to their diversified entrepreneurship (gold mining, import and export, land colonization, family banks, later coffee and the textile-based industrialization of the regional capital Medellín) (Botero, 2013). They were never far removed from regional public affairs, forming part of the local elite since the late eighteenth century (Twinam, 1982). And in the present era, the large family business groups located in the main cities (Bogotá, Medellín, Cali and Barranquilla) not only routinely provide financial support to various presidential candidates, but also enjoy privileged access to senior public officials; lobby the executive and legislative powers; are owners of – or partners in – media groups; participate in large state contracts, and at times have members holding high public office by appointment (presidential advisors, state ministers, ambassadors and so on). In addition, they have never been far removed from negotiations to resolve the armed conflict that has plagued Colombia for the past 25 years (Rettberg, 2013). The ways that entrepreneurial families (presidential or not), and also non-family-owned business groups, interact with politics and the state – to a greater or lesser extent, in one combination or another, or at this or that moment in time – depend on the formation, modification and evolution of the country's institutional framework, referred to in this chapter. Within this structurally turbulent context, they display, at each specific time and place, various functions that are productive, non-productive or destructive in terms of economic development (Baumol, 1968; Torres, 2003).

For the smaller and less powerful family business groups, as well as entrepreneurial families who operate small- and medium-sized businesses, there is a clear lesson: without strategic handling of the relationship with politics and the state, even at a local level, an entrepreneurial family has very little room to manoeuvre (even the task of legally registering its companies becomes difficult). It should be added that participation in politics, in the discharge of public office (both by election and appointment), what is known colloquially as 'the revolving door' (the step from private sector to temporally holding public office), has among its costs the frictions, conflicts of interests and hostilities that inevitably arise from decision-making, which in the long term can effect the relationship with other families and business sectors.

In presidential families, as well as in any large family business group, the social network (through marriage, kinship, elite schools and universities, professionals, social clubs, regional identification, immigrant colonies and so on) continues to play a crucial role.

Important to mention, in the context of Latin America the case of conflict-ridden Colombia in the last half century (1960–2010) is singled out for the complex and continuing armed conflict ('a prolonged and degraded war') wherein illegal groups (guerrillas, drug traffickers and their networks, paramilitaries and alliances and counter-alliances among some of them) paradoxically coexist with a robust record of economic growth and internationally acknowledged macroeconomic stability. Undeniably, in the destructive entrepreneurial activities deployed by all such groups, families have been a central actor. Not only in this 'narco-stained nation'[8] the drug cartels typically have been family-based, but also in financial scandals, political corruption and in general the 'capture of the state', especially at the local and regional levels, entrepreneurial families have long played a central role. However, entrepreneurial families condemned for their illegal activities, families praised for their contribution to economic development and family business groups that are blazing trails in the globalization process are all subjects for future scholarly empirical research. This is a far better option than depicting such diverse entrepreneurial families with a broad stroke as all-powerful, ever present, 'extractive oligarchies'.

This study also clearly shows that the entrepreneurial family as the unit of analysis used here is different from the family firm and deserves room in the family business scholarly literature. It would be worthwhile continuing to research the entrepreneurial family, as much in its endogenous factors (structure, education, values, the role of kinship and its reproduction, division of work among members, succession, intergenerational transition, the family as reservoir of entrepreneurship and so on) as in the handling of and adaptation to the contexts through which the entrepreneurial family passes from generation to generation. This chapter hopes to contribute in this aspect. For this we have to turn to historical research, especially business history, as well as the traditions of sociological and anthropological studies on family (for example, Lomnitz and Pérez-Lizaur, 1987). As previously noted, entrepreneurial families should be studied in diverse contexts of economic development (comparative research between advanced and emerging economies, but also within the latter, for example, among various Latin American countries, and also between these and Spain).

It would seem that, in addition to engaging in dialogue with critics of family structures in the corporate governance of businesses groups (Morck, 2010; Morck and Steier, 2005), and with the critics of families as oligarchical institutions who only have their own interests at heart (Acemoglu and Robinson, 2012), the subject explored in this chapter, that is, the crucial role of the relationship of entrepreneurial families with politics and the state, can contribute to the current interest in the varieties of capitalism (VoC) (Business History Review, 2010, pp. 638–74; Schneider, 2009), not only at a global level, but even to distinguish 'sub-varieties' thereof within Latin American countries (Miller, 2010a).

NOTES

* Like all chapters in the present volume this work is an outcome of the international comparative project described in the Introduction. The support of the School of Management at the University of the Andes and the History, Business and Entrepreneurship Research Group is appreciated. I thank in particular two of its members, doctoral students Holmes Páez and Ana Milena Fayad (now a student at El Colegio de Mexico) as well as doctoral student Julia Díaz who collaborated in the initial stage of the research. The comments and suggestions from the editors of the book, Paloma Fernández Pérez and Andrea Lluch, on a previous version of this chapter were very helpful. The author has sole responsibility for its limitations.

1. Other than the coffee (agro-exporter) and oil sectors, a pioneer in internationalization is a family group from the sector of office and graphic art materials (Carvajal), founded in 1904 that began to internationalize in the late 1950s in the midst of substitution of imports (Caballero, 2013).
2. In his most recent work (Baumol, 2010, chapter 8) deals with two, instead of three, types of entrepreneurship: 'productive/innovative wealth seeking' and 'redistributive wealth seeking'.
3. This paragraph draws on Torres (2003), who complements and expands the ideas of Baumol (1968), especially in relation to institutional change.
4. For an insightful critique of Acemoglu and Robinson's book, see Boldizzoni (2015).
5. These characteristics are widely documented by historiography for the period under study, among which the following are basic references: Grupo de Memoria Histórica (2013), Meisel and Ramírez (2010), Ocampo (1984, 1987), Palacios (1979, 2011, 2012), Safford (2002, 2011), Safford and Palacios (2002), Robinson and Urrutia (2007). A number of expressions associated with this country will help to understand its evolution: 'fragmented land, divided society'; 'not an immigrants's land'; 'coffee republic'; 'country of regions'; 'country of cities'; 'El Dorado country'; 'one of the most underdeveloped countries of the region throughout the XIX century'; 'secondary periphery'; 'country in which the nineteenth century lasted until 1920'; 'a nation despite itself'; 'cradle of political violence'; 'country unfit for military dictatorships'; 'exclusive society'; 'high concentration of wealth'; 'bipartite regime'; 'modest public enterprise'; ' narco-stained nation'; 'country in armed conflict since the mid twentieth century'; 'land of the drug cartels'; 'formal electoral democracy'; 'notable macroeconomic stability throughout the twentieth century'.
6. Due to space limitations, the bibliographical references for the six families on which this section is based are not detailed in any systematic way. The principal sources are as follows. On the López family: Dávila (2012), Rueda (2010), Raymond (2008), Randall (2007), Iragorri (2012), Noguera (1986), Tirado (1986), Zuleta (1966); on the Ospina family: Pardo (1946), Ramírez (1996), Molina (2008); on the Restrepo family: Alvarez

(1999), Restrepo (1992, 2011); on the Samper family: Dávila (2012), Pascualy de Gómez et al. (1994), Sanz de Santamaría (1983); on the Santos family: El Tiempo (2011), Marín (1976), Santos (1936, 2013); and on the Reyes family: Lemaitre (1952), Perico (1974).

7. The great coffee-growing expansion began in 1905 and saw average yearly growth rates of 7.5 per cent (Pizano, 2003, p. 1111); traders with foreign connections (Palacios, 1979), such as the López, Samper and Ospina families, played an important role in this.
8. This label applied to Mexico in a recent *Time* magazine cover story (Time International Edition, 2014); it also fits well for Colombia.

REFERENCES

Acemoglu, D. and J.A. Robinson (2012). *Why Nations Fail: The Origins of Power, Prosperity and Poverty*. New York: Crown Business.

Allende, F. (2009). 'Poor Thomas Buddenbrook! Family Business in Literature' *Business and Economic History On line*, available at http://www.thebhc.org/publications/BEHonline/2009/allende.pdf, accessed March 18 2015.

Alvarez, V. (1999). Restrepo Jaramillo. Familia empresa y política en Antioquia, 1855–1966. Medellín: FAES.

Barbero, M.I. (2008). 'Business history in Latin America: a historiographical perspective'. *Business History Review* **82–3** (Autumn), 555–75.

Baumol, W.J. (1968). 'Entrepreneurship in economic theory'. *American Economic Review* **58** (2), 64–71. Reprinted in M. Casson (ed), *Entrepreneurship*. Aldershot, UK and Brookfield, VT, USA: Edward Elgar, pp. 49–59.

Baumol, W.J. (2010). *The Microtheory of Innovative Entrepreneurship*. Princeton, NJ: Princeton University Press.

Boldizzoni, F. (2015). 'Do nations really fail? Reconceptualizing the history of development'. Inaugural lecture (17 February). Terceras Jornadas de Historia Económica, El Colegio de México, Mexico City.

Botero, M.M. (2013). 'Las casas comerciales: empresas de familia en una economía preindustrial. Antioquia (Colombia), 1850–1910'. In C. Dávila (ed.), *Empresarios bananeros y tierra, casas comerciales y navegación a vapor en tres regiones de Colombia (1850–1930)*. Bogotá: Universidad de los Andes, Facultad de Administración. Monografías, No. 109, pp. 39–69.

Business History Review (2010). 'Varieties of capitalism roundtable'. *Business History Review* **84** (4) (December), 637–74.

Caballero, C. (2013). 'La internacionalización temprana de Carvajal & Cía y el papel de Manuel Carvajal Sinisterra'. Bogotá: Universidad de los Andes, Escuela de Gobierno, documento de trabaj.

Casanova, L. (2008). *From Multilatinas to Global Latinas; The New Latin American Multinationals*. London: Palgrave Macmillan.

Chandler, A. (1977). *The Visible Hand*. Cambridge, MA: Harvard University Press.

Chandler, A. (1992). 'Organizational capabilities and the economic history of the industrial enterprise'. *Strategic Management Journal* **12**, 33–48.

Chrisman, J.J., J.H. Chua and P. Sharma (2005). 'Trends and directions in the development of a strategic management theory of the family firm'. *Entrepreneurship Theory and Practice* **29** (5) (September), 555–76.

Colli. A. (2011). 'Business history in family business studies: from neglect to cooperation?'. *Journal of Family Business Management* **1**, 15–25.

Colli, A. (2013). 'State of the art. Family firms between risks and opportunities: a literature review'. *Socio-Economic Review* **11**, 577–99.

Colli, A. and M. Rose (2007). 'Family business'. In G. Jones and J. Zeitlin (eds), *The Oxford Handbook of Business History*. New York: Oxford University Press, pp. 194–218.

Colli, A., E. García-Canal and M. Guillen (2013). 'Family character and international entrepreneurship: a historical comparison of Italian and Spanish "new multinationals"'. *Business History* **55** (1) (January), 119–38.

Dávila, C. (2010). 'Entrepreneurship and cultural values in Latin America, 1850–2000: from modernization, national values and dependency theory towards a business history perspective'. In J.L. García-Ruiz and P. Angelo Toninelli (eds), *The Determinants of Entrepreneurship: Leadership, Culture, Institutions*. London: Pickering & Chatto, pp. 143–60.

Dávila, C. (2012). *Empresariado en Colombia: perspectiva histórica y regional*. Bogotá: Universidad de los Andes, Ediciones Uniandes.

Dávila, C. (2013). 'The current state of business history in Latin America'. *Australian Economic History Review* **53** (2) (July), 109–20.

Davis, G. and J.A. Cobb (2010). 'Resource dependence theory: past and future'. *Research in the Sociology of Organizations* **28**, 21–42.

de Jong, A., D.M. Higgins and H. van Driel (2015). 'Towards a new business history?'. *Business History* **57** (1), 5–29.

Dinero (2013). 'Los grupos', 5 mil empresas, No. 423 (14 June), 92–123.

Donadio, A. (1983). *Banqueros en el banquillo*. Bogotá: El Ancora Editores.

Donadio, A. (1984). *Por qué cayó Jaime Michelsen?* Bogotá: El Ancora Editores.

Echavarría, H. (1983). *El escándalo de los Fondos Grancolombiano y Bolivariano en el gobierno del Dr. Turbay Ayala*. Bogotá: Editorial Andes.

El Tiempo (2011). Publicaciones en conmemoración a sus 100 años de existencia (11 February).

Fernández Pérez, P. (2003). 'Reinstalando la empresa familiar en la Economía y la Historia. Una aproximación a debates teóricos recientes'. *Cuadernos de Economía y Dirección de Empresas* **17**, 45–66.

Fernández Pérez, P. (2012). *La última globalización y el renacer de los grandes negocios familiares en el mundo*. Bogotá: Universidad de los Andes, Facultad de Administración, Cátedra Corona, No. 23, p. 21.

Fernández Pérez, P. and A. Colli (2013). 'Introduction. A global revolution: the endurance of large family businesses around the world'. In P. Fernández Pérez and A. Colli (eds), *The Endurance of Family Businesses: A Global Overview*. New York: Cambridge University Press, pp. 1–11.

Fernández Pérez, P. and N. Puig (2010). 'Dynasties and associations in entrepreneurship: An approach through the Catalan case'. In J.L. García-Ruiz and P. Toninelli (eds), *The Determinants of Entrepreneurship: Leadership, Culture, Institutions*. London: Pickering & Chatto, pp. 105–25.

Friedman, W. and G. Jones (2011). 'Business history: time for debate'. *Business History Review* **85** (1), 1–8.

Grupo de Memoria Histórica (2013). *Basta Ya¡ Colombia: Memorias de guerra y dignidad*. Informe general Grupo de Memoria Histórcia. Bogotá: Imprenta Nacional.

Herrigel, G. and J. Zeitlin (2010). 'Alternatives to varieties of capitalism'. *Business History Review* **84** (4), 667–74.

Iragorri, C. (2012). *Felipe López. El hombre detrás de la revista Semana*. Bogotá: Planeta.

Iversen, M.J. (2010). 'The "varieties of capitalism" approach as an analytical tool for business historians'. Varieties of Capitalism Roundtable. *Business History Review* **84** (4), 464–6.

Kobrak, C. and A. Schneider (2011). 'Varieties of business history: subject and methods for the twenty-first century'. *Business History* **53** (3), 401–24.

Landes, D.S. (2006). *Dynasties: Fortunes and Misfortunes of the World's Great Family Businesses*. New York: Viking Press.

Lemaitre, E. (1952). *Reyes*. Bogotá: Editorial Iqueima.

Lomnitz, L.A. and M. Pérez-Lizaur (1987). *A Mexican Elite Family*. Princeton, NJ: Princeton University Press.

Lubinsky, C. et al. (2013). *Family Multinationals. Entrepreneurship, Governance, and Pathways to Internationalization*. New York: Routledge.

Marín, F. (1976). *El tío*. Bogotá: Tomo y Lomo Editores.

Meisel, A. and M.T. Ramírez (eds) (2010). *La economía colombiana del siglo XIX*. Bogotá: FCE, Banco de la República.

Miller, R. (2010a). 'Latin American business history and varieties of capitalism'. *Business History Review* **84** (4), 653–7.

Miller, R. (2010b). *Foreign Firms and Business History in Latin America*. Bogotá: Universidad de los Andes, Facultad de Administración, Cátedra Corona, p. 18.

Molina, L.F. (2008). 'Ospinas & Cía. S.A. 1932–2008. Una empresa con historia'. In L.F. Molina, R. Gutiérrez, A. Saldarriaga et al., *Urbanismo, arquitectura, patrimonio, Ospinas 75 años*. Bogotá: Ospinas, Zona, pp. 14–39.

Morck, R.K. (2009). 'The riddle of the great pyramids'. NBER Working Papers Series, Working Paper 14858 (April). National Bureau of Economic Research, Washington, DC.

Morck, R.K. (2010). 'Loyalty, agency conflicts and corporate governance'. In H.K. Baker and J.R. Nofsinger (eds), *Behavioral Finance: Investors, Corporations, and Markets*. New York: Wiley, pp. 453–73.

Morck, R.K. and L. Steier (2005). 'The global history of corporate governance: an introduction'. In R.K. Morck (ed.), *A History of Corporate Governance Around the World: Family Business Groups to Professional Managers*. Chicago, IL: University of Chicago Press, pp. 1–64.

Noguera, A. (1986). *Aproximación a Alfonso López: testimonios para una biografía*. Bogotá: Banco de la República.

Ocampo, J.A. (1984). *Colombia y la economía mundial, 1830–1910*. Bogotá: Siglo XXI.

Ocampo, J.A. (ed.) (1987). *Historia económica de Colombia*. Bogotá: Siglo Veintiuno Editores de Colombia, Fedesarrollo.

Palacios, M. (1979). *El café en Colombia, 1850–1970. Una historia económica, social y política*. Bogotá: Editorial Presencia.

Palacios, M. (2011). *De quién es la tierra? Propiedad, politización y protesta campesina en la década de 1930*. Bogotá: Fondo de Cultura Económica, Universidad de los Andes.

Palacios, M. (2012). *Violencia pública en Colombia, 1958–2010*. Bogotá: Fondo de Cultura Económica.

Pardo, J.A. (1946). *Tres presidentes de Colombia y semblanzas de personajes de la familia Ospina*. Bogotá: Editorial Santafé.

Pascualy de Gómez, E., M. Estrada, C. Hernández and A. Barajas (eds) (1994). *Los Samper. Un libro abierto*. Bogotá: Editorial Colombia Nueva.

Perico, M. (1974). *Reyes de cauchero a dictador*. Tunja: Universidad Pedagógica y Tecnológica de Colombia – Ediciones La Rana y el Águila.
Pfeffer, J. and G.R. Salancik (1978). *The External Control of Organizations: A Resource Dependence Perspective*. New York: Harper & Row.
Pizano, D. (2003). 'El sector cafetero colombiano en el siglo XX'. In C. Dávila (ed), *Empresas y empresarios en la historia de Colombia. Siglos XIX y XX. Una colección de estudios recientes*. Bogotá: Editorial Norma, Ediciones Uniandes, Facultad de Administración, Universidad de los Andes, pp. 1107–46.
Portafolio (2013). 'Élite empresarial de Colombia 2013'. *Separata* (31 May), 1–46.
Ramírez, J.E. (1996). 'La construcción del poder económico: La familia Ospina, 1850–1960'. *Innovar, Revista de ciencias administrativas y sociales* (July–December), 133–55.
Randall, S. (2007). *Alfonso López Michelsen, su vida, su época*. Bogotá: Villegas Editores.
Raymond, P. (2008). *Mucha tela que cortar: la saga de una fábrica textil y la pugna de las familias Caballero y López por su control*. Bogotá: Editorial Planeta.
Restrepo, J.A. (1992). *Retrato de un patriarca antioqueño. Pablo Antonio Restrepo Escovar, 1815–1899. Abogado, político, educador y fundador de Andes*. Bogotá: Banco de la República.
Restrepo, N. (2011). *Empresariado Antioqueño y Sociedad 1940–2004. Influencia de las élites patronales de Antioquia en las políticas socioeconómicas colombianas*. Medellín: Editorial Universidad de Antioquia.
Rettberg, A. (2003). *Cacaos y tigres de papel. El gobierno de Samper y los empresarios colombianos*. Bogotá: Facultad de Ciencias Sociales, Departamento de Ciencia Política, CESO, Universidad de los Andes.
Rettberg, A. (2013). 'La construcción de paz bajo la lupa: una revisión de la actividad y de la literatura académica internacional'. *Estudios Políticos*, **42** (enero–junio), 13–36.
Robinson, J. and M. Urrutia (eds) (2007). *Economía colombiana del siglo XX. Un análisis cuantitativo*. Bogotá: FCE, Banco de la República.
Rodríguez-Satizábal, B. (2010). 'Beyond the large business enterprise: the rise of business groups in Colombia, 1974–1998'. MSc (Economic History) dissertation, London School of Economics and Political Science.
Rueda, M.I. (2010). *Casi toda la verdad*. Bogotá: Editorial Planeta.
Safford, F. (2002). *Los valores socioculturales, las estructuras y las políticas públicas en el desarrollo colombiano*. Bogotá: Universidad de los Andes, Facultad de Administración, Cátedra Corona, p. 5.
Safford, F. (2011). 'Pautas en la vida empresarial de Colombia en el siglo XIX'. In F. Safford et al., *Visión y actuación del empresariado en Colombia, 1820–1950*. Monografías de Administración, Universidad de los Andes, Facultad de Administración, No. 106, May, pp. 1–54.
Safford, F. and M. Palacios (2002). *Colombia. Fragmented Land, Divided Society*. New York: Oxford University Press.
Santiso, J. (2013). *The Decade of the Multilatinas*. Cambridge: Cambridge University Press.
Santos, E. (1936). *Periodismo: Eduardo, Enrique y Gustavo Santos*. Bogotá: Editorial Minerva.
Santos, F. (2013). *Rebelde con causa*. Bogotá: Fundación Confianza Colombia.
Sanz de Santamaría, C. (1983). *Historia de una gran empresa*. Barcelona: Editorial Gaudi – Benjamín Villegas & Asociados.

Schneider, B.R. (2009). 'Hierarchical market economies and varieties of capitalism in Latin America'. *Journal of Latin American Studies* **41** (August), 553–75.
Scranton, P. and P. Fridenson (2013). *Reimagining Business History*. Baltimore, MD: Johns Hopkins University Press.
Semana (1989). 'Qué tan culpable es Michelsen?' (15 June).
Semana (2013). 'Faceta desconocida', No. 1644 (4 November), p. 17.
Superintendencia de Sociedades (1978). *Conglomerados de sociedades en Colombia*. Bogotá: Superintendencia de Sociedades.
Thurow, L.C. (1989). 'An establishment or an oligarchy?' *National Tax Journal* **42** (4), 405–11.
Time International Edition (2014). 'Save Mexico', Cover story (24 February).
Tirado, A. (1986). *El pensamiento de Alfonso López Pumarejo*. Bogotá: Biblioteca del Banco Popular.
Torres, E. (2003). 'Funciones empresariales, cambio institucional y desarrollo económico'. In C. Dávila (ed.), *Empresas y empresarios en la historia de Colombia. Siglos XIX y XX. Una colección de estudios recientes*. Bogotá: Editorial Norma, Ediciones Uniandes, Facultad de Administración, Universidad de los Andes, pp. 3–32.
Twinam, A. (1982). *Miners, Merchants and Farmers in Colombia*. Austin, TX: University of Texas Press.
Zuleta, E. (1966). *El presidente López*. Medellín: Albón – Interprint.

8. From the domination by family elites to the presence of multiple players: capitalism in Costa Rica in the twentieth century

Juan Carlos Leiva and Erick Guillén Miranda

8.1 INTRODUCTION

The aim of this chapter is to contribute to the knowledge of family businesses, specifically large family businesses (LFB), in Costa Rica. In particular, the chapter will discuss the causes that can help to understand the continuity and survival of LFB in Costa Rica in the twentieth century. This period in the economic history of Costa Rica can be divided into three identifiable phases and these will provide the basis on which the chapter is organized. With the first period covering 1870 until 1948, followed by another spanning 1948 to 1978 and concluding with a third that comprises 1978 to the present day, this chapter shows how the Costa Rican economic scenario has transformed from being dominated by a small elite of families to one where multiple players are in competition and LFB play a relatively smaller role.

Generally speaking, little is known about family businesses and LFB in Costa Rica. The Costa Rican Observation Center for Micro, Small, and Medium-sized Companies points out that 50 per cent of these types of company are family-run (Brenes and Govaere, 2009). With respect to LFB in particular, even less is known. Nevertheless, it is possible to put a dimension on the phenomenon. In Costa Rica today, 95 per cent of companies are classified as micro, small and medium-sized (MEIC, 2013). If we consider that there are approximately 49 000 companies in total, the group of large businesses would add up to about 2450 firms. This group of large companies (5 per cent of the registered total), can be divided in turn into two blocks: companies with foreign capital established in Costa Rica and those with local capital. It is on this latter group that our research will focus.

From a theoretical perspective, the survival and longevity of LFB can be understood through two approaches. The first is based on resources and capacity (Chrisman et al., 2005); it shows that companies have a number of resources and capacities (valuable, rare, imperfectly imitable and irreplaceable) that help to explain the causes of the differences in the performance of the companies. The second looks at the influence of the competitive environment (McGahan and Porter, 1997). Its proponents point out that resources and capacities explain no more than a third, statistically speaking, of the differences in companies' performances. Therefore, the environment becomes an important element.

Our baseline argument is that the social and political environment in present day Costa Rica can be defined as dispersed, atomized and with multiple power groups, both emerging and traditional (Lizano, 2008). In this analytical framework, we consider that the sector of LFB and entrepreneurial families is similar and constitutes a reflection of this environment. As shall be seen, Costa Rica went from a situation in which the economy was dominated by an elite of entrepreneurial families to one in which multiple players act together in a dispersed and atomized arena.

Returning to the theoretical perspective, it is clear how the two above-mentioned theoretical approaches come together. The surviving LFB developed a series of capacities that successfully adapted to the changes in the environment, making the focus of our attention the way this affected the continuity and longevity of LFB as well as the entrepreneurial families behind them.

Likewise, it is important to mention from the theoretical perspective that the analysis of family businesses in general raises many questions that are so far unanswered. From the most basic, such as the consensual and shared definition of family businesses, to more concrete subjects like the forms of approach and theoretical frameworks from which the objects of study can be analysed (Chrisman et al., 2005).

Thus, our work faces various theoretical challenges. The first is the definition of the object of study. We will visualize family businesses as those that, with structural and legal variations, are managed through a strategic vision that seeks to organize certain resources and values shared by entrepreneurial families that lead to the survival of these businesses. The second is the specificity of the context. As in all countries, Costa Rica is the product of a series of its own circumstances that marks the course of its development. The third constitutes the conceptual conflict between entrepreneurial families versus family businesses. Chrisman et al. (2005) emphasizes this aspect as a prominent factor in empirical as well as theoretical works on family businesses. In our case, this conflict occurs in various points in the chapter, but we see it as an intrinsic part of the phenomenon under study.

Given our objective, the methodology used is by force qualitative, specifically based on case study. It is important to point out some methodological challenges that were faced. Firstly, access to information. In Costa Rica there is almost no academic work in our topic of interest. Nor are there relevant secondary sources of information, specifically with a historical focus. Furthermore, there is a very low participation of these types of local firms in the stock market and they are, in addition, very reticent about providing information about their companies (Camacho, 2012).

A significant part of our work is therefore directed to the study of the 20 most relevant Costa Rican LFB today, and these form our representative sample for study. Taking into account the lack of information sources available, we take as prime reference the annual publication made by the journal *EKA* on the 500 most important (by turnover and number of employees) organizations (both private and public) that are operational in Costa Rica (see Table 8.1 at the end of the chapter). As a complement to the above, we use case studies of companies that were also identified as being important in other historical moments by specialist publications in economics and finance.

To reach our aim, we first present an analysis of the development of the socio-economic history of Costa Rica over a number of phases, and its impact on the LFB we are studying. Then the current situation is outlined and finally we offer some conclusions and reflections.

8.2 HISTORICAL DEVELOPMENT OF FAMILY CAPITALISM

The socio-economic development of Latin America can be divided, according to Bertola and Ocampo (2010) into long historical periods, although the complexity of this task, given the heterogeneity between countries, should not be forgotten. They qualify the first phase as 'independencies, liberal reforms and industrial revolution'. They then outline a period denominated 'globalization, institutional strengthening and primary export development'. The third period is defined as 'State-directed industrialization'. This is followed by the fourth, 'reorientation towards the market'. These periods are clearly seen in Costa Rica, albeit with delay in some cases with respect to the time frame proposed by the authors.

Thus, from the perspective that interests us in this work, the Costa Rican nation can be divided into various clearly identifiable time lapses. According to the consulted literature, each of these periods can be positioned within a particular development style (Rovira, 2004). This way, then, we can divide the recent socio-economic history of Costa Rica into clearly identifiable stages. One begins in 1870 and lasts until the 1940s, with a clear culmination in 1948 when the last armed revolution in Costa Rica took place. The next begins at this point and ends with the Costa Rican financial crisis in 1978, which saw Costa Rica default on its debt repayments to international financial institutions. Finally, a third phase covers the period from the 1980s to the present day (Hidalgo, 2003; Rovira, 2004).

8.2.1 Agro-export and Family Capitalism Dominated by an Elite of Families: From the Beginning of the Century to 1948

This phase of Costa Rican socio-economic development can be classified as delayed in comparison to the rest of Latin America. In their proposal, Bertola and Ocampo (2010) define the years between 1930 and 1980 as industrialization led by the State, whereas in Costa Rica the situation at that time was more connected to previous stages such as globalization (albeit in very few sectors), institutional strengthening and primary export growth. State-led industrialization began in Costa Rica some years after the armed revolution of 1948.

This way, in the years prior to 1948, Costa Rica was influenced by aspects such as the transport revolution in the economy, that is, the reduction in the cost of product transportation; likewise, by the increase in global demand for food and raw materials by the industrialized world; in the national context, the consolidation of liberal reforms, which were basically the commercial exploitation of land, labour mobility and others, as well as the consolidation of political power structures (Bertola and Ocampo, 2010). As the 1940s gradually approached, other factors mentioned by the authors emerged, such as the appearance of new players: for example, the working class and the State.

Economically, there reigned in Costa Rica an agrarian capitalism linked to two export products: coffee and banana (Hidalgo, 2003). The following data illustrates this: in 1915 the two products represented 81 per cent of total exports; in 1925 it was 96 per cent; in 1935, 85 per cent and in 1945, 84 per cent. It is interesting, in turn, to see the family nature of these enterprises; for example, between 1930 and 1950, approximately half of the 25 per cent of coffee producers were family firms (Peters, 1984). In the case of the banana, its production was linked to foreign capital, mainly from the USA and within a system of enclave, or to put it another way, 'behind the back of the rest of the economy' (Hidalgo, 2003).

The economic predominance of a small elite of entrepreneurial families constitutes a primary element of this period. These families, mainly coffee producers in origin, took over the decision-making and benefits in economic policies, acting in predominantly three sectors: agro-export, trade imports and banking (Hidalgo, 2003).

From a social perspective, it should be mentioned that these families were interconnected, wielded substantial power and dominated participation in government bodies; and they were not without their periods of infighting over positions of dominance (Hidalgo, 2003). This small socio-economic elite had among its members not only the creole elite originating from colonial times and with strong internal bonds (Stoner, 1975), but also immigrant groups (mainly Germans, British, Jews and North Americans) attracted by the opportunities offered by the young nation of Costa Rica.

In this context and in light of our study, it seems we should talk of dominant entrepreneurial families rather than LFB, in this period. Two facts illustrate this. As seen in Table 8.1, only two of the 20 most important LFB that are still active today emerged at this time. Additionally, as another study showed, out of the 14 centenarian Costa Rican companies still active today (therefore founded within the scope of this work) only four did not remain small or medium-sized (less than 100 employees) (Leiva, 2012d).

These entrepreneurial families, dominant in the period we are analysing, have shown diverse patterns of development. One group of families has remained important in the Costa Rican economic arena through strategies of economic diversification, alliances and acquisitions. The Sánchez, Dent, Peters and Orlich families, for instance, appear among the main exporters of coffee in the period 1930–50 and are currently connected to a large number of businesses such as real estate, finance, urban development and shopping malls.

On the other hand, there are entrepreneurial families that closed their businesses. This was due to both external and internal factors. Among the former we can mention the world economic crisis of 1929, the coffee crisis in 1933 and World War I. Among the internal factors a number of regulations issued by the Costa Rican government in 1936 can be mentioned that substantially restricted coffee export, as well as the declaration as 'national enemies' and confiscations that many foreigners (especially Germans) and their descendants suffered because of World War II (Peters, 1984).

From this we conclude that this first phase in our historical and economic division of Costa Rica was characterized by the presence of an elite of dominant entrepreneurial families, with entrepreneurial activities that were strongly linked to an agro-export model prevailing at the time. Although this did not result in many specific LFB surviving until the present day, we do find some families that have evolved and that are now involved in diverse economic activities, allowing them to remain important players in the Costa Rican socio-economic arena. The causes of the previous situation have their origin both in elements within the families themselves, that is, in their capacity to implement diverse entrepreneurial strategies (diversification, acquisitions, alliances), as well as in adjustments to the external environment (political, economic, social).

8.2.2 Substitution of Imports Model and Family Capitalism with New Players: From 1948 to 1978

In 1948, Costa Rica went through its last armed revolution, in which two politically opposing forces confronted each other and its outcome marked a change in the development style of Costa Rica (Lizano, 2008). Without dwelling on the political reasons for the revolution, in economic terms we can state that the winning group attempted to move the country away from a primary agro-export model and towards substitution of imports.

In relation to Latin America, it can be seen how Costa Rica at this moment adopted a development style that other countries already had. Thorp (1998), for example, defines it as 'industrialization and expansion of the role of the State' (positioning it between 1945 and 1973), while Bertola and Ocampo (2010) call it 'State-directed industrialization' (1930–80). Three factors characterize this phase according to these authors: industrialization as the first step towards development; the participation of the State in wider areas of economic and social life; and the focus on the internal market.

According to the same authors, during a second sub-phase of this period, approximately from the end of World War II until 1980, the strongest growth in productivity and the economy was seen in Latin America. In our case, it positioned what we call the golden period of Costa Rican LFB. The fact that 13 of the sampled 20 LFB were created in this time is a clear example of this.

In Costa Rica specifically, this change of model was introduced by the winning group in the revolution; it stimulated a new economic vision based on a strong business and welfare State, promotion of industrialization through substitution of imports, laws of industrial development, incorporation (albeit late) into the Central American common market and great interest from foreign capital in the process.

In terms of the winning and losing social groups, the panorama changed. Among the winners we can count several national industrial entrepreneurial groups and small traders, closely linked to the small urban intellectual bourgeoisie; likewise foreign industrial capital. Among the losers we can include the powerful old groups like the agro-exporters and the importer traders linked to the coffee-producing oligarchy, as well as workers, especially from the banana sector, unified in the communist party (Lizano, 2008).

Parallel to this internal context, the external context was characterized by the following aspects: a long period of economic growth and a process of Central American integration stimulated by the United States. Likewise, the price of coffee, the main export product, reached high levels on the international market.

This is the breeding ground where many of the LFB in our study were created. The sectors in which they emerged are a faithful reflection of the changes in the environment: trade, services and production of goods.

It is interesting to note that though it may be true that the State intervened considerably in national life in the period analysed, it does not seem to compete in the economic sectors known implicitly as private capitalist (Rovira, 2004). It is within this framework that many of the LFB that still survive today were born, and also many others that initially grew at a remarkable rate but later, in the next period of our economic historical division, succumbed through acquisitions or mergers, a subject that we shall return to later.

Regarding the sectors, it was within trade that most companies were created, according to our representative sample of 12 LFB. In fact, the five commercial enterprises that emerged in this period occupy the top five positions by turnover in our ranking. These companies were located in areas that were 'non-competitive' with the State (sale of home appliances, automobiles and mass market consumer goods production).

Analysing the origin of these, we made some interesting discoveries. For example, in 1971 two partners, Carlos Monge Herrera and Servio Flores Arroyo, opened a home appliances retail store called El Gallo más Gallo. With a strategy of sale on credit (counting on high volumes and low margins) and directed towards rural areas, this store marked the birth of two of the most important LFB in our ranking: Grupo Monge (first position) and Gollo (third position). Three years after the founding of the company and with eight stores in their possession, the partners decided to separate, dividing the stores equally between them (Barahora, 2006).

Monge Herrera was a public servant with 'trade in his blood'; he had tried but failed with other businesses and had used his personal savings to open the store (Barahona, 2006). Flores Arroyo was a former employee of an international company producing mass market consumer goods (Leiva and Guillén, 2012). What is interesting in both cases is that they were entrepreneurs coming from the 'emerging' social sectors and, as far as the evidence shows, not associated with traditional groups of economic power (León, 2010). Something similar occurred with the family behind the company in position two of our ranking: Grupo Purdy Motor, which had as its core business the representation of Toyota in Costa Rica and small operations in other countries. Its founder was Xavier Quirós Oreamuno, an agricultural engineer who decided to import two Toyota cars for his work but, on discovering the ease with which he could sell them, decided to enter the automobile business (Leiva and Guillén, 2013).

These three cases seem to be a product of their historical context, that is, an emerging middle class that recognized business opportunities in Costa Rica at that time. Without doubt, these companies knew how to take advantage of the opportunities and to position themselves as the powerful entrepreneurial families that they are today, undergoing generational transitions, professionalization and internationalization of their operations in the process. We shall come back to this later.

In the industrial sector there are also LFB that were created in the processes of change that Costa Rica underwent during the years of this analysis. Four companies emerged in areas with no competition from the State (for example, food manufacturing and household cleaning products). An example is the Irex company, founded by Ricardo Amador Céspedes, an agricultural and construction worker who started up his enterprise practically from nothing (Leiva, 2012a). Another case that demonstrates this social diversity is Envases Comeca, founded by Víctor Mesalles Cebriá, an expatriate ex-executive of a foreign company located in Costa Rica (Summa, 2006).

In the services sector we also have examples like Meco, which in the present day is the largest construction company in the country, founded by Carlos Cerdas Araya in association with his father Ángel Américo Cerdas, a small trader of stone and construction materials as well as machinery rental. In this case, the role played by the Costa Rican Institute of Electricity, as client of the business in its beginnings, was fundamental (Leiva, 2012b).

So far, we have looked at cases that emerged with the social changes and that can be defined as 'winners' in the process, but we also have cases of groups that are 'losers', but that nevertheless maintain an important presence in the business world. Examples of these are the Nación group that, although officially created in 1946, is directly linked to entrepreneurial groups coming from the said losing elite; a similar case is Televisora de Costa Rica canal 7 (Robles and Voorend, 2011).

To conclude this historical period, we can state that the social and economic changes produced after the 1948 revolution opened up a whole range of opportunities that some prominent entrepreneurs from the 'winning' social classes managed to capitalize on and that their offspring consolidated, as we shall see later. Along with this, we find notable entrepreneurs from among the 'losing' social groups who also experienced a process of growth and consolidation in their LFB.

8.2.3 Economic Opening and Reconfiguration of Family Capitalism: From 1978 to the Present

The economic history of Costa Rica had another turning point towards the end of the 1970s and early 1980s, when the country went through one of the most complex economic crises of its history. Classified as structural not cyclic (Hidalgo, 2003), this crisis can be explained from various perspectives.

From the external point of view, Hidalgo (2003) identifies two fundamental economic upheavals: a rise in international interest rates and in the value of the dollar. The increase in international interest rates had two results: it blocked the entry of foreign capital and caused the local capital to leave the country. The rise in value of the dollar forced a devaluation of the national currency, the colón, with its consequent increase in foreign debt expressed in colóns and the rise in price of imports as well as the transfer of inflation to the economy as a whole. All these factors together, repeated in various Latin American countries, triggered the debt crisis of the 1980s, Costa Rica being in 1981 the first country to fall into a state of moratorium or to default on its foreign debt.

This phase fits very well with that defined by Bertola and Ocampo (2010) as 'reorientation towards the market', which in Latin America began in 1980, as well as with the definition given by Thorp (1998) as 'growth through debt, disaster and reorientation', from 1973 onwards. Both approaches coincide in pointing out that changes in paradigm, adjustment and opening of markets were the prevailing tendency in Latin American countries.

An additional and important element of the external context was that during this time a reconfiguration of the international division of work was begun, which among other things produced an expansion in the large corporate company (usually of developed countries), which in its search for efficiency began to internationalize a great number of its processes, both administrative and productive (Rovira, 2004). As shall be seen later, this had an enormous impact on countries and especially on the LFB of our analysis.

Similarly, it is important to point out the significant role played in Costa Rican politics by institutions such as the International Monetary Fund (IMF), the World Bank (WB), the Inter-American Development Bank (IDB), as well as the US cooperation Agency for International Develoment (AID), which in one way or another have been classified as key players in the change of development model that occurred in Costa Rica during the period of our analysis (Rovira, 2004).

Along with the external upheavals, the development model adopted by Costa Rica showed certain structural weaknesses that conspired with the external elements. In the words of Hidalgo (2003, p. 67), 'the model of industrialization by substitution of imports had generated a very rigid socio-economic structure that was only able to maintain its stability, despite its internal contradictions, in a stable and complementary environment.' For example, the country was still dependent on the foreign market but its pattern of integration was not the most suitable. This is because raw materials, intermediate and capital goods were imported; while agricultural products of little added value and little diversification were exported. To this we can add the activity of the State as entrepreneur and responsible for welfare; this reached its peak, as we saw, in the 1970s.

Other important elements were the anti-export bias of the industrial protectionist policies and the reduced internal – and even Central American – market; also highly significant were a series of socio-political factors such as the civil conflict in Nicaragua, against the backdrop of the Cold War and with a powerful country like the USA seeing Costa Rica as an ally on this front.

In response to the crisis, Costa Rica changed its development model and adopted a more neoliberal approach. Concrete examples of the measures taken as part of the new model are the various programmes of structural adjustments signed by the government of president Monge (1982–86), as well as the liberalization of foreign trade, expressed in five areas: the dismantlement of protectionism; the advancement of non-traditional exports; development of touristic activities; the abandonment of a fixed exchange rate; and new forms of economic integration (Hidalgo, 2003).

Some facts that contextualize the change: in 1945, coffee and banana were 85 per cent of Costa Rican exports. In 1980 the traditional exports (basically coffee, banana, sugar, meat and a few other agricultural products) represented 57 per cent of the total, while in 2003, export of non-traditional products was 87 per cent leaving only 13 per cent for the traditional exports. These non-traditional products were basically new agricultural (for example, pineapple, melon, yucca) as well as industrial (Rovira, 2004).

In the present day, this model still prevails. To name but a few characteristics. The export basket has diversified remarkably; dependency on traditional products is minimal; the opening of markets is generous; many free trade agreements have been signed (Canada, Mexico, Central America, Unites States, Chile, Europe, Singapore, China); tourism is one of the main generators of currency and the schemes for attracting foreign direct investment in services and industry have been strengthened. Nevertheless, it is generally agreed that the development model is still in debt regarding many social indicators (Estado de La Nación, 2010).

In retrospect, studies concurred (Hidalgo, 2003; Lizano, 2008; Robles and Voorend, 2011; Rovira, 2004) in pointing out certain groups as winners in the change of model: new agro exporters; the financial system; tourism sector; trade sector; transnational capital. On the side of the losers we have the protected industrial sectors and the agricultural and livestock producers for the internal market. In an intermediate position there are the traditional exporters. Despite this, we should for our purpose perhaps talk more of winning and losing activities, given the remarkable economic diversity of the entrepreneurial family businesses in the time frame studied.

It is in this context, then, that the LFB and their entrepreneurial families have had to develop, with differing results. On the one hand, there are the 15 companies created in the two previous phases as described above. These companies have grown and become strengthened by processes of improvement in their competitiveness, professionalization, alliances, as well as some internationalization processes. On the other hand, many of the LFB created in the previous period ceased to exist due to mergers, acquisitions or takeovers by other – usually international – companies, who established operations in Costa Rica in light of the new development model. In addition, there are companies that have emerged within this historical period itself.

Firstly, let us look at the companies that emerged in the previous blocks and are still active as family businesses today. In this sub-group of firms, what can be emphasized is that they have known how to adapt easily to the changes in the development model and the new constraints. There have been various strategies: formalization and professionalization, internationalization, diversification and the signing of strategic alliances.

An example of a case of formalization and professionalization is the Monge Group, which since 1995 implemented a model of corporate governance with non-family members on its executive board, a process that took place in parallel with a generational transition. This group could also be an example for internationalization, but other firms such as Purdy Motor, Comeca, Meco, Grupo Nación, Britt and Irex also took this path. Regarding diversification, we can mention Comeca as an example, a company that began as a producer of packaging and today is active in industry, trade, services and agriculture (Summa, 2006). Concerning the establishment of strategic alliances, the firm Cefa is a good example, recently forming an alliance with a Chilean family pharmaceutical group that held a philosophy and entrepreneurial vision very similar to its own (Leiva, 2012c).

Regarding the companies that ceased to exist as family-managed, we see an interesting phenomenon. In some cases, the families abandoned their enterprise, usually the most prominent and long-standing, but they continued actively participating in other branches of economic activity.

Then, what occurs is a transfer of activities. In many cases, investments are made in 'winning' activities of the new development model, such as tourism, real estate, personal services, among others. As an example we can mention the Uribe family that, after many years as owners of a supermarket chain (founded by the father, first generation in the 1960s), formed an alliance with the transnational Walmart to whom (after some years) sold the totality of its shares. Nevertheless, the family founded the company Grupo Cuesta Moras, involved in various businesses in the area of financial services, real estate, tourism, among others (Morales, 2006). The company Durman Esquivel went through a very similar process; created in 1959 as a manufacturer of piping, it formed a first strategic alliance with the Belgian company Aliaxis that later took it over entirely. Despite this, the Durman Esquivel family remained active in agro-industry, finance, service, technology and real estate, among others, through its company Grupo Montecristo (Mercados y Tendencias, 2010).

In parallel to the above, the entrepreneurial family of LFB underwent another process in this context, that of 'managerialization' (Robles and Voorend, 2011), a phrase coined to denote the process by which the chairman and owner of a LFB takes on the position of the company's country manager when the LFB passes into the hands of the transnational firm. In the two previous cases, the Uribe and Durman families, this was exactly what occurred. Similarly for the Liberman family when it sold the Interfin bank to the Canadian ScotiaBank. The pattern was the same in the three cases: the sale was preceded by the signing of a strategic alliance, followed by the purchase of the majority shares and then finally the shares were sold in their entirety.

This chameleon-like behaviour by entrepreneurial families had a very interesting aspect: its integration into the private financial system, specifically banking. We have found various studies that analyse this integration from within a social and anthropological framework, from the perspective of trying to understand the formation of groups with power and social domination (León, 2010; Robles and Voorend, 2011). What is more, we must not ignore that some researchers have questioned this strengthening process of the financial sector, it having occurred, in some cases, in a context of soft loans and donations given by AID in the 1980s (Robles and Voorend, 2011), some even classifying it as 'not at all competitive nor glamorous' (León, 2010).

For our work, without wanting to dismiss the importance of previous approaches, it is interesting to note how many of the entrepreneurial families analysed began activities in the financial sector, especially banking, at a specific moment in time (after the change of model between 1978 and 1984) and then later, when having to face changes in the environment (the entrance of global megabanks from 2006 onwards), were seen to modify their strategies of participation or to get out of the banking activity entirely.

For example, around the mid 1990s, there were 21 private banking institutions. Out of these, four were foreign and the rest local; among these latter we find as shareholders several of the families of our analysis (Jiménez, Quirós, Garnier, Sánchez, among others) (León, 2010). If we look again at the Costa Rican private finance sector after 12 years, in 2007, we find there were 12 private banking groups left, of which only two were national and the rest foreign. These foreign groups entered by acquiring or taking over the old national groups. Likewise, as part of the reaccommodation in the financial sector, two new players emerged very forcefully: a group of cooperatives as well as institutions called 'finance groups from the non-private banking sector'. In this latter group we find some of the previously mentioned entrepreneurial families.

So, as we can see, the entrepreneurial families adopted diverse response strategies when facing changes in the environment. Some decided to continue in the core business but diversified to some degree; they professionalized, signed alliances and became internationalized. In contrast, there was another group that sold its flagship companies and relocated its capital into winning enterprises, even, in some cases, entering and exiting 'rapidly' from some activities (that is, financial banking system).

Regarding the emergence of new companies in this period, we have an interesting fact – there were only five and all of them were founded before 1989. That is, there is a distinct lack of firms among the LFB in our study sample that could in any way be regarded as young.

Among these five companies, two are involved in trade, two in services (a bank and a construction firm) and one in production. As in the previous phase, this composition could be said to reflect the new configuration of the Costa Rican economy. That is, a predominance of service and trade companies, to the detriment of manufacturers and agriculturalists. Likewise, the heterogeneity of the origin of the families behind the companies is maintained.

For example, we have Banco Improsa, which is part of an eponymous financial group; it was created in 1986 as a financier and converted into a bank in 1995. Headed by the Ortuño family, representatives of the traditional coffee-growing oligarchy (Pérez, 1997) and with a long entrepreneurial tradition, it emerged through the previously mentioned reforms in the Costa Rican financial system and has remained until today one of the few financial groups that has not been taken over by global megabanks.

At this time there were also 'new sector' companies that emerged, such as Extralum, whose founder came from the middle classes, with no entrepreneurial antecedents or family tradition.

Finally, we have the completely novice entrepreneurs. A good example is the Britt group. This company was formed by Steve Aronson Fletcher, a US economist involved in business from an early age, who decided to settle in Costa Rica and found his business (Summa, 2006). The interesting feature of this case is that it reflects various facets. At the beginning, the company focused on 'traditional businesses', and is recognized as having contributed to the innovation in this sector. Later, its diversification strategy allowed it to become involved in other commercial areas, such as chocolate, tourism and gift shops in airports, which has now become its core business (Santana, 2011).

8.3 THE CURRENT SITUATION OF LARGE FAMILY BUSINESSES IN COSTA RICA

This section presents an outline of the current situation of Costa Rican LFB, using the representative sample of the 20 most important companies according to the journal *EKA* (2010).

A first analysis of the situation of these LFB (Table 8.1 at the end of the chapter) shows that in the year under study this group of companies had a total turnover of US$ 2597 million, which is equivalent to an average annual turnover of US$ 129 million. The company with the greatest turnover reached US$ 575 million and the one with the least, US$ 55 million. Regarding number of employees, the 20 firms together employ approximately 18 500 people, with an average of 927 employees per company. The largest company reached 286 employees, and the smallest, 217. The average age of the companies is 44.5 years, the oldest being 81 and the youngest 22.

Regarding sectors, services and trade prevail, followed by production or manufacturing. Specifically, eight companies are involved in services (three in construction, two in communications, two in distribution and one in banking); seven in trade (all in mass market consumer products like home appliances, cars, medicine); and five in production or manufacturing (food, household domestic products like soap and intermediate industrial goods).

An interesting point for analysis is the position of the family companies in the ranking of the journal from where the information is obtained (EKA, 2010). Although it is true that the ranking has its limitations (for example, much of the data is an estimate), it is the most serious and systematic effort that has been made in the context of Costa Rica. In addition, it covers a wide area and includes private companies as well as all types of organizations (for example, State companies) that are operational in the country. This is why it is remarkable that we had to 'reach position 122' in order to complete the 20 family businesses of the sample. Even if it is true that the first LFB of our group is number 5 in the general ranking (an excellent position), if we see it in proportion with the rest of the companies or organizations, the figure 122 implies that only 16 per cent of the companies in this section are LFB.

When aiming to contextualize the phenomenon of entrepreneurial families in the international environment, we should say that Costa Rica represents only a tiny portion. Proof of this is the turnover level and number of employees. In comparison to other countries, it is clear that the Costa Rican LFB are for the main part 'small players' in the Latin American arena, not to mention the global.

More evidence of this appears when we compare with other Latin American countries; the international incursion of Costa Rican family business groups into the international arena is 'timid' and limited to the national environment (Camacho, 2012). Various explanations have been put forward in this respect (social, political, economic), but the truth remains that the size of these family groups in the international context is small, as can be appreciated when comparing the other countries incorporated in this volume.

8.4 CONCLUSIONS

This chapter has aimed to provide a contribution to knowledge on LFB in Costa Rica. As a general conclusion, we can point out that the continuity and longevity of these businesses reflect to a large extent not only the socio-political and economic conditions that have marked them in the Costa Rican context, but also a series of resources and capacities of their own that have allowed them to adapt to these conditions.

One of the baseline arguments was that the Costa Rican socio-political arena could be defined as disperse, atomized and with multiple power groups, both emerging and traditional (Lizano, 2008) and that the LFB constitute a reflection of this.

If we take as a sample the 20 most important LFB, as well as others that were important in the past but no longer exist now, we can see a reflection of this scenario. Thus, there are old companies that came from the traditional elite, coexisting with firms emerging from the 'winning' groups

Table 8.1 The 20 largest family companies by turnover in Costa Rica (turnover in thousands of US$)

Name	Sector	Founding	Turnover (US$ thousand)	Employees
Grupo Monge	Trade	1971	573 196	2086
Purdy Motor	Trade	1957	331 604	700
Gollo	Trade	1974	186 698	1300
Cefa Comercial	Trade	1955	158 378	1695
Grupo Constenla	Trade	1956	152 933	1749
Constructora MECO	Services	1977	129 048	1257
Grupo Nación	Services	1946	121 155	1500
Grupo Farmanova Intermed	Trade	1984	110 544	320
Grupo HA (Humberto Alvarez)	Services	1930	98 736	221
Distribuidora Pedro Oller	Services	1960	91 320	400
Banco Improsa	Services	1986	83 310	217
Alimentos Jack's de Centroamérica	Production	1963	72 002	672
Volio & Trejos Asociados	Services	1983	70 730	480
Envases Comeca	Production	1978	63 058	583
Extrusiones Aluminio (Extralum)	Production	1989	62 720	590
Grupo Britt	Trade	1985	60 987	850
Sardimar	Production	1973	60 931	1174
Canal 7 Televisora de Costa Rica	Services	1958	59 276	1100
Const. Van der Laat y Jiménez	Services	1969	55 937	700
Irex de Costa Rica	Production	1957	55 393	946

Source: Journal *EKA*, web pages of the companies and interviews with founders or managers cited in the bibliography.

that succeeded after the big changes in Costa Rican development style, as well as with immigrant companies that, in different moments in time, took advantage of the opportunities created by this environment.

Undoubtedly, the environment is important but, as shown by the theoretical approach of resources and capacities, it alone does not explain everything. In this spirit, we can appreciate how the capacity for adaptation to the environment and its changes explain to a large degree the continuity and longevity of Costa Rican LFB.

Some concrete examples of this were the processes of professionalization, diversification and signing of strategic alliances that could be seen among the sample of LFB analysed. Theoretically, this means that there is a number of resources and capacities behind these processes.

This work also has its limitations just like any other of its kind. As was mentioned, the lack of information and the selection of companies by convenience should lead to a cautious reading of the results.

ACKNOWLEDGEMENTS

We are grateful to all the chief executive officers of the companies that participated in the interviews; it was an enormous learning experience for us, as authors. We would also like to thank our colleagues Arnoldo Araya Leandro and Rodolfo Carrillo Mena for their support in the elaboration of the chapter.

REFERENCES

Barahora, V. (2006). 'Un gallo con mucha espuela'. *Revista Summa* **141**, 34–6.

Bertola, L. and J.A. Ocampo (2010). 'Desarrollo, vaivenes y desigualdad: una historia económica de América Latina desde la independencia'. Secretaría General Iberoamericana. http://segib.org/publicaciones/files/2010/12/Historia-Economica-AL-ESP.pdf (accessed 16 July 2014).

Brenes, L. and V. Govaere (eds) (2009). *El estado nacional de las mipymes costarricenses formales*. San José: editorial UNED Costa Rica.

Camacho, A.C. (2012). 'Capital tico se queda en casa'. *Semanario El Financiero*. http://www.elfinancierocr.com/ef_archivo/2012/marzo/18/enportada3101030.html (accessed 16 July 2014).

Chrisman, J., J. Chua and P. Sharma (2005). 'Trends and directions in the development of a strategic management theory of the family firm'. *Entrepreneurship Theory and Practice* **29** (5), 555–75.

EKA (2010). 'Informe de las 500 EKA'. http://www.ekaenlinea.com (accessed 16 July 2014).

Estado de La Nación (2010). *Decimosexto Informe Estado de la Nación de Costa Rica*. http://www.estadonacion.or.cr/ (accessed 23 September 2014).

Hidalgo, A. (2003). *Costa Rica en evolución*. San José: Editorial de la UCR y de la Universidad de Huelva.

Leiva, J.C. (2012a). 'Entrevista realizada a Ricardo Amador Céspedes, Presidente y fundador de la empresa IREX' (22 February). Oficina IREX, San José, Costa Rica.

Leiva, J.C. (2012b). 'Entrevista realizada a José Alfredo Sánchez Zumbado, Vicepresidente de la empresa MECO' (30 January). Oficina MECO, San José, Costa Rica.

Leiva, J.C. (2012c). 'Entrevista con Denise Garnier, Presidenta de la empresa CEFA' (29 May). Oficina CEFA, San José, Costa Rica.

Leiva, J.C. (2012d). 'Aprendiendo de los viejos'. *Semanario El Financiero* **873** (June). http://wvw.elfinancierocr.com/ef_archivo/2012/junio/24/negocios3190743.html (accessed 16 July 2014).

Leiva, J.C. and E. Guillén (2012). 'Entrevista realizada a Servio Flores Cacho. Presidente de Grupo Gollo' (14 June). Oficina Grupo Gollo, Alajuela, Costa Rica.

Leiva, J.C. and E. Guillén (2013). 'Entrevista realizada a Javier Quirós de Anaya. Presidente de Grupo Purdy Motor' (10 April). Oficina Grupo Purdy, San José, Costa Rica.

León, A. (2010). 'Los grupos de poder económico costarricense: quiénes y cómo son? El caso del sector financiero'. Informe final de investigación del Instituto de Investigaciones Sociales, UCR.

Lizano, R. (2008). 'Quién manda en Costa Rica'. *Revista Poder*. http://www.poder.cr/inicio/2011/07/%C2%BFquien-manda-en-costa-rica/ (accessed 16 July 2014).

McGahan, A. and M. Porter (1997). 'How much does industry matter, really?'. *Strategic Management Journal* **18** (Summer special), 15–30.

MEIC (Ministerio de Economía, Industria y Comercio) (2013). *Estado de situación de las pymes en Costa Rica*. http://www.meic.go.cr (accessed 23 September 2014).

Mercados y Tendencias (2010). 'Costa Rica: Grupo Montecristo adquiere control accionario del Hospital Clínica Metropolitana'. *Revista Mercados y Tendencias*. San José. http://www.revistamyt.com/negocios/1629-costa-rica-grupo-montecristo-adquiere-control-accionario-del-hospital-clinica-metropolitana- (accessed 16 July 2014).

Morales, S. (2006). 'Rodrigo Uribe se aleja de las góndolas'. *Semanario El Financiero*. San José. http://www.elfinancierocr.com/ef_archivo/2006/diciembre/17/negocios921895.html (accessed 16 July 2014).

Pérez, A. (1997). 'Sombra de abolengo'. *Revista Dominical del diario La Nación*. http://wvw.nacion.com/dominical/1997/marzo/02/vida.html (accessed 16 July 2014).

Peters, G. (1984). 'Empresarios e Historia del Café en Costa Rica (1930–1950)'. In H. Pérez Brignoli and M. Samper (eds), *Tierra, café y sociedad*. Costa Rica: FLACSO, pp. 495–589.

Robles, F. and K. Voorend (2011). 'Los dueños de la palabra en Costa Rica en un contexto de reforma neoliberal'. *Revista Rupturas* **1** (2), 144–61.

Rovira, J. (2004). 'El nuevo estilo nacional de desarrollo de Costa Rica 1984–2003 y el TLC'. In M. Flórez and G. Hernández (eds), *TLC con Estados Unidos: contribuciones para el debate. Debe Costa Rica aprobarlo?* San José: Instituto de Investigaciones Sociales, Universidad de Costa Rica, p. 309.

Santana, V. (2011). 'Café Britt: un negocio, diversas identidades'. *Revista Summa* **207**, 54–6.

Stoner, S. (1975). *La Dinastía de los Conquistadores*. San José: editorial Universitaria Centroamericana.

Summa (2006). *Especial sobre los 100 empresarios de América Central más grandes, exitosos, prestigiosos e innovadores* (June). Costa Rica.

Thorp, R. (1998). *Progreso, pobreza y exclusión. Una historia de económica de América Latina en el siglo XX*. Washington, DC: Banco Interamericano de Desarrollo.

9. Large family businesses in Honduras: the influence of State intervention and immigration in the twentieth century

Allan Discua Cruz, Concepción Ramos Rodas, Claudia Raudales and Lourdes Fortín

9.1 INTRODUCTION

This chapter focuses on the origin and development of large family business in Honduras throughout the twentieth century. While family businesses have dominated the economic landscape in Honduras, little research has been conducted on how and why large family businesses developed in Honduras. Prior research advocates that this is due to lack of appropriate definitions and reliance on theories developed in culturally different contexts (Discua Cruz, 2010; Discua Cruz and Howorth, 2008). To advance understanding this chapter defines family business using broad criteria, including the participation and influence of family members in the control and development of a family firm over time (Chrisman et al., 2005). Defined historical periods in Honduras in the twentieth century are used to pinpoint exogenous and endogenous aspects that influenced the emergence and growth of family businesses (Amaya, 2006, 2011; Barahona, 2005; Becerra, 2011; D'Ans, 2011). To complement existing historical evidence this study relies on interviews with members of families that founded and/or control large family businesses in Honduras. The contribution of this chapter is identifying that State interventions, related to development paradigms (Ocampo, 2008; Ocampo and Ros, 2011) and immigration (Sánchez Alonso, 2007) are closely linked to the development of large family business in Honduras in the twentieth century.

9.2 REVIEW OF THE LITERATURE

9.2.1 A Brief Historical Summary after Independence from Spain

After independence (1821), Honduras continued as a peasant society with a subsistence family-related economy, conducted by a dispersed population and based on agriculture and exploitation of natural resources.[1] Trade was dominated by activities linked to agriculture, livestock (Sarmiento, 2006; Squier Ephraim, 1870; Wells, 1857) and mining (Euraque, 2001). By the end of the nineteenth century such context remained unaltered featuring social conflict and political instability, limited national markets and restricted opportunities in the global markets (Bendel, 1993; D'Ans, 2011).

9.2.2 Late Nineteenth Century and Early Twentieth Century: The Liberal Reform and Immigration

In the late nineteenth century, the Liberal Reform, considered the first development paradigm (Ocampo, 2008; Ocampo and Ros, 2011) implemented in Honduras, was introduced to mitigate political instability and to centralize power around the State (Barahona, 2005, p. 28). At the start of the Liberal Reform, families in dispersed villages subsisted on informal trade exchanges around agricultural and livestock products (Charles, 1890). By 1889, the population reached approximately 300000 inhabitants, yet dispersed in rural areas. Most trade activity continued to be predominantly informal. Marco Aurelio Soto (President of Honduras 1876–83) implemented the reform to foster exports of Honduran products (Bendel, 1993). Natural resources were promoted overseas to attract foreign investment and immigration aiming to boost agricultural exports and mining products (D'Ans, 2011; Stokes, 1947). Such an approach was inspired by processes of industrialization in the United States and Europe, attempting to modernize production and increase exports of primary products (Euraque, 2009). The Liberal Reform sought to diversify production and opened spaces for immigrant families[2] to the new independent country.

The reform allowed the emergence of large local family businesses dedicated to agricultural trade. The Liberal Reform allowed the accumulation of land for intensive agriculture and introduced favourable policies for the agricultural sector (Stokes, 1947; Thorpe, 2002). Some families involved in agricultural and livestock trade managed to accumulate large areas of land, creating large farm-based family businesses (Roscoe et al., 2013). Yet the emergence of local and large farming family businesses was limited to basic and similar products, in sparsely populated areas and with small consumer markets.[3] To further support growth some creole families[4] established *casas comerciales* or trading houses, located in the centre of villages, close to the village hall, church and markets (Cruz Reyes, 1984). These trading houses functioned as establishments for the exchange and commercialization of agricultural produce (Euraque, 2009; Euraque and Aguilar, 2008).

High production costs and the geography of the country made the support for the cultivation of new products very difficult (Barahona, 2005; Euraque, 1991). One of the activities that received most support was the production of non-traditional products such as coffee and the trade of tobacco in the region of Copán by families of Spanish immigrants (D'Ans, 2011). One creole family in particular, the Bueso family, linked to trade in a wide range of merchandise and later to the tobacco trade, founded La Casa Bueso, in 1880 in the city of Santa Rosa de Copan[5] with great success around the commercialization of tobacco.

State intervention aimed to increase foreign capital and the number of immigrants. Immigration was seen as a way to facilitate foreign direct investment, the transfer of technology, an enterprising culture and the possibility of better mix of races (Amaya, 2011, p. 30). State policies fostered the creation of local manufacturing activities by immigrant families.[6] The most desired immigration was from the United States and Europe to develop productive areas in the country (Amaya, 2011, p. 34).

It was during the presidency terms of Luis Bográn (1883–91), Ponciano Leiva (1891–93) and Policarpo Bonilla (1894–99), when immigration was most stimulated. On 1 April 1895, the Law of Immigration was introduced.[7] The Political Constitution enacted in 1895 gave equal civil rights to Hondurans and immigrants (Lemus and Bourgeois, 1897). Foreign investment security was offered, with generous legal and commercial advantages for immigrants in comparison to their countries of origin (Lombard, 1887; Morrison, 1883). It is precisely after the introduction of this law that the highest levels of foreign immigration to Honduras occurred, mainly North American, British, German, French, Italian and later Arabs and Chinese (Amaya, 2011, p. 35). Immigrants settled mostly around the export areas of the country. Yet Arab and Palestinian immigration dominated the end of the nineteenth century,[8] with immigrants settling mostly on the productive northern coast of Honduras (Euraque, 1997).

In the early twentieth century, Honduras was promoted as the country of greatest natural wealth in Central America with clear advantages such as low labour costs, diversity in agriculture, trade and mining, particularly emphasizing the northern and central areas of the country (Scott, 1909). Immigration from the United States and Europe was the most sought after by the State (Sánchez Alonso, 2007), reaching significant levels in industry and trade (Euraque, 2001). In 1906, another Immigration reform was introduced by the State, fuelling immigration during the first three decades of the twentieth century. This law complemented a parallel productive process, the growing banana production on the northern, or Atlantic, coast of Honduras (Euraque, 2001). By 1911, the participation of European families (mainly from Germany, Italy and France) is significant in the lists of trading, manufacturing and distribution companies, particularly in the northern area of the country (Fletes, 1911). By this time the primary Honduran export produce was banana, coffee, wood, gold and silver. Imports came directly from the countries of origin of European immigrants (Koebel, 1917). State interventions to promote immigration (Sánchez Alonso, 2007) and support of new export products influenced the emergence of immigrant family businesses in specific geographical areas.

In summary, the Liberal Reform allowed Honduras to join the global economy in the late nineteenth and early twentieth centuries with significant influence in the emergence and development of family businesses. Early policies helped some local creole families to develop agricultural and trading enterprises, particularly in the more sparsely populated areas of the country. Nevertheless, the eagerness to establish the Liberal Reform emphasized foreign investment and immigration in the north of the country, which led to the emergence of immigrant-based family businesses, yet isolated many developing creole family businesses from the areas of rapid economic growth (with a few exceptions[9]). The growth of banana exports led to the next period in Honduran history relevant for the development of large family businesses.

9.2.3 The Banana Enclave (1912–29)

The banana enclave, meaning the establishment of a State within a State, occurred due to the State turning on foreign investment to address the lack of resources for national development (D'Ans, 2011). During the first three decades of the twentieth century, the influence of companies dedicated to the cultivation and export of bananas was substantial due to large concessions given by the State in exchange for foreign capital investment in national development. Gradually these transnational companies dominated the political and economic landscape of the country becoming first a monopoly and then an oligopoly (Garcia Buchard, 1997; Striffler and Moberg, 2003). These companies introduced various institutions and instruments, such as banks and own currency linked to the rapid development of the northern area of the country and separated from State control.[10] The focus by the State in the northern area of the country meant limited investment or support policies in other regions where established family businesses were growing.[11]

In 1914, the First World War broke out in Europe. This did not have many economic repercussions in Honduras[12] in contrast to other countries (Ocampo, 2008) yet fuelled immigration (Amaya, 2006, 2011). Jewish immigration, although small relative to other countries of origin, increased after the First World War as a consequence of the economic crisis in Europe.[13] European immigration at this time originated mainly from Poland, Romania and Russia, related to mining extraction and banana exports (Amaya, 2011).

By 1918, the greatest percentage of immigrants, who eventually established family businesses, was of Arab or Palestinian origin (Amaya, 2006). The settlement pattern of the Arabs and Palestinians was from the very beginning very linked to the transnational companies. The Arab immigration originally aspired to the accumulation of resources and envisioned the return to the country of origin.[14] This aspiration was, in some cases, cultivated in the following generation.[15] The Arab immigrants organized themselves around 'patriarchs' who concentrated information, influence and resources among people of the same ethnic group and ensured solidarity among their members (Amaya, 2006).

In the 1920s, national exports relied mostly on bananas.[16] Although members of some families linked to the State[17] managed to become minority shareholders of companies related to the banana industry, the few commercial opportunities allowed by transnational companies were quickly grasped by immigrant families with knowledge in local and international trade and with ethnic networks providing information and resources to exploit them (Euraque, 2001). This thwarted the already scant participation of local creole families (Leyva, 2000, p. 42) to the extent that the elite landowning local Honduran families, who had formed businesses in previous periods in rural areas, did not have the slightest control over the cultivation, processing and export of the only product able to provide them with a niche in the global market (Euraque, 1991, p. 9).

As immigrant-based family businesses grew, the local perception of immigration to the country was characterized mainly by animosity, particularly towards the 'Arabs'. Local business families linked to the government pressured the then President Vicente Mejía Colindres (1929–33) to enact a new immigration law in 1929, which, in contrast to previous ones, was characterized by xenophobia and racism (Amaya, 2006). These laws limited the arrival of 'Arabs' and demanded greater contribution of capital for trade activities further encouraging the immigration of 'white' Europeans and North Americans. To counteract the effects of the new immigration laws, the Arab immigrant families diversified their investments, applied their know-how and turned to ethnical support practices.[18] This diversification allowed the development of family business groups compared to the approach of business families in rural regions, who lost the opportunity to develop existing capabilities or diversify (Leyva, 2000). The Bueso family was one of the very few that were able to compete with Arabs and Palestinian families for commercial control and turned to novel approaches to diversify their products and businesses.[19]

Thus, the development of the banana enclave encouraged the emergence and development of immigrant-based family businesses, yet limited the development of local family businesses located outside the northern area of the country. While local families could not compete against transnational companies to gain new business opportunities their remaining influence forced the State to condition the influx of immigrants. As a result, existing family businesses started by immigrants and those started in this period were forced to diversify into new areas.

Until 1929, disputes between two transnational banana companies, the Cuyamel Fruit Company and the United Fruit Company, marred the economic and political life of the country in order to control public power and obtain land concessions for expanding banana plantations. Yet such influence was thwarted by the global economic crisis of 1929, which damaged the financial balance of Latin American countries (Ocampo, 2008) including Honduras,[20] and forced the two transnational companies to merge.[21] As transnational banana companies restructured they supported the transition into the longest lasting government in Honduran history (Euraque, 2004).

9.2.4 The Regime of General Tiburcio Carías Andino (1933–48)

The regime of General Tiburcio Carías Andino began in 1933. Through reforms in 1936 and 1939, he continued in power until 1948 due to the crisis originating from the Great Depression and the Second World War (Euraque, 1991). This period was mostly characterized by strong development of much needed national infrastructure (Argueta, 2008), which would facilitate distancing from bananas as the principal export product. In the 1930s, the population reached over one million, but it continued to be predominantly rural. With the decrease in banana exports, support was channelled to areas previously neglected, allowing the economy to remain productive and in a healthy state after the Second World War (Cáceres Rivera and Zelaya Carranza, 2005), which encouraged the development of small family businesses at a national level.[22]

The Second World War resulted in different outcomes for family firms in Honduras. First, it fuelled a new immigration wave (D'Ans, 2011) making this period relevant for the emergence of new family businesses. During this period, mining in the central areas of the country fostered the creation of small manufacturing companies by immigrants (Euraque, 1991, p.26). Jewish immigration found new impetus, as a result of the persecution by the Nazi regime in Germany and the immigration law of 1929 which sought to halt the immigration of Arabs, Chinese and Africans and in return promote the immigration of 'white' Europeans (Amaya, 2011). One of the most exemplary cases of family businesses started by Jewish immigrants is found in the Rosenthal family. By 1929, Yankel Rosenthal arrived in the country and began working as an employee in a company that exported crocodile leather.[23] Eventually he became an employee in a prominent trading house in the north of the country: Casa Barrett,[24] founded by a US immigrant without heirs. In 1934, two Jewish immigrants, Isaac Weizemblüt and Boris Goldstein,[25] appeared in the trade register of northern cities, gradually entered into trade and the start-up of various companies (Amaya, 2011).

Second, the Arab and Palestinian immigrant community, motivated by the xenophobia of the previous period and a new found protection under General Carías Andino,[26] engaged in business diversification, redirecting investments to other sectors of the economy such as tobacco, light manufacturing, textiles and sugar (Amaya, 2006). All these industries prospered in the years after the Great Depression and before and during the Second World War. Furthermore, the development and diversification of creole family businesses was timid in comparison with immigrant families, with a few exceptions (for example, the Bueso family[27]); this is due to passive reaction to opening spaces in the national economy and a continued focus on surplus of agricultural and livestock production.

Finally, as a result of the Second World War several growing family businesses established in previous periods experienced an abrupt demise. Families of German and Italian origin were forced to abandon the country and expropriated of their assets due to the alliance with the United States in the war effort (D'Ans, 2011).

In summary, this period fostered the development of some family businesses due to a clear influence and protection from the State, concentrated in one individual. In contrast to the consolidation phase of some family businesses others saw their demise or stagnation. With the end of the Second World War, the need for a regime was reduced, paving the way for a new period in history.

9.2.5 The Transition to a Developmental State (1949–79)

In the mid twentieth century, Honduras was just coming out of a long regime, State intervention aimed at formalizing economic policy and stimulating industrial diversification to facilitate the transition to what was termed a Developmental State (Barahona, 2005). On 1 January 1949, Juan Manuel Gálvez, War Minister during the General Carías Andino regime and lawyer of a transnational banana company, became president (Barahona, 2005). By 1950, the population reached almost a million and a half inhabitants; yet 69 per cent of the population was still rural and only 20 per cent lived in urban centres with more than 2000 inhabitants (Flores Fonseca, 2010). During Gálvez's presidency, the national banking system was established through the Banco Central de Honduras and the Banco de Fomento.[28] Furthermore, the State introduced a process of industrialization based on substitution of imports (ISI) (Posas and Fontaine, 1980) yet different to, and later than, other countries in the region (Dávila, 2009).

Family businesses started by Arab and Jewish immigrants responded differently to these transitional interventions. The Arab and Palestinian families expanded and took economic advantage of the ISI,[29] investing in the industrial, trade, financial and agricultural sectors (Amaya, 2006, p. 141). The participation of family businesses led by Jewish families was almost non-existent as subsequent generations focused on the growth of existing companies and the preparation of successors abroad.[30]

By 1952, large surviving local family businesses involved in agricultural production continued in the hands of a few dispersed families (Barahona, 2005, p. 200). Creole families, like the Bueso family, supported the growth of existing firms through the incorporation of professional family members.[31] It is during this period that one of the largest family businesses by creole families in Honduras was founded. On 1 September 1951, the Banco de Occidente was established in the city of Santa Rosa de Copán by Manuel Bueso Pineda and Jorge Bueso Arias;[32] joining forces with members of other local families.[33]

After the presidency of Gálvez the State entered into the construction of national capital as a Developmental State (Barahona, 2005). It began with the government of Dr Ramón Villeda Morales (1957–63), followed by the military governments of Oswaldo López Arellano (1963–65, 1965–71, 1972–75) and Juan Alberto Melgar Castro (1975–78).[34] It marked a reorientation towards State functions and State interventions in the economy, including new judicial frameworks created for social relations, and the strengthening of social, economic and political players. The presidency of Villeda Morales introduced the national labour law corresponding to the development of capital.[35] During this period, principally between 1958 and the latter years of the 1970s, the emphasis was on policies of industrialization through substitution of imports and a project of regional economic integration as a paradigm of development (Ocampo and Ros, 2011). By 1975 the export of coffee and livestock would exceeded banana exports.

During military governments in the 1960s, some family businesses were shut down by government intervention.[36] During this period, few local families expanded their businesses,[37] immigrant-based family businesses established in previous periods consolidated their companies and joined forces with local entrepreneurs to defend their interests. It is during this period of collaboration among immigrant and local families that large family businesses in Honduras started their consolidation. The National Association of Industrialists (Asociación Nacional de Industriales, ANDI) was founded (1958) by entrepreneurs involved in the area of textiles, knitwear, beverages and footwear. A decade later (1967), during military governments the Honduran Council of the Private Enterprise (Consejo Hondureño de la Empresa Privada, COHEP) was established, led by entrepreneurs from the northern area of Honduras and oriented towards collaboration with ANDI to support a national plan for the country (Argueta and Posas, 2002). Thus, associations represented the means of national investors, grouping together large family businesses that during this period were facing internal social conflicts and external pressures.[38]

It is in this period when some of the largest family businesses led by Jewish families took shape in Honduras. The Rosenthal family began their major economic expansion through the leadership of Jaime Rosenthal Oliva. Yet, while the Rosenthal family businesses expanded they could still not compete with their Arab counterparts. According to Jaime Rosenthal Oliva, having to confront this situation prompted them to join forces with members of the Arab, Jewish and immigrant communities.[39] By 1975, the Rosenthal family, led by Jaime Rosenthal Oliva, founded Inversiones Continental and began a diversification and consolidation process of the group of family businesses including banking, industry, trade and agricultural activities. At the same time, the Goldstein family, close partners of the Rosenthal family, diversified and became one of the most important economic groups of the country,[40] particularly due to their previous incursion into share ownership of banking institutions and the benefits of national industrialization (Amaya, 2011, p. 108). It should be mentioned that the Goldstein and Rosenthal families also entered national politics, supporting and gradually becoming leaders of various political parties, mainly to protect their family business interests (Amaya, 2011; Becerra, 2011). Although some Jewish immigrants formed associations with local families to launch new businesses, in comparison to the Goldstein and Rosenthal families, the rest of the Jewish immigrant community remained involved in small and medium-sized businesses (Amaya, 2011, p. 123).

At the end of the 1950s new family businesses of Arab and Palestinian immigrants emerged spurred by another process of immigration: the Cuban crisis of 1959. Among the families that arrived were the Atala family who started out in the wood processing sector and gradually penetrated into the financial sector (Romero, 2009, p. 77). Established family businesses started by Arab families consolidated one of the largest family businesses in Honduras. Corporacion Dinant, led by Miguel Facussé Barjum, which started a chemical-based plan in the 1960s, expanded operations into the whole of Central American accumulating 64 per cent of the regional market for household cleaning products (Illescas, 2009, p. 279).

By 1975 the military regimes that ruled the country provided a new infrastructure for the country. The State went on to sponsor the creation of a group of nationally owned companies in sectors such as cement, milk processing, meat packing, sugar mills, flour mills and factories of textile and shoe manufacturing. Such a development caused a considerable impact on the country's external debt that provided the starting platform for the next period in history (Barahona, 2005).

9.2.6 From the Developmental State to the Neoliberal State (1980–2000)

In the last 20 years of the twentieth century, a new paradigm of development was introduced in Honduras: neoliberalism (Ocampo and Ros, 2011). This period is influenced by internal and external factors. First, a democracy monitored by military power due to crisis spurred on by abysmal ideological differences in Central America (Dabène, 1993) and an economic crisis that labelled the 1980s as a 'lost decade': years of paralysis and strong economic shrinkage (Mudrovcic, 2009). The economy had shrunk, the economic crisis triggered an informal economy due to lack of employment, investments were reduced and there was a higher dependency on external sources of capital, technology and aid, which generated a vicious circle of economic deterioration. Several external factors such as an increase in the global price of petrol, protectionist trade policies in developed countries, high interest rates in the international financial markets, as well as a reduction in foreign investment and growing foreign debt exacerbated the situation in the country (Barahona, 2005). Internally, Honduran private businesses had little capacity to support growth and development.

In 1982, at the start of the government of Roberto Suazo Córdova (1982–86), the government opened the national economy, promoted non-traditional exports, controlled the fiscal deficit and divested State-owned companies (Hernández, 1987, p. 105). This process continued during the presidency of Jose Azcona Hoyo (1986–90). Yet, this decade was a conflictive time and the country's economy was in turmoil; few entrepreneurial families managed to sustain and develop their companies.

In the late 1980s, families of Jewish origin grew economically and politically (Amaya, 2011; Becerra, 2011). The Goldstein and Rosenthal families controlled about 40 companies, contributing to a large percentage of financial and industrial national investment (Amaya, 2011). The Grupo Continental, led by Jaime Rosenthal Oliva, managed to expand and consolidate further in different areas of business: financial, agriculture, communications, among others. The Arab and Palestinian descendant community turned into a financial elite, controlling 26.47 per cent of financial investments, higher than the investment of transnational companies (22.51 per cent) of total national financial investment (Flores, 1990, p. 81).

In the last decade of the twentieth century, the greatest challenge for Honduras was economic management. Honduras was then led by Rafael Leonardo Callejas (1990–94), Carlos Roberto Reina (1994–98) and Carlos Roberto Flores Facussé (1998–2002). In comparison to previous decades, the aim was to help the Central American region to integrate efficiently with the international economy, particularly with North America, through an increase in the flow of trade and investments (Segovia, 2006, p. 520). A number of very severe economic measures were introduced[41] with the launch of the Programme for Economic Structural Adjustment. The most important objectives were market liberalization, reduction of inflation and fiscal deficit, reduction of the State's size and the privatization of State companies started in previous periods (Becerra, 2011, p. 305). This phase is similar to development paradigms in Latin America (Dávila, 2009). The economic reforms and the push towards a free market economy allowed new opportunities for family businesses.

Despite what the neoliberal model and the free market could offer, local entrepreneurial families did not achieve the level of competitiveness demanded. Yet, family businesses of immigrant descent, which by this period had both incorporated their ethnic customs and adapted to the local culture (Cranshaw, 1998), were best situated to pursue new opportunities. This can be attributed to various factors. First, compared to immigrant counterparts, the majority of creole large family businesses remained in areas far from State institutions and political participation, which offered guidance on benefits of new reforms. Several families gradually developed their investments in rapidly developing sectors.[42] Institutions such as ANDI and COHEP fiercely defended the interests of associated members with a growing and close link to State institutions (Becerra, 2011). Second, immigrant-based families had knowledge of trade in other areas of the world and access to key information and resources thanks to the ethnic family networks (Euraque, 2001), which allowed them to diversify often as a result of deliberate team effort. Lastly, the preparation of successors by immigrant families in previous periods invigorated existing businesses and opened up the opportunities for new business to be created often as a team effort (Discua Cruz et al., 2012).

At the end of the twentieth century, the largest family companies of Honduras were owned and controlled mostly by descendants of Jewish or Arab and Palestinian immigrants that arrived in the country at the beginning of the century.

9.3 CONCLUSIONS

This chapter has shown that the development of the largest family companies in a country cannot be adequately understood without appreciating the historical processes and the voices of the families behind them. The contribution of this chapter is to present, with a longitudinal focus, elements that show the beginnings and the evolution of the large family companies in Honduras in the twentieth century.

In each of the presented historical phases, we show that State intervention, whether intended to boost the export of traditional or non-traditional agricultural products for most of the twentieth century or sponsoring for a short time models that aimed for industrial diversification (for example, ISI), were crucial for the emergence and development of large family businesses. Furthermore, the influence of transnational companies cannot be overlooked as they influenced further immigration and national development. State intervention (or lack of it) supported reforms intended to increase economic development through foreign investment and immigration. In doing so, State intervention fostered, probably inadvertently, the rapid development of some large family business, while limiting the growth or causing the demise of others. The waves of immigration that had been arriving since the end of the nineteenth century, particularly of Arabs and Palestinians – and later, to a lesser extent of Jewish families, show that these processes also fuel the emergence and development of large family businesses.

In the course of the twentieth century, regardless of the origin of the largest family businesses in Honduras, it is clear that only families that capitalized on resources provided by kinship and ethnic fabric, formed alliances with others, diversified and prepared their successors professionally were able to react to, participate in and even influence the interventions by the State. The results of this study present a challenge to researchers in family business to carry out more in-depth investigation into the impact of global historical processes in the world while at the same time acknowledge contextual State interventions and the complexity of immigration to understand how and why large family businesses develop in a country.

ACKNOWLEDGEMENTS

We are grateful to members of the Rosenthal, Handal Facusse and Bueso families for their invaluable information. To Gina Kawas for facilitating information about the ANDI; postgraduate students at the UNICAH for compiling data; Professor (Ret) Mary Rose, University of Lancaster, for guidance in accessing historical archives of the British Library; and finally Professors Paloma Fernández Pérez and Andrea Lluch for guidance in the development of this chapter.

NOTES

1. Characteristic of most countries in Latin American after independence (Acemoglu et al., 2001).
2. Travel costs and protection was offered (Oquelí, 1980, p. 331).
3. The development of trade was gradual. At the beginning of the twentieth century, what existed was a 'barter market'. Non-traditional agricultural produce, such as cotton, sugar and coconut oil, appeared in the north of the country (D'Ans, 2011).
4. Descendants mainly from immigrants, born in Honduras (D'Ans, 2011).
5. Established by Manuela Cuellar de Bueso and her sons, Julio and Abraham Bueso Cuellar. After her death, and after the youngest brother of Julio and Abraham, Manuel Bueso Cuellar joined the business. It was later named Empresa Bueso y Hermanos. Interview with Jorge Bueso Arias (third generation) and revised by Manuel Bueso (fourth generation) in November 2013.
6. Derivatives of non-traditional cultivations such as tobacco or the fibre extracted from agave. Principally artisan activities by immigrants with small capital (D'Ans, 2011).
7. The first immigration law was enacted in 1866 (Amaya, 2011).
8. Foreigner Registers reported that by 1910, 6117 foreigners were registered, of which 200 were Arab and Palestinian (Amaya, 2006). 'Arabs' included Turks, Lebanese, Syrians and Palestinians (Euraque, 2001).
9. The Bueso family founded a retail shop in San Pedro Sula in 1910. Interview with Jorge Bueso Arias.
10. Two currencies were in circulation: on the northern coast, the dollar; in the rest of the country, silver (pesos). The Banco Atlantida was founded (1913) by the banana company Vaccaro Brothers, later named Standard Fruit Company (Amaya, 2011, p.108). By 1918, the legal currency was the US dollar.
11. Some families strengthened their family businesses: the Bueso family invested in the development of their core business between 1914 and 1917.
12. Banana became the main product for export. Tax revenue increased by more than 15 million bunches of bananas between 1911 and 1920 (D'Ans, 2011).
13. It did not occur as Jewish immigration, but as immigration of individuals of Jewish faith (Amaya, 2011).
14. The majority of Palestinian immigrants were Christians, coming from Bethlehem and its surroundings villages, and they were not, as commonly believed, peasants, but rather sophisticated street peddlers, historically linked to European trade networks long before the nineteenth century (Euraque, 2001, p. 82).
15. Interview with Edgar Handal Facussé, third generation of Arab immigrants in October 2013.
16. By 1923 Honduras was the greatest global exporter of bananas (Arancibia, 2001, p. 40).
17. Family of President Luis Bogran (Euraque, 2001).

18. Interview with Edgar Handal Facussé.
19. In the 1920s, Casa Bueso was established as a North American company with head office in New York, named Bueso Brothers Inc. and incorporated under US law, recognized by the State of Honduras as a legal entity on 12 December 1923 by Government Agreement No. 862. Interview with Jorge Bueso Arias.
20. Banana exports shrank 75 per cent, going from US$23 million in 1929 to US$6 million in the years immediately after the crisis (Barahona, 2005, p. 96). One of the effects of the crisis was the incapacity to pay external debts and as a solution for monetary stability it was decreed in 1930 that the lempira (Lps) would be the national currency (Euraque, 1996).
21. The United Fruit Company merged with the Cuyamel Fruit Company.
22. Local family landowners created new companies related to the cultivation of coffee. Nevertheless, the coffee market came to be controlled by families of Arab immigrants, meaning that local family companies gained little from the benefits of its trade (Euraque, 1991, p. 19).
23. Yankel Rosenthal, in the search for his brother, went from Ecuador to the United States on a banana boat. During a stopover at Puerto Cortés, he was forced to leave the ship. Interview with Yani Rosenthal Hidalgo (3rd generation) in May 2012.
24. Alvin Barret was a North American immigrant who in 1919 founded the company Alvin M. Barrett y Compañía; in 1936 it became Casa Barrett and in 1954, Agencia Barrett. Interview with Jaime Rosenthal Oliva (2nd generation) in October 2013.
25. The former born in Berlin in 1905 and the latter of Polish origin, born in 1909, scribe by profession. The Goldstein family began with a small cobbler's workshop (Amaya, 2011).
26. The result of a strong friendship between Arab patriarchs and General Carias. Interview with Edgar Handal Facussé.
27. The brothers Abraham and Manuel Bueso Pineda (2nd generation) and heirs of Julio Bueso Pineda legally registered Casa Bueso in 1936. Jorge Bueso Arias (born 1919, 3rd generation), studied in England and the United States. In 1946, the sons of Julio Bueso separated from the partnership; the only remaining partners were brothers Abraham and Manuel Bueso Pineda, who focused on reorganizing the original family business.
28. Founded 1 July 1950: nationalization of payment methods and reorientation of monetary, exchange and credit policies. See http://www.bch.hn/historia_bch.php (accessed 15 May 2014).
29. In 1950, the Canahuati family began operations in textile and clothing manufacturing, founding Lovable, a group of family businesses (Interiano, 2011). The Facussé family capitalized Textiles Rio Lindo through the sale of shares to the family. Interview with Enrique Handal Facussé.
30. Yankel Rosenthal becomes partner of Agencia Barret (46 per cent). The Rosenthal family's knowledge of international markets increased through the relationship between Alvin Barrett and Yankel Rosenthal. In this phase, the Rosenthal family was involved in grocery stores and tyres, through the Agencia Barret. The next generation (Jaime Rosenthal Oliva) studied at the Massachusetts Institute of Technology in the United States.
31. In 1951 the lawyer Jorge Bueso Arias, and in 1953 his brother Enrique, joined the tobacco plantation business.
32. Authorized on 30 August 1951, through Agreement No. 500 of the Ministry of Finance and Public Credit.
33. Jorge Bueso Arias, Presidential Speech, http://www.bancocci.hn/mensajepresidente.html (accessed 20 March 2015).
34. The governments of military juntas reached power through coups d'état and the transition to a democratic State (Pozas and Cid, 1980).
35. The Labour Code was passed in 1959, the Law of Agrarian Reform in 1962 and the incorporation of social security in the new Constitution in 1957.
36. Diario La Prensa, founded by Arab and local entrepreneurs together, was closed in 1968

due to criticism made of the military government. As a condition for its reopening, the Rosenthal family were forced to sell their part of the business.

37. In 1961, Casa Bueso supported the introduction of the cultivation of Havana tobacco to Copán for cigars, pioneers being the engineers Héctor and Enrique Bueso Arias, sons of Manuel Bueso Pineda and Lastenia Arias de Bueso. In the 1960s and 1970s, Banco de Occidente had its greatest growth. Interview with Jorge Bueso Arias.
38. This association emerged out of events occurring in the mid 1950s as a response of the industrial sector to the boom of workers associations that after the strike of 1954 and during the regime of Ramón Villeda Morales had increased in strength, and also as a product of the attempts already being made to establish the Central American Common Market (MCCA). Source: Gina Kawas, ANDI.
39. On his return to Honduras from the United States, Jaime Rosenthal Oliva, through Agencia Barrett, become involved in insurance sales for a transnational company. A legal ban prompted the organization of the company Seguros La Continental, which in 1968 became known as Seguros Continental. The founding partners of the company were Alvin Barret, Yankel Rosenthal, Boris Goldstein, José Brandel, Edmond L. Bográn, Yude Canahuati and Antonio Mata.
40. This family managed to build an economic and political emporium. Both Rosenthal and Goldstein families developed strategic alliances in various sectors (Amaya, 2011, p.108).
41. In this decade, the economic figures were grim: inflation in 1990 was 23 per cent, in 1991, 36 per cent and between 1994 and 1996 it remained at 20 per cent (UAT, 1999). Foreign debt increased and unemployment fluctuated between 35 per cent (1993) and 26.5 per cent (1998).
42. BCH, Report on the Maquiladora industry, 2001.

REFERENCES

Acemoglu, D., S. Johnson and J.A. Robinson (2001). 'The colonial origins of comparative development: an empirical investigation'. *American Economic Review* **91** (5), 1369–401.

Alonso, B.S. (2007). 'The other Europeans: immigration into Latin America and the international labour market (1870–1930)'. *Journal of Iberian and Latin American Economic History* **25** (3), 395–426.

Amaya, J. (2006). *Los árabes y palestinos en Honduras (1900–1950)*. Tegucigalpa, Honduras: Editorial Guaymuras.

Amaya, J. (2011). *Los Judíos en Honduras, 2nd edn*. Tegucigalpa, Honduras: Editorial Guaymuras.

Arancibia, C.J. (2001). *Honduras, un estado nacional?*, 3rd edn. Tegucigalpa, Honduras: Editorial Guaymuras.

Argueta, M. (2008). *Tiburcio Carías: Anatomía de una época*. Tegucigalpa, Honduras: Editorial Guaymuras.

Argueta, M. and M. Posas (2002). *Honduras: Visiones históricas de país*. Cuadernos Visión de mi País. Tegucigalpa, Honduras: PNUD.

Barahona, M. (2005). *Honduras en el siglo XX: Una síntesis histórica*. Tegucigalpa, Honduras: Editorial Guaymuras.

BCH (2001). *La Actividad Maquiladora en Honduras 2001*. Reporte del Banco Central de Honduras. Tegucigalpa, http://www.bch.hn/download/maquila/maquila-2001.pdf. (accessed 1 June 2012).

Becerra, L. (2011). *Evolución Histórica de Honduras*, 21st edn. Tegucigalpa, Honduras: Baktun Editorial, Litografía López.

Bendel, P. (1993). 'Honduras'. In D. Nohlen (ed.), *Enciclopedia electoral de Latinoamérica y el Caribe*. San Jose, Costa Rica: IIDH, pp. 398–411.
Cáceres Rivera, M. and S. Zelaya Carranza (2005). 'Honduras. seguridad productiva y crecimiento económico: la función económica del cariato'. *Anuario de Estudios Centroamericanos* **31**, 49–91.
Charles, C. (1890). *Honduras: The Land of Great Depths*. Chicago, IL and New York: Rand, McNally & Company.
Chrisman, J.J., J.H. Chua and P. Sharma (2005). 'Trends and directions in the development of a strategic management theory of the family firm'. *Entrepreneurship Theory and Practice* **31**, 555–75.
Cranshaw, W. (1998). *Las empresas familiares en Honduras*. San Pedro Sula, Honduras: Grafica S. de R.L.
Cruz Reyes, V. (1984). 'La casa solariega del siglo XIX como símbolo de posición social: el caso de la familia Fortin'. *Yaxkin, Revista del Instituto Hondureño de Antropología e Historia (IHAH)* **7** (1), 61–80.
D'Ans, M.A. (2011). *Honduras: Difícil emergencia de una nación, de un estado*, 7th edn. Tegucigalpa, Honduras: Litografía Lopez.
Dabène, O. (1993). 'La invención y remanencia de una crisis: Centroamérica en los años 80'. *Anuario de Estudios Centroamericanos* **19** (2), 25–50.
Dávila, C. (2009). 'Entrepreneurship and cultural values in Latin America, 1850–2000. From modernization and dependency theories toward a business history perspective'. Paper presented at the XV World Economic History Congress, International Economic History Association (IEHA), Utrecht, the Netherlands, August.
Discua Cruz, A.F. (2010). 'Collective perspectives in portfolio entrepreneurship: a study of Honduran family business groups'. *EDAMBA Journal* **8**, 91–105.
Discua Cruz, A.F. and C. Howorth (2008). 'Family business in Honduras: applicability of agency and stewardship theories'. In V. Gupta, N. Levenburg, L. Moore, J. Motwani and T. Schwarz (eds), *Culturally-sensitive Models of Family Business in Latin America*. Hyderabad, India: ICFAI University Press, pp. 222–43.
Discua Cruz, A.F., E. Hamilton and S.L. Jack (2012). 'Understanding entrepreneurial cultures in family businesses: a study of family entrepreneurial teams in Honduras'. *Journal of Family Business Strategy* **3** (3), 147–61.
Euraque, D.A. (1991). '"La Reforma Liberal" en Honduras y la hipótesis de la "Oligarquía Ausente: 1870–1930"'. *Revista de Historia* **23**, 7–56.
Euraque, D.A. (1996). 'La Creación de la Moneda Nacional y el Enclave Bananero en la Costa Caribeña de Honduras: En Busca de una Identidad Étnico-Racial?'. *Yaxkin, Revista del Instituto Hondureno de Antropologia e Historia (IHAH)* **14** (1, 2), 138–50.
Euraque, D.A. (1997). 'The Arab-Jewish economic presence in San Pedro Sula, the industrial capital of Honduras: formative years, 1880s–1930s'. *Immigrants and Minorities* **16** (1–2), 94–124.
Euraque, D.A. (2001). *El capitalismo de San Pedro Sula y la historia política hondureña (1870–1972)*. Tegucigalpa, Honduras: Editorial Guaymuras.
Euraque, D.A. (2004). *Conversaciones históricas con el mestizaje y su identidad nacional en Honduras*. Tegucigalpa, Honduras: Centroeditorial.
Euraque, D.A. (2009). 'El significado del Mesón Casa de los Bueso y el Centro Histórico de Santa Rosa de Copan'. *Yaxkin, Revista del Instituto Hondureño de Antropología e Historia (IHAH)* **25** (1), 121–63.
Euraque, D.A. and J.M. Aguilar (2008). 'Significado historico del pueblo de

Manto, Olancho y la Casa Güell como parte del patrimonio cultural de Honduras'. *Yaxkin, Revista del Instituto Hondureño de Antropología e Historia (IHAH)* **24** (2), 89–101.
Fletes, E. (1911). *Commercial Directory of Honduras, 1911*. Hamburg, Germany: Schröder & Jeve.
Flores, M. (1990). *El capital financiero en Honduras*. Tegucigalpa, Honduras: UNAH.
Flores Fonseca, M.A. (2010). 'Descalzos, sin pan y en petate: preguntas especiales en el censo de población de Honduras de 1950'. *Revista Población y Desarrollo: Argonautas y Caminantes* **6** (6), 14–25.
García Buchard, E. (1997). 'Empresa bananera e intervención política en Costa Rica (1899–1939) y Honduras (1912–1933)'. *Revista de Historia* **35**, 9–41.
Hernández, A. (1987). *El neoliberalismo en Honduras*, 2nd edn. Tegucigalpa, Honduras: Editorial Guaymuras.
Illescas, J. (2009). 'Los grupos de poder y los sectores industrial y agrícola'. In V. Meza, L. Salomón, R. Romero, M. Torres Calderon and J. Illescas Oliva (eds), *Honduras: Poderes Fácticos y Sistema Político*, 3rd edn. Tegucigalpa, Honduras: CEDOH, pp. 241–307.
Interiano, J.R. (2011). *Historia de la maquila en Honduras*. Asociación de Maquiladores de Honduras, San Pedro Sula. http://www.ahm-honduras.com/wp-content/uploads/2011/08/historia-maquila-honduras.pdf (accessed 1 June 2012).
Koebel, W.H. (1917). *Central America: Guatemala, Nicaragua, Costa Rica, Honduras, Panama, and Salvador*. London: T. Fisher Unwin.
Lemus, M. and H.G. Bourgeois (1897). *Breve noticia sobre Honduras: Datos geográficos, estadísticos e informaciones prácticas*. Tegucigalpa, Honduras: Tipografía Nacional.
Leyva, H.M. (2000). *Hacia una dinámica cultural del desarrollo en Honduras*. Tegucigalpa, Honduras: PNUD.
Lombard, T.R. (1887). *The New Honduras: Its Situation, Resources, Opportunities and Prospects, Concisely Stated from Recent Personal Observations*. Chicago, IL and New York: Brentano Publishers.
Morrison, W K. (1883). *Prospectus of the Honduras Colonization and Commercial Co*. California: Honduras Colonization and Commercial Co.
Mudrovcic, M.A. (2009). 'En busca de dos décadas perdidas: la novela latinoamericana de los anos 70 y 80'. *Revista Iberoamericana* **LIX**, 445–68.
Ocampo, J.A. (2008). 'Los paradigmas del desarrollo en la historia latinoamericana'. In O. Altimir, E.V. Iglesias and J.L. Machinea (eds), *Hacia la revisión de los paradigmas del desarrollo en América Latina*. Santiago, Chile: CEPAL and Secretaría General Iberoamericana, pp. 19–57.
Ocampo, J.A. and J. Ros (2011). 'Shifting paradigms in Latin America's economic development'. In J.A. Ocampo and J. Ros (eds), *The Oxford Handbook of Latin American Economics*. Oxford: Oxford University Press, pp. 3–25.
Oquelí, R. (1980). *José Cecilio del Valle*. Tegucigalpa, Honduras: Editorial Universitaria.
Posas, M. and R. Fontaine (1980). 'Honduras at the crossroads'. *Latin American Perspectives* **7** (2–3), 45–56.
Pozas, M. and R.D. Cid (1980). 'Honduras: Los límites del reformismo castrense (1972–1979)'. *Revista Mexicana de Sociología* **42** (2), 607–48.
Romero, R. (2009). 'Los grupos financieros y el poder político'. In V. Meza, L. Salomón, R. Romero, M. Torres Calderon and J. Illescas Oliva (eds), *Honduras:*

Poderes Fácticos y Sistema Político, 3rd edn. Tegucigalpa, Honduras: CEDOH, pp. 55–118.
Roscoe, P., A. Discua Cruz and C. Howorth (2013). 'How does an old firm learn new tricks? A material account of entrepreneurial opportunity'. *Business History* **55** (1), 53–72.
Sánchez Alonso, B. (2007). 'The other Europeans: immigration into Latin America and the international labour market (1870–1930)'. *Revista de Historia Económica* **25** (3), 395–426.
Sarmiento, Jose A. (2006). *Historia de Olancho 1524–1877*, 3rd edn. Tegucigalpa, Honduras: Editorial Guaymuras.
Scott, L.S. (1909). *Honduras: The New el dorado*. New Orleans: J.G. Hauser.
Segovia, A. (2006). 'Integración real y grupos centroamericanos de poder económico: implicaciones para la democracia y el desarrollo regional'. *ECA Estudios Centroamericanos* **61** (691–2), 517–82.
Squier Ephraim, G. (1870). *Honduras: Descriptive, Historical, and Statistical*. London: Trübner & Co.
Stokes, W.S. (1947). 'The land laws of Honduras'. *Agricultural History* **21** (3), 148–54.
Striffler, S. and M. Moberg (2003). *Banana Wars: Power, Production, and History in the Americas*. Durham, NC: Duke University Press.
Thorpe, A. (2002). *Agrarian Modernisation in Honduras*. Lewiston, NY: Edwin Mellon Press.
UAT (1999). *Estudio sobre el gasto en servicios sociales básicos. Iniciativa 20/20. Secretaria de Estado en el Despacho Presidencial*. Resumen Ejecutivo, Tegucigalpa, Honduras, p. i.
Wells, W.V. (1857). *Explorations and Adventures in Honduras, Comprising Sketches of Travel in the Gold Regions of Olancho and a Review of the History and General Resources of Central America*. London: Sampson, Low and Co.

PART IV

Business families between dictatorship and democracy (Spain, Peru, Chile): from narrow regulated markets to the global market

10. Between power and the market: an approach to the historical evolution of large family businesses in Spain in the twentieth century

Paloma Fernández Pérez and Pablo Díaz Morlán*

10.1 INTRODUCTION: A LONG-TERM PERSPECTIVE

Family-controlled businesses dominate Spanish business history, but no official statistics exist, nor have long-term studies using comparable and rigorous methodology ever been done. This chapter is a pioneering contribution, gathering together indicators that allow the documentation of some historical transformations in Spanish family capitalism between the mid twentieth century and early twenty-first century. These transformations are particularly found in organizational structures and growth strategies adapted to technological and political changes and the new opening of markets. We also provide evidence of continuities, such as the predominance of activities related to services and the enduring specialization of some families in industrial sectors like construction and auxiliary industries.

The work is organized chronologically into three significant phases of Spanish economic history: the first third of the twentieth century, with its industrial consolidation and slowing down; the Franco era (1939–75); and the last phase, with crisis, the entry into Europe and accelerated internationalization (1976 until the present). In each phase, we identify the families that have formed the so-called elite of Spanish family capitalism. Also, we provide for each phase the indicators of the evolution of the largest family businesses, be it decline or expansion, analysing the main exogenous and endogenous determinants that would explain why some businesses endure while others end up disappearing or transforming themselves. For the period between the 1960s until the present, the identity of the key names and family businesses comes from a unique historical database with the 232 largest family businesses and groups in Spain (Fernández Pérez, 2013 in http://econpapers.repec.org/paper/ahedtaehe/1307.htm). Qualitative information since the early 1900s are published biographies and monographs, as well as authors' own research.

There are in Spain many publications on family businesses and groups in the export sector, families in finance and in media, and families that have been successful and have survived until today. But are there really so many entrepreneurial families that have survived the twentieth century? What factors explain why, out of the families that controlled the 50 largest groups of the 1960s, only two still have companies ranked among the top businesses in 2010? Why, in the same sector and time period, are there families who stay in the elite and others who retire, decline or fall? Is it due to profiteering, managerial incapacity, family conflicts, end of the natural cycle for the original business, incapacity to cumulate social capital? Are successful families of today the successful families of past times? And for what reasons?

In the following pages, we will try to find answers to these questions, with qualitative and quantitative information for years before the 1960s, and with our sample of the 232 largest family-controlled business and groups in Spain within the 437 largest business and groups of the country in those years.[1] This sample confirms the relevance of this organizational structure in Europe with data for Spain (Fernández Pérez and Colli, 2013).

In this work, and in keeping with the other chapters in this book, we use a flexible definition for the term family business, taking into account the changing life cycle of families and family business (Chrisman et al., 2005). We consider that a company is a family business if the ownership lies with one or more families for more than one generation, and when at least two members of the same family who have total or partial ownership hold a decisive position in strategic management of said business. A major conclusion, in agreement with that of the other chapters, is that in Spanish history, often business families have survived not by maintaining but by selling or reducing ownership of businesses created by founders.

10.2 LARGE FAMILY BUSINESSES IN SPAIN BEFORE THE CIVIL WAR, 1900–36

Catalonia, Basque Country, Madrid and, to a lesser extent, Andalucia, Asturias and Galicia, had the greatest concentration of large family businesses in Spain, which before the Civil War was an agricultural country, barely industrialized, and with an enormous lack of infrastructure and education.

In Catalonia, the years between the end of the nineteenth century and the first third of the twentieth, were an era of boom and crisis for sectors and businesses linked to steam power and the new sectors of electricity, banking and the export of quality consumer goods (Cabana, 2006). Notable was the Comillas-Güell group, established by the Cantabrian Antonio López y López, born in 1818, who after living in Cuba, had returned in 1853 to Spain and founded Antonio López y Compañía, later Compañía Trasatlántica, the largest shipping line in Spain. After that would come Crédito Mercantil, the Hispano Colonial Bank and the Compañía General de Tabacos de Filipinas, as well as participation in the Compañía del Norte. In the final years of his life, his two sons formed part of the executive board of the businesses he had founded, but the early death of his eldest son, Antonio, meant that total responsibility fell on Claudio López Bru. His great achievement was the adaptation of his business conglomerate to the loss of the colonies at the dawn of the twentieth century. When he died without descendants in 1925, the interests of the Comilla group were passed on to his nephews, the Güell López brothers, who in the first third of the century expanded the interests of the group to Morocco and secured a strategic connection with the Ybarra-Zubiría through the Spanish Society of Shipbuilding (Cabana, 2006; Rodrigo y Alharilla, 2001).

The arrival of electricity in the early twentieth century led to the collapse of artisan families like the ones dedicated to the repair of nineteenth-century steam engines, forcing their disappearance or their search for new directions. A paradigmatic case was that of the blacksmith family Roca Soler, from Manlleu, who transformed the old smithy set up by their great-grandfather Ignasi Soler in 1830, into a huge factory of sanitaryware in the 1920s, and became an internationalized business group in the 1970s, and today among the largest Spanish – and global – businesses in its activity sector. Another enterprising family who started out in the first third of the twentieth century was the paper manufacturer Torras Hostench, number two company in the paper sector during the Franco era, no longer active today. Also worth mentioning is the paper manufacturer Miquel, world leaders today, who have managed to retain family control through the generations.

International and internal demand in the early twentieth century was fertile ground for family wine business (the Raventós brothers in Codorniu), for the cotton industry (the Sedó family), the chemical industry (Amadeo Cros, whose business was abruptly cut short with the unexpected death of his two sons before his own death in 1916) and pharmaceuticals

(José Antonio Grifols Roig founded in 1909 the Institute of Central Analysis as a precedent to the family holding company that today is world leader in blood derivative products). The firm of Salvador Andreu was also created in these years, and in the early 1970s would become the third largest pharmaceutical firm in Spain. The manufacture of construction materials, stimulated by industrialization and urbanization, was another big business that in the first third of the twentieth century was developed by Catalan families such as the brothers José María and Manuel Roviralta (Uralita), as well as the families that created the companies that preceded the current FCC and Acciona (Torres, 2011). Another fledgling business was the financial activity of the Recasens brothers, founders of Banco de Cataluña, which along with other banks of the country, won the tender for the oil monopoly in 1928.

In the Basque Country, there was a dense network of family businesses in the province of Guipúzcoa, even though these businesses tended to be smaller in size than the large businesses founded by the Biscay bourgeoisie, who in the twentieth century expanded through mining, steelworks, the maritime sector and shipping, banking, electric power, insurance, construction, chemical industry, cement, paper and other business activities. The leading family group in Biscay in the first third of the twentieth century was the Ybarra- Zubiría clan. The founder, José Antonio Ybarra de los Santos, with his sons Juan María and Gabriel and his son-in-law Cosme Zubiría, reached a position of dominance in the mineral and steel trade in the mid nineteenth century. The alliance between these three, another brother, José María, based in Seville, and the son-in-law of Gabriel, the Catalan engineer José Vilallonga, determined the success of the group in mining, steel and shipping. Although the third and fourth generations had grown in size, mechanisms were introduced to unify share participations and also to unify opinions on the executive board. Tomás Zubiría Ybarra was in charge of the steel business and chairman of Altos Hornos de Vizcaya from 1902, and the Spanish Society of Shipbuilding from 1907. Fernando de Ybarra, Marquis of Arriluce, dedicated himself to the new electricity business and was the most visible of the clan, and of the whole provincial bourgeoisie, in Vizcaya Bank and its subsidiaries, Hidroeléctrica Ibérica and Hidroeléctrica Española, as well as in electrical equipment manufacturing such as in the subsidiaries of Babcock Wilcox and General Eléctrica based in Biscay (Díaz Morlan, 2002).

In the first third of the twentieth century, in the Basque Country, dozens of members of the Ybarra-Zubiría clan married into other families with surnames that were destined to become well known, such as Churruca, Arteche, Oriol or Careaga. Others, such as the Chávarri brothers, managed to join the leading business group by participating with the merger of their

Biscay steelworks to form AHV at the beginning of the century (Alonso Olea, 2005). Ramón de la Sota, with his relatives, the Aznar, created in the 1880s one of the most powerful business groups of the province, with notable positions in shipping, iron ore mining and, from 1900, shipbuilding (Euskalduna) (Torres, 1998). Another family, the Martínez Rivas, sold their inherited businesses to the emporium AHV-SECN just after the First World War and at a very good price (Díaz Morlán, 2004, 2005). Finally, the first third of the twentieth century saw the rise and fall of the family group Echevarrieta, victim of an ambitious diversification strategy that dragged it to its ruin in the 1930s, and caused its disappearance from the Biscay and national business elite (Díaz Morlán, 1999a, 1999b). The de Sota group also did not cope well in the crisis that began in 1929, being forced to close its Sagunto steelworks and deal with the death of its founder, Ramón, in August 1936. Finally, at the outbreak of the Civil War, it was the extended nucleus of the Ybarra-Zubiría clan that emerged the winners among the Biscay elite.

The highest concentration of large family groups involved in finance, construction, energy and the most capital intensive industries was to be found in Madrid. Prominent was the Urquijo family group, one of the most powerful in Spain until the early 1980s, which in the early twentieth century was led by the nephew of the founder, Juan Manuel Urquijo Urrutia, and his three sons, Estanislao, Juan Manuel and Luis Urquijo Ussía, operating through the banking firm Urquijo y Compañía. After the death of their father, in 1918 the three brothers transformed the family partnership into the Banco Urquijo, and three years later gave positions on the executive board to their brothers-in-law Francisco de Cubas and Juan Tomás Gandarias. They participated in all strategic sectors of the Spanish economy, whereby all three brothers, as well as the two brothers-in-law and their right-hand man, Valentín Ruiz Senén, held positions of resposibility in dozens of large companies, among them MZA and Norte Railways, the electrical companies Chade and Unión Eléctrica Madrileña, the steelworks Altos Hornos de Vizcaya and Duro Felguera, the Spanish Society of Shipbuilding (together with the Comillas-Güell and Ybarra-Zubiría groups), and the monopolies of the Compañía Arrendataria de Tabacos (since 1887, and also after its conversion into Tabacalera in 1945), the Compañía Telefónica Nacional de España and oil (Campsa, since 1928). Very close to the Urquijo and in alliance with them were the brothers Francisco and José Luis Ussía Cubas, who were behind the founding of the Banco Central and present at the creation of the Banco de Crédito Industrial. Without doubt, the Urquijo group and its relatives, Gandarias and Ussía, were the largest Spanish family group in the first third of the twentieth century (Díaz Hernández, 1998; Puig and Torres, 2008).

The expansion of Madrid at the beginning of the century consolidated the wealth of some old family groups such as the two Figueroa Torres brothers. Both Gonzalo and Álvaro, Count of Romanones, invested in Moroccan mining, forestry (for resin and timber), wineries, railways, and the list goes on, using the extensive agricultural and mining properties that they had inherited from their father, the Marquis of Villamejor, considered one of the wealthiest men in Spain (Bahamonde and Otero, 1989; Moreno Luzón, 1988; Parejo, 2011). The Mahou family were prominent in the brewing industry. Originally from Zaragoza, the second generation of the Escoriaza clan arrived in Madrid in the first third of the twentieth century under the initiative of the brothers Nicolás and Manuel, who invested in railway rolling stock and tram and railway companies, and participated in the boom of urban public services, positioning themselves close to the sphere of influence of the Banco Urquijo. Also with one foot in Aragon and the other in Madrid was the Lozano family group, creators of the sugar producers Azucarera del Ebro, one of the three oligopolistic firms of the sector, and also present in Eléctricas Reunidas de Zaragoza and companies of gas, railway, cement and banking (Germán, 2009; Parejo, 2011; Torres, 2000).

In Andalucia, the five Ybarra González brothers, sons of José María Ybarra from Bilbao who was in Seville around 1843, took advantage, through the Casa Ybarra, of the connection with their Basque cousins, based around the shipping line of the same name, by investing in mines and extensive agricultural projects that led to the development of a powerful agri-food industry still active today (Díaz Morlán, 2002; Sierra Alonso, 1992; Ybarra, 2002). The Osborne group was also prominent in the agri-food sector (wines, La Cruz del Campo brewery), remaining a family venture until its acquisition by a foreign group in the 1990s (Parejo, 2011). Notable in the financial sector were the three brothers from Granada, Manuel, José María and Miguel Rodríguez-Acosta, whose eponymous bank was in the family's hands until being taken over by Banco Central in 1946 (Titos Fernández, 2004).

In Galicia, the initiatives of Pedro Barrié de la Maza were prominent; he was part of the family group that controlled the financial institution Sobrinos de José Pastor (Banco Pastor in 1925), after which he got involved, together with a cousin of his father, in the fishing and electrical industry and, after the war, founded the shipyard Astilleros del Noroeste (Astano) and Fuerzas Eléctricas del Noroeste (Fenosa) (Carmona, 2006). In Asturias, the Herrero family, dedicated almost exclusively to banking since the nineteenth century, became involved, under the direction of the three Herrero Vázquez brothers, in the coal business and subsequently took part in the founding of mining-steel company Duro-Felguera, in 1902. Ten years later the business became a public limited company with the name Banco Herrero, it remained under family control and was passed on to the next generation, represented by Ignacio Herrero de Collantes, who will be mentioned again in the next phase, becoming as he did a central figure in Spanish business (Anes and Otazu, 1987; Torres, 2000).

This apex of Spanish family capitalism in the first third of the twentieth century was, in reality, no more than a tiny fraction of the network of family businesses that controlled the majority of economic activities in Spain. The canning sector has not been mentioned, dominated by family businesses all along the Cantabrian coast (Carmona, 2011); nor the already developed industrial districts in the provinces of Valencia and Alicante that encompassed most of the industrial activity in the area and continued to do so until the next phases (Vidal, 2005).

10.3 LARGE FAMILY BUSINESSES IN THE FRANCO ERA (1939–75)

The Civil War changed the rules of the game, and the effect of the subsequent dictatorship – as with other countries dealt with in this book that had dictators like Chile or Peru – was to seriously undermine the survival of some families but also make possible the rise of others, old and new.

In 1964, among the top 42 large businesses controlled by families in Spain, 12 were in Barcelona, seven in Madrid, seven is Biscay, five in Asturias and the rest dispersed over a few other provinces. However, when we examine the 20 largest family businesses and groups in the country, six were in Biscay, five in Madrid and three in Asturias.

The Catalan family groups and companies, with head offices in Catalonia, did not form part of the elite of family capitalism during the Franco era, and, in fact, until the consolidation of the autonomic regional governments and the entry into Europe in the mid 1980s were not visible at all in the top 20. Until 1989, family businesses and groups located in the Basque Country and Madrid had the highest percentage of employment and own resources among the largest family businesses and groups of the country. They were close to banking and utilities, and to power, during the Franco dictatorship.[2]

The two steel companies that were at the top of the ranking of Spanish family business elite by employment in 1964 were Duro Felguera and Altos Hornos de Vizcaya, represented by the Urquijo group, which also appears in Hulleras del Turón and in the Basconia, the latter through the Gandarias family. Four companies in the top 20 by number of workers in 1964 had members of the Urquijo group in executive positions or as part of the ownership organization; they had remained in the electrical companies founded earlier and entered in the shipping line business through an alliance with the Aznar family. The Urquijo Ussía brothers had paid a high price in the Civil War: three of Estanislao's sons and one of Luis's died in the struggle. The professionalization of management that had been developed in the previous phase continued during francoism and the control of the bank at this time was in the hands of Juan Lladó Sánchez-Blanco, under whose direction the Banco Urquijo focused increasingly on industry and became the top private business group in the country. However, and despite the fact that in 1976 it was still in number four position among family groups, it could not survive the industrial crisis of the 1970s and ended up being taken over in 1983 (Puig and Torres, 2008; Torres, 2000).

Three other outstanding family groups leading Spanish businesses before the war, the Comillas, the Ybarra-Zubiria and the Sota Aznar groups, suffered and declined with the abrupt political change of Franco dictatorship. The second Marquis of Comillas had died in 1925 and the business conglomerate founded by Antonio López in the nineteenth century did not survive the Franco era as an independent and unified group. The Banco Hispano Colonial was taken over by Banco Central in 1950 and the rest of the businesses passed into public hands. The Güell family, heirs to the interests of the Comilla group, continued with the Asland cement plant and, although Count Güell went into exile after the Civil War, his son, Juan Claudio Güell Churruca, kept the entrepreneurial spirit of the family alive by founding the Banco Atlántico in 1946 and a series of new companies in the emerging sectors of oil and tourism. But still they remained outside the family group elite (Cabana, 2006; Rodrigo y Alharilla, 2001; Torres, 2000).

The third family of the leading triangle before the Civil War, Ybarra-Zubiría, suffered tragically in the war. The three sons of the Count of Zubiría were murdered in June 1937. The Marquis of Arriluce, together with his son and two nephews, was murdered in the massacre on the prison ship *Cabo Quilates* in 1936. Many other members of the family, up to 40, died on the front or in the rearguard. Despite the terrible losses, this enormous clan forms part of the business that is ranked second among the largest family businesses in 1964, AHV, and also with the number ten, La Papelera Española (Lape), since Alfonso Churruca Calbetón is directly related to them (married to a Zubiría). In Lape, Churruca coincided with the Aresti family, heirs of Enrique de Aresti y Torre, one of the founders of the firm of paper manufacturers that would stay among the top business groups during the Franco period, although its family-controlled status was lost in the crisis of the 1970s (Valdaliso, 2002a). The surviving members of the Ybarra family, especially Javier Ybarra Bergé and Luis María Ybarra

Oriol, kept their positions of responsibility in companies that were central to the national economic life in finance and energy in the 1940s and 1950s, such as the Banco de Vizcaya and the electricity companies Iberduero and Hidroeléctrica, which had few employees when compared to industrial and mining companies, but high turnover and capital. Later, in the 1960s, Fernando Ybarra López-Dóriga joined the executive board. In the following decade, it was the turn of Emilio and Santiago Ybarra Churruca, sons of the murdered Santiago Ybarra Zapata de Calatayud (Díaz Morlán, 2002).

The future of the de Sota and Aznar group was also cut short by the Civil War. The son and heir of Ramón de la Sota was forced into exile because of the family's nationalist connection. The heirs of Eduardo Aznar, royalists and also francoists, took the place of their relatives in the businesses of the group in such a way that the shipping line Sota y Aznar became converted to the shipping line Aznar and the shipyard Euskalduna (ranked third by number of workers in 1964) and the remaining businesses came under their control (Valdaliso, 2002b, 2006).

The most powerful families in the first third of the twentieth century that were still part of the Spanish business elite in 1964 through their industrial and mining companies (seven out of 20 by number of workers) kept their top positions until the early 1970s due to their control of capital-intensive businesses (banks, iron and steel and shipbuilding companies). They inevitably lost their dominance due to the 1970s crisis that caused the majority of industrial firms to disappear from among the largest ranked companies.

The loss of dominance of the mining, steel and iron companies also affected some families that were either from Asturias or had wide-ranging interests in the economy there, such as the Figaredo, Heredia, Rivière, Pidal and Tartière, related to the Fábrica de Mieres, Santa Bárbara, Minas de Langreo y Siero, Duro Felguera and Uninsa, who were among the largest family groups in 1964 and 1969 but no longer there in 1976. The same happened with the Biscay family Echevarría, in the steel industry, who were in seventh position in 1964 by number of employees, through S.A. Echevarría.

These formally powerful families began to be replaced by others with roots in the pre-civil war era. In 1969, we find the Lozana family from Aragon with its sugar company Ebro, and some descendants of the chemical group Cros, as well as the Catalan paper manufacturers Torras Hostench. The Cantabrian group Quijano remained thanks to its steel factory Nueva Montaña Quijano, but lost its place in the elite with the fall of the industry and had disappeared completely by 1976. Another Cantabrian group, Botín, became increasingly important and managed to place Banco de Santander ahead of its old competitors, the Vizcaya and Urquijo Banks, and had an extraordinary future ahead (Martin Aceña, 2007). Continuing in the banking sector, another surname with roots in pre-war companies is that of Herrero, represented during the Franco era by Ignacio Herrero de Collantes, who raised the profile of the bank whose chairmanship he had inherited and, at the same time, acted as chairman of Hidroeléctrica del Cantábrico, the Banco Hispano Americano, Tabacalera and Unión Española de Explosivos. We can also find once again, with his business centred on a bank founded before the Civil War, Pedro Barrié de la Maza, who died without descendants (Carmona, 2006). Still within the banking sector, four Catalan brothers should be mentioned: Félix, Pedro, Luis and Javier Valls-Taverner, who, since joining Banco Popular in the 1950s through their cousin Félix Millet and their uncle Pedro Arnó, had climbed to seventh position in the ranking of family groups in 1969 and sixth in 1976, managing to maintain their independence and family-owned status as a financial institution almost until the present day (Tortella et al., 2011).

During the Franco period, renowned entrepreneurs converted their business groups into family businesses when their heirs joined the management and the organizations of ownership representation. The most famous of these was without doubt Juan March Ordinas. After his death in 1962, two sons replaced him, through the shipping line Transmediterránea and the Banca March, the latter also present in the business elite of 1976 together with Uralita, who acquired the Roviralta brothers in the 1960s (Cabrera, 2011).[3] The entry of descendants to the holding company comprising more than 50 companies, Ildefonso Fierro, was already a reality after the death of the founder in 1961 (monopolies in matches and tobacco, Banco Ibérico, present in the ranking of large family businesses in 1969 and 1976) (San Román, 2011).[4]

After the Stabilization Plan of 1959, the golden age of growth favoured opportunities for new entrepreneurs and their families. The expansion of the middle classes and the general increase in purchasing power of the Spanish population in the 1960s stimulated the appearance of numerous business opportunities in retail trade, and consumer good distribution, for perishable as well as durable products. This was the case for the family firms Galerías Preciados, El Corte Inglés and El Águila. In 1969, Galerías Preciados already occupied 13th position in the ranking of greatest family businesses in the country, rising to seventh in 1976, while El Corte Inglés in this latter year rose to second position within Spanish family groups. Curiously, the origin of both of these companies and groups is with Spaniards who had been in the Americas and had brought back new organizational and business ideas in the distribution sector.

Entrepreneurship resulting from a mixture of ideas from immigrants was also a very common feature in the commercial distribution sector of various Latin American countries in the twentieth century. In the case of Galerías Preciados, José (Pepín) Fernández Rodríguez transferred the model of the department store El Encanto, of La Havana, where he had worked until he was forty (he opened his first shop in Madrid in 1934 and nine years later the first department store with Galerías Preciados). The founder of El Corte Inglés, Ramón Areces, had a career path in some ways parallel to that of his fellow countryman, Fernández: his uncle was manager of the Cuban department store El Encanto, where he too had had his first professional experience before returning to Spain and becoming concessionary of a tailor shop in Madrid called El Corte Inglés. In hard competition with Galerías Preciados, El Corte Inglés ended up overtaking Fernández's company thanks to capital contributed by his uncle and his opting for diversification. Areces died without offspring in 1989, but the management of the family group had already been in the hands of his nephew, Isidoro Álvarez, for quite a number of years (Toboso, 2000). Another important family group during the Franco years was created by the businessman Augusto Comas y Blanco, founder in 1900 of the brewery El Águila, whose success catapulted it to 12th position in 1976, years before being sold to the foreign group Heineken (Gutiérrez, 1997).

A singular case was a new family holding created right after the Stabilization Plan of 1959: Rumasa. In contrast to the three previously mentioned entrepreneurs, who were already well known before the outbreak of the Civil War, José María Ruiz Mateos was a newcomer, whose holding company, Rumasa, would very quickly climb to the top of Spanish family businesses in 1976. Rumasa, created in 1961 when its founder was thirty, reached a total of 65000 workers in the 1970s thanks to a strategy of acquiring and relaunching businesses with financial troubles in the sectors of wine production, hotel and catering, laboratories, and finance. He had shares in more than 200 companies, some as important as Galerías Preciados, Laboratorios Hubber and Loewe. He was expropriated in 1983 (Tamames, 1995).

In the expansive decade of the 1960s, construction and its auxiliary industries opened up opportunities for families that had managed businesses in this sector before the war, like Huarte. Also, for new families who would start very enduring businesses (Aguirre with Agromán, and Entrecanales). Some of them still lead the sector and are global companies, like Entrecanales. The engineer José Entrecanales Ibarra, together with Manuel Távora, created his construction company in 1931. Távora died in 1940 and Entrecanales was in charge until 1969, when he left the management of the company to his two sons. Business continuity and skilled management, together with the boom in civil engineering and construction in the 1990s, has allowed it to remain active until the present day (Nesco that since 1997 has channelled the construction activities of the Acciona group; the current CEO is José Manuel Entrecanales, part of the third generation). Agromán, for its part, was created in 1927 by Alejandro San Román and José María Aguirre Gonzalo. In the 1960s and 1970s it was the number one construction company in the country and currently forms part of the Ferrovial company.

Félix Huarte had founded Huarte y Compañía before the war, in 1931 in Navarra, and became family-controlled in the 1940s when his sons joined. During the Franco period, it was a group composed of more than 60 companies when its founder retired in 1963, eight years before his death. In the hands of this new generation, however, the family holding company could not maintain its positions and in the 1990s would be part of the merger directed by Juan Miguel Villar Mir, which formed the origins of another family-controlled construction group: the OHL group.

In the cement industry, the Serratosa family, who had founded a factory of artificial cement in Valencia in 1917, took advantage of the climate of growth. By 1976, José Serratosa Nadal and his three sons were basing their expansion on export and horizontal integration, with backing from Banesto (García Ruiz, 2007; Torres, 2000, 2009a). Above them in the ranking of Spanish family business elite that year was the company Asland, created by the Güell family in the previous phase.

10.4 POLITICAL TRANSITION, ECONOMIC CRISIS AND INTERNATIONALIZATION, 1975–2010

The death of Franco and the transition towards the new democratic regime coincided with the arrival in Spain of the economic crisis that had been spreading through the whole of the developed industrial world since the oil price increase in 1973 and 1974. It was a period of rupture that profoundly affected the main family groups. The statistical data gathered for 1976 and 1986 illustrates how traditional industry (textile, mining, steel, iron, shipbuilding) was becoming less important, as were the sectors that had been sheltered under the protectionism of the previous phase. In contrast, there was a strengthening of business groups involved in distribution, food and activities related to construction, including cement and bathroom equipment. In 1989, 1998, 2005 and 2010, the data clearly confirms the tendency of the most powerful family groups to concentrate on distribution, food and construction. Other groups also joined them, those that had benefited from the restructuring of traditional industries and of newer sectors like fashion, hotel and catering, gambling and transport.

The opening up towards Europe after joining the European Economic Community (EEC) in 1986 determined the evolution and growth of businesses, depending on their degree of involvement in exports and their capacity to compete against foreign groups in the internal market; and the housing boom between 1996 and 2008 stimulated family groups dedicated to construction to fight with distributors for top positions in the ranking.

Financial institutions disappeared from the elite of family business because banks were being eliminated, either through bankruptcy (the case of Urquijo, whose assets were passed on to March and then to a foreign group) or through takeovers when bankruptcy was imminent (the case of Ibérico), or because huge expansion had made them lose their family-controlled status, and they were now controlled by professional managers (the case of BBVA and, with small differences, Santander). Thus, the banking industry, so much a central part of family business elite before the transition, became sidelined ten years later, although the exceptions should be mentioned: Banco Popular and, to a certain extent, Emilio Botín's Santander (Martín Aceña, 2007; Tortella et al., 2011). The electrical firms continued to provide a safe and profitable haven for some old names from previous phases (Ybarra, Oriol) but the managerial character of these companies limited the influence of the family members on executive boards, rarely allowing them to be heard.

The three activity sectors of distribution, food and construction comprised the 20 largest family-controlled businesses and groups of Spain in the years for which we have elaborated rankings of top family businesses: 1986, 1989, 1998, 2005 and 2010. The expropriation and subsequent break-up of Rumasa put El Corte Inglés in first position in the ranking of family groups in 1986 and 25 years later, it was still there. In second place in 2010, behind the business directed by Isidoro Álvarez, was Mercadona, having had success with the launch of its own brand, cheap but good quality thanks to long-term agreements with leading suppliers from each food sector. Behind this supermarket emporium is Juan Roig and, to a lesser degree, his brother Fernando; when they inherited the business from their father after its founding in 1981, it comprised only eight supermarkets, all of them in the city of Valencia; 30 years later, Mercadona had 1400 establishments and 70000 workers, and covers 13.5 per cent of Spain's distribution industry (Blanco and Gutiérrez, 2008). Another important distribution company is Caprabo, founded in 1959 by three Catalan families – Carbó, Prat and Botet, later to be joined by Elías. It opened its first supermarket in Barcelona, copying the North American model of self-service and free customer choice, at that time a concept practically unknown in Spain. After almost half a century of expansion, it was one of the main family groups in 2005 with 400 establishments and more than 10 000 workers, but in 2010 it no longer appeared in the ranking after having lost a good part of its family status with its 75 per cent acquisition in 2007 by Eroski (Cabana, 2006). The three cited businesses, El Corte Inglés, Mercadona and Caprabo, have all known how to adapt, each in their own way, to changes brought about by the arrival of competition from the big French hypermarkets and the aggressive strategies of the powerful foreign groups since Spain joined the EEC and the markets were liberalized (Maixé-Altés, 2009).

In close proximity to the sector of distribution is the food sector, with a strong family tradition in Spain. In 1986, no less than three of the 14 main family groups were active in the brewing sector, although they would all end up in foreign hands a few years later: Comas y Blanco's El Águila, Osborne's La Cruz del Campo and Damm.[5] Beer aside, in 1989 the importance of the agri-food sector in Spain was clearly seen in the ranking of the 20 principal family groups, with six of them present in that year: Pescanova, Panrico, Campofrío, Pascual, Osborne and Nutrexpa. However, in 1998 only two groups remained, Agrolimen and Campofrío, and both would disappear by 2005, when only Ebro Puleva remained among the top 20 family businesses in Spain. The data confirms that the food sector has been one of the favourite areas for acquisitions by foreign multinationals. There are still today some important family-controlled companies in the food sector, but in many cases they are battling with serious financial problems; Pescanova is one example, created in 1960 by the Galician entrepreneur José Fernández López, whose son, Manuel Fernández de Sousa Faro, took over the presidency in 1980 (Carmona, 2006). Panrico, in contrast, created in 1962 by Andrés Costafreda and the Rivera family, reinforced its family status when the second generation of the Costafreda family acquired all shares after the death of the founder in 1998, but finally it was sold in 2005 to the venture capital firm Apax Partners for 900 million euros (Cabana, 2006). Campofrío, a meat processing company created in 1952 in Burgos by José Luis Ballvé, also underwent a complex process of mergers and selling of shares to foreign groups. The policies of alliances and mergers (with Navidul in 2000), and the entry of Smithfield Foods with the acquisition of 22.4 per cent of the capital, finally led to the founding in 2008 of Campofrio Food Group (Moreno, 2009).

The second generation of the Pascual family also kept control of the group after the death of its founder, Tomás Pascual Sanz, from Burgos, in 2006; a similar case is the Osborne family whose group, after a 200-year history, still retains family status, being in the hands of Tomás Osborne Gamero-Cívico and his cousin, Ignacio Osborne Cólogan (Torres, 2000).

The ownership of the Catalan Nutrexpa also continues in the hands of the founding family (Javier Ventura and the Ferrero Jordi brothers in equal parts), even though it has undergone an intense process of management professionalization, putting it into outside hands, and has diversified its lines of business. In Agrolimen, for its part, 100 per cent of ownership is in the hands of the six Carulla brothers, sons of the founder, who are active in the management, despite half a century ago giving executive positions to professionals outside the family (contracting Juan Cornudella as CEO) (Cabana, 2006).[6] Ebro Puleva, lastly, is a unique case. Coming from the merger in 2000 of Azucarera Ebro and the dairy company Puleva, it has recently let go of its traditional sections, that is, sugar and milk, but is structuring a food group with the Hernández family holding 15 per cent of the shares, as well as position of chairman, thus allowing it to still claim a certain amount of status as a family firm.

Despite many families specialized in food having retained their family status, or at least not abandoned it completely, they have been replaced in the elite of Spanish family capitalism by those dedicated to construction and auxiliary industries: as many as nine are among the main family groups in the ranking of 2005, and ten in 2010, no doubt a reflection of the boom in property development and construction that Spain underwent between 1996 and 2008. Among the veterans, the Roca family is prominent, originating from the first phase and converted at the turn of the century into the second group worldwide specialized in the bathroom equipment sector. Ownership continues in family hands but the management has been professionalized since the 1970s with outsiders in management (Fernández Pérez, 2006). The third generation of the Serratosa family, represented by Emilio Serratosa Ridaura, sold Valenciana de Cementos in 1992 to the Mexican group Cemex. Ten years later, he and his sons Javier and Gonzalo took over the control of Uralita through their financial vehicle corporation Nefinsa. Another group already mentioned is that of the Entrecanales family, who through Nesco are majority owners of the construction company Acciona, the result of the merger in 1997 of Entrecanales y Távora with Cubiertas y Mzov, and whose members dominate the executive board and occupy positions of greatest reponsibility. Their huge international expansion and their diversification and specialization in infrastructures, energy and water management has meant they could avoid excessive exposure to the risks in the Spanish construction industry and property market. Also remaining among the top positions is the Ferrovial group, founded by the del Pino family in 1952. In the 1990s it took over the ailing Agroman, linked to Banesto, and continued with its international expansion, specializing in the construction and management of airports and highways worldwide. Four offspring of the founder remain on the executive board and one of them, Rafael del Pino Calvo-Sotelo, has been chairman of the group since 2000.[7]

Among the new groups, the case of Juan Miguel Villar Mir is one of the most interesting. After being chairman of Altos Hornos de Vizcaya, he bought from his ex-company its old and failing subsidiary, Obrascón, for one peseta in 1985 when he was fifty-five years old, and from this moment on the rise was unstoppable, with the merger with the Navarra companies Huarte and Laín to form OHL, of which 51 per cent belonged to the Villar Mir Group. The entry of his sons into executive positions has catapulted the group into the elite of family businesses, in such a way that in 2010, 25 years after becoming an entrepreneur, Villar Mir dominated three out of the top 20 businesses, thanks to minimizing the exposure to the risks of property development and opting for international expansion, with more than 50 subsidiaries located around the world (Ximénez de Embún, 2005). For its part, the ownership of the construction group Fomento de Construcciones y Contratas (FCC), which remains among the highest ranked family groups, passed into the hands of the two Koplowitz sisters, Esther and Alicia, on the death of their father. During the 1970s and 1980s, the company managed to position itself among the top constructors and property developers of the country. Although the company went through total professionalization of management, the family character of FCC remained, until end of 2014, because ownership and control continued partially unified, and Esther's 54 per cent of capital allowed her control of the executive board (Torres, 2009b). The entrance of the Mexican family Slim in the ownership of FCC confirms family control of the group, but now under two families, one the Spanish Koplowitz, the other the Mexican Slim, a sign of new times of globalization of the so-called *multilatinas* studied in Lourdes Casanova's chapter in this volume. Without leaving the construction sector, we must finally mention Abengoa, until 2015 a success story that also began in the post-war years, with its founding in 1941 by the engineers Javier Benjumea and José Manuel Abaurre. After national expansion in the 1960s, Abengoa began in the 1970s to open up to outside markets and in the 1980s formed part of the family business elite, where it is still to be found today, in the sectors of environment and renewable energies (Torres, 2000).

These three sectors aside, there is one case that stands out as almost unique: Inditex. After its ninth position ranking in 1989, it climbed to third place in 2010, ahead of it only El Corte Inglés and Mercadona. The success of Amancio Ortega is based on innovation and the agility to respond to market demands at a moderate price. The first Zara shop opened in 1975 in La Coruña, and 35 years later the group has opened 5500 establishments in more than 400 cities around the world, and has 110000 employees. In the last years, even though the professionalization of management is very advanced (the CEO of the group is Pablo Isla, a professional outside the family), the founder has been preparing the ground for his probable successor, his daughter Marta, to take up an executive position (Blanco and Salgado, 2004).

As with the fashion industry, family business groups have also evolved in the tourism sector. Globalia Corporación Empresarial was founded in 1997 from businesses created by Juan José Hidalgo, who had taken his first steps in the sector in 1965. Halcón Viajes, Air Europa, Travelplan and, since 2003, Viajes Ecuador are some of the iconic family holding companies that have forcefully entered the market of hotel acquisition and management. Iberostar Hoteles y Apartamentos, in turn, is the result of a veteran travel agency that the second generation of the Fluxá family, originally from Mallorca, acquired in 1956.[8]

Also in these years, the boom of gambling, security and communication in the 1980s began to be reflected in the companies that appeared in the ranking: in gambling, Cirsa y Recreativos Franco; in security, Prosegur, created by Herberto Gut in 1976; and in communication – and recently very affected by the crisis caused by new communication channels – Prisa, Planeta, Godó, Vocento (of the Ybarra and the Bergareche families), Zeta (of Asensio, with a brief appearance in the ranking of 1989) and Moll (Editorial Prensa Ibérica) (Cabana, 2006; Fernández Moya, 2012; Parejo, 2011; Torres, 2000).

Family groups are not only prominent in services, but also in industrial activities. One example is Técnicas Reunidas, a group dedicated to engineering, design and construction of big industrial plants, above all oil and gas, having built more than a thousand in its 40-year history; the main shareholders are the Lladó family.[9] In the chemical industry, there are Sarrió and Ercros, the latter the result of the merger between Unión Explosivos Río Tinto and the veteran company Cros, giving rise to the first Spanish chemical company, but now no longer family-owned. In the steel industry, five business groups dedicated to steel appear in the ranking between 1986 and 2010. Two of them in the 1980s: Patricio Echeverría from Guipuzcoa and Laminados Velasco from Biscay. The former took advantage of the restructuring process to concentrate on the manufacture of agricultural machinery, investing heavily abroad.[10] The latter became involved with another private group in 1986 and with the public sector in 1997. The three other powerful steel manufacturing groups with important outside investments were founded between the 1950s and 1960s, but their expansion took place in the 1980s and 1990s, a clear indication of their capacity to survive the metal crisis of the 1970s: Celsa, Gonvarri and Ros Casares. The brothers José María and Francisco Rubiralta founded the

Compañía Española de Laminación (Celsa) in 1967, based on the experience of their father, an iron wholesaler, and it was Francisco who directed the company from then on. Both Francisco and his brother have recently deceased and it is their sons who must deal with the current difficulties in the global steel industry (Cabana, 2006, pp. 719–24; *El Confidencial*, 2 July 2012; *El País*, 21 May 2012; *Expansión*, 18 November 2010; Fernández Pérez, 2003, 2004). At a level below Celsa is the group founded in 1954 by Francisco Ros Casares, dedicated above all to the distribution of steel products. After being partly transferred to other hands, the Ros Casares family recuperated all the capital in 2001 and proceeded with its expansion in Spain. Currently, just as with Celsa, it is facing difficulties in dealing with the decline in the market and debt accumulation (*El País*, 4 May 2012).[11] The Gonvarri group, lastly, was created by an entrepreneur from Burgos, Francisco Riberas Pampliega, who began with a first production plant in 1958 and expanded into the international market in the 1990s, opening installations in Brazil, Italy, Morocco and Portugal. At the same time, he took advantage of the boom in the automotive sector in Spain to become involved in component manufacture, taking over a bankrupt business, Gestamp Automoción, and converting it into market leader. His two sons are currently in charge of the group's management, and have been since before the death of their father in 2010; the group has recently entered the sector of renewable energy (*Diario de Burgos*, 5 April 2010; *El País*, 6 April 2010; *Expansión*, 23 February 2011).

The automotive industry was the developmental powerhouse of Spain during the Franco years, dominated by foreign multinationals but fuelling powerful national family groups (and also groups in other countries, such as Argentina, through auxiliary industries). One of these, Irausa, founded by Avelino Antolín Toledano together with his brother José in the late 1950s, subsequently reached an agreement with a German group to manufacture automobile parts. Avelino died in 1995 and his brother José, together with his nephew, took over control, continuing with a big international expansion that has established them in 12 countries and positioned them as market leaders in car roof manufacturing (*El País*, 23 and 25 March 1995).[12] Another old family business, Bergé y Compañía, took advantage of the boom in the manufacture and sale of automobiles in Spain to expand its traditional activity as shipping agent (since 1870), becoming a top import-export company in Spain, present in all the main Spanish ports since its origin in Bilbao, bringing it into the elite of family businesses at the start of the twenty-first century. Its subsidiary, Bergé Automoción, developed in the 1980s with the entry of Spain into the EEC and the consequent liberalization of vehicle imports. Currently it is the largest automotive distributor in the Iberian Peninsula and Latin America, at the same time developing other areas of related business.[13]

In summary, since the democratic transition at the end of the 1970s, until almost today, the Spanish family business elite: (1) comprises more groups than businesses; (2) has leading head offices in Madrid, and secondarily in the outlying provinces; (3) is dedicated to light industries linked to the boom in distribution, food, construction, engineering and services, illustrating the increased purchasing power registered in the country (fashion, information technology, tourism, leisure, security, finance) and the innovation and internationalization of Spanish industry (vehicle components, steel). The opening up to outside markets is, finally, a common characteristic of practically all the groups studied in this phase, and one of the fundamental motives of their success and survival. For some of the family groups studied, the national market represents no more than a fifth of their turnover and often other emerging countries have become more important for their revenues than the homeland.

NOTES

* Paloma Fernández Pérez acknowledges the financial support, at different stages of the research and writing process, of an Icrea Academia Award, a FBBVA grant and a public research project of the Spanish Ministry HAR2013-41453-P.

1. For details, see http://econpapers.repec.org/paper/ahedtaehe/1307.htm (accessed August 2012).
2. Fernández Pérez (2013). http://econpapers.repec.org/paper/ahedtaehe/1307.htm (accessed August 2012).
3. There are at least six biographies on Juan March, the latest by Mercedes Cabrera (2011).
4. http://econpapers.repec.org/paper/ahedtaehe/1307.htm (accessed August 2012).
5. 'El Águila. Una historia centenaria'. http://www.fundacioncruzcampo.com (accessed August 2012).
6. http://www.nutrexpa.es (accessed August 2012); Cabana (2006).
7. For more information on the expansion of construction companies, see Torres (2009a).
8. http://www.globalia.com; http://www.grupoiberostar.com (accessed August 2012).
9. http://www.tecnicasreunidas.es (accessed August 2012).
10. http://www.bellota.com (accessed August 2012).
11. http://www.froscasares.es (accessed August 2012).
12. http://www.grupoantolin.com (accessed August 2012).
13. http://www.bergeycia.es (accessed August 2012).

REFERENCES

Alonso Olea, E.J. (2005). *Victor Chávarri (1854–1900): Una biografía*. San Sebastián: Sociedad de Estudios Vascos.

Anes, R. and A. Otazu (1987). *El Banco Herrero 75 años de Historia. 1912–1987*. Oviedo: Banco Herrero.

Bahamonde, A. and L.E. Otero (1989). *La sociedad madrileña durante la Restauración (1876–1931)*, Vol. I. Madrid: Comunidad de Madrid.
Blanco, M. and S. Gutiérrez (2008). 'El empleo del modelo de gestión de la Calidad Total en el sector de la distribución comercial en España: el caso de Mercadona'. *Universia Business Review* **17**, 40–63.
Blanco, X. and J. Salgado (2004). *Amancio Ortega, de cero a Zara: El primer libro de investigación sobre el imperio Inditex*. Madrid: Esfera de los Libros.
Cabana, F. (ed.) (2006). *Cien empresarios catalanes*. Madrid: Lid.
Cabrera, M. (2011). *Juan March (1880–1962)*. Madrid: Marcial Pons.
Carmona, X. (ed.) (2006). *Empresarios de Galicia*. Coruña: Fundación Caixa Galicia.
Carmona, X. (2011). *Las familias de la conserva. El sector de las conservas de pescados a través de sus sagas familiars*. Pontevedra, Spain: Fundación Cluster de Conservación de Productos del Mar.
Chrisman, J.J., J.H. Chua and P. Sharma (2005). 'Trends and directions in the development of a strategic management theory of the family firm'. *Entrepreneurship Theory and Practice* **31**, 555–75.
Díaz Hernández, O. (1998). *Los marqueses de Urquijo. El apogeo de una saga poderosa y los inicios del Banco Urquijo, 1870–1931*. Pamplona: Eunsa.
Díaz Morlán, P. (1999a). *Horacio Echevarrieta, 1870–1963. El capitalista republicano*. Madrid: Lid.
Díaz Morlán, P. (1999b). 'Aeroplanes, torpedoes and submarines: German interests in Spain in the inter-war period'. *International Journal of Maritime History* **XI** (2), 31–59.
Díaz Morlán, P. (2002). *Los Ybarra. Una dinastía de empresarios (1801–2001)*. Madrid: Marcial Pons.
Díaz Morlán, P. (2004). 'Tras las huellas del empresario schumpeteriano: el caso de José Martínez Rivas (1872–1913)'. *Revista de Historia Económica* **1**, 39–64.
Díaz Morlán, P. (2005). 'Capitalismo rentista y decadencia empresarial: la desaparición de la casa Martínez Rivas (1913–1921)'. *Revista de Historia Industrial* **29**, 117–38.
Fernández Moya, M. (2012). 'Creating knowledge networks: Spanish multinational publishers in Mexico'. *Business History Review* **86**, 69–98.
Fernández Pérez, P. (2003). 'Reinstalando la empresa familiar en la Economía y la Historia Económica. Una aproximación a debates teóricos recientes'. *Cuadernos de Economía y Dirección de la Empresa* **17**, 45–66.
Fernández Pérez, P. (2004). *Un siglo y medio de trefilería en España. Moreda y Rivière*. Barcelona: Trivium.
Fernández Pérez, P. (2006). 'Josep, Maties, Martín i Àngela Roca Soler'; 'Francesc Rubiralta, de CELSA'; y 'Francisco Rivière'. In F. Cabana (ed.), *100 empresarios catalanes*. Madrid: LID Editorial, pp. 407–13, 481–7, 719–24.
Fernández Pérez, P. and A. Colli (eds) (2013). *The Endurance of Family Businesses: A Global Revolution*. New York: Cambridge University Press.
García Ruiz, J.L. (2007). 'BANESTO, 1902–1993: auge y decadencia de un gran banco mixto'. *Revista de Historia de la Economía y de la Empresa* **1**, 141–61.
Germán, L. (ed.) (2009). *Grandes empresarios aragoneses*. Madrid: Lid.
Gutiérrez Marcos, J. (1997). 'La fábrica de cervezas "El Águila" de Madrid/España'. *Informe de Construcción* **49**, 23–30.
Maixé-Altés, J.C. (2009). 'La modernización de la distribución alimentaria en España, 1947–1995'. *Revista de Historia Industrial* **41** (3), 109–44.

Martín Aceña, P. (2007). *1857–2007. Banco Santander, 150 años de historia*. Madrid: Turner.
Moreno Lázaro, J. (2009). 'Formación e internacionalización de la gran empresa cárnica española, 1944–2008: Campofrío'. *Investigaciones de Historia Económica* (Spring), 103–40.
Moreno Luzón, J. (1988). *Romanones, caciquismo y política liberal*. Madrid: Alianza Editorial.
Parejo, A. (ed.) (2011). *Cien empresarios andaluces*. Madrid: Lid.
Puig, N. and E. Torres (2008). *Banco Urquijo. Un banco con historia*. Madrid: Banco Urquijo Sabadell Banca Privada.
Rodrigo y Alharilla, M. (2001). *Los Marqueses de Comillas 1817–1925. Antonio y Claudio López*. Madrid: Lid.
San Román, E. (2011). *Ildefonso Fierro. La aventura de un emprendedor*. Madrid: Lid.
Sierra Alonso, M. (1992). *La familia Ybarra, empresarios y políticos*. Sevilla: Muñoz Moya y Montraveta.
Tamames, R. (1995). *La economía española: 1975–1995*. Madrid: Temas de Hoy.
Titos Fernández, M. (2004). *Rodríguez-Acosta. Banqueros granadinos, 1831–1946*. Madrid: Lid.
Toboso, P. (2000). *Pepín Fernández 1891–1982, Galerías Preciados, el pionero de los grandes almacenes*. Madrid: Lid.
Torres, E. (1998). *Ramón de la Sota, 1857–1936. Un empresario vasco*. Madrid: Lid.
Torres, E. (ed.) (2000). *Los 100 empresarios españoles del siglo XX*. Madrid: Lid.
Torres, E. (2009a). 'Las grandes empresas constructoras españolas. Crecimiento e internacionalización en la segunda mitad del siglo XX'. *Información Comercial Española. Revista de Economía* **849** (July–August), 113–27.
Torres, E. (2009b). 'La internacionalización de dos grandes empresas constructoras españolas: FCC y Dragados (c. 1960–1992)'. *Revista de Historia Industrial. Economía y Empresa* **40**, 155–87.
Torres, E. (2011). *Origen, crecimiento e internacionalización de las grandes empresas españolas de la construcción (1900–2008)*. Bogotá, Colombia: Universidad de los Andes-Cátedra Corona.
Tortella, G., J.M. Ortiz-Villajos and J.L. García Ruiz (2011). *Historia del Banco Popular. La lucha por la independencia*. Madrid: Marcial Pons.
Valdaliso, J.M. (2002a). 'Comerciantes e industriales en México, banqueros e industriales en Vizcaya. Unas notas sobre los indianos Aresti, López de Letona, Hernández Mendirichaga y Maíz'. *Illes i Imperis* **6** (Summer), 51–66.
Valdaliso, J.M. (2002b). 'Grupos empresariales, marco institucional y desarrollo económico en España en el siglo XX: los negocios de la familia Aznar (c.1937–c.1983)'. *Revista de Historia Económica* **3** (XX) (Autumn–Winter), 577–624.
Valdaliso, J.M. (2006). *La familia Aznar y sus negocios (1830–1983). Cuatro generaciones de empresarios en la España contemporánea*. Madrid: Marcial Pons.
Vidal, J. (ed.) (2005). *Cien empresarios valencianos*. Madrid: Lid.
Ximénez de Embún, M.Á. (2005). *Juan Miguel Villar Mir: rigor y audacia en los negocios*. Madrid: Ediciones Internacionales Universitarias.
Ybarra, J. (2002). *Nosotros, los Ybarra. Vida, economía y sociedad (1744–1902)*. Barcelona: Tusquets.

11. Evolution of the Peruvian large family business, 1896–2012

Martín Monsalve Zanatti

This chapter analyses the evolution of Peruvian large family businesses from 1896 to 2012. The variables that guide this study are the changes in the investment strategies of the large family firms, the relationship between the family firms and the financial system, and their capacity to react and adapt to the challenges represented by government economic policies. Taking these variables into account, the aim of this chapter is to show which factors have determined the evolution of Peruvian family firms, the longevity of some of them and their capacity to face the current challenge of the internationalization process.

This study is divided into three periods that correspond to characteristics of the Peruvian economy and politics: (a) the formation of the large family businesses (1896–1960); (b) family business and the formation of new business groups during State-driven development (1960–90); and (c) restructuring of the Peruvian large family business (1990–2012). The proposal of this chapter is that economic-political changes generate different types of managerial attitudes in family businesses and that the longevity of a firm depends on the skill of its leaders to interpret the periods of change, and the capacity of the company to adapt to them.

In methodological terms, this analysis is based on the annual reports of the companies, journalistic sources for the different periods and secondary sources. For the first period it is harder to obtain statistical sources, which is why the study is more qualitative than quantitative. In addition, following the guidelines of the editors, included within the term 'family business' are firms (1) that are owned by one or more families, or one family is majority shareholder and (2) where representatives of the same family hold decisive positions on the executive board and in the company's management.

In the case of Peru, especially after the 1960s, entrepreneurial families diversified their investments, sometimes randomly, forming what we know as business groups. These we can define, following Guillén (2000) and Khanna and Yafeh (2007), as interdependent firms, operating in multiple industries, frequently unconnected to each other, unified by formal and informal links. Generally, Peruvian economic groups operate through a company under majority control of the family, constituting its core business. For this reason, when the occasion demands, Peruvian large family businesses are studied in the context of the economic group of which they form part.

11.1 THE FORMATION OF LARGE FAMILY BUSINESSES, 1896–1960

It was only around 1896 that the Peruvian economy managed to recuperate from the economic consequences of the Pacific War (1879–83) and the subsequent civil wars. The recuperation was linked as much to the new political stability as to the boom in export based on the diversification of exported products (minerals, sugar, cotton, rubber and oil). Here begins a long period in Peruvian entrepreneurial history, characterized by: (1) the predominance of direct foreign investments in extractive industries; (2) economic policies that favoured free foreign trade; and (3) the creation of large family businesses that preferred to invest in sectors of high profitability (agro-industry, real estate and finance).

Economic policies that favoured the growth of the internal market were inconsistently developed only between the years 1930 and 1948, but these did not significantly harm the exporting sector or direct foreign investment. Likewise, the action of the government did not affect the land ownership system and the financial system retained its structure throughout this period. Therefore, there were no radical changes to the way family businesses in Peru were managed at this stage.

During this period, the majority of family businesses were to be found in the agro-industrial sector (sugar and cotton), in trade, and a smaller group was in industry. In addition, it is important to point out that 23 per cent of family businesses at this time originated from abroad, mostly from Europe (Portocarrero, 2010, pp. 41–3). Even if businesses of single ownership predominated, it was not unusual for families to form alliances; nor to find partners from outside the family context.

The running of agro-industrial businesses was the responsibility of the patriarch of the family, who took all the decisions relating to the business directly. On his death, it was common for his heirs to form a new company responsible for managing the acquired assets. In this way, the division of the company was avoided, but also allowed the brothers to make their own investments. For example, the Aspílliga Anderson Brothers Company owned the Negociación Agrícola Cayaltí y Palto. The brothers invested the surplus from their sugar exports in the financial sector (the Banco Italiano, popular and international banks, and the insurance firms Internacional and Rímac) and in the real estate sector in the city of Lima (Portocarrero, 2010).

Investments in the financial sector and in the trading houses were aimed at ensuring the families had access to a rare asset: credit. For this reason, around the end of the 1920s the majority of companies dedicated to sugar and cotton production owned shares in the Banco del Perú y Londres, the most important financial institution in Peru until 1930 (Quiroz, 1989).

Similarly, the cattle ranchers of the central mountain range invested the surplus of their businesses in the financial sector. For example, the Olavegoya brothers, founding partners of La Sociedad Ganadera del Centro SA (later Laive SA) invested considerable sums in insurance companies such as Rímac, Compañía Internacional de Seguros and Compañía de Seguros Italia. But their most important investment in this sector was in the Banco Italiano, of which Domingo Olavegoya became chairman (Portocarrero, 2010; Quiroz, 1989). The agro-industrial entrepreneurs also invested their surplus in textile manufacturing. The most emblematic case was with the Fábrica Nacional de Tejidos La Victoria (1899), owned by the Pardo family, landowners of Tumán. The Pardo family were very important in the political sphere, their leader José Pardo being President of Peru on two occasions (1904–08 and 1915–19). Nevertheless, despite their social and economic influence, they did not manage to maintain control of their textile factory, Fábrica Nacional de Tejidos la Victoria, and ended up selling the majority of their shares to the US firm W.R Grace & Co. in 1903. The agro-export families preferred to invest in shares of industrial companies rather than manage them themselves (Monsalve, 2011).

However, this does not mean that there were not families who used industry as the basis for their business. The Prado family, to name one, another family with presidents in their history, had as core business the Fábrica Nacional de Tejidos de Lana Santa Catalina (1899). Originally, the factory was founded by an Italian immigrant, Bartolomé Boggio, and a US citizen, Enrique Price, in 1889. One year later, Juan Manuel Peña y Costas, and Mariano Ignacio Prado decided to invest in the factory by buying out Price and creating a new company with Boggio. According to Portocarrero, the positive business results encouraged Peña and Prado to make a greater investment and expand their business to include cotton textile production and flour production (Portocarrero, 1995).

The modernization of the business included substituting hydraulic power with electric. This brought with it the creation of the Empresa Transmisora de Fuerza Eléctrica and the construction of the Santa Rosa power plant. These two companies subsequently became the Empresas

Electricas Asociadas, one of the few listed companies at this time (Portocarrero, 1995, pp. 71–3). As well as the textile factories and energy production, the Prado family controlled the Banco Popular (1898), which guaranteed them access to commercial loans and attracted finance from foreign investors. This advantage allowed them to expand their interests to the cement sector through the founding of the Compañía Nacional de Cementos Portland (1916). This diversification in their investments allowed the family to raise capital from other family groups who in turn were looking to expand their financial horizons.

The history of the Prado family's investments was closely linked to the leadership of the heads of each generation. Mariano Ignacio Prado Ugarteche, the founder of the group, managed the consolidation of the businesses acquired from 1889 until the 1930s in the industrial sector (textile, energy and cement). This economic power allowed the leader of the second generation, Mariano Ignacio Prado Heudebert, to have almost unlimited influence in the business world, which he was able to complement with a rise of influence in the political sphere, thanks to his uncle Manuel having been twice president of Peru (1939–45, 1956–62). Taking advantage of this favourable environment, Prado Heudebert used the privileged access to credit that the Banco Popular provided him to accelerate a disorganized process of business expansion that included real estate. Ultimately, between 1960 and 1970, Mariano Ignacio Prado Sosa was running the family business in a very irresponsible way, at a time when the financial crisis of the Banco Popular prevented this institution from being the core business of the family; the family was then forced to take refuge in real estate (Portocarrero, 1995).

Apart from the Prado family, the greatest group of industrialists comprised Italian immigrants. For example, the textile factory San Jacinto was founded in 1896 by Gio Batta Isola in partnership with fellow Italian Giacomo Gerbolini. The company is one of the few that still exists under the control of the same family.

Despite representing only a very small part of the population of Lima (less than 3 per cent according to a survey from 1908), Italian immigrants were particularly active in the process of the launch of industry. By 1906, immigrants had formed 975 companies, of which 624 were dedicated to trade, while 131 formed part of the industrial sector, the majority manfacturing noodles, some producing wine (Durand, 2004). But the 'comparative advantage' of the immigrants lay not in their 'entrepreneurial' or 'innovative' spirit that the sociologist Francisco Durand contrasted with a traditional and rentier 'criolla' elite. Their advantage was that they were a social group organized around a financial institution, the Banco Italiano (1888). For this reason, the traders and industrialists of Italian origin had comparatively more secure access to bank loans, a great privilege in the late 1900s. Thus, it is essential to analyse the consequences of the restructuring of the financial system in the early industrialization of Peru.

Beside the Italians, other European immigrants arrived, among them the Englishman 'José' R. Lindley who in 1910 established the Fábrica de Aguas Gasificadas Santa Rosa. At the beginning it produced beverages similar to those found in England (lemon squash, orange squash and so on). By 1928, the elder son José was in control of José R. Lindley e Hijos SA and under his management Inka Kola was created in 1935. He died not long after and was replaced by his brother Nicolás (Chumpitazi and Rodríguez, 2010).

In the trade sector the presence of immigrants can also be seen, such as the Wiese brothers, originating from Austria. They began working in the Casa Wagner, later creating Casa A. y F. Wiese SA. When Peru entered the Second World War, there was a change in the investments of the Wiese brothers: they acquired Banco Trasatlántico Alemán, which in 1943 received the name Banco Wiese (Portocarrero, 2010, p. 138).

Peruvian family businesses at this time had their basis in agro-industry, in the financial sector and in their influence on political power. The entrepreneurial families with greatest access to financial capital and/or political power specialized in the industrial sector that provided no short-term profits and needed constant investment. This is how the Italian immigrants were able to concentrate on the industrial sector. But it was the combination of political and financial power that made the textile business of the Prado family the most important in Peru.

Due to the weakness in the financial sector, the networks between families and trading houses became the most important method of obtaining capital for the development of the company. This made the patriarch of the family the centre point of the family's social and financial network. It was a 'señorial' style of management in which the fate of the business was linked to the type of investments made by the patriarch, as shown in the case of the Prado family.

This period reached its end when the dictatorship of the Military Junta expropriated the lands of the agro-industrialists and a large part of the banking sector came under the control of the government, thus leaving the family businesses without their economic base. Nevertheless, in this period emblematic companies were formed that still remain under family ownership and management, such as the textile factory San Jacinto (Isola family) and the bottling plant José R. Lindley e Hijos SA (Lindley family).[1] Similarly, other family groups were created at that time that would have a central role in the following phase, for example, the Wiese, Romero and Brescia families, among others.

11.2 THE FORMATION OF NEW FAMILY GROUPS AND THE DEVELOPMENT TOWARDS THE INTERIOR, 1960–90

The years between 1968 and 1990 were particularly complicated in the political and economic panorama of Peru. The country went from military dictatorship that transformed the system of ownership and State intervention in the economy, to a fragile democracy that had to deal with a global economic crisis, hyperinflation and the threats of the subversive guerrilla group, Shining Path (Parodi, 2000; Thorp and Bertram, 1985).

During these 22 complicated years, entrepreneurial families that were considered second tier in the previous period took on a central role; such was the case of the Brescia and Romero families. Likewise, faced with economic difficulties and political instability, the entrepreneurial families developed a 'reactive' style of management that consisted in designing investment strategies that would protect them from the risks that the implementation of economic policies could bring. An important part of these risk aversion tactics was the diversification of investments and a link to financial capital in order to cope with the liquidity crises that were so common at this time.

Thus, through the 1980s the investments of entrepreneurial families became increasingly diversified while those of the State diminished. For this reason it should be of no surprise to find that in the ranking of the top 500 businesses in Peru in 1989, 346 firms were family-owned and only 47 State-owned (Campodónico et al., 1994, p. 116). The majority of the former type of company was linked to what we at the beginning of this chapter call an economic group. This is why it is impossible in this period to separate the study of the family business from the group of which it forms part.

The most important family groups operating in Peru numbered 13. Among them, three were foreign: the Grupo Fierro from Spain; La Fabril of the Bunge y Born group from Argentina; and the Hochschild group from England.[2]

Among the Peruvian groups, the Romero and Brescia families owned the largest number of businesses, followed by the Ferreyros group. Likewise, the diversification in the groups was quite high, half of them investing in more than three economic sectors. The most diversified are the Romero (six sectors), Brescia, Nicolini and Wiese (five sectors) and Backus-Bentín and Ferreyros (four sectors) (Campodónico et al., 1994, p. 125).

The majority of the economic groups of this period have their origins in family businesses that were founded by the patriarchs, most of them immigrants, in the previous phase. This was the case of the Brescia and the Romero families. At that time, as suggested by the research of Vásquez (2000a) and Durand (2003, 2004), the family was fundamental in the founding of the company or companies that then became the core of the business.

During the period 1960–90, the majority of the companies that were considered the core of the family business were found in the industrial or trade sector. The centre of economic activity of the family group could change if better investment perspectives appeared in other sectors, or if the family needed to protect itself from some action by the Peruvian State. But in general, what the families were looking for was to increase the market participation of their principal business in order to thus improve their negotiating power with the government of the day in the implementation process of economic policies (Váquez, 2000a).

The economic and political uncertainties made access to financial resources a very important issue for all large family businesses. This has given rise to very significant debate among Peruvian academics. For Alcorta (1990), Anaya (1990) and Campodónico et al. (1994), the economic power of family groups can be measured by the control they have over financial capital. For this reason, their research emphasizes the study of investments made by entrepreneurial families in banks and insurance companies. Meanwhile, for Vásquez, economic groups organize themselves around a family business that constitutes the core business, and from there it expands to the financial sector as a way of guaranteeing access to capital (Váquez, 2000a).

According to Alcorta, through financial control the economic groups developed a pyramidal structure to their businesses, which allowed them access to cheap loans for their companies and to make internal transfers between them. The bigger their financial capacity, the more the groups could benefit from tax exemptions and access to cheap loans that the government was giving out at this time to companies established in the economic sectors and/or geographical regions it was interested in developing (Alcorta, 1990, pp. 134, 213).

Vásquez, for his part, focuses more on the company (or companies) that functioned as core business of the economic group. This type of company was usually managed by the family and could take the form of a holding company. In the period 1960–90, the majority of core businesses were to be found in the manufacturing industry (textile, food or beverages) and were commercially oriented to the internal market (Váquez, 2000a, p. 273).

The move from one core business to another depended on many factors: from generational changes in the running of the company, to the drying up of the business itself, expropriations and/or sudden changes in the economic policies of the government of the day. Thus, for example, the

Romero family went from the production of cotton to edible oil; the Brescia family from real estate to mining, then to textile, returning towards the end of this period to real estate; the Wiese family replaced their commercial activities with banking; and the Ferreyros went from consumer goods to capital goods and so on (Váquez, 2000a, p. 275).

Using the core business as a base, the families managed their investment portfolio. The level of diversification often depended upon the reaction to changing policies of the government in power, which meant that it was a diversification that sought to minimize risks and ensure the liquidity of the family group. This required an organizational flexibility in the companies that would allow them to adapt to new investments and expand their participation in the markets (Guillén, 2000). For Vásquez, family groups expanded towards the financial sector to obtain access to funds and information, but also to expand social and political networks (Váquez, 2000a, p. 283). These networks, combined with the size of the core business' market share, allowed the economic groups to increase their capacity of negotiation with the government in power.

Towards the end of this period, some important changes began to appear in the business structure of the large family groups. It was the start of a process of professionalization of the family members in charge of the companies, and there was an increase in holding companies that would ensure family control of the firms despite a rise in the contracting of managers or the incorporation of new shareholders not linked to the family.

11.3 RESTRUCTURING OF THE PERUVIAN LARGE FAMILY BUSINESS, 1990–2010

In the 1990s, there was another sudden shift in economic policies, oriented towards a market economy that gave priority to free trade of food and the consequent price 'justification', the privatization of State companies, the reinsertion of the country into the global financial market and the control of inflation. The adjustment policies increased the recession that the Peruvian economy was undergoing and inflation was not fully brought under control. It wasn't until 1993 that the economy began to recover and GDP grew 6.4 per cent; inflation was maintained at 39.5 per cent, to fall the following year to 15.4 per cent. This growth continued in the following years but generated an overheating of the Peruvian economy, which raised the deficits in the balance of trade and made the Peruvian economy very vulnerable to the 'Asian Crisis of 1998' (Parodi, 2000). Nevertheless, after the year 2000, an economic cycle driven by the rise in price of raw materials brought sustained growth in the Peruvian economy, reaching an average yearly GDP growth rate of 5.7 per cent for the period 2000–10.

After almost 30 years of being accustomed to a reactive management style, to a diversification based on risk aversion and to negotiation with the government to obtain tariffs or tax exemptions, it is valid to ask oneself how the large family businesses adapted to the changes in economic policies.

For Francisco Durand (2007, p. 149), the first years of market reform strengthened foreign companies; they benefited from privatization and invested directly in the primary export sector, above all in mining. The national family groups became junior partners to the multinationals through the process of acquisition of private companies.

Five of the 19 Peruvian economic groups went bankrupt (Galski, Lucioni, Nicolini, Picasso Salinas, Wiese), two were taken over by foreign companies (Bentín and Wong) and three (Piaggio, Piazza and Wu) saw their economic positions downgraded. This process of diminishing economic power of the important entrepreneurial families is what leads Durand to argue that there is a process of foreign takeover in the Peruvian economy (Durand, 2007).

The data on the participation in the total sales of the first 65 companies in Peru seems to confirm this position. For example, in 2005 the participation of Peruvian family businesses reached only 35 per cent compared to 49 per cent by foreign companies. The years 2008 and 2009 were the hardest for Peruvian family firms, their participation sinking to 27 and 28 per cent, respectively. However, around 2010 a process of rapid recovery began, with 41 per cent participation in sales (Peru Reporting, 2010).

The sectorial analysis for 2010 shows that the mining sector represented 28 per cent of turnover, the hydrocarbon sector 22 per cent and the finance sector 13 per cent. It should therefore be of no surprise that the four companies that registered the largest turnover and profits were Petróleos del Perú SA, Refinería La Pampilla SA, Southern Peru Copper Corporation and Compañía Minera Antamina SA. The first is a State-owned company and the other three foreign-owned (the last with a small participation of national capital). The only companies owned by Peruvian families that appear in the top ten are the financial holding companies linked to the Rodríguez Pastor family (IFH Perú Ltd) and the Romero family (Credicorp), both with a head office in the Bermudas (Peru Reporting, 2010).

In this general panorama, it does not signify that the Peruvian large family groups have lost their competitiveness. Quite the contrary; many of them, since the start of the new century, have initiated a process of internationalization. The questions that immediately arise are: What were the strategies followed by the family groups that successfully coped with changes initiated in the 1990s? Have new family business groups emerged?

The families in mining, like the Benavides group, began in the 1990s to implement policies of strategic alliances or joint ventures, with the aim of obtaining capital for large mining projects such as Yanacocha with the New Mont company.

The Brescia group also established alliances with foreign companies in order to guarantee access to capital so that it could expand its investments. The most important of these companies was the one it formed with BBVA Bank in order to participate in the privatization of Banco Continental, one of the most important of Peru. This allowed it to enter the business of Private Administration of Pensions (*Administradoras Privadas de Pensiones*), AFP Horizonte, and to strengthen its investments in the insurance company Rímac Seguros. The revitalization of its financial portfolio allowed Brescia to buy the Sipesa company from the Galsky group in 2005, and to manage it together with the company Tecnológica de Alimentos SA (TASA), one of the world's largest producers of fish meal and fish oil, as well as canned food. Similarly, the family continued the expansion of its mining investments through Minsur SA, a company involved in the exploitation of tin (Vásquez, 2000b). The Brescia family maintained its pattern of diversification of investments, expanding in the last years into the Chilean market with the acquisition of companies manufacturing cement and paints, as well as the acquisition of Chilean real estate.

The Romero family, which along with the Brescia family continues to be the most influential group, concentrated firstly on strengthening its core business in order to launch, in recent years, an aggressive process of internationalization. The changes in economic policies coincided with the transfer of the control of the business from the third to the fourth generation, a smooth and well-planned process that culminated in 2001.

The initial strategy of the Romero family in the face of economic policy changes was to merge the companies it owned in the food processing sector, and acquire the companies of its competitors who had become weakened through being unable to adapt to these changes. In this way, it took over part of the business of the Nicolini and bought the company La Fabril. By 1997, it had founded a new company called Alicorp SA that had as its base Calixto Romero y Cía and Industrial Perú Pacífico Company, in addition to the recently acquired companies. In the following years, Alicorp became consolidated while the family diversified into other businesses such as the production of biofuels and the acquisition of Repsol's service stations that went on to form the Primax company (Revista Poder, 2012).

The Alicorp company began a more aggressive internationalization process. In 2008 it bought The Value Brand Company (TVB), the third most important company in the production of household products and personal care in Argentina after Procter & Gamble y Unilever. On the basis of this company, Alicorp Argentina was established, and continued to grow in the next years with the acquisitions of Sanford (giving it access to the cookie market through Okebon) and of Italo Manera and Pasta Especiales. The founding of Alicorp Argentina signified the diversification of the Peruvian company into other areas and the control of a distribution chain that covered 25 countries. That year, Alicorp Peru bought Productos Personales SA (Propesa) and Eskimo, both with good distribution chains, and from there it has founded Alicorp Colombia and Alicorp Equador, respectively (Revista Poder, 2012).

The other important groups formed alliances with companies from abroad. For example, Ferreyros SA specialized, through partnership with Caterpillar Co., in the sale of capital goods and services for the large-scale mining industry. The Lindley family sold the Inka Kola brand to Coca Cola Co. in exchange for a percentage of the sales and the role of bottler and distributer of the US company in Peru. The construction company Graña y Monetero SA diversified considerably and established an alliance with Odebrecht of Brazil. Finally, Aceros Arequipa of the Cillóniz family and Cementos Lima SA (today UNACEM) of the Rizo Patrón family have also increased the range of their operations and begun processes of internationalization.

But the most extraordinary event in this period is the consolidation of new family groups such as the Rodríguez family from the Gloria SA group, the Añaño family of the Aje Group and the Belmont family of Belcorp y Yambal (Infante, 2010; Revista Poder, 2012; Rivera, 2011). In addition, there are also Carlos Rodríguez Pastor from the Interbank group. Using financial capital, Rodríguez Pastor have successfully expanded into the retail sector, supermarkets, cinema chains, fast food, pharmacies, hotels and education – both basic and superior.

The most interesting entrepreneurial families from this period, however, are the Rodíguez Rodríguez and the Añaño Jerí, because they come from a middle-class sector from the south of the country and accumulated capital that allowed them to make a fortune at the worst economic and political moment in the country, the second half of the 1980s. In addition, their companies had undergone a rapid process of internationalization. These families represented the opposite case to that of the Nicolini or Wiese families, who lost their core business during the process of market opening.

The Rodríguez Rodríguez family are the leaders of the Gloria group, a holding company that includes dairy production, cement plants, paper works and sugar plantations destined for the production of biofuels. The business of the family began with the father, José Rodríguez Banda, who had a small company of freight forwarders that his son transformed into a company for the transport of materials for the mines of Arequipa. The business, José Rodríguez Banda SAC (Jorsa) still exists and acts as a holding company for the family businesses in dairy production.

One of the elements that characterize the Gloria group is that, in the 1990s and 2000s, it underwent a process of diversification very similar to that of a classic economic group. That is, on some occasions it invested in businesses linked to the dairy company; on others it took advantage of the opportunities that presented themselves. For example, during the process of privatization, it decided to buy Cementos Yura and Cementos Sur. However, there are four areas in which it concentrates the majority of its investments: dairy, paper, sugar and cement. Each of these areas is organized around a holding company.

The expansion into the area of dairy products and articles for daily use started very early with the acquisition of the Sociedad Ganadera Luis Martín, which allowed it to enter the production of ready-to-eat processed foods and yoghurt. Only two years later, they bought the factories of Pil Andina in Bolivia. Subsequently, at the start of the new century, they begin an aggressive expansion policy in the region, buying Suiza Dairy Co. (Puerto Rico), Compañía Regional de Lácteos Argentina SA (Argentina), Algarra SA (Colombia), Lechera Andina SA (Edcuador) and Ecolat SA (Uruguay). The expansion into cement, as already commented above, was more a reaction to the opportunities offered by privatizations rather than a strategic plan. The acquisition of the paper works, and carton and box factories, on the other hand, does correspond to a project for gaining independence in the production chain and improving the packaging of their products (Revista Poder, 2012, p. 27). The investments in sugar were a result of the constant search for diversification and the opportunity that the production of biofuels could represent for the future.

The case of the Añaño family has some similarities with the previous case. The Añaño family had no links with the government or foreign multinationals, nor did it have financial capital; nevertheless, it managed to create two firms that today compete in the local and international market against large multinationals. The two companies in which the family is involved are: (a) Industrias San Miguel, founded by two married couples, Eduardo Añaño-Mitha Jerí and Jorge Añaño-Tania Alcázar; and (b) Aje Group formed by the other Añaño Jerí brothers.

As with the Rodríguez Rodríguez case, the Añaño family's process of raising and accumulating capital happened not only in the worst moment of the Peruvian economy, but also in the geographical centre of the armed conflict that shook Peru in the 1980s and 1990s. Industrias San Miguel was founded in Huamanga, Ayacucho in 1988 thanks to the company of the above-mentioned spouses Añaño Jerí y Añaño Alcázar. The first brand, Kola Real, was sold in five flavours all over the Ayacucho region, using recycled beer bottles. The internal war restricted the distribution capacities of bottling plants based in Lima, raising the demand for trade in low-cost drinks in the southern and central mountain range. This resulted in the growth of Industrias San Miguel in 1991 towards Andahuaylas (Apurímac) in order to supply the Cusco region. It was at this time that Jorge Añaño reached an agreement with his brothers for them to set up a plant in Huancayo in the central mountain range. This factory was the beginning of the Aje Group, trading in the same products as Industrias San Miguel. Both companies had the same strategy of remaining a low-cost company, but the markets they chose for expansion marked the difference in their evolution.

The market in the southern mountains was bigger but also needed more working capital to remain competitive, and the next step after being established in the south was usually to put a plant in Lima, as the Rodríguez family had done with Gloria milk. Indeed, in 1993 Industrias San Miguel opened a plant in Huara, to the north of the capital with the aim of competing in the largest Peruvian market. Aje Group continued a different strategy; it was not concerned with expanding its participation in the Peruvian market, but rather in consolidating its operations. For this, it sought to repeat the experience of Ayacucho and Huancayo in a smaller market, but also a much cheaper one in terms of working capital and transaction costs. This was how it decided to open a second plant in the small town of Bagua in the northern Peruvian Amazon. The geographical location of Bagua offered various advantages. The first was that the entire Amazonian region was exempt from both income tax and value added tax. The second was that from Bagua one could reach the mountains and the northern Peruvian coast and establish a small regional market; which is what effectively happened with the plant set up by the Aje Group in Sullana (Rivera, 2011).

Towards the end of the 1990s, the Añaño brothers of the Aje Group decided that in order to maintain their growth in the long term, it was not worth competing to get greater participation in the Peruvian market, and decided to take their production and commercialization model to Venezuela. Their strategy of internationalization consisted in setting up their own plants and not competing for large market participation, but rather, once they had consolidated the business, to move on to another country. But the most important step for the company was the entry to Mexico where reaching 7 per cent of the Mexican market gave them more profit than the whole of their Peruvian businesses put together (Rivera, 2011).

Once the objectives in Mexico were reached, the Añaño brothers proposed a greater challenge: to enter with the same model into the Asian market. But since this implied a greater growth of the company, they could not do this by themselves, and for the first time they contracted a manager from outside the family to be in charge of operations. The first test was done in Thailand and the success they achieved encouraged them to put a plant in Vietnam and Indonesia, and recently they have opened another in India. The Asian investments enabled the Aje Group to establish an office in Spain in order to have a management 'bridge' between the American continent and Asia. In addition, the expansion brought with it the employment of a greater number of high-ranking members of staff from outside the family, even though the family continues being in control of ownership and administration. As in the case of the Gloria Group, Aje made no capital increases using external funds, thus avoiding the entry of non-family partners, and for the same reason neither are they listed on the stock market. The biggest novelty in this respect was the issue of corporate bonds in 2012 (Rivera, 2011).

Industria San Miguel successfully continued its strategy of ensuring its participation in the Peruvian market, and in the last years has initiated a process of industrialization with the construction of a plant in the Dominican Republic and another very large one in Salvador de Bahía, Brazil.

The cases briefly described in this section allow us to demonstrate that after a difficult period of adaption to reforms in the market, Peruvian family groups began a new process of diversification and internationalization, the latter constituting the main difference with the two previous phases. The tendencies that prevail are that the large entrepreneurial families have a greater participation in the sectors linked to the extraction of natural resources (mining and fishing), sugar cane production, finance, cement and the beverage and food industries.

The groups whose fortune originated in the previous phase tend to keep a close connection with finance capital as a way of strengthening their investments. In contrast, the new groups, such as Belmont, Añaño and Rodríguez Rodríguez, tend not to be too interested in investments in finance capital; in fact, only the latter group owns companies that are listed. Likewise, these families are reticent about making capital increases that would involve the entry of partners from outside the clan, the reason for their preference to issue corporate bonds when they are in need of greater access to capital.

The internationalization of the companies and the growth of their operations have led Peruvian families to found holding companies in order to maintain family control of ownership as well as of the administration.

This by no means contradicts the increase in the use of professional managers that have no family links with the owners of the company. It is precisely the structure of holding companies that allows the combination of family-based administration and the 'managerial revolution'.

11.4 CONCLUSIONS

One of the first curious facts is that large Peruvian family companies seem to be relatively short-lived. The only two companies that have lasted longer than a hundred years and are still in the hands of Peruvian entrepreneurs are the Corporación Lindley and Tejidos San Jacinto (Isola family). For this reason it is important to emphasize that, despite none of their businesses (Banco de Crédito del Perú brings together various groups) being older than a hundred years, the Romero family has managed to remain active in the Peruvian business world for four generations. Interestingly, one of the oldest family firms is Gloria, which in the 70 years of its existence was first a transnational company with minority participation of Peruvian capital, then a family business after its acquisition by the Rodríguez brothers in 1986. Backus & Johnston followed an inverse path, being bought up by foreign companies.

A possible explanation for the relatively short life of the companies could rest with the sudden changes in economic policies of the governments, especially in the 1970s and 1990s. But it could also be due to generational changes in the leadership of the businesses established at the beginning of the twentieth century. The companies founded in the second half of the twentieth century have laid much more importance on the professional training of their members and the mechanisms of transition.

Another important element in understanding the history of large family businesses is their relationship to foreign capital and the sectors in which they specialize. With the exception of the second period, foreign investments have dominated the most productive sectors of the Peruvian economy. For this reason, in the early twentieth century as well as in the early twenty-first, Peruvian family businesses have established joint ventures with multinational companies in order to guarantee the necessary capital for their investments or for allowing access to new technology. Similarly, Peruvian businessmen used to invest in the economic sectors that foreign companies were not interested in or where legal matters made their participation difficult, such as insurance companies.

Nevertheless, in the third period we have seen an important change in this respect. The Rodríguez family buys a company from a multinational and uses it to compete in other markets. In the same way, Alicorp begins to enter areas that were generally controlled by Unilever or Proctor & Gamble, and the Añaño family also represents a similar case. This is not to say that the majority of extractive industry is not still controlled by multinationals. The sectors in which the more solid family businesses are specialized tend to be linked to finance, food and beverage processing, agro-industry, mining and fishing and, to a lesser extent, textiles.

Another element that stands out from the three periods is the forms of diversification of the investments of Peruvian large family businesses. There are three basic patterns. The first, represented best by the Brescia family, is based on a diversification that seeks different opportunities for investment in order to protect it from changes in the Peruvian economy. This diversification is possible thanks to links with financial capital. Another style is that of the Romero family, or Gloria Group, that from a core business looks for investments with which it can control an important part of the market. Only in the last period have very specialized industrial groups appeared, like the Belmont in beauty products and the Añaño in beverages.

Finally, an element that characterizes all three periods is the close links to the financial system and family groups. Banco Italiano, later Banco de Crédito del Perú, played a fundamental role in this story since it was, and is, the financial arena in which many entrepreneurial families interact. Since the 1970s it has been under the control of the Romero family, which has allowed the family to retain a certain predominance in the financial world. The acquisition of part of Banco Continental by the Brescia family, together with its participation in the insurance company Rímac, have been fundamental for the expansion of the family's business and its internationalization.

NOTES

1. The company Laive SA, from this period, is no longer under the control of the Moreyra family since the majority shareholder is a Chilean company. A similar case is represented by the brewery Compañía Nacional de Cerveza Backus y Johnston that now belongs to SAB Miller.
2. This latter group generated mixed feelings because its main source of accumulation was found outside Peru, but its political and social interests were within the country. Currently, the group is managed by a new generation with Peruvian nationality and has the majority of its investments in the country, criteria enough to call it a local group.

REFERENCES

Alcorta, L. (1990). *El nuevo capital financiero: grupos financieros y ganancias sistemáticas en el Perú*. Lima: Fundación Friedrich Ebert.

Anaya, E. (1990). *Los grupos de poder económico: un análisis de la oligarquía financiera*. Lima: Horizonte.
Campodónico, H., M. Castillo and A. Quispe (1994). *De poder a poder: grupos de poder, gremios empresariales y política macroeconómica*. Lima: Desco.
Chumpitazi, R. and G. Rodríguez (2010). *Corporación Lindley, Inkacola. El dulce sabor de la peruanidad*. Lima: Empresa Editora El Comercio SA.
Durand, F. (2003). *Riqueza económica y pobreza política: Reflexiones sobre las elites del poder en un país inestable*. Lima: Pontificia Universidad Católica del Perú Fondo Editorial.
Durand, F. (2004). *El poder incierto. Trayectoria política y económica del empresariado peruano*. Lima: Fondo Editorial del Congreso del Perú.
Durand, F. (2007). *El Perú fracturado. Formalidad, informalidad y economía delictiva*. Lima: Fondo Editorial del Congreso.
Guillén, M. (2000). 'Business groups in emerging economies: a resource-based view'. *Academy of Management Journal* **43** (3), 362–80.
Infante, J. (2010). *Belcorp; L'Bel, Ésika y Cyzone: Belleza que trasciende*. Lima: Empresa Editora El Comercio SA.
Khanna, T. and Y. Yafeh (2007). 'Business groups in emerging markets: paragons or parasites?'. *Journal of Economic Literature* **45** (2), 331–72.
Monsalve, M. (2011). 'Industria y Mercado Interno, 1821–1930'. In C. Contreras (ed.), *Compendio de Historia Económica del Perú*. Lima: Banco Central de Reserva del Perú, Instituto de Estudios Peruanos, pp. 239–303.
Parodi, C. (2000). *Perú 1960–2000. Políticas económicas y sociales en entornos cambiantes*. Lima: Universidad del Pacífico Centro de Investigación.
Peru Reporting (2010). *Peru Top*. Lima: Peru Reporting.
Portocarrero, F. (1995). *El Imperio Prado: 1890–1970*. Lima: Centro de Investigación de la Universidad del Pacífico.
Portocarrero, F. (2010). *Wealth and Philanthropy: The Economic Elite in Peru 1916–1960*. Saarbrücken, Germany: VDM Verlag Dr Müller Aktiengesellschaft & Co. KG. Spanish edition published 2013, Lima: Fondo Editorial de la Universidad del Pacífico.
Quiroz, A.W. (1989). *Banqueros en conflicto: Estructura financiera y economía peruana, 1884–1950*. Lima: Centro de Investigación de la Universidad del Pacífico.
Revista Poder (2012). *Cinco historias emprendedoras*. Lima: Poder.
Rivera, D. (2011). 'El sueño de los Añaño'. *Poder* (November), 22–32.
Thorp, R. and G. Bertram (1985). *Perú 1890–1977. Crecimiento y políticas en una economía abierta*. Lima: Universidad del Pacífico, F.F. Ebert y Mosaca Azul.
Vásquez, E. (2000a). *Estrategias del Poder: grupos económicos en el Perú*. Lima: Centro de Investigación de la Universidad del Pacífico.
Vásquez, E. (2000b). 'Estrategias competitivas de grupos económicos en el Perú en un contexto de apertura de mercado y reformas estructurales: 1990–1995'. In E. Vásquez and D. Sulmont (eds), *Modernización empresarial en el Perú*. Lima: Red para el desarrollo de las ciencias sociales en el Perú, pp. 15–58.

12. Large entrepreneurial families in Chile: their characteristics and contribution to the country, 1830–2012

Jon Martínez Echezárraga

12.1 INTRODUCTION

The aim of this chapter is to highlight the contribution that entrepreneurs and their families have made to economic development in Chile since its beginnings as an independent nation. It focuses especially on large entrepreneurial families – large in terms of equity – and their relevance as significant players in the economic life of the country. Although information on the nineteenth century is included, gathered from various sources, the main focus is on the twentieth century and the start of the twenty-first, this being the more relevant historical period for the purpose of this book.

This work makes no attempt to be a detailed nor exhaustive account of the contribution of entrepreneurial families to the economic history of independent Chile. Instead, it gives priority to identifying the broad tendencies and the players involved rather than a precise telling of events. Furthermore, the author offers his own interpretation to explain the evolution and development of Chilean entrepreneurial families during the years of the analysis. It is quite possible that other authors have a different interpretation of the processes under study.

As one of the conclusions of this chapter is that there is an apparent link between the economic environment and the development of entrepreneurial families in Chile, we begin by describing the economic situation in Chile since the beginnings of its republican life, around 1830, to the present day in the twenty-first century.

12.2 THE CHILEAN ECONOMY FROM 1830 TO 2012

The Chilean economy has undergone profound changes during the history of Chile as an independent nation. In aggregate terms, the Chilean economy in the twentieth century saw substantial growth, with a gross domestic product (GDP) that grew 25 times and a GDP per capita multiplied by five (Massad, 2001). However, as commented by Schmidt-Hebbel (2006), the GDP per capita grew at an average annual rate of only 1.5 per cent between 1810 and 1990, but in contrast, between 1991 and 2005 this rate leapt to 4.1 per cent. These were indeed profound changes.

There is no consensus among historians and economists regarding the periods into which the economic history of Chile can be divided. Nevertheless, according to the author's interpretation of the events, tendencies and results that have marked these last two centuries, at least five significant periods can be clearly identified since independence. Below is a description of these periods. For a complete analysis of Chilean economic life in the time before independence, that is, in colonial times, see De Ramón and Larraín (1982).

12.2.1 Exports of Raw Materials in the Republic (1830 to 1880)

After Chile's declaration of independence in 1810, the country was at war with Spain for a decade before it gained definitive freedom. The 1820s were years of regulating and the start of its existence as a republic and independent nation.

Nevertheless, between 1830 until 1880, Chile saw significant economic growth, stimulated by its integration into the world economy as an exporter of raw materials from mining (silver and copper) and agriculture (wheat and flour), and importer of manufactured goods derived from the industrial revolution. This process allowed the emergence of a new entrepreneurial elite, different from the traditional mercantile and landowning elite of colonial origin, and able to rapidly take control of the most dynamic areas of the economy. It was this social group that introduced modernization measures characterized by the establishment of an exporting industrial mining complex; the emergence of a transport infrastructure for land (railway) and sea (steamboats and ports); urban renovation (tramways and new residential areas); the creation of a financial system (banks and limited companies); and the modernization of certain agricultural activities (vineyards and windmills).

12.2.2 The Boom of 'Salitre' (1880 to 1930)

After the War of the Pacific (1879–82) between Chile and Peru-Bolivia, the sodium nitrate (saltpetre) mines in the areas conquered during the war became a huge source of revenue that was directed towards imports, public work projects, education and, less directly, the expansion of a fledgling industrial sector.

This period in Chile's economic history was dominated by export of saltpetre (known as salitre by the Chileans) that was used mainly for the manufacture of explosives and as a natural fertilizer for agriculture in developed countries. At the beginning of this industry, in 1860, Chilean entrepreneurs began the exploitation of nitrate deposits in the provinces of Tarapacá and Antofagasta, which at that time belonged to Peru and Bolivia. The control of the deposits, the most important source of nitrates in the world in the late nineteenth century, led to the War of the Pacific. Later, foreign investment, principally British, was necessary for the large-scale exploitation and export of nitrate (Vial, 1981).

The Chilean GDP per capita had sustained growth at the end of the nineteenth century, at a rate similar to that of the United States and exceeding the GDP per capita of Spain and Argentina in 1880 (Braun-Llona et al., 2000).

Between 1890 and 1924, the export of saltpetre accounted for approximately a quarter of the GDP of the country. In fact, in 1913 these exports represented 71.3 per cent of Chile's total exports, while copper was only 7 per cent (Bulmer-Thomas, 1998). Around 1910, Chile had established itself as one of the prosperous countries in Latin America.

However, the decline of the saltpetre boom began with the manufacture of synthetic sodium nitrate during the First World War. The final blow came with the Great Depression in 1929, when the value in dollars of nitrate export fell almost to the level of 1880.

12.2.3 From the Great Depression to Allende's Government (1930 to 1973)

The impact of the Great Depression of the 1930s on the Chilean economy was so devastating that it produced a complete change in the country's strategy: an 'inward-oriented development' replaced the 'outward-oriented development'. Chile was the country most profoundly hit by the world crisis, according to a report by the League of Nations, given that its GDP fell 38 per cent in 1932 with respect to the average of the period 1927–29, and its exports were reduced by 78 per cent (Meller, 1996).

Industrialization came to be considered the formula for the development of the national economy, becoming the driving force for growth, and industrialization based on substitution of imports marked the first stage in this new process of development. Meller (1996) commented that due to the relatively slow reaction of the private sector, and the generalized perception that large basic industries in key sectors of energy and intermediate supplies were a prerequisite for the success of the new model, the State began to take on an increasingly important role in the economic process. Thus, in 1939 Corporación de Fomento de la Producción (CORFO) was created as a State entity for the furthering of industrialization in the country.

This new model of imports substitution via industrialization of the country and inward-oriented development, instead of towards the exports that marked the previous periods until 1930, was not exclusive to Chile, since various Latin American nations developed the same model, promoted and conceptualized later by the Comisión Económica para América Latina (CEPAL), a body of the United Nations (Prebisch, 1964).

The CORFO became the main vehicle for promoting growth through development policies, and towards the end of this period it had become a conglomerate of State companies that dominated almost every area of the national economy. During the government of Eduardo Frei Montalva (1964–70), the State's participation in mining was 13 per cent, in manufacturing 3 per cent, public services 25 per cent, transport 24 per cent, communications 11 per cent and 0 per cent in financing, with a general average of 14.2 per cent (Hachette and Lüders, 1987).

However, at the end of this period, during the socialist government of the Unidad Popular, led by Salvador Allende (1970–73), the huge majority of private companies were nationalized, making the State's participation in mining reach 85 per cent in 1972, 40 per cent of manufacturers, 100 per cent of public services, 70 per cent of transport, 70 per cent of communications and 85 per cent of the financial sector. The general average of the country was already 35 per cent in the hands of the State (Hachette and Lüders, 1987). This is without considering the Agrarian Reform, initiated in 1962 and expanded by Allende's government, with extensive expropriations of agricultural land and property (Cáceres, 1974).

Simultaneously, the State increased its wide repertoire of economic controls. Thus, there appeared in succession differentiated tariffs, licences and pre-export deposits; freezing of prices, interest rates, wages and salaries; limitations on the physical volume of production, taxes on resource allocation, subsidies and multiple exchange rates and so on. All this contributed to the growing power of the State and the restriction of private initiative (Ibáñez, 1983).

Lastly, this period is also characterized by a rising interest rate. From an annual average of 5.8 per cent in the 1930s, inflation shot up to an average

38.4 per cent in the 1950s and in the government of Allende it ran out of control at 255.2 per cent in 1972 and 605.9 per cent in 1973 (Ibáñez, 1983).

12.2.4 The New Model of Market Economy (1973 to 1990)

On 11 September 1973, armed forces took control of the country and overthrew the government of Allende, thus beginning a new period in the economic history of Chile. At this time the country found itself in a very delicate economic situation. GDP fell 5.6 per cent in 1973, inflation rocketed, as mentioned earlier, and fiscal deficit reached 24.7 per cent of GDP, with an over-bloated and interventionist State. Price freezing and other controls on goods and services led to the flourishing of rationing, the black market, hoarding and long queues for acquiring even the most basic goods. As commented by Ibáñez (1983), what had been produced was total economic collapse.

The government led by General Augusto Pinochet, which covers the entirety of this period, put into practice an economic programme designed by a group of ten economists known as the 'Chicago Boys', since most of them had done postgraduate studies at the University of Chicago (Bardón et al., 1985). This programme brought about a fundamental economic transformation in Chile and for this reason is denominated the 'Chilean economic miracle'. Nevertheless, Hernán Büchi, the last Interior Minister of this government, insists it was not a miracle but rather the result of a carefully prepared programme.

Büchi (2008) states that this programme was based on opening the Chilean economy to the world and revitalizing the languishing private sector. A tariff-only system was established for imports and State companies were privatized. The list of initiatives that were adopted was endless: control inflation, create an autonomous Central Bank, balance the fiscal accounts, make room for the private sector, create a new system of pensions with individual capitalization instead of a pay-as-you-go system, decentralize education and develop support systems for the most vulnerable, with emphasis on human capital, among many others (Büchi, 2008).

This new economic model, completely the opposite of the previous period, put Chile at the head of economic development in Latin America. Even if the results took a little longer in coming, given there was a lot to regulate and reconstruct, towards the end of the 1970s, Chile's growth rate was between 7 per cent and 10 per cent. However, the policy of fixed exchange rate produced an enormous disequilibrium in the balance of payments, which ended in crisis in 1982 with a fall of 14.1 per cent in GDP. The subsequent exchange relaxation and other adjustments provoked a new upswing, this time definitive, and thus the Chilean economy saw an average annual growth rate of 7.2 per cent between the mid 1980s and 1997, when the Asian crisis struck.

12.2.5 The Return to Democracy (1990 to 2012)

With the arrival of democracy in 1990, the centre-leftist and leftist governments of the *Concertación* (alliance of parties for democracy) were faced with the dilemma of whether to retain the existing economic model – that was giving such good economic results to the country – or to change it to one that was more in accordance with their ideology. They opted for the former, with a large dose of pragmatism, and the country continued on its path of growth until 1997, reaching a yearly average of 7.7 per cent. Boosted by the economic reforms of the previous period, this was the time in which the first free trade agreements were signed and efforts were made to open the export markets.

Nevertheless, between 1998 and 2009, growth was moderated to an average yearly 3.5 per cent. If we discount the last two years that were affected by the global crisis resulting from the 'sub-prime' crisis in the United States, the average yearly growth was 4 per cent. Büchi (2008, p. 325) attributes this reduction to 'the ideological soul of the governments of the *Concertación* managing to override the pragmatic soul. In doing so, it destroys [the companies'] incentive to employ and invest'.

With the change of government towards an alliance between centre-right and right in 2010, there was a renewed economic boost to the Chilean economy and investments and employment were strongly revitalized. Thus, Chile grew an average of almost 6 per cent in the period 2010–12, despite the great earthquake that hit the country in February 2010.

12.3 ENTREPRENEURIAL FAMILIES IN INDEPENDENT CHILE

Let us recall that in the years 1830–80, Chile had significant economic growth, stimulated by its integration into the world economy as exporter of raw materials of mining and agriculture, and as importer of manufactured goods. This process allowed the emergence of a new entrepreneurial elite – different from the traditional mercantile and landowning elite of colonial origin – that took control of the most important areas of the economy. The new entrepreneurship, dynamic and progressive, was being established on the basis of an emerging bourgeoisie that began to replace the traditional dominance of the landowning elite with its aristocratic mentality.

The work of these entrepreneurs is valued highly by the historian Sergio Villalobos who comments:

> what would have become of Chile if there had not been in the twentieth century a dynamic group of copper and silver miners in Atacama, pioneers of railway and steam navigation, risk-taking industrialists and active bankers. It was they who gathered capital, made investments, explored the territory, introduced techniques and machinery and exposed their fortune to daring business ventures. Without them, one would have to imagine a backward and rural country. (Villalobos, 1980, p. 77)

Nevertheless, the majority of large entrepreneurial families of the nineteenth century did not survive the passing of time or generations. Only isolated cases like Edwards or Cousiño managed to continue, but towards the second half of the twentieth century both families' influence and relative equity had become greatly diminished. It should be mentioned that these were the most prominent families in the nineteenth century, as seen in Table 12.1, where five members of both families appear among the top six fortunes in Chile.

The case of the Cousiño family, for example, is very interesting. This family is very closely linked to the history of Chile as an independent republic. Since Matías Cousiño began his entrepreneurial activities in 1835, six generations have passed. This is without counting two further generations, since the first Cousiño arrived in Chile in 1760, from Galicia, Spain. Don Matías was the precursor of many industries in Chile, such as coal in Lota, railway, viticulture and so on. He also worked in the silver mine in Chañarcillo and founded the Association of Millers of the South. His only son, Luis, developed the businesses even further, but died young at 38. His wife, Isidora Goyenechea, mother of seven, proved to be a great entrepreneur and continued to expand the businesses of the family. In the present day, the brothers Carlos, Emilio and Arturo Cousiño Valdés, descendent of the youngest of these seven offspring, are the only ones continuing this successful family saga. Successive distributions of property among the seven branches of the family, in addition to the various upheavals in the country's economy during the twentieth century, have eroded the family fortune, once among the largest of Chile. Its businesses today are focused on the wine industry, through the prestigious Cousiño Macul vineyard, and in the real estate sector, with Inmobiliaria Crillón, based on the land of the family hacienda in Macul.

At the end of the 1950s, the majority of the large economic groups or conglomerates in Chile were associated with banking. Table 12.1 shows the results of a study by Ricardo Lagos – ex President of Chile – in his years as a law student, on the concentration of economic power and the

Table 12.1 The largest economic groups in Chile in the late 1950s

Group	Controlling families	No. of companies	% of total capital invested in limited company
Banco Sudamericano	(1) Alessandri-Matte; (2) Salinas and Fabres; (3) Cooperativa Vitalicia; (4) independent	126	39.90
Banco de Chile	Various shareholders	45 + 29	35.80
Banco Edwards	Edwards	61	20.80
Punta Arenas	Families from Punta Arenas (linked to the succession of Sara Braun)	40	15.30
Banco Nacional del Trabajo		35	8.00
Grace-Copec		21	8.00
Banco Español	García Vela and other 'Spaniards'	32 + 10	4.40
Banco Continental	Furman, Pollack & Lamas	35	2.90
Cosatán	Family of Norte Grande	17	2.60
Banco de Crédito e Inversiones	Yarur	11	1.90
Banco Panamericano	Said & Hirmas	13	1.80

Source: From Lagos (1960).

principal groups (Lagos, 1960). From the 11 identified groups, eight are linked to banks, and another eight are associated with entrepreneurial families. As we shall see later, this scenario changes radically in the subsequent decades.

Other research by Garretón and Cisternas (1970) shows that in the late 1960s there were approximately 20 economic groups in Chile. Table 12.2 shows these groups. The authors point out that the top three were large in size, and the remaining 17 were smaller. Now the names of banks have disappeared, with the exception of Banco Hipotecario, to be replaced by the names of individual entrepreneurs and entrepreneurial families. It is interesting to see how in only ten years the names have changed so much, excepting Edwards, Matte, Yarur and Said, who were already the big entrepreneurial families of the time.

On the subject of changes, it is interesting to look at the more detailed

Table 12.2 The largest economic groups in Chile in the late 1960s

1	Agustín Edwards
2	Eliodoro Matte
3	Banco Hipotecario (Javier Vial, Fernando Larraín and Ricardo Claro)
4	Familia Menéndez Préndez
5	Anacleto Angelini
6	Said Kattan brothers
7	Nicolás Yarur Lolas
8	Yarur Banna brothers
9	Teófilo Yarur Asfura
10	Hirmas Atala brothers
11	César Sumar Pachá
12	Furman Levy brothers
13	Hernán Briones
14	Pollack Ganz brothers
15	Roberto Lepe, Pierre Lehman and Helios Piquer
16	Marín family
17	Carlos Vial Espantoso
18	Andrónico Luksic
19	Pedro Ibáñez
20	Francisco Soza

Source: Garretón and Cisternas (1970).

Table 12.3, which shows the largest economic groups in Chile ten years later, that is to say, at the end of the 1970s. The top two groups, Cruzat-Larraín and BHC, with Javier Vial as head of the group, were together in third place a decade before. Since the 1960s, they had been known as the 'pirañas'. After them come the group of the Matte family, who remain among the top positions, and lower down the families Said and Yarur reappear. The Edwards family group, once the most important in Chile and, we recall, originating in the nineteenth century, is now somewhat reduced. Other families have also lost significance and new ones have emerged, all this in only ten years. What had happened? Why so many changes? Over and above the problems of succession in families, conflicts, management mistakes, failed investments or investments in declining sectors and so on, it is possible that the economic and political environment of the 1960s and 1970s and the change from a State-run economic model to one focused on the social market economy can help explain part of it.

Many entrepreneurial groups and families knew how to adapt to an environment that needed more management, more competitiveness and

Table 12.3 The 20 largest economic groups in Chile in the late 1970s

Group	Controlling person or family	No. of companies	Equity (US$ million)
Cruzat-Larraín	Manuel Cruzat Infante & Fernando Larraín Peña Sub-group: Ricardo Claro Valdés Sub-group: Patricio García Vela Allied Group: Francisco Soza Cousiño	109	1000
BHC	Javier Vial Castillo Sub-group: Carlos Vial Espantoso Sub-group: Carlos Cruzat Paul Sub-group: Marín Larraín Family	65	520
Matte	Eliodoro Matte Ossa	45	360
Angelini	Anacleto and Gino Angelini Fabbri	26	140
Edwards	Agustín Edwards Eastman	40	74
Luksic	Andrónico Luksic Abaroa and sons Andrónico and Guillermo Luksic Craig	31	150
Yarur Banna	Hermanos Jorge, Amador and Carlos Yarur Banna	12	100
Yarur Lolas	Nicolás Yarur Lolas and sons Alfredo, Fuad and Nazri Yarur Kasakia		
Hochschild	Mauricio Hochschild	12	60
Said	José Said Saffie, Antonio Said Kattan, Domingo Said Kattan and Jacobo Said Kattan	28	
Briones	Hernán Briones Gorostiaga		55
Puig	Brothers Vicente and Tomás Puig Casanova		40
Gálmez	Juan Gálmez Couso and sons Juan Antonio y José Miguel Gálmez Puig		95
Lepe, Piquer y Lehman	Roberto Lepe Flaraud, Helios Piquer Melija and Pierre Lehman Chaufour		70
Sumar	Hermanos César and Fernando Sumar Pachá		26
Abalos y González	Patricio Abalos and Ricardo González C.	20	
Mustakis	Constantino Mustakis Kotsilini	18	22
Schiess	Guillermo Schiess		40
Andina	Orlando Sáenz Rojas, Alejandro Bañados Morandé, Sergio Vergara Bruce, Santiago Cummings Marín and Carlos Joannon Fernández	23	
Sáenz	Orlando Sáenz Rojas		

Source: Dahse (1979).

less protectionism, while others did not, and remained entrenched in an environment with more protectionist business practices and more influence from the State.

Three decades later, Table 12.4 presents a list of – in my opinion – the 20 most important entrepreneurial families in Chile at the time of writing.

It is possible that I have unintentionally omitted some families that should have been included on the list. I have, however, excluded some important entrepreneurs, individual leaders of a group or family, because, in my opinion, they do not yet constitute an entrepreneurial family. This is the case, for example, of Julio Poce, controller of SQM, world leader in specialized fertilizer, iodine and lithium.

There are some obvious conclusions to be drawn from Tables 12.1 to 12.4.

There have been many changes to the map of most important entrepreneurial families in Chile in the last six decades. Many reasons could contribute to explaining what occurred. Among these, dramatic changes in the economic and political environment, good or bad investments, exit from or remaining in dying sectors, successful or failed management, good or bad dealing with succession and other family matters and so on.

The majority of families that were important at the end of the 1950s, 1960s and 1970s are no longer so, or have lost a great deal of their equity, either in absolute or relative terms. The most illustrative case is that of the Edwards family that, as we recall, was one of the most important families of the nineteenth century, and that in the twentieth century was in control of a large number of companies. At the start of the twenty-first century, its core company is the *El Mercurio* newspaper and other newspapers that are part of this journalist company. Other examples are families of Arab and Jewish origin that owned important textile companies in Chile. With the boom in textile manufacturing in Asia and particularly in China, many of these families saw their equity significantly reduced.

In the last 60 years, only three families still remain among the top 20: Matte, Yarur and Said. The case of the Matte family is interesting in that, as mentioned by the historian Vicuña-Mackenna (1882), they already appeared among the most important families in 1882. Although the present day Matte are only distant relatives, all are part of the same family that arrived in Chile from Cantabria, northern Spain. Also interesting is the case of the Yarur and Said families. Both families, of Palestinian origin, had significant participation in the textile industry, but knew to get out in time and diversify into banking, financial services and other businesses, in the case of the former; and in the case of the latter, shopping malls, beverages, banking and health services.

Many of the largest entrepreneurial families today were small at the end

Table 12.4 The 20 largest entrepreneurial families in Chile in 2012

Family	Main companies	Industries	Generation of family
Luksic	Banco de Chile, CCU, CSAV, Antofagasta Minerals	Banking, beverages, maritime, mining	2nd
Angelini	Copec, Arauco	Wood pulp, forestry, fishing, fuel	2nd
Matte	CMPC, Colbún, Entel	Wood pulp, forestry, energy, telecommunications	2nd–3rd
Paulmann	Cencosud	Retail, finance	1st–2nd
Solari y Cuneo	Falabella, Sodimac	Retail, finance	3rd–4th
Del Río	Falabella, Sodimac, Derco	Retail, finance, automotive	2nd
Cueto	LATAM Airlines	Airlines	2nd
Yarur	Bci, Salcobrand	Banking, insurance, pharmacies	3rd–4th
Said	Parque Arauco, Andina, BBVA, Cruz Blanca, Edelpa	Malls, beverages, banking, health, packaging	3rd–4th
von Appen	Ultramar, Ultragas	Shipping line, port services	2nd–3rd
Saieh	CorpBanca, SMU	Banking, retail	1st–2nd
Fernández León	FFV, Consorcio Financiero, Pucobre, Entel, Banmédica	Real estate, insurance, mining, telecommunications, health	2nd
Hurtado Vicuña	Entel, Consorcio Financiero, Pucobre	Telecommunications, insurance and pensions, mining	2nd
Vial	Agrosuper	Food	1st–2nd
Bofill	Carozzi, Costa, Ambrosoli, Agrozzi	Food	4th
Délano y Lavín	Cuprum, Penta, Banmédica	Pension funds, banking, insurance, health	1st–2nd
Schiess	Transoceánica	Investments, real estate	2nd
Calderón	Ripley	Retail, finance	2nd
Marín	CGE, Gasco, Metrogas	Energy	2nd
Guilisasti	Concha y Toro, Emiliana, Viconto	Wine growing, fruit growing	2nd

Source: Author's elaboration based on various sources.

of the 1960s and 1970s. The most interesting cases to analyse are those of Anacleto Angelini and Andrónico Luksic. The former, born in Italy, was pioneer in the Chilean forestry and fishing industries. Since he had no heirs, his nephew Roberto took the reins in 2007. The latter, Croatian by origin, began his development in mining in Antofagasta, but later, together with his sons Andrónico, Guillermo and Jean-Paul, expanded into many other sectors, such as banking, manufacturing industry, food and beverages, and has recently entered maritime transport through the gradual takeover of Cía. Sudamericana de Vapores (CSAV), which because of financial problems was being sold off by the Claro family. This is not to mention the copper mine where the Luksic family has expanded enormously through Antofagasta Minerals, the company that is listed in the London stock market. Both groups, Angelini and Luksic, together with Matte, are the three principal economic groups in Chile, and the three most important entrepreneurial families.

Several of the families prominent in the present day developed only 20 or 30 years ago, or even later. Significant cases are, for example, the entrepreneur Horst Paulman, born in Germany and founder of Cencosud, a retail giant in Chile and neighbouring countries; the Solari, Cúneo and Del Río families, controllers of Falabella and Sodimac, two more retail giants in South America; the Cueto family, important shareholder and manager of LAN Airlines, today LATAM, after the merger with TAM of Brazil; and the von Appen family, also of German origin, that has grown enormously in the shipping and port services industry. These families were born and developed in a highly competitive environment and knew how to remain strong and grow thanks to good management, good corporate governance, aligned shareholders and families that have known how to remain on good terms in order to succeed in business.

Figure 12.1 shows the changes in some of the most prominent entrepreneurial families and economic groups in the last 50 years.

Apart from the gradual decline of the Edwards family, reflected in Figure 12.1, it is interesting to note the rise and fall of the 'pirañas': Cruzat-Larraín, Javier Vial and Ricardo Claro, who in the 1960s began together in the Banco Hipotecario de Chile and later separated. However, it is important to point out that, more than entrepreneurial families, these three were economic groups with entrepreneurs in the first generation. Manuel Cruzat and Fernando Larraín, who were indeed related, being brothers-in-law, built the largest economic conglomerate of the country with more than 100 companies, Javier Vial remained with Banco Hipotecario and starting from it he built another huge conglomerate, called Grupo BHC. Together, they controlled companies that represented around 50 per cent of the equity of listed companies (Jones and Lluch,

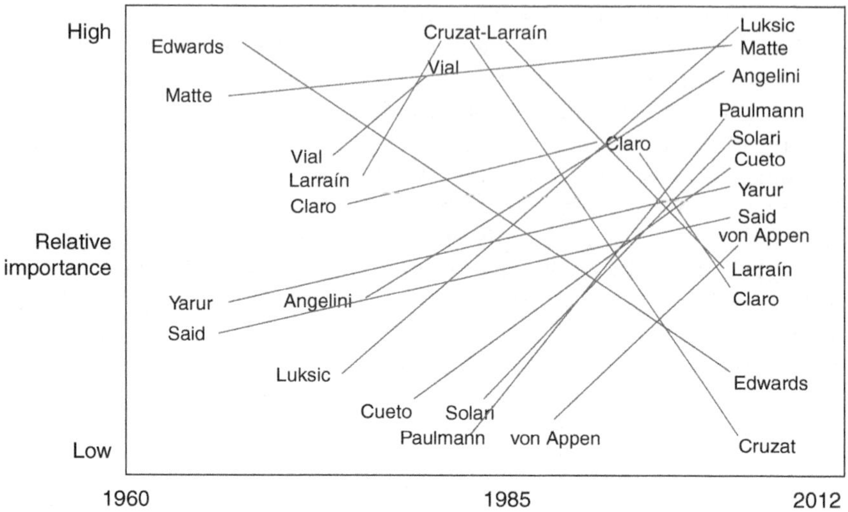

Figure 12.1 Map of entrepreneurial families and groups in Chile, 1960–2012

2011). Both groups were deeply in debt in dollars at the time of devaluation with the end of the fixed exchange rate in 1982 and the government had to intervene, since, moreover, transactions had been made between their companies and the banks they controlled. Javier Vial never managed to recover; he died 20 years later. Manuel Cruzat and Fernando Larraín separated and each continued with their sons, becoming what we know as entrepreneurial families. Cruzat was relaunched in the 1990s but failed again. In contrast, Fernando Larraín and family managed to form a smaller, but significant and healthy group, with companies such as Watt's, Santa Carolina, Larraín Vial and CIC. For his part, Ricardo Claro, who was also one of the 'pirañas', took over the control of various prominent companies, such as Cía. Sudamericana de Vapores, Elecmetal, Megavisión, Viña Santa Rita and Cristalerías de Chile, among others. Nevertheless, after his sudden death in 2008, the 'flagship' company of his group, the shipping line, had to hand over control to the Luksic family due to its enormous debt and the fall of the global market of maritime transport. This without a doubt weakened the group of the Claro family considerably. It is interesting to note that neither Ricardo Claro nor Anacleto Angelini, another great entrepreneur, had offspring. However, the former had brothers and the latter nephews, to succeed them.

12.4 CHARACTERISTICS OF LARGE ENTREPRENEURIAL FAMILIES IN CHILE

Chilean entrepreneurial families present a series of very prominent characteristics, especially if we refer to the 20 most important families that appear in Table 12.4. Even if we extend the number to the top 50, these features would be maintained. They are described below.

Firstly, they are relatively young or recent. The large majority is in the second generation, or in the transition from founder to the second. Only very few are in the third or fourth generation.

Although I have not presented data on their equity, this being private and not known in any detail, some of these families appear in the global ranking of Forbes. If we consider that Chile is a country of close to 17 million inhabitants, the Chilean presence is quite astonishing; without doubt it is the largest in Latin America in relation to the size of the country. This speaks volumes of the great development achieved by the principal Chilean entrepreneurial families.

Even though diversification is predominant, especially in the top three family groups (Luksic, Angelini and Matte) who own many companies in sectors unrelated to each other, some of the entrepreneurial families of greater size present more focus and concentration on one sector or on adjacent sectors. This is the case of the Paulmann, Solari-Cúneo-del Río and Calderón families in retail; Cueto in airlines; von Appen in shipping and ports; Vial and Bofill in food; Guilisasti in wines and so on.

Table 12.5 shows the internationalization of the 20 largest entrepreneurial families in Chile. As is evident, not only the retail companies have made significant progress in internationalization, but also companies involved in food, beverages, wines, financial services, shipping lines and so on.

Furthermore, these families are generally in control of well-managed and efficient companies. In fact, two studies have concluded that companies controlled by families and trading on the Santiago stock market have greater profitability than non-family companies (Bonillla et al., 2010; Martínez et al., 2007).

Another important characteristic of large entrepreneurial families in Chile is their austerity and low profile. In relation to their growing equity, the Chilean families tend to be more austere and have a lower profile than other Latin American entrepreneurial families, as far as I can tell from my experience as consultant to many of these families in various countries of the region. The principal Chilean entrepreneurs and their families protect their privacy very jealously and in general tend to avoid the press, except when commenting on mergers, acquisitions or important achievements on a national or international level.

Table 12.5 Internationalization of the 20 largest entrepreneurial families

Family	Internationalization and investments abroad
Luksic	Banco de Chile has offices all around the world; CSAV has offices in 25 countries; CCU operates in Argentina, Paraguay and Uruguay; Antofagasta Minerals in Pakistan; Luksic family owns large hotel chain in Croatia; 20 per cent of Nexans in France
Angelini	Forests and plants of wood pulp in Argentina, Brazil and Uruguay
Matte	Plant and forests in Brazil; forests in Argentina and Uruguay, Americatel Peru
Paulmann	Important investments in retail (through brands like Jumbo, Paris and Easy) in Argentina, Brazil, Colombia and Peru
Solari y Cuneo	Important investments in retail (through Falabella and Sodimac) in Argentina, Brazil, Colombia and Peru
Del Río	Important investments in retail through Falabella and Sodimac in Argentina, Brazil, Colombia and Peru. Three of the brothers are owners of Derco, automotive distributor with investments in Bolivia, Peru and Colombia
Cueto	LAN has operations in Argentina, Ecuador, Peru and now in Brazil with TAM
Yarur	Bank in the United States and minority percentage in Banco de Crédito de Perú
Said	Important percentage of ownership in shopping malls in Argentina; operations of Andina in Argentina and Brazil
von Appen	Investments in ports of Argentina, Brazil, Peru and other Latin American countries
Saieh	Bank in Colombia
Fernández León	Real estate investments in Argentina, Americatel Peru, clinics in Peru and Colombia through Banmédica
Hurtado	Americatel Peru
Vial	Export of chickens and turkeys to various countries
Bofill	Manufacturing plants and trade offices in Argentina, Peru and the United States; exports to a large number of countries worldwide
Délano y Lavín	Clinics in Peru and Colombia through Banmédica
Schiess	Real estate investments and hotels in Uruguay
Calderón	Important retail investments in Peru and Colombia (through Ripley)
Marín	Investments in energy in Argentina
Guilisasti	Vineyards and operations in the United States (Fretzer) and Argentina; exports to a large number of countries worldwide

Source: Author's elaboration based on companies' annual reports and websites, and articles in newspapers.

The offspring of these family entrepreneurs usually have very sound training in business in general. Many of them have studied economics, engineering or law in the best universities in Chile, and many of them do postgraduate studies abroad, especially MBAs in renowned business schools in the United States and Europe.

With some exceptions, Chilean large entrepreneurial families do not tend to actively participate in politics and even though they may have defined preferences, the majority avoids publicly supporting determined parties or candidates. In contrast to other countries, especially in the north of Latin America, the large economic groups in Chile do not directly influence the politics of the country.

Another feature that sets them apart is that, generally speaking, Chilean entrepreneurial families are socially responsible. The majority of companies have programmes of corporate social responsibility (CSR) and a significant proportion of the families have non-profit foundations for supporting issues such as education, health, the fight against poverty, art and so on.

Lastly, Chilean large entrepreneurial families are concerned about the continuity and training of their successors. Many of them have participated in programmes of family business and have hired consultants to help in planning their succession, both at a management level and in terms of equity. For more than 20 years, programmes of this type have been carried out in Chile, a pioneering country in this subject in Latin America.

12.5 THE CONTRIBUTION OF ENTREPRENEURIAL FAMILIES TO CHILE

We have seen that throughout the history of Chile as an independent nation, entrepreneurial families have played a prevailing role in the economic development of the country. Let us look now at some statistics and evaluations of its current importance.

According to the National Institute of Statistics (INE), there are 750 000 companies in Chile (INE, 2009). From this galaxy of companies we can estimate that around 80–90 per cent are family-run, that is, owned and managed by families.

However, the INE indicates that only 8000 of the 750 000 have a turnover of more than US$5 million a year. These 8000 are considered medium and large-sized companies. Of these – according to a recent study – a little more than two thirds are family businesses (Martínez, 2010). Furthermore, around 60 per cent of the companies listed on the Santiago stock market are controlled by families (Bonilla et al., 2010; Martínez et al., 2007).

With the above statistics, we can make a conservative estimate that family companies generate between 50 per cent and 70 per cent of the GDP of Chile, and provide a similar proportion of employment. This makes them the veritable spinal cord and driving force of the country's economy.

Apart from their role in economic growth and the creation of employment, entrepreneurial families have been the main source of creation and development of small, medium and large private companies. The enormous contribution they have made to the development of large, efficient and competitive companies in the Chilean market is remarkable; and they have also led the integration of Chile into the global environment, particularly through exports and direct investment.

These family-controlled companies have provided Chile with a highly significant volume of exports, and they have contributed to a large part of Chilean direct investment abroad, especially in Latin America.

These companies, owned and controlled by entrepreneurial families, have introduced and developed state-of-the-art technology, innovation and highly professional management skills to Chile. This has been fundamental for the companies to be able to achieve a higher performance than the non-family companies, according to the previously mentioned studies.

Furthermore, entrepreneurial families have improved the image of Chilean entrepreneurs through the many examples of CSR of its companies, and the disinterested contribution – often anonymous – of foundations and social and philanthropic works by the families themselves.

Last, but not least, entrepreneurial families have contributed very significantly to the economic stability of Chile – at least in the last 30 years – and have been the veritable driving force of the model of social market economy that has had such good results in the development of Chile in the last decades.

12.6 CONCLUSIONS

The family company is the predominant form of entrepreneurial organization in Chile and constitutes the true driving force of the country's economy. The entrepreneurial families who control and manage these companies have made – and are still making – a fundamental contribution to the economic development and stability of Chile.

Particularly, it has been the large entrepreneurial families that have made a decisive contribution. The large entrepreneurial families active today are relatively new, since many of the families that emerged in the nineteenth and large part of the twentieth centuries were forced to confront an adverse economic and political environment, as well as serious internal problems within the companies and families themselves, preventing them from surviving or prospering.

In the second half of the nineteenth century, Chile was one of the strongest economies of Latin America. The Chilean GDP per capita saw continual growth at a rate similar to that of the United States, and even managed to exceed that of Spain and Argentina in 1880.

But after the Great Depression of the 1930s and until the arrival of the Military Government in 1973, Chile languished in a profound lethargy, the consequence of protectionist and State-controlled economic policies.

Nevertheless, appropriate economic policies established by various governments in the last quarter of the twentieth century and first decade of the twenty-first allowed a decisive contribution by family companies, and more specifically, by the entrepreneurial families behind these companies, making them symbolic of responsible private companies that stimulated economic growth in the country.

We can, therefore, conclude that the development of entrepreneurial families seems to be closely linked to the development of the Chilean economy. It was in the periods of economic liberalization and stability and the subsequent boom when the entrepreneurs and their families flourished, developed, created employment and gave greater dynamism to the country. The opposite seemed to have occurred in the periods in which the State played a more dominant and nationalizing role.

As a result of the well-managed macroeconomics of the country in the last 30 years, Chile today finds itself at the door to development. Since 2010, Chile has belonged to the Organisation for Economic Co-operation and Development and is close to reaching development. At the end of 2012, its GDP per capita was at US$18 350, adjusted by purchasing power parity, becoming the only country in Latin America to reduce the gap with developed countries in the last 30 years (Corbo, 2012). In the next three to five years it hopes to reach US$20 000–25 000, which would make it the first Latin American country to obtain the category of developed country. As a result, the index of poverty in the country has been significantly reduced in the last 30–40 years, from close to 40 per cent of the population to less than 15 per cent. Chilean entrepreneurial families can feel very satisfied to have collaborated with an enormous grain of sand to these achievements.

REFERENCES

Bardón, A., C. Carrasco and A. Vial (1985). *Una Década de Cambios Económicos. La Experiencia Chilena 1973–1983*. Santiago: Editorial Andrés Bello.

Bonilla, C., J. Sepúlveda and M. Carvajal (2010). 'Family ownership and firm

performance in Chile: a note on Martinez et al.'s evidence'. *Family Business Review* **2** (23) (June), 148–54.
Braun-Llona, J., M. Braun-Llona, I. Briones, J. Díaz, R. Lüders and G. Wagner (2000). 'Economía Chilena: 1810–1995. Estadísticas Históricas'. Documento de Trabajo, Instituto de Economía, Pontificia Universidad Católica de Chile (January).
Büchi, H. (2008). *La Transformación Económica de Chile. El Modelo del Progreso*. Santiago: Aguilar Chilena de Ediciones SA.
Bulmer-Thomas, V. (1998). *La Historia Económica de América Latina desde la Independencia*. México: Fondo de Cultura Económica.
Cáceres, C. (1974). 'La Economía de Chile durante el período de Gobierno de la Unidad Popular'. *Escuela de Negocios de Valparaíso*, Fundación Adolfo Ibáñez (March).
Corbo, V. (2012). 'La transformación económica de Chile y los retos futuros'. Artículo publicado por diario *El Mercurio* (18 November).
Dahse, F. (1979). *Mapa de la Extrema Riqueza: Los Grupos Económicos y el proceso de Concentración de Capitales*. Santiago: Editorial Aconcagua.
De Ramón, A. and J.M. Larraín (1982). *Orígenes de la Vida Económica Chilena 1659–1808*. Santiago de Chile: Centro de Estudios Públicos.
Garretón, O. and J. Cisternas (1970). 'Algunas Características del proceso de toma de decisiones en la Gran Empresa: la dinámica de la concentración'. Servicio de Cooperación Técnica (March).
Hachette, D. and R. Lüders (1987). 'El proceso de Privatización de Empresas en Chile, 1974–1982'. *Boletín Económico* **22**, Instituto de Economía, Pontificia Universidad Católica de Chile.
Ibáñez, P. (1983). *Hacia una Moderna Economía de Mercado. Diez Años de Política Económica 1972–1983*. Escuela de Negocios de Valparaíso, Fundación Adolfo Ibáñez (July).
INE (Instituto Nacional de Estadísticas) (2009). *Metodología Muestral Encuesta Longitudinal de empresas año contable 2007*. Santiago de Chile (October).
Jones, G. and A. Lluch (eds) (2011). *El Impacto Histórico de la Globalización en Argentina y Chile: empresas y empresarios*. Buenos Aires: Editorial Temas.
Lagos, R. (1960). *La Concentración del Poder Económico. Su Teoría. Realidad Chilena*. Santiago de Chile: Editorial del Pacífico.
Martínez, J. (2010). 'Cómo ha impactado la Globalización a las Empresas Familiares en Chile?'. *Revista del ESE Business School*, Universidad de los Andes (December).
Martinez, J., B. Stöhr and B. Quiroga (2007). 'Family ownership and firm performance: evidence from public companies in Chile'. *Family Business Review* **XX** (2) (June), 83–94.
Massad, C. (2001). 'Economía Chilena: Experiencias de un Siglo'. Presentación como Presidente del Banco Central de Chile (November).
Meller, P. (1996). *Un siglo de economía política chilena (1890–1990)*. Santiago de Chile: Editorial Andrés Bello.
Prebisch, R. (1964). 'Nueva Política Comercial para el Desarrollo'. Fondo de Cultura Económica, México.
Schmidt-Hebbel, K. (2006). 'El Crecimiento Económico de Chile'. Documento de Trabajo, Banco Central de Chile (June).
Vial, G. (1981). *Historia de Chile (1891–1973)*. Vol. I. Santiago: Editorial Santillana.

Vicuña-Mackenna, B. (1882). 'Principales fortunas chilenas'. Carta publicada en *El Mercurio de Valparaíso* (26 April).
Villalobos, S. (1980). *Los comienzos de la historiografía económica de Chile: 1862–1940*. Santiago: Editorial Universitaria.
Villalobos, S. (1993). *Chile y su Historia*. Santiago: Editorial Universitaria.

Conclusions

Paloma Fernández Pérez and Andrea Lluch

One of the conclusions of this book, in line with the recent theoretical approaches of Pramodita Sharma, Jess Chua and Mattias Nordqvist, is that the real protagonists of family-controlled businesses are, in the long term, the families and not necessarily, nor always the companies.

Another important theoretical conclusion of the reflections in this book is that the organizational structures that families in Latin America and Spain adopted in the long term were flexible adaptations to regulatory, institutional, financial and market uncertainties. The structure of a legally independent company, or of a holding, or a formal or informal business group, or an association in districts with a regional base, would be – from a historical perspective – a non-essential organizational component in the long-term strategies of family businesses, using the terminology of Sharma and Chua. What has been, and still remains, the most essential factor for the largest business families in these countries is the capacity and the intention (successful or not) to match resources over time with the willingness to endure in the business, using the organizational structure that is most efficient and best suited to the various external environments and the changing internal evolution of the families.

Thirdly, the 22 researchers from 11 countries, who collaborated as an interdisciplinary team, combining tools from historical methodology with those of analysis of family business management – in contrast to many works by consultants who analyse only the keys to success for large family businesses – demonstrate above all experiences of change, transformation, disappearance, divestiture, mergers, failures and chameleon-like adaptation of large family firms, belonging to the most outstanding entrepreneurial families of eight Latin American countries (Brazil, Mexico, Argentina, Colombia, Peru, Chile, Costa Rica, Honduras) and Spain, over the course of more than a century. The presentation of the nine national cases was organized into three broad parts according to specific features of the countries involved, ordered by size of market and the type of insertion into the global economy in the long term.

As the reader will have observed, the embracing of such a huge and diverse area allows for a wealth of cases to be explored, in contrast to the widespread tendency to identify a 'Latino standard' of family capitalism. Indeed, what becomes apparent in these pages is a rich territorial and cultural mosaic in which experimentation, change, success and failure predominated. It is precisely this diversity that has been noticed, also, in comparative studies of large family business in other regions of the world like Asia (Okochi, 1984) and Europe (Colli et al., 2003; Fernández Pérez and Colli, 2013; James, 2006; Jones and Rose, 1993).

Taken together, the comparative works of the first part and the national approaches of the other three large parts of this book contribute to clarifying and putting into context recent debates on the diversity of cultural standards in business structure that exist worldwide (Hofstede et al., 1990), and the proclaimed existence of institutional standards that predetermine certain types of national capitalism and a particular form of company with 'standards' that belong to the Anglo-Saxon, Germanic, Asian or Mediterranean territories. Above all for this latter debate, and concerning what is known as 'Varieties of Capitalism' (VoC), the findings reinforce the limitations of orthodox ideas on the organization of institutions that affect businesses around the world. According to the initial proposals by Hall and Soskice (2001), there are two major kinds of institutional frameworks that condition two ideal types of capitalism: one inspired by the USA and the UK, based on liberal market economies (LME), and another inspired by Germany and Japan, based on corporatist market economies. This excessive simplification and polarization of what constitutes institutions that affect businesses in the world led its authors and other specialists to diversify the influential institutional frameworks, to include mixed market economies (MME), Mediterranean and Southeast Asian capitalisms and hierarchical market economies in Latin America (Hancké et al., 2007; Herrigel and Zeitlin, 2010; Iversen, 2010; Miller, 2010; Schneider, 2009). Critics of the original version of the debates on VoC insist not only that the institutional reality is much more complex than these simplifications, but also that there exists a huge diversity of national and regional cases within the supposed continental or national monolithic blocks (Herrigel and Zeitlin, 2010).

The evidence gathered in this book is significant, considering that the specific 'variety' proposed for Latin America, called hierarchical market capitalism, was characterized – among other factors – by the dominance of diversified family business groups in both large and small economies (Schneider, 2009). However, no conclusive empirical evidence has as yet been found to support these claims, nor has any previous research covered an area of geographical diversity comparable to this work. Furthermore, and in contrast to these general viewpoints, the chapters on Peru, Chile,

Brazil and Argentina show that the dominance of business groups has been changing, as well as their level and type of diversification. The chapters on Mexico and Spain, for instance, emphasize the regional diversity, an aspect that over the course of more than a hundred years has conditioned regional frameworks where institutions, companies and markets can interact in opposition to national dynamics.

In line with some critics of the orthodoxy of the VoC paradigm, the chapters of this book dwell on two other elements with new data and arguments. On the one hand, that institutional frameworks change, they are not immutable or neutral, as Herrigel and Zeitlin (2010) indicated; and, on the other hand, that the main players (companies, entrepreneurs) often have – and this confirms the ideas of Baumol (2010) – active roles and are not merely passive in the configuration of institutional frameworks supposedly created by an invisible hand. Moreover, and as many chapters of this work reveal, these roles and functions have been dynamic (even during the lifetime of a single company and/or family), and unlikely to be found in any 'pure form'. This book also shows that business families have often been highly visible in their contribution to the configuration of institutional frameworks, in some periods, in some countries, either putting pressure on governments or sometimes occupying positions of control within the governments at the top level, or within official departments in charge of granting projects and subsidies to private firms.

The inexistence of rigid and immutable national institutional frameworks that determine different ways of doing business over time, as well as the diversity of profiles and strategies of the entrepreneurial players, are founded on another key element in this book: the periodization proposal. The majority of chapters identify three or four large periods of change in the eight Latin American countries, and also in Spain. These large periods are linked to the impact of external shocks and to the changeable insertion of the region into the global economy, but also to internal processes that changed the ground rules for foreign and national investors, and to the institutional and legal frameworks that shaped the opportunities for public and private companies. The years between the 1930s or 1940s – depending on the country – and the 1980s were characterized by strong public intervention in the economy, with institutional frameworks that cannot simply be named as 'hierarchical markets' exclusive to Latin America, but rather were changing contexts in which the States promoted public companies and, furthermore, in Latin America, industrial growth through import substitution. Nevertheless, the diversity of situations within Latin America, as well as the regional differences within each country, the changes in developmental paradigms and the progress and setbacks in the implemented programmes all make it impossible to support the existence of a common institutional framework for the whole Hispanic-American area, even though a widespread feature of successful family business in the majority of countries and regions studied is their ability to adjust to rapid environmental changes.

With regard to the active role of business agents in the shaping and change of institutional frameworks, the chapters on Colombia and Peru are paradigmatic in showing how the sectorial specialization of some families (particularly in the media business) facilitated the conquest of the presidency and the elite of political parties with national, regional and local public powers, from where they could participate directly in the shaping of rules and regulations that would determine their business.

Supporting the ideas of Baumol (2010), this book provides evidence that the institutional framework, in contrast to what orthodox neoclassic economics usually imply, is not an external agent of economic activity that conditions or even determines it. Sometimes economic agents capture the institutions and steer local, regional and national economies. The chapters on Colombia, Chile and Peru clearly show that the capture of political power must be understood in light of historical research, and with no dogmatism. At times, the control of institutions and sudden changes in who wielded this control meant an end to traditional business, as seen in the chapters on Chile, Spain, Argentina and Peru, due to the imposition of military dictatorships or sudden changes in economic policies. But controlling institutions can sometimes also be the basis for accelerating technology transfer, under the leadership of entrepreneurs and families who are well connected to foreign centres of innovation, in periods of weakness of government revenue and corruption, as at times seen in the cases of Mexico, Argentina, Spain, Chile, Colombia, Costa Rica, Honduras and Brazil.

The chapters in this book also represent a contribution to recent debates on the longevity and survival of large family business. The sections relating to the history of family-controlled business in Spain, Peru, Argentina, Mexico, Chile, Honduras and Brazil reveal that some well-known families from the nineteenth and early twentieth centuries, who founded their business at that time, managed to find the balance between maintaining a harmonious relationship within the extended family and adapting to new business environments in countries where there was often great political and macroeconomic instability. The replacement and disappearance of family firms is a common feature of almost all the cases analysed. Nevertheless, branches of some families mentioned in the book, such as the Botín, the Wiese, the Zambrano, the Yarur, the Braun, the Wolmann-Arrieta, the Matte, the Edwards, the Rosenthal and the Gerdau, are still active today, transforming themselves, changing profiles, creating new companies, albeit not always with the same impact as their forebears. Their accumulated know-how and their contact networks have allowed them to survive, and have influenced their financial capacity in the sectors in which they invest and in the companies through which they established partnerships or mergers. Furthermore, all the chapters show that, gradually and with differing dynamics, the process of modernizing the management system of successful large family businesses became strengthened, hand-in-hand with their progressive internationalization. Likewise, some authors suggest that contact with centres and consultants specializing in family business in the USA and Europe would have played a significant role in the professionalization of family business. In some cases, such as in Spain, the connection with local family-controlled service companies would also have been important in the professionalization and internationalization of large family businesses in the last three decades, as suggested by evidence obtained in recent research for Catalunya, and relevant for the rest of Spain (Fernández Pérez, 2013).

Many books and articles analyse the keys to success of entrepreneurial families that have survived over time. However, family business historians and consultants know that only a small minority of families manages to maintain the continuity of their firms in the long term. Indeed, each chapter uncovers only a tiny number of cases with the capacity to survive for a century. The overwhelming majority of businesses legally registered as companies disappear after two generations. A failure, apparently. Many consultants and global consultancy partnerships of family business, as well as institutions such as the European Union itself, are putting energy and effort into studying how to avoid the legal disappearance of family-controlled companies. Notwithstanding, this historical research covering nine countries, indicates – through in-depth study of public and private archives, interviews with surviving members of business families from the past, and print and digital newspaper archives – that in the business history of Latin America and Spain there was an abundance of entrepreneurial and business families that disappeared from one company and appeared in others, but continuing the activity over decades, often diversifying into sectors with greater profitability or security, thus changing the legal name of the business, the organization chart and the corporate governance blueprint. With its long-term perspective, this book reveals, among other things, that if there is a problem that affects family businesses, it is not the historical disappearance of legal companies controlled by families, but rather that the families disappear from the productive entrepreneurial activity. This conclusion is important and suggests that it is of priority to study, and nurture, entrepreneurial and business families in our countries, seeking not necessarily to protect certain legal forms of company, but instead the frameworks that facilitate the flexible adaptation to changes that take place within families and within the political, technological and market environments.

Using historical sources and methods, we can affirm, in line with what some experts in family business theory such as Pramodita Sharma and Jess Chua have suggested, that some families (and not necessarily their firms) survive precisely because they sacrifice companies legally registered by their grandparents and parents, and they diversify, establish partnerships, change name, become structurally more complex (and even move to other countries). The analysis of strategic shareholders of large businesses often shows the continuity of families. In reality, they are the key to a country's wealth, more than the companies on the Trade Register. For this reason, in the study of family business in a region, sector or continent, researchers must pay close attention – as we have done in this book on Latin America and Spain – to the evolution of the families, to their adaptability to changes in the environment. As indicated by Sharma and Chua, the history of entrepreneurial families in Latin America and Spain reveals that often the 'components' of a family business change over time, in order to maintain the 'essence' or objectives of the family (Chrisman et al., 2005; Chua et al., 1999; Nordqvist and Melin, 2010).

In line also with the emphasis put by family business theorists on the importance of analysing the context and the environment in order to understand the survival or disappearance of companies, in this book the chapters on Mexico, Argentina, Chile, Spain and Peru confirm the deeply rooted relationship some families have with their respective districts, be they agricultural, industrial or service-based. This element is clearly illustrated in the chapter on families in the north of Mexico, and in the chapter on Spain, dealing with the evolution of the largest family firms and groups in the industrial areas of the Mediterranean and northern Spain during the second half of the twentieth century and the beginning of the twenty-first.

The importance of the environment is also fundamental for understanding the enormous influence of the State in creating conditions that support or stifle the families' entrepreneurial initiatives over time, a point we have already referred to in these pages. In this respect, long-term analyses and the comparative chapter of Javier Vidal Olivares encourage one not to apply stereotypes or dogmatisms. On the one hand, the chapters on Argentina, Chile, Spain and Peru highlight the upheaval caused by various dictatorships to pre-existing business families: within the very different contexts of each country, the abrupt changes of the ground rules that occurred with the arrival of the dictatorships obstructed the development of some families in traditional businesses, or in businesses that clashed with the strategic interests of the new governments. This book, nevertheless, shows that the relationship between business families and authoritarian governments is not straightforward: some authoritarian political projects encouraged the rise and accumulation of family firms and groups of national origin, and in some Central American countries, the legislation explicitly protected the creation and growth of immigrant groups over the protection given to local groups, in this way determining the accumulativc process of expansion of some family groups and companies until the present day.

Another complementary finding emerging from the national and comparative analyses of this book is that the period known as *desarrollismo* (developing process) and *aperturismo* (opening up) in Spain, and State-driven industrialization in a large part of Latin America – a period that generated so many contradictory opinions in the economic literature – could also represent an environment with certain favourable financial, labour and tax conditions for the growth of many business families that had invested, in a modest way in consumer goods and service industries in the previous decades.

Whether under democratic or military governments, interventionist or neoliberal, an element that clearly stands out from this research is the strong link between State and family business and how sudden changes in the macroeconomic and institutional conditions brought with them great challenges for family firms. A clear example of the negative combination of external and internal shocks was the foreign debt crisis in Latin America in 1982, an event that caused the disappearance of large family groups and businesses and the reworking of economic policies that changed the internal make-up of the family-controlled business elite in many countries, boosting new faces up to top positions, as in the case of the Slim family in Mexico. This direction was confirmed in the 1990s with the embracing of the paradigm of market reform. Another example is the late impact of the energy crisis of the 1970s in Spain, due to the death of Francisco Franco (in 1975) and the transition to democracy, combined with the external shocks of the price of energy, which delayed adjustments of business practice and led Spain, as all of Europe, to a reorganization and the proliferation of business 'groups' from the 1980s onwards (Fernández Pérez, 2013).

Nevertheless, since no process is straightforward, changes in monetary, labour, fiscal and foreign trade legislation presented an opportunity for some business families who were capable of adapting to complex environments. Furthermore, the chapters on Brazil, Argentina and Peru indicate that not all families and businesses benefited from the same promotional programmes and, in general, these policies encouraged a pattern of business diversification (at least until the 1990s), which seemed to be an adequate strategy for remaining active and growing in turbulent markets, as long as the diversification did not reach unmanageable levels.

State subsidies for the promotion of some industrial sectors – as seen in the case of support given by BNDES in Brazil to its major private businesses, whether controlled by families or not, illustrated in the chapters on Brazil by Armando Dalla Costa, Carlos Eduardo Drumond and José María Las Heras, and also in the chapter on *multilatinas* by Lourdes Casanova – is paradigmatic of the great importance that channelling of public borrowing in recent decades can have for the growth and internationalization of medium and large family businesses. Indirect tax or monetary policies might also be useful to them, as clear from the analysis of the different impacts of the Argentinian and Brazilian monetary policies within MERCOSUR since the 1990s. In this regard, internationalization, a direction that various companies took after the 1970s and especially in the last decades, seems to be a route taken by those experiencing successful growth, since it meant a higher degree of independence from local macroeconomic conditions.

Regarding the influence of the massive influx of foreign capital, work and business organizations in Spain and Latin America, this book confirms what experts in the history of globalization have generally pointed out: that the inflow of new resources was very unevenly distributed. In Honduras, Costa Rica, Brazil, Peru, Argentina and Spain, since the late nineteenth and early twentieth centuries, multinationals boosted the entrance of foreign direct investment for the production and export of commodities, and for the construction of an emerging national transport network, infrastructure and services. This way, broadly speaking, a distinctive specialization was created between foreign capital and large local family capital. The greater presence of the State in the economies studied in this book, as previously mentioned, later encouraged the rise (with varying degrees of success) of public or private 'national champions' who developed production activities that were considered strategic and that attempted to reduce foreign dependence. Foreign multinationals, however, continued to occupy a fundamental position, as analysed in the chapters on Brazil and Argentina. In more recent decades, other works in this book emphasize the importance of the partnerships between large family groups and foreign capital for the development of strategic businesses, as illustrated in the chapters on Mexico, Chile, Peru and Spain.

One factor that no doubt boosted the development of family business in Central American countries, and in Argentina, Chile and Peru, was immigration, especially from Europe, and secondly from regions in the Near East (Syria, Lebanon, Palestine, Armenia) and, with a lesser impact on large Latin American business, from Asia and Africa. The entrepreneurial dynamics of many immigrant communities that used local and transnational networks for the flow of capital, know-how, human resources and merchandise or services was pointed out a long time ago by historians, sociologists and anthropologists who took an interest in their presence and activity in Latin America. Until the mid-twentieth century, their businesses were often initially focused on relatively low capital-intensive sectors such as food and beverage manufacturing and distribution, textile, construction, financing of consumer industries, fishing and canned food, paper mills, river and road transportation, as well as auxiliary industries to multinationals (in transport, energy, communications). In addition, they were very closely linked to the media and communications sector, creating conditions that favoured the entrance of business families into politics, as masterfully shown in the chapter on Colombia, and in the cases of the Planeta group in Spain, Clarín in Argentina, El Mercurio in Chile and El Comercio in Peru, to mention only a few examples. This book has illustrated how migratory flows were a fundamental factor in the creation of entrepreneurship and family dynasties, with the various waves of immigrants that moved through Latin America, and the different phases of emigration registered in Spain, since the late nineteenth century. Although the influx of European immigration to Latin America and the Spanish emigration to America gradually diminished, especially around the middle of the twentieth century, it is interesting to highlight that various chapters portray a strong link, even in the mid twentieth century, between medium and large-sized family business and migrations in Latin America and Spain.

In summary, this book brings together the first long-term, interdisciplinary overview of the origins and evolution of large family-controlled business in Latin America and Spain from the late nineteenth century to the present day. It is also an incomplete book, full of gaps and difficulties that current and future research must address. It bears the burden of some blame and defects by being the first of its kind in trying to achieve two goals that until now no researcher had been able to do alone, as it required a lifetime of work, or an efficiently coordinated international team. In order to meet the intended objectives, the support of the Fundación BBVA was fundamental, as was the cohesion and effort of the research team, and the task of coordination. The results obtained represented two major breakthroughs.

The first, as we have highlighted, is a relatively acceptable and standard methodology that delivers solid empirical evidence in order to gain a complete picture of the current importance of the largest family-controlled firms and groups in Latin America and Spain. The second breakthrough is the presentation of a retrospective analysis of local entrepreneurial dynamics, dominated by families, over the course of more than a century. In these pages, the topics that have been the focus of debates on family business in the last years have found historical and current evidence, analyses and comparisons: organizational structures, performance, corporate governance, management, succession and generational transition, survival and longevity, links between families and company, contexts and institutional frameworks, conflicts and partnerships, professionalization, internationalization, innovation, philanthropy in family firms, political power, ethnicity and immigration; regions, State and family business. And within the context of long-term studies and taking a narrative perspective, not only do the 'hows' abound, but also the 'whys' (Fernández Pérez and Colli, 2013). Overall, this book represents a first cooperative attempt to address the challenges, the obstacles and the greater or lesser importance of business families in the development of different regional and national economies and, in some cases, in the creation of large global giants.

REFERENCES

Baumol, W.J. (2010). *The Microtheory of Innovative Entrepreneurship*. Princeton, NJ: Princeton University Press.

Chrisman, J.J., J.H. Chua and P. Sharma (2005). 'Trends and directions in the development of a strategic management theory of the family firm'. *Entrepreneurship Theory and Practice* **29** (5), 555–75.

Chua, J.H., J.J. Christman and P. Sharma (1999). 'Defining the family business by behavior'. *Entrepreneurship Theory and Practice* **23** (4), 19–39.

Colli, A., P. Fernández Pérez and M. Rose (2003). 'National determinants of family firm development? Family firms in Britain, Spain, and Italy in the nineteenth and twentieth centuries'. *Enterprise and Society* **4** (1), 28–64.

Fernández Pérez, P. (2013). 'De hereus a profesionales. La transición de un modelo tradicional a un modelo moderno de gestión en la empresa familiar catalana'. In P. Fernández Pérez (ed.), *La profesionalización de las empresas familiares*. Madrid: LID, pp. 35–72.

Fernández Pérez, P. and A. Colli (eds) (2013). *The Endurance of Family Businesses: A Global Overview*. New York: Cambridge University Press.

Hall, P. and D. Soskice (eds) (2001). *Varieties of Capitalism: The Institutional Foundations of Comparative Advantage*. Oxford: Oxford University Press.

Hancke, B., M. Rhodes and M. Thatcher (eds) (2007). *Beyond Varieties of Capitalism: Conflict, Contradictions, and Complementarities in the European Economy*. New York: Oxford University Press.

Herrigel, G. and J.H. Zeitlin (2010). 'Alternatives to varieties of capitalism'. *Business History Review* **84** (4), 667–74.

Iversen, M.J. (2010). 'The "varieties of capitalism" approach as an analytical tool for business historians'. Varieties of Capitalism Roundtable. *Business History Review* **84** (4), 464–6.

James, H. (2006). *Family Capitalism: Wendels, Haniels, Falcks, and the Continental European Model*. Cambridge, MA: Harvard University Press.

Jones, G. and M.B. Rose (1993). 'Family capitalism'. *Special Issue on Family Capitalism. Business History*, **35** (4), 1–16, (ed. G. Jones and M.B. Rose).

Miller, R. (2010). 'Latin American business history and varieties of capitalism'. *Business History Review* **84** (4), 653–7.

Nordqvist, M. and L. Melin (2010). 'Entrepreneurial families and family firms'. *Entrepreneurship & Regional Development* **22** (3–4) (May–July), 211–39.

Okochi, A. (ed.) (1984). *Family Business in the Era of Industrial Growth: Its Ownership and Management*. Tokyo: University of Tokyo Press.

Schneider, B. (2009). 'Hierarchical market economies and varieties of capitalism in Latin America'. *Journal of Latin American Studies* **41** (August), 553–75.

Index